GOD AS LOVING GRACE

The Biblically Revealed
Nature and Work of God

Barry L. Callen

Evangel Publishing House
Nappanee, Indiana

Cover Design: Barbara Thompson

ISBN: 0-916035-65-4

Library of Congress Catalog Card Number: 95-61999

Printed in the United States of America

5 4 3 2 1

Dedicated to

Ian Patrick Callen

a fresh and wonderful gift
from the God of loving grace

Gratitude is expressed for the generous
support received for this book from:

James and Ethel Eckman
Raymond and Caroline McCutcheon
Robert and Patricia McCutcheon

TABLE OF CONTENTS

PREFACE

Celebrating the God of Loving Grace

God's gracious love for us humans is our only hope of salvation. The sheer wonder of this biblically revealed truth of who God is and what God has and is doing on our behalf moves us to poetry, parable, praise, and song.

Two of Jesus' parables are especially dramatic in teaching us about the character of God. One, the story of the laborers in the vineyard (Matt. 20:1-16), is clear about the Jewish view of God as loving grace. Is God like an employer who pays a wage? Is he like someone who holds a gun to a person's head demanding certain actions or else? The parable beautifully portrays the grace of God, "a concept so integral to Jewish thought during the time of Jesus and yet very difficult to grasp."[1] The other parable is about the compassionate Father and his two lost sons (Lk. 15:11-32). The Father allows his sons to take premature advantage of their inheritance, victimizing the father who allows freedom of choice to the sons despite the related vulnerability to the father, the rightful owner of all. Jesus is drawing a vivid story-picture of God. God also loves, risks, suffers, sacrifices, and finally welcomes home with a loving grace wholly undeserved.

Thinking biblically, divine grace is known through the history of its disclosure. We know God as loving grace because of the graceful way God has demonstrated love along the troubled road of our human history. The reality of grace "precedes and conditions

---

[1] Brad Young, *Jesus: The Jewish Theologian* (Peabody, Mass.: Hendrickson Publishers, 1995), 129.

9

every discrete Christian inquiry into the meanings of creation, redemption, and consummation. Grace is presupposed in every serious call to repentance, faith, new birth, and holy living."[2] Grace is the rich soil in which we are enabled to participate in any redeemed future. It makes possible a proper understanding of God. The pattern of loving initiatives taken by God inspires our realization that such love, such grace, is central to the very being of God.

Charles Wesley was inspired to write, and Christians all over the world often sing:

> Love divine, all loves excelling,
> Joy of heaven, to earth come down,
> Fix in us thy humble dwelling,
> All thy faithful mercies crown!
> Jesus, thou art all compassion,
> Pure, unbounded love thou art;
> Visit us with thy salvation!
> Enter every trembling heart.
>
> Come, almighty to deliver,
> Let us all thy grace receive;
> Suddenly return, and never,
> Never more thy temples leave.
> Thee we would be always blessing,
> Serve thee as thy hosts above,
> Pray, and praise thee without ceasing,
> Glory in thy perfect love.

---

[2] Thomas Oden, *The Transforming Power of Grace* (Nashville: Abingdon Press, 1993), 24. Note that the title of Ray Dunning's systematic theology (Kansas City: Beacon Hill Press, 1988) is *Grace, Faith and Holiness*--grace necessarily coming before all else.

Finish then thy new creation,
Pure and spotless let us be;
Let us see thy great salvation
Perfectly restored in thee;
Changed from glory into glory,
Till in heaven we take our place,
Till we cast our crowns before Thee,
Lost in wonder, love, and praise.[3]

What love and grace! They constitute the "Ananias" approach to God and God's work in our world. This name is the Greek form of Hananiah, meaning "God has dealt graciously." In Acts 9 we meet a man of this name. While difficult and presumably dangerous to do, Ananias obeyed the divine call and befriended Saul in Damascus. Saul, the then notorious enemy of the young church of Jesus, now was unexpectedly yielded to Christ and waiting a promised healing and commissioning. Ananias set aside his suspicion and fear of potential cost to himself and became the agent of redeeming, healing, and sending love. God indeed has dealt graciously, is gracious, and offers to us all a renewing grace that leads to risky responsibility.[4]

Truly it is amazing. There probably is no more universally loved Christian song than "Amazing Grace" by John Newton, a former slave trader who himself was saved by the gracious and loving God.[5] Such grace characterizes the very being of God, enables human salvation, and inspires praise to God that will never end. It is this grace, this God, this amazing love that we celebrate! So Paul prayed and this book has been written:

---

[3] This hymn text is quoted as it appeared in *A Collection of Hymns for the Use of the People Called Methodists* (1780). See *The Bicentennial Edition of the Works of John Wesley* (Nashville: Abingdon Press, 1984 onward), 7:545-46. It is present in many contemporary hymnals.

[4] See Randy Maddox, *Responsible Grace: John Wesley's Practical Theology* (Nashville: Kingswood Books, Abingdon Press, 1994).

[5] See the PBS home video *Amazing Grace* by journalist Bill Moyers, 1990, for numerous examples of this song of John Newton being sung with great appreciation in many cultures.

I pray that, according to the riches of his [God's] glory, he may grant that you may be strengthened in your inner being with power through his Spirit, and that Christ may dwell in your hearts through faith, as you are being rooted and grounded in love. I pray that you may have the power to comprehend, with all the saints, what is the breadth and length and height and depth, and to know the love of Christ that surpasses knowledge, so that you may be filled with all the fullness of God (Eph. 3:16-19).

As one approaches consideration of the biblically revealed nature and work of God, the proper attitude is that conveyed by the first line of a much beloved hymn: "I need Thee every hour, Most *gracious* Lord."[6]

---

[6] Hymn "I Need Thee Every Hour" by Annie Hawks and Robert Lowry. Emphasis added.

INTRODUCTION

Augustine, an early and very influential Christian theologian (354-430), is said to have been walking one day along the shore of the Mediterranean Sea. As the story goes, he noticed a little boy pouring sea water into a hole made in the sand. Time after time the little hands were filled with a bit of dripping water that was carried quickly and emptied into the hole. Questioned by the older man, the boy claimed that he was moving the sea into the hole. When told that he was wasting his time at an impossible task, the boy announced with wisdom beyond his years: "Well then, so are you wasting your time writing about God. You'll never get him into a book!"

Of course, neither will this book accomplish impossibilities. Any "god" who can be captured and contained by mere humans is not God. Nevertheless, surely some ways of approaching a human understanding of God are more appropriate than others. Especially if God desires to be known and chooses to assist in the knowing process, some meaningful level of human knowing is possible. The goal, rather than squeezing God into a book or creed, is to be transformed by obedient awareness of the ultimate reality, God, who in loving grace chooses to be known.

Those people willing to be instructed by the Bible concerning the God-knowing task soon encounter Mark 12:29-30. Here are words said to be from Jesus himself about the most important commandment of all: "The first is, 'Hear, O Israel: the Lord our God, the Lord is one; you shall love the Lord your God with all your heart, and with all your soul, and with all your mind, and with all your strength.'" Yes, of course; but how does one do this? Who is this God to be so loved? What is there about God that is so worthy of our human love? What has God done that makes possible our human awareness of the divine and thus the possibility of our loving response? What is the significance of the man Jesus in knowing God rightly? What of the amazing claim that Jesus actually was God actively present and Self-revealing among us so that we might really know and thus be changed forever?

In these pages "loving grace" is at the center of the answer to all of these questions. According to the biblical revelation, such divine grace defines God's character, explains why we humans can know the divine, clarifies the reason Jesus came, and is our only hope as sinful persons standing before a holy God. Here is good perspective: "Christian spirituality is the formation of life in response to the divine Spirit as that is known in Jesus Christ. The divine Spirit is God. Hence, what we believe about God determines our spirituality."[1] Knowing God as loving grace is to know God aright and sets the believer on the path to abundant life. Walking this path with the believer is God, the loving-grace God who stands above, stoops below, suffers, sacrifices, enlightens, enables, and finally saves.

In 1995 I authored a biography of Daniel Warner, primary nineteenth-century pioneer of a contemporary movement among Christians popularly known as the Church of God (Anderson). The book's title is *It's God's Church!*[2] It intends to convey that those who belong to Christ by redemption belong to each other in the family of Christ. All is of God, from God, for God, a particular God, the God of loving grace. To be God's church, believers must know and respond in obedient gratitude to God's being, will, and way.

No Christian teaching is more central than that about who God is and how God works in our world. Teaching about God deeply affects one's understanding of divine sovereignty, creation, election, and providence, human salvation and history, the past and the future, and especially the meaning of the divine incarnation in Jesus Christ. If we who believe are to be holy as God is holy, a central biblical expectation (Lev. 11:44), it is essential that we explore, to the limit of our divinely enabled ability, the ways in which God is holy. Who God is guides who we are to be. How God works is the pattern for how God's children should function as agents of the divine Spirit.

It is tragic that in common understanding probably no teaching has been so influenced, even perverted, by ideas not central to bibli-

---

[1] John Cobb, Jr., *Can Christ Be Good News Again?* (St. Louis: Chalice Press, 1991), 152.

[2] Published by Warner Press (Anderson, Ind., 1995). A companion volume published the same year is *Contours of a Cause: The Theological Vision of the Church of God Movement (Anderson)* (Anderson University School of Theology).

cal thought as has the teaching about God. What kind of God created this world? What kind of world has been created? What is its relation to the ongoing work of God? Who decides who will be saved--and on what basis? The answers depend on one's perspective on the divine. Unfortunately, the perspective that has prevailed in much of Christian church history has been shaped by more than the biblical witness.

The message of the Bible is intended to be really *good news* about divine grace and human restoration. Why then has it often become *bad news* for so many people? Usually the problem has been with a faulty understanding of who God is and how God works. In fact, most of the problems in Christian theology root in a range of inadequate understandings of the distinctive character, intentions, and way that God now is present in the world. The only adequate understanding of God is the one revealed in the biblical narrative. Biblical revelation is to be the central authority for Christians.[3] This authority lies not in itself, but in its pivotal function of pointing to the God of loving grace. In the Bible we are confronted by a richly diverse, yet consistent picture of God. Ultimate reality is the being of God who is active in our world as loving grace.

Very often the biblical vision of God is thought of as placing priority on God's sovereignty, majesty, glory, and unchanging, irresistible will. God is said to be righteous, the One who will not tolerate or forgive sin unless divine justice is fully satisfied. Whatever God dictates comes to pass. While God cares deeply about the fallen creation, the divine remains essentially unaffected by worldly sorrow, suffering, and sin. God, it is argued, stands outside the turmoil of our times. Such a picture of God has come to be conventional among a large portion of "conservative" Christians.

Given the vast and varied biblical material, it is admittedly easy to support this conventional view with a series of scattered texts. Recently, however, a call has gone out for contemporary Christians to recover a more biblically balanced and faithful vision of God, a

---

[3] Note, however, that biblical authority depends on the adequacy of its interpretation, which in turn relies in part on human reason, experience, and church tradition. See Donald Thorsen, *The Wesleyan Quadrilateral* (Grand Rapids: Zondervan, 1990).

vision that would influence in fresh ways all else that is believed. Referred to as "creative love theism,"[4] this vision of God is based on the affirmation that "whoever does not love does not know God, for God is love (1 Jn. 4:8). The central features of this biblical perspective on the divine are:

> First, it celebrates the grace of God that abounds for all humanity. It embraces a wideness in God's mercy and rejects the idea that God excludes any persons arbitrarily from saving help. Second, it celebrates Jesus' category of "father" to express God's openness and relationality with us. God seeks to restore relationships with estranged people and cannot be thought of primarily as a Judge seeking a legal settlement. Third, it envisions God as a mutual and interrelating Trinity, not as an all-determining and manipulative transcendent (male) ego.[5]

These defining features of the divine consciously seek to replace their opposites that have been so influential, even standard in conservative Christianity. The intent now is still to conserve, but only what is biblically faithful, not what is rooted in much theology that evolved long after the Bible's composition, theology that has been equated falsely with biblical teaching. The new attempt to be biblically faithful opposes a minimizing of divine grace, an exaggeration of the legal dimension of human salvation, and a misrepresentation of the meaning of God's sovereignty. A replacing of these negatives results in a more dynamic theological perspective focusing on the "openness" of God. It takes this general form, the elements of which are elaborated in the following chapters:

---

[4] This phrase was introduced by Robert Brow in an article in *Christianity Today* (Feb. 19, 1990). Its implications now have been developed in Clark Pinnock and Robert Brow, *Unbounded Love: A Good News Theology for the 21st Century* (InterVarsity Press, 1994), and in Clark Pinnock and others, *The Openness of God: A Biblical Challenge to the Traditional Understanding of God* (InterVarsity Press, 1994).

[5] Pinnock and Brow, op. cit., 8. Regarding emphasis on "father" as a designation for God, see chapter two of this present volume for a discussion of gender language for God. For consideration of the concept of "trinity" in relation to God, see chapter four.

God, in grace, grants humans significant freedom to cooperate with or work against God's will for their lives, and he enters into dynamic, give-and-take relationships with us. The Christian life involves a genuine interaction between God and human beings. We respond to God's gracious initiatives and God responds to our responses...and on it goes. God takes risks in this give-and-take relationship, yet he is endlessly resourceful and competent in working toward his ultimate goals..... God does not control everything that happens. Rather, he is open to receiving input from his creatures. In loving dialogue, God invites us to participate with him to bring the future into being.[6]

Who is God? God is the ultimate One who is characterized best as loving grace. God is the One who is "open" to the world, who loves *all sinners*, just as Christians are to weep over the lost (Rom. 9:1-3, 10:1). God is not the One who needs placated before it is possible for a divine loving and forgiving of us sinners. Rather, God is the One who chooses out of unbounded love to seek restored relationship while we are yet sinners. God is the One who, though God, chooses to be vulnerable, open, risking, suffering and rejoicing with us, always interacting with rather than manipulating the creation. Modern atheism is not so much a denial of the existence of God as the denial of the God so often preached by Christians. What is needed now is not "arguments for God's existence but clarification of God's gracious character and actual identity."[7] What follows here is dedicated to this crucial task of clarification.

In the process of clarification, there are insights from "process" theology that prove helpful (and others that do not). Particularly

---

[6] Pinnock and others, *The Openness of God*, 7.

[7] Ibid., 10. The inappropriate vision of God often championed by Christians is described on p. 11 as: "What we are opposing is that development in Western theology which twists the gospel into legalistic terms, conceiving sin as primarily a disturbance of God's justice and salvation primarily as a propitiation of God's wrath. This forensic reading of the gospel portrays God not as the passionate lover of humankind, but as an implacable judge. It also depicts the cross not as the revelation of a compassionate God, but as an instrument of God's revenge."

helpful is the theological tradition rooted in the significant theological work of John Wesley (1703-1791). Wesley illumined the whole of the God-world relation by a careful balancing of divine grace and human responsibility.[8] He resisted the common view of most of his contemporaries in the eighteenth century, including Descartes and Newton, that pictured the universe in machine-like terms. This common view identified God as the maker of all who, having made, stands outside the creation and acts on it from the high throne of absolute and semi-detached sovereignty. The God of loving grace, however, while certainly transcendent of creation, was judged by Wesley also to be "the Soul of the world who pervades and actuates the whole of creation, and who enlivens, enlightens, and liberates all people, calling them to strive toward personal and social perfection, and empowering their efforts."[9]

Accordingly, belief in the ongoing work of the Holy Spirit is critical to adequate Christian faith and life. Rigid views of predestination are rightly brought into sharp question. Also brought into question is our modern preoccupation in the West with the "usefulness" of God. When the Bible is taken seriously, we learn of the one and only God who cannot be manipulated by us creatures, but who chooses in loving grace not to manipulate us.

Is the will of God the final explanation for all that happens? Can anything hinder the accomplishment of God's purposes? Why did God come to us in the Christ and what did Jesus accomplish on the cross? To these and many other God-related questions we now turn.

One guide used here is the content of the Nicene-Constantinopolitan Creed (381), probably the most widely recognized witness to the centrally held content of the apostolic faith of Christians.[10]

---

[8] See Randy Maddox, *Responsible Grace: John Wesley's Practical Theology* (Nashville: Abingdon Press, Kingswood Books, 1994).

[9] John Cobb, Jr., *Grace & Responsibility: A Wesleyan Theology for Today* (Nashville: Abingdon Press, 1995), 51.

[10] For helpful commentary on this creed, see *Confessing the One Faith: An Ecumenical Explication of the Apostolic Faith as it is Confessed in the Nicene-Constantinopolitan Creed* (381), new revised version (Geneva, Switz.: World Council of Churches Publications, Faith and Order Paper No. 153).

Structured around the complex being of God as biblically revealed according to apostolic understanding, this creed's content is reproduced as headers to the several chapters of this book.

The little boy of long ago was right. God will never fit in any hole we humans dig, or in any creed we write or church structure we create. We humans have, by our sin, brought into being a destructive situation that we cannot ever escape alone. Into this circumstance comes God, the creating and re-creating God, the God of loving grace. Now nothing need remain the same. Why? Because of grace.

What is grace? It is a pattern of divine presence and activity that identifies for us the essence and intention of God. We learn the meaning of grace from the grace-full acts of God among us. Though we are sinners, God is willing to meet us. Though we are deaf, God is willing to enable us to hear. Though we are far away, God is willing to come to us and bring us to our true home. Though Christ was rich, yet for our sakes he became poor. Such initiatives define the meaning of divine grace.

Our knowledge of God is more a gift of divine revelation than an achievement of human reason. Our status before God is something given, not earned. Said Paul on behalf of us all: "By the grace of God I am what I am" (1 Cor. 15:10). This is God at work, the God of loving grace.

CHAPTER ONE

GOD IN TODAY'S MARKETPLACE

—

"We believe in one God..."

—

To fix one's attention on God and on the biblical record of God's nature and working in history is to rise above self-preoccupation and the tyranny of the present time and place. However, many current Christian leaders express deep concern:

> We confess that we have often lost the fullness of our Christian heritage, too readily assuming that the Scriptures and the Spirit make us independent of the past. In so doing, we have become theologically shallow, spiritually weak, blind to the work of God in others and married to our cultures.[1]

The task of Christians is to be focused on God, the God who is understood best in Christ as active and loving grace. This focus will keep in right perspective the Christian church, its mission, and its theology as they function in any culture.

---

[1] From "The Chicago Call: An Appeal to Evangelicals," as in *Christianity Today* (June 17, 1977). An ad hoc group of forty-six "evangelical" Christian leaders met in a Chicago suburb in May, 1977, to express their concerns and share their faith through this statement. For theological development of the themes of this Call, see Robert Webber and Donald Bloesch, *The Orthodox Evangelicals* (Nashville: Thomas Nelson, 1978).

Christian Theology and Mission

The church of God is the family of God's loyal disciples. It exists for mission.[2] The church has been called to recognize, live out, and extend the benefits of the divine kingdom of God that already have arrived in Jesus Christ. Therefore, among Christians there should be no destruction of the faith's historic foundations, no capitulation to a current culture, no dominance of non-mission matters. There is good news about God. It is from God, resides primarily in Christ, and is to be shared with all people. God is active in our time on behalf of all the world. This is not a time for preoccupations that distract believers from Christ's commission (Matt. 28:18-20). Believers are to *be* disciples and to *make* disciples. Christian theology has to do with explaining this *being* and *making*. It rests on a particular understanding of God and God's ongoing relation to this world.

Unfortunately, distractions are common. Usually they involve too heavy a focus on the maintenance of the church's institutions or on an inordinately felt burden to pass on the speculative minutia sometimes associated with the church's formalized doctrines. Proper perspective is constantly vulnerable to perversion, to status-quo sterility. In the service of mission, the church is best thought of as a *verb* as much as a noun. The body of Christ's disciples is less an organization and more an *organism*, a dynamic, living reality rooted in the person and work of God. "Movement" is a better metaphor than "machinery." "Inspiration" is a more flexible and powerful concept than "institution." "Dynamic" suggests more aliveness than does "dogmatic."

Priority belongs to spreading news of the kingdom of God and being obedient to the demands of actual life in the kingdom. Although still awaiting the arrival of this divine kingdom in its fullness, the wonderful news is that it already has arrived in Jesus Christ. This

---

[2] Note especially the Lausanne Covenant, a widely circulated affirmation of Christian faith and mission that emerged from the International Congress on World Evangelization (July, 1974, Lausanne, Switzerland) sponsored by the Billy Graham evangelistic association. This writer was privileged to be a representative from the United States, joining some 3,000 Christian leaders who came from 150 countries.

"already" presence should be central in the church's teaching and kept obvious in the church's theology and life in the world, even while the "not yet" of the kingdom is readily admitted and anxiously anticipated. While waiting, the point is serious discipleship and Christian witness. To be authentic, these must be rooted in encounter with the God who confronts, transforms, defines, and sends (Isa. 6).

What is Christian theology? A simple question like this soon leads to complex considerations. To respond briefly, the church of Jesus Christ is a community of shared experience and discourse, a body of believers gladly receiving divine grace and intentionally embracing a divinely offered new life. The church has its own shaping memories and distinctive terminology, its own values, and a particular narrative of experience and perceived meaning that transforms and directs its life in the world. Words like sin, salvation, and the lordship of Christ are understood in a certain way within the church, a way that often sounds like a foreign language to those outside its borders.

One theologian recently offered this definition of theology in general: "Theology is the creative reconstruction of inherited symbols, the construction of a tradition's future from the resources of its past."[3] Theology remembers with loyal appreciation a faith community's heritage and envisions with creative courage concerning that heritage. Always this envisioning is to be done in vital continuity with the inherited tradition, although the central focus is on its future. The key questions for Christian theologians have to do with defining the nature of the "inherited symbols" and the necessary boundaries, if any, of the task of "creative reconstruction."

Christian theology is a careful examination and expression of the church's historic view of reality, a view believed to be divinely inspired. It is a rehearsing, refining, and, as necessary, a translating of the church's distinctive story, the biblical story of redemption. It is a continuing conversation among believers and between believers and the surrounding people and culture, a conversation about the substance and implications of the belief of the church about God's being

---

[3] Delwin Brown, *Boundaries of Our Habitations: Tradition and Theological Construction* (Albany: State University of New York, 1994), 148.

and work in the world.[4] Theology is "orthodox" when it rightly perceives and faithfully maintains the faith's historic and enduring substance; it is "radical" when it rightly reforms and courageously puts into actual practice faith's mission implications.[5] Central to it all, of course, is God. The very word "theology" makes this clear. "Theo" (God) and "logos" (word) refer to a speaking about God.

Such theological speaking about God today has acquired many descriptive adjectives that highlight differing perspectives and agendas. In one recent book[6] there are article entries on *biblical* theology, *black* theology, *confessional* theology, *death of God* theology, *dogmatic* theology, *empirical* theology, *feminist* theology, *historical* theology, *liberation* theology, *narrative* theology, *natural* theology, *philosophical* theology, *political* theology, *postmodern* theology, *practical* theology, *process* theology, *sacramental* theology, *systematic* theology, and *womanist* theology. Each, while representing a special angle of approach, a particular concern, involves in its own way a focus on God and our world. Who is God? How does God relate to our world now? What are the implications for us that come from God's identity and ongoing work in our current circumstances?[7] Such are the central questions of Christian theology.

The Christian theological enterprise usually leads to specific teachings framed with care and then considered in some sense authoritative for the church's faithful. Such doctrines, however, basic as they are, can be a significant distraction from the fulfillment of Christian

---

[4] For broad perspective on the range of current understandings of the nature and task of Christian theology, see Theodore Jennings, Jr., ed., *The Vocation of the Theologian* (Philadelphia: Fortress Press, 1985). The contributors to this survey speak of theology's task variously as (1) providing a clear and comprehensive description of the faith, (2) translating the faith into terms intelligible to today's culture, (3) thinking about pressing social and moral issues from a Christian perspective, and (4) reflecting on and motivating Christian life in the midst of communities of oppressed people.

[5] Says Delwin Brown: "Theology accepts as a starting point what a tradition has been, accepts as a goal what it might be and should become, and accepts as an obligation the advocacy of that potential realization" (op. cit., 148).

[6] *A New Handbook of Christian Theology* (Nashville: Abingdon Press, 1992).

[7] The "current circumstances" of the global community at the end of the twentieth century are identified and explored helpfully by Howard Snyder in *EarthCurrents: The Struggle for the World's Soul* (Nashville: Abingdon Press, 1995).

mission. An intellectual preoccupation with theological precision can sap energy, short-circuit honest questing, and reduce faith to mind games about secondary matters. A legalistic creedalism easily can paralyze a people, turn them inward on themselves, and shut out others, thus stopping translation and transmission of the biblical revelation. Theology, while foundational, easily deteriorates into an obstacle to obedient discipleship and credible witness to the truly good news about God in Jesus Christ.

Nonetheless, in spite of the danger, and as Acts 2 clearly shows, God's "adding to the church those who were being saved" (mission) was not separate from the church giving careful and regular attention "to the apostles' teaching." In other words, the commissioning of the church for mission always has been related closely to the church's convictional foundation, especially the news about who God is and what God has done in Israel and in the life, death, and resurrection of Jesus. Spreading and building God's kingdom is not possible without awareness of the nature of God and the kingdom. Knowing the nature of the kingdom is dependent on knowing the King whose realm it is. Mission slips into mere enthusiasm for some personal or group preference if there is no divinely initiated message that transcends human limitations. Failing to keep focus on God is to push our own human agendas, no matter how heavily we cover them with religious language and ritual.

Theology can be a trap, an escape from the practical, a cognitive quagmire, if God, discipleship, and mission do not remain central. Christians are called to real faith, truly transformed lives, sacrificial service, and an aversion to pointless and fruitless abstractions. Did St. Paul not say that the Kingdom of God is power and not talk (1 Cor. 4:20)? What is needed, the voices of laypersons tend to insist, is less theology and more real religion. These voices are right, at least in the warning that theology should not exhaust itself and the church with detached, intellectualized sidetracks. They are wrong if religious "experience" is allowed to interfere with disciplined conversation about the nature and implications of the being and work of God, the core task of theology in any time.

The Believers' Church or radical reformation tradition, for instance, is anything but an escape from the practical. Not long after the Protestant Reformation of the sixteenth century, there evolved an Orthodoxy-Pietism split.[8] Contrary to the intention of either of these movements, the evolving tendency was to separate the discipline of doctrinal reflection from the direct obedience of Christian life. Right belief became rationalized by many orthodox Lutherans into a scholastic creedalism, while reacting Pietists typically focused primary attention on life application, even devaluing theological reflection.[9]

Today the widespread concern for "relevance" is strong. Many voices understandably call for life and world application, insisting on understanding Christian theology as a *practical* discipline. Theology is "not merely the intellectual findings of professional thinkers, but requisite knowledge for doers–disciples of the Lord who need to know whom they follow and why they are following him."[10]

We still are living in the wake of the revolutionary 1960s. That decade spawned influences on Christian theology of major proportions. These influences tend toward the practical, linking more closely theology and ethics, reflection and action, church tradition and immediate spiritual experience. The characteristics of much current theology, therefore, include *participation*, *process*, and *public issues*.

Theology is being shaped now by many new voices that reflect, often in case-study or narrative fashion, on the paths of particular human experiences. Rather than humans receiving a defining set of "facts" of divine revelation, these voices think it better to say that we humans are being encountered by the God who comes in loving grace to redeem broken relationships. Accordingly, theology now is being pursued commonly through categories that are *relational* and *process* in orientation. Given these dynamic categories, the doing of

---

[8] See the helpful discussion in Justo González, rev. ed., *A History of Christian Thought* (Nashville: Abingdon Press, 1975, 1987), III:300ff.

[9] Note the judgment of John Downame. The best of theology is "that which consisteth more in experience and practice than in theory and speculation; and more principally tendeth to the sanctification of the heart than the informing of the judgment and the increasing of knowledge" (as quoted by F. Ernest Stoeffler, *The Rise of Evangelical Pietism,* Leiden: E. J. Brill, 1965, 70).

[10] Stanley Grenz, *Revisioning Evangelical Theology* (InterVarsity Press, 1993), 58.

theology is not being limited to a churchly realm, but is taking into account social and political realities and is working for practical consequences. Theology is seeking "to norm not only ideas and confessions but Christian action in the world."[11] Especially since the 1960s, Christians have heard the frequent call to go beyond the classroom. Believers are to hit the streets, adding shoeleather to times of worship and theological reflection. Action should compliment adoration. Theology, however, need not and should not disappear in the midst of the action. Theology is inevitable and basic to the life of faith and the mission of the church. People inevitably live out of that to which they are really committed. The story of reality that is believed will shape the life stories of those who believe. Doctrine and discipleship are always linked.

The New Testament invites the community of believers to think through its faith (Matt. 22:37; 2 Cor. 10:5; 1 Pet. 3:15). Christians are instructed to bring their lives and their every thought into the captivity of Christ (2 Cor. 10:5). Since theology seeks to further this reflection on the faith, the theological enterprise is to be valued as a vital function in the life of Christian discipleship. When faith responds to the biblical revelation of God's work of loving grace, theology soon enters as reflection on the church's language and practice of faith. When theology is trying to translate the exercise of faith into a language that can impact the contemporary culture, it is engaging in the church's mission. One important task of "systematic" Christian theology, then, is to develop and share a coherent and timely presentation of the faith, a thoughtful retelling of the biblical story of God-with-us, a witnessing styled with the deepest human hungers of the times in mind.[12]

---

[11] Randy Maddox, "The Recovery of Theology as a Practical Discipline," *Theological Studies* 51:4 (December 1990), 666.

[12] *Biblical* theology studies directly the writings of the Hebrew and New Testament Scriptures. *Historical* theology reviews the many ways the faith has been formulated over the centuries (see, e. g., the excellent three-volume work *A History of Christian Thought* by Justo González, Abingdon Press, 1975, 1987). *Practical* theology applies the substance of the faith to the tasks of preaching, counseling, educating, etc. *Philosophical* theology examines the faith in light of reason, experience, and contemporary modes of thought.

Authentic church growth always rests on distinctively Christian ground. Evangelizing and church planting call for believers to understand the nature and mission of the church itself, as well as the lives and languages of those to be reached. The good news to be shared has particular and essential theological content. This content is the distinctive biblical revelation of the God of loving grace who brings salvation to all the world in Jesus Christ.

It is sadly true that Christian theology over the centuries often has become speculative, legalized, culture-bound, divisive, distracting from mission, boring to the average believer. Even so, the enduring substance of the teachings of the biblical prophets, historians, and apostles has not been rendered meaningless or optional. As Gabriel Fackre aptly puts it: "If we are to get the story *out*, we must first get the story *straight*."[13] That always begins with knowing who God really is and how God works in our world.

Being nurtured as a Christian disciple always should include Christian theology (God-talk) as a central consideration. When lacking a clear vision of the apostolic teachings that give it distinctive definition, the church drifts into being little more than another human organization reflecting its own context and establishing its own "religious" agenda.[14] The teaching of the apostles, on the other hand, insures a focus on God and the divine agenda, a focus that makes the church truly *God's* church and the church's mission truly that of realizing the Kingdom of God on earth as it is in heaven. This teaching is less a pre-set body of intellectual formulas of the faith and more a hearing and faithful entering into the story of God in Israel and in Jesus Christ, founded on the reporting and reflections of those who were closest to the origination of the story.

The initial call of Jesus was for hearers to repent, be converted to a significantly new set of will and mind, and therefore look in a dif-

---

[13] Gabriel Fackre, *The Christian Story*, rev. ed. (Eerdmans, 1978, 1984), 2.

[14] The church growth movement, so prominent in North American Christianity in recent years, has been vulnerable to such drifting. For a critique of this movement and its tendency toward cultural accommodationism, see Philip Kenneson, "Selling [Out] the Church in the Marketplace of Desire," *Modern Theology* 9:4 (October, 1993), 319-348.

ferent direction so that a new reality could be recognized, a new story about life read, embraced, and shared.[15] This reality, this dramatic story of Jesus, is the biblical narrative of the invading presence of the reign of God into this troubled world. Only an awareness and understanding of this redemptive presence brings the potential of all things becoming new.

The early apostolic focus, however, was on more than the divine presence and agenda. The spotlight also was on the divine being. Who is this God whose mission we are called to join? What are we to believe about the nature of God, of humankind, and of the destiny that awaits all creation? What view of ultimate reality puts in proper perspective the mass of data and experiences that pile up around us like blinding and burdening mountains? What hope should grip our lives so that we can resist the control of the prevailing culture and risk our all in selfless service? What adds the radical dimension to what is orthodox?

The sincere seeker after answers to such basic questions is invited into the arena of Christian theology. Donald Bloesch puts it well: "Theology endeavors to present a true picture of the activity of divinity that serves to illumine the pilgrimage of faith." Since, however, the goal of theology moves beyond illumination to actual life and mission, Bloesch continues: "God has provided a revelation of himself sufficient for us to think deeply and rightly concerning his will and purpose so that we may implement his plan for the world in faithful service."[16]

Credo is Latin for "I believe." To believe is to confess that one sees and affirms a foundation for life, something that gives human life meaning, direction, and hope. Far more than just a rational theory, by faith this foundation becomes a living reality for the believer, a guiding force, the vision and framework for life itself. Christians who first said *credo* did not do so lightly. They often risked their lives by submitting to a baptism that declared openly their highest understanding and ulti-

---

[15] Walter Brueggemann illustrates this effectively by reconstructing the biblical scene (Joshua 24) in which Joshua retold publically the story of Israel, now safely in the promised land by the grace of God. His was an evangelistic testimony to a divine process in history that others could and, he hoped, would decide to join (*Biblical Perspectives on Evangelism*, Abingdon Press, 1993, chapter two).

[16] Donald Bloesch, *A Theology of Word & Spirit* (InterVarsity Press, 1992), 116.

mate allegiance. To really believe is to present one's life a living sacrifice in divine service (Rom. 12:1). While always more than mere rationalism, "doing theology is praying in the rational mode"[17] or praying with the mind (1 Cor. 14:13-15). It is a vision of life consciously explored by the mind and chosen by the will.

Apostolic tradition assumes that a believer being baptized understands the essence of the faith being confessed. The "I believe" has a substantive reference. In fact, "the purpose of Christian theology...[is] to clarify the ancient ecumenical faith into which Christians of all times and places are baptized. It is expected of all who are baptized," concludes Thomas Oden, "that they will understand what it means to believe in God the Father Almighty, in God the Son, and in God the Spirit...."[18] The theological task is to explore such understanding for the purpose of knowing the triune God in a way that leads to personal commitment, that in turn should lead to mission. Theology thus serves the very purpose of the church's life.

A belief in the triune God, Father, Son, and Spirit, is the threefold plan around which several major theological works of recent years have been developed.[19] These significant works join in recognizing that the Nicene-Constantinopolitan (381 C.E.) creed, itself organized around these three designations of the full being and work of God, is (1) the most widely recognized of the ancient faith confessions of Christians, (2) a concise summary of the early apostolic "teachings," and (3) models well the evangelistic goal set forth in Matthew 28:19. For this reason, this classic creed is reproduced in the several chapter headings of this book.[20]

---

[17] C. Norman Kraus, *God Our Savior* (Scottdale, Pa.: Herald Press, 1991), 14.

[18] Thomas Oden, *The Living God* (Harper & Row, 1987), 11.

[19] Examples are H. Ray Dunning, *Grace, Faith and Holiness* (1988), Theodore Jennings, Jr., *Loyalty To God* (1992), Thomas Oden's three-volume systematic, *The Living God* (1987), *The Word of Life* (1989), and *Life in the Spirit* (1992), Wolfhart Pannenberg, *The Apostles' Creed* (1972), and Hans Küng, *Credo: The Apostles' Creed Explained for Today* (1992).

[20] The Apostles' Creed is also a compact and widely celebrated summary of New Testament teaching. Its present form dates as far back as the sixth century after Christ. Closely related to it is the Old Roman Creed, an early Christian statement used in connection with baptism and dating back to the latter part of the second century.

Christians, says the risen Christ, are to be serious about the substance of their faith. Why? Such seriousness is for the sake of their mission for Christ in this world. We who believe are commissioned to teach, make disciples, and baptize "in the name of the Father and of the Son and of the Holy Spirit." So Christian teaching is God-oriented baptismal teaching based on the biblical narrative of God acting and being Self-defined in Israel and Jesus Christ. It seeks to explore the nature of the divine good news and the basis for the baptismal commitment. It ponders the marvelous and mysterious, the pivotal and profound. Finally, it focuses on the being of the God who, so the biblical revelation reports, chose to come among us in love and grace, and now intends to send us out into the world the same way.

The writers of the four Gospels were themselves theologians, receiving and reexpressing the Jesus Story for their several times and audiences. The Gospel of Matthew, for instance, is a helpful model as one begins to explore the tasks of Christian theology today. Matthew apparently wrote with two reading communities in mind, even two differing cultures. He sought to be a bridge between them and the transforming potential of the Jesus Story. The ancient Jewish tradition provided for Matthew a prophetic foundation; the Gentile world was the extensive new mission field. The Jewish tradition of faith and hope always has to be understood and appreciated if the Christian community is to retain its historic roots and distinctive identity. These early chapters of the biblical revelation, the "first testament," are essential for understanding the rest of the revelation (especially Jesus as the fulfilling climax). The Gentile world, however, always is the new challenge. So Matthew is known as the "Jewish" Gospel on the one hand and the "missionary church" Gospel on the other.

The ongoing task of Christian theology is similar. One foot is to be set solidly on the soil of the historic tradition of the whole Christ event; the other foot should step out with a measured wisdom and a missionary motive to place its print in the shifting sands of the current culture. Theology serves the church in each time and place of its existence by "reflecting on and applying the one faith of the church to the world in which contemporary disciples live and engage in ministry in Christ's name."[21] Such theological service attempts to interrelate the enduring Christian gospel, the yet evolving tradition of the church's past life, and the circumstances and thought forms of the immediate setting. The intended result is "to articulate the unchanging confession of Jesus in a changing context and thereby to speak to the issues of succeeding generations."[22] Given the culture of the Western world as the twentieth century comes to an end, this theological task is indeed a major challenge.

Elements of the Theological Task

What follows is an attempt to focus the minds and hearts of contemporary Christians on the vital substance and current implications of Christian theology, particularly its understanding of God and God's work in the world. Good theology and faithful mission are inseparable. One working assumption of these pages is that the essence of authentic Christian theology was formed in the experience and carried in the proclamations of those earliest apostles who already are seen in action in Acts 2.[23] Thus, present theological thinking has a "restorationist" flavor, a recovery of the early "teachings" for the sake of the integrity of today's church and the reclamation of today's world. The classic creeds, including the Apostles' and Nicene, are instructive milestones of Christian believing, although they are not themselves the originating dynamic or formative center of Christian belief. The center is always the God of Israel who has chosen to be known most fully in Jesus the Christ.

Another working assumption deals with the spiritual "experience" underlying those primal apostolic proclamations. There is crucial wisdom in the "lodestar" of Emil Brunner's theological thought, so influential especially in the middle decades of the twentieth cen-

---

[21] Stanley Grenz and Roger Olson, *20th Century Theology* (InterVarsity Press, 1992), 9.

[22] Ibid.

[23] This assumption is not meant to ignore the essential foundation of the Hebrew's historic experience and resulting faith as known to us through the Hebrew Scriptures ("Old" Testament).

tury. The biblical concept of truth is inseparable from seeing "truth as encounter." One cannot really understand the Hebrew experience or the Christian gospel "apart from being personally engaged in an I–Thou encounter with God."[24] Truth moves beyond the semi-arid abstractions of objects and ideas to the enlivened arena of actual divine-human relationship. To be spiritually *informed* requires being spiritually *involved* and *formed.*

God has chosen, first in Israel and especially in Jesus, to communicate key characteristics of the divine being and directions of the divine will. Thus revelation, rather than the unaided quest of human reason, is theology's proper and necessary starting point. God has chosen to communicate. In its essence, this communication is not a list of religious concepts that intellectually define the divine. Revelation is received and understood only when a woman or man is engaged in the relational encounter where Self (divine) and self (human) come near, where a hot coal off the divine altar touches the human mouth, absolves the "woe is me!" and inspires a "here am I, send me!" (Isa. 6:6-8). One approaches the Christian theological task best by coming, not merely with the strain of the brain, but also and significantly with an enlivened spiritual discernment that is expanded by the warmth and vision of a divine-human relationship.

What prime motive is best for engaging in the Christian theological task? Instructed again by Emil Brunner, a committed Christian should labor philosophically and theologically for the sake of the gospel's proclamation. Brunner's own publications over his lifetime totaled about four-hundred (!), with about two dozen of the books translated into English. He is said to have regarded all his books as "a paraphrase on Romans 1:16."[25] Brunner had learned in part by personal experience. He was anxious to expound theology for the sake of proclaiming the good news encountered in Jesus. He was "not ashamed of the gospel; it is the power of God for salvation to everyone who has faith" (Rom. 1:16).

---

[24] J. Edward Humphrey, *Emil Brunner* (Waco, Tx.: Word Books, 1976), 20. See Brunner's influential book titled *Truth As Encounter* (Westminster Press, 1964).

[25] Ibid., 20.

This bold affirmation necessarily is more than an intellectual statement. It has relational depth and is theologically foundational. There is a crucial joining of divine revelation, human spiritual experience, and the task of theology, with all three oriented toward church mission. Put simply, the purpose of theology is "to make it possible for the gospel to be heard in our time."[26] But there is an additional task of the Christian theologian. Reflecting the Believers' Church tradition, the task, beyond evangelism, is *discipleship.* Theology is "the Christian community reflecting on and articulating the faith of the people who have encountered God in God's activity as focused in the history of Jesus of Nazareth and who therefore seek *to live* as the people of God in the contemporary world."[27]

Participate, Reflect, Express. The definition that John Macquarrie gives to the nature and task of Christian theology is helpful in all these regards. He defines theology as "the study which, through participation in and reflection upon a religious faith, seeks to express the content of this faith in the clearest and most coherent language available."[28] The three elements of this definition deserve highlighting.

First, theology proceeds "through participation in." Christian theology is continuous with faith because it participates in faith and speaks from the standpoint of faith–from a particular faith arising from a given community of faith formed by the biblical narrative that focuses finally on Jesus. Thus, one can distinguish the theologian from the more detached philosopher of religion. The theologian is not motivated only by academic interest or personal preference, association, or experience, but functions within a given faith tradition and is guided by the distinctive bases, goals, and community disciplines of that tradition.

[26] Sallie McFague, *Speaking in Parables* (Philadelphia: Fortress Press, 1975), 1.

[27] Stanley Grenz, *Theology for the Community of God* (Nashville: Broadman & Holman Publishers, 1994), 10. Emphasis added.

[28] John Macquarrie, *Principles of Christian Theology* (N.Y.: Charles Scribner's Sons, 1966), 1.

Second, theology necessarily "reflects upon" that given faith in which the theologian actively participates. While theology rises out of a specific faith and does not speak in a detached manner from outside this faith, it nevertheless takes a step back from the immediate claims and experiences of faith. Such a step enables the theologian to subject the faith to careful thought and possibly even to fresh conceptualization and expression. Such rethinking and re-expressing usually describe and interpret the faith's foundations and traditions, though at times they may be critical and innovative.

Third, theology's intention is to express thoughtfully the content of the faith in which the theologian participates and upon which he or she reflects. For the sake of effective communication, the experienced and refined faith seeks expression "in the clearest and most coherent language available." In this sense theology shares the character of all intellectual enterprises, aiming at intelligibility and consistency. In seeking verbal expression of faith and employing our common language, theology implicitly claims to have its place in the total intellectual endeavor of humankind. It is both continuous with other disciplines of the mind and with faith.[29] The purpose for such clear and coherent expression is to strengthen the church's own understanding of the faith as it witnesses to the world about the good news of God in Jesus Christ.

Priority of Past or Present? Of particular concern is a tension always found in relation to this third aspect of the theological task. The tension is a form of the in-the-world-but-not-of-the-world paradox. With mission a primary motive for theological work, naturally the theologian is very concerned to make meaningful contact with the contemporary mind and experience. However, how does one address effectively the world of alternate faith or non-faith communities, bringing to bear the distinctive Christian faith, without that Christian faith being reduced to merely an echo of the questions and answers of the world?[30] Paul Tillich's "method of correlation" has been one

---

[29] Ibid., 3.

[30] C. Norman Kraus says the task of theology is "to contextualize the message of Scripture so its true meaning can be communicated." By contextualization he means "the

prominent attempt to pursue Christian theology by coordinating the world's current questions and the faith's relevant answers. Unfortunately, this approach usually has led to a degree of accommodation to "the world" that risks altering as much as communicating the faith.

When does accommodation to the form and content of the questions of the world constitute such an adapting of the theological content and agenda that the result is no longer a distinctively Christian proclamation? This is one of the more basic of all questions related to any Christian theology that is actively on mission for the church. Note how Delwin Brown describes the contrast between the theological methods of "conservative" and "liberal" Christianity:

> ...conservative Christianity at its best will say, "We ought to listen to the hypotheses of the present and take from them what we can, but ultimately the truth has been given to us in the past, particularly in Jesus, and the acceptance of that is our ultimate obligation. Everything the contemporary world might say must be judged by its conformity to biblical revelation."[31]

What does the "liberal" tend to assume? She or he is prepared to honor the significance of the Christian past. Nonetheless:

> ...finally we must live by our best modern conclusions. The modern consensus should not be absolutized; it, too, is always subject to criticism and further revision. But our commitment, however tentative and self-critically maintained, must be to the careful judgments of the present age, even if they differ radically from the dictates of the past.[32]

---

reformulation of theological statements in the context of the world's varying cultures so the message truly conforms to the original gospel of Jesus." Kraus witnesses to his own pilgrimage from a "sheltered Mennonite community" to active ministry in Asian and African cultures and now the "postmodern" culture of our Western world (*God Our Savior*, Herald Press, 1991, 17-19).

[31] Brown in Clark Pinnock and Delwin Brown, *Theological Crossfire* (Grand Rapids: Zondervan, 1990), 23.

[32] Ibid.

Brown clearly prefers the liberal tilt of this tension. Preferring the conservative tilt is Clark Pinnock. His view was reflected by a representative group of "evangelicals" who issued "The Chicago Call" in 1977.[33] They affirmed that "in every age the Holy Spirit calls the church to examine its faithfulness to God's revelation in Scripture." Today, in part because of excessive yielding to the competing authority claims of our own human reason and contemporary culture, these conservative Christians lament that "evangelicals are hindered from achieving full maturity by a reduction of the historic faith." A rush for relevance can easily become a deluge of distortions.[34]

For this reason Donald Bloesch, echoing Pinnock's concern, judges: "The real battle lines in the future will be between those who espouse a revisionist theology bent on updating theology and bringing it into greater harmony with contemporary experience, and those who uphold a confessional theology that witnesses to the claims of the gospel as presented in Scripture and church tradition."[35] To be revisionist is to be guided so much by the contemporary that little or no distinctively Christian good news is left to be communicated.

A revisionist theology will not be espoused here to the extent of allowing contemporary experience to set the theological agenda and effectively determine what finally is acceptable faith content for Christians. But the inevitable tension remains. The dual task of a responsible theologian, the necessary past-present balance, is reflected well in Thomas Oden's statement of his own writing mission: "to deliver as clearly as I can that core of consensual belief...that has been shared for two hundred decades...[and] seek language that makes plausible today the intent of classical Christianity."[36] The consensual belief core is "orthodox"; the clarity of current communication (in language and life) is "radical." The challenge of adequate Christian theology is to be both.

---

[33] See the text in *Christianity Today*, June 17, 1977, 28-29.

[34] It also is true that a rush to remain rigidly in the historic faith can easily become a deluge of other distortions, including being commonly perceived as irrelevant to the times.

[35] Donald Bloesch, *A Theology of Word and Spirit* (InterVarsity Press, 1992), 267.

[36] Thomas Oden, *The Word of Life* (Harper, 1989), x.

This dual theological task also is reflected clearly in Donald Bloesch's statement of definition. He understands Christian theology to be "the systematic reflection within a particular culture on the self-revelation of God in Jesus Christ as attested in Holy Scripture and witnessed to in the tradition of the catholic church." Theology in this sense, Bloesch concludes, is "both biblical and contextual. Its norm is Scripture, but its field or arena of action is the cultural context in which we find ourselves."[37]

Bloesch's definition certainly is mission minded, but not in the sense found in the writing of Gustavo Gutiérrez, the influential liberation theologian who identifies theology as "a critical reflection on historical praxis."[38] By "praxis" Gutiérrez means direct involvement in the current class struggle to build a new and more just society. Bloesch, by contrast, although not without deep sympathy for human justice, rightly sees theology's role as expressing the significance of the new creation that already has broken into this world in Jesus Christ. This divinely enabled new creation is highly relevant to the social dilemmas of our fallen world. The only point to be made is that this world and our actions in it are not in themselves the *source* and *norm* of Christian theology. They certainly are its context and concern.

---

[37] Donald Bloesch, *A Theology of Word and Spirit*, 114. The associated dilemma, of course, is that the shape of even this confessional theology is and should be impacted by assumptions made about the nature of revelation, the church, and Christian ethics. Note James McClendon, Jr., who claims we need: "(1) To find and focus upon that theological center, the vision around which our constructive work can be done. Honoring the past (but not too much!), we must trust God to lead us into the future (and not too late!); (2) We need to do this by acknowledging the rich resources for theology in the narrative common life of that vision; and (3) We need to seize the appropriate point of departure for reflection upon this narrative and common life in theological ethics" (*Ethics: Systematic Theology*, vol. 1, Abingdon Press, 1986, 27).

[38] See Bloesch, op. cit., 115, footnote 39. Note, however, the clarification of Gutiérrez that his emphasis on *orthopraxis* "is not to deny the meaning of *orthodoxy*, understood as a proclamation of and reflection on statements considered to be true. Rather, the goal is to balance and even to reject the primacy and almost exclusiveness which doctrine has enjoyed in Christian life and above all to modify the emphasis, often obsessive, upon the attainment of an orthodoxy which is often nothing more than fidelity to an obsolete tradition or a debatable interpretation" (Gutiérrez, *A Theology of Liberation*, rev. ed., Maryknoll, N.Y.: Orbis Books, 1988, 8).

Focusing on the longstanding "consensual belief" (Oden) is to express reverent respect for the Bible as the defining wellspring of Christian existence. It also is to respect highly the work of the Holy Spirit in assisting the church to be a faithful interpreter of the Word of God as it seeks to relate to and facilitate redemption in the modern world.[39] Highlighting language that is "plausible today" reflects a genuine concern for Christian mission. Oden is right in observing that "works of systematic theology have not characteristically been written in our time as intentional companions to evangelical witness."[40] But his own theology is intended as such a companion, and this one also hopes to be. These pages seek to recover the ancient wisdom of Christian faith, with the Bible accepted as the central norm and contemporary witness a prominent motive.

Prayer and Personal Bias. How can one be responsible theologically? How does one (1) *participate* in the faith, (2) *reflect* upon it–even critically, and (3) *express* the faith's enduring meaning in currently relevant ways, all without distorting the faith itself and aborting faith's crucial mission in today's world? The theological task, necessarily comprising all three of these dimensions, is as demanding as it is essential. Especially is this the case in the contemporary setting.

Note the warning sounded by Kenneth Leech. There is a large and dangerous gulf between the "mystical" theology of the early church theologians and the common academic approach to theology today. The early pattern was to begin and end theological work in prayer, so that "they wrote from what they had seen with the eyes of their spirit, and loved from the depths of their hearts. Their theology flowed from their mysticism and their mysticism flowed from their theology."[41]

---

[39] See chapters six and seven.

[40] Thomas Oden, *The Word of Life* (Harper, 1989), xiii.

[41] Kenneth Leech, *Experiencing God* (Harper & Row, 1985), 344, quoting Harvey Egan, SJ, "The Christian Mystics and Today's Theological Horizon," in *Listening* 17:3 (1982), 204. Compare: "We declare to you what was from the beginning, what we have heard, what we have seen with our eyes, what we have looked at and touched with our hands, concerning the word of life..." (1 John 1:1).

Theological work again should be acknowledged as "interior spiritual progress, not simply a movement which occurs in the realm of ideas." The work of theology itself "needs to be rescued from the intellectual ghettos, and reintegrated with the struggles for justice in the world and for personal and corporate holiness."[42] Beyond concept refinement, theology should be a process of spiritual formation. Recalling Macquarrie's three-fold analysis of theology's central tasks, *participating in* rightly precedes, though never replaces, *reflection on* and *expression of.*

It is to be granted that one always analyzes participation in faith from some personal-cultural vantagepoint, an inevitability that can be a strength or weakness. To some degree we all practice "standpoint theology." Feminist theologians have been right in pointing out the negative results of the dominance of males in the history of biblical interpretation and theological writing. This dominance has led to much false interpretation that obscures the role of women in sacred history and misuses the Bible to keep women subordinated to the wisdom and rule of males. Numerous recent studies have shown that women enjoyed equal discipleship and service in the company of Jesus and in the earliest New Testament church, an equality soon lost in cultural accommodation.[44]

One such study is Elizabeth Fiorenza's *Bread Not Stone*,[45] judged by Elizabeth Achtemeier "a brilliant historical survey which sets squarely before the church its culpability in wandering from its gospel."[46] Achtemeier, however, properly goes on to warn that fem-

---

[42] Leech, *Experiencing God*, 345.

[43] In critique of the first draft of this volume, J. Denny Weaver expressed the caution, characteristic of the Anabaptist (Believers' Church) tradition, that "participating in" not be limited too much to the mystical dimension of the interior spiritual life. There is much external about living within and living out the revelation of God in Jesus. In part, one comes to understand the Jesus Story only by participating in a process of being shaped by and intentionally living out its substantial implications.

[44] See, e.g., Sharon Pearson, "Women in Ministry: A Biblical Vision," *Wesleyan Theological Journal* 31:1(Spring 1996).

[45] Elizabeth Fiorenza, *Bread Not Stone: The Challenge of Feminist Biblical Interpretation* (Boston: Beacon Press, 1984), chapter four.

[46] Elizabeth Achtemeier, "The Impossible Possibility: Evaluating the Feminist Approach to Bible and Theology," *Interpretation* (January, 1988), 46.

inists bring to the interpretative task as much perverting bias as males when, as women, they make their own experience and rightful desire for liberation the measure of the Word of God. She insists that the Bible is not anti-woman. It stands in judgment on the weaknesses of all our human limitations as interpreters. Theologians necessarily operate from their own personal-cultural vantagepoints. This fact can be turned into a constructive tool for making the faith relevant. It also calls the theologian to constant self-examination, humility, and prayer.

A Sea of Human Opinions

God is reported to have said to King Solomon: "If you will walk before me as David your father did, with integrity of heart and uprightness...then I will establish your royal throne over Israel forever" (1 Kings 9:4-5a). Such a divine announcement was both comforting and demanding. How good it is to know that God is present and prepared to establish and maintain forever those who are faithful, those whose integrity before God remains sound and whole. And yet, how challenging is the expectation that disciples of the sovereign God should come to know what is upright and then consistently walk that narrow path with true integrity of heart and life.

The issue is integrity, the integrity of belief and action. The task of Christian discipleship centers in bringing life into conformity with the will of God. Only when there is true congruence between God's life and ours (holy as God is holy) can God be seen in us and thus can God's mission be accomplished through us. That will of God highlights the divine concern for reestablishing the intended divine-human relationship and the healing of all creation. Such covenant intention, however, is only possible when one views God properly, grasps God's central intention clearly, and receives and interprets rightly what God has done in Christ and wishes done in and through those who believe. All of this comprises the substance of Christian theology. All is dependent on divine revelation, not singularly, but primarily, and in relation to the enlightening experience of faith.

The goal is mission. The church's task, as covenant partner with God, is to be an agent in the redemption of a lost world. Doctrine certainly should not dominate or divide believers in premature or unnecessary ways, a disastrous diversion that easily sidetracks the task and devastates the church.[47] Even so, since Christian faith presupposes a particular understanding of God and of human life and destiny, theology should stand on center stage in the church's life.[48] Being on center stage with a definitive theological script to follow, however, has become especially awkward these days. While a viable Christian theology must be in living relation to who God is and what God is seeking to do in this world, understandings of divine identity and activity now are multiple, even inside the Christian community.

Today Christian theology seems to be "drowning in a sea of human opinions and modern trends, having lost touch with the substance and standards of the faith as historically confessed by the churches."[49] The tragedy of this loss is that the church loses its intended identity and becomes hindered in its mission. Many Christian writers of recent years have urged that the church rediscover the unique biblical base of its own existence and counter-cultural message.[50] One must *be* before one can *do*. One must *know* before one can *share*. Meaning derives from the biblical revelation when it is accepted by faith as describing best what reality is and what yet can be in this fallen world.

The circumstance is complicated further by the Christian faith now having to function in secular societies like those of the United

---

[47] See Barry Callen's *It's God's Church! Life and Legacy of Daniel S. Warner* (Anderson, Ind.: Warner Press, 1995) for an example of one Christian leader who spoke prophetically about the negative impact of Christian disunity.

[48] What should be is often not the case. Too many groupings of Christians have so deemphasized the theological base of their lives that they have become little more than socially appreciated community organizations that seek to help with a wide range of personal and public needs (and get tax credit for it). Rather than alternative communities shaped by a vision of reality different from that of the surrounding culture, bodies of Christian people commonly adjust to prevailing public values and expectations, thus subtly becoming tools of the secular status quo.

[49] Clark Pinnock, *Tracking The Maze* (Harper & Row, 1990), ix.

[50] Such a call to clarified identity is found in *Resident Aliens* by Stanley Hauerwas and William Willimon (Nashville: Abingdon Press, 1989). Gabriel Fackre wrote his narrative interpretation of basic Christian doctrine, *The Christian Story* (Eerdmans, 1978, 1984) for this very purpose. He says: "The task of Christian Story-telling is to keep alive

States and Western Europe. Being "dogmatic" about any belief is commonly judged to be arrogant, to infringe on the rights of others with one's private opinion (the place to which all religious beliefs are now said to belong). Reflects Lesslie Newbigin: "As long as the church is content to offer its beliefs modestly as simply one of the many brands available in the ideological supermarket, no offense is taken. But the affirmation that the truth revealed in the gospel ought to govern public life is offensive." [51]

Equally offensive today, given the high value placed by the public on tolerance and personal rights, is any claim that Jesus Christ is *decisive* for faith, the *final* revelation, and the *only* way to God. Welcome indeed is Carl Braaten's recent insistence that apart from Jesus there is no other gospel.[52] This insistence joins the New Testament witness (Acts 4:12; Gal. 1:6-9; 2 Cor. 11:1-6) instead of reducing itself to today's crowded marketplace of relative perceptions. Yes, all perceptions are historically conditioned; but Christian faith still insists that there is a difference between truth and falsehood, and that truth is seen best in Jesus Christ, however limited may be our present perception of that truth and whatever truths can be learned from other religious leaders.

Basic to all this modern confusion is the transitional nature of our times. The twentieth century has been turbulent and troubled. People have sought to "come of age" by throwing off much that in the past has defined the good and the right. This century also has witnessed a vast array of cultural shifts and Christian theological innovations. These ten decades have been a questing and very unsettling time, "an age of transition from so-called modern culture, inaugurated by the Enlightenment, to postmodern culture."[53] Understanding this transition is very important.

---

this set of counter-perceptions so the church may be what it is and see what it is called to see, rather than be made over in the image of the regnant culture" (2).

[51] Lesslie Newbigin, *The Gospel in a Pluralist Society* (Grand Rapids: Eerdmans, 1989), 7.

[52] Carl Braaten, *No Other Gospel!* (Minneapolis: Fortress Press, 1992). See the section "Pluralism and Particularity" in chapter three.

[53] Stanley Grenz and Roger Olson, *20th Century Theology* (InterVarsity Press, 1992), 9.

The "Modern" Mentality. The Enlightenment, an era that began about the end of the seventeenth century, signaled a significant shift in the intellectual history of Europe and America. It tended to reverse the cultural synthesis of the Middle Ages. That synthesis saw the church as the custodian of supreme authority on earth. God was firmly believed to be transcendent in heaven, and faith was dependent on divine revelation. The reverse of this synthesis then emerged with a determination that, free of the control of church institutions and religious dogma, people could exercise their native intellectual abilities in unfettered, individual integrity. Thus was elevated the status of humans and the exercise of human capabilities that were presumed worthy and capable even apart from the direct assistance of God. Now humans would be on center stage, not a transcendent God, a dominating church, or a divine revelation assumed by definition to be authoritative.

Sometimes called the "Age of Reason," the Enlightenment began in part as a response to the religious wars of the seventeenth century. Unbridled emotion for too long had fired religious fanaticism. Could not such conflict be ended by placing more focus on reason? Beyond the Bible, God now was said to have a "second book," nature. Thus "Deism" arose in England. Surely, it now was insisted, religion could be identified as a set of essentials to which all reasonable people could agree. The scientific writings of Isaac Newton (1642-1727) popularized the perspective that the universe is ruled by natural laws. Christianity, then, can and should rest on a rational foundation.

The heart of this new "Enlightenment" experiment was the presumed authority of human reason. It was assumed that one can gain knowledge dispassionately. A person, as an unconditioned scientific observer, can view reality objectively. Religious belief was not necessarily to be discarded. What was different was the shift of focus. The importance of God now was to be determined according to God's perceived *value* for the lives of human beings. The old maxim of Anselm, "I believe in order that I may understand," was reversed so that the quest for knowledge was more, "I believe what I can understand."

A leader of this new, "enlightened" approach to knowledge was Rene Descartes (1596-1650). He was intent on devising a method of philosophic investigation that would lead to discovery of truths that could be said to be absolutely certain. The human self would be its own point of reference. The primary place of beginning would be reasoning humans and not the revealing divine. The authority of the past was thus repudiated in favor of the presumed power of humans to find truth for themselves.

In Enlightenment thinking, so influential to the present time, what is reasonable and scientifically measurable becomes the standard of truth. The whole of reality is said to be a harmonious unity that can be penetrated by reason since the structures of reality and of the human mind correspond. The goal is to bring human life into conformity with the laws of nature that can be identified by reason. Once identified and followed, continuous improvement in personal and social life is possible, even likely. Rational "objectivity" supposedly is possible and sets one free of church authority and on the path of probing and controlling the world for good.

The British empiricist John Locke (1632-1704) was influential in arguing that Christianity, freed of unnecessary dogmatic baggage, is the most reasonable form of religion. Christian theology became a discovery and cataloging of the "facts" of revelation found in the Bible. The faith itself came to function like a science, with religious knowledge turned into rational propositions that have logical coherence. The Bible, in effect, was "modernized." It became "more mechanical, more precise, more impersonal, less mysterious, more subject to human mastery. It became less the living voice of God calling people into communion with the divine and more a collection of precise propositions subject to scientific verification."[54]

It is ironic that the most conservative forms of contemporary Protestantism rely heavily on aspects of Enlightenment methodology in an effort to resist many assumptions and conclusions associated with the Enlightenment. Alexander Campbell, the influential Dis-

---

[54] C. Leonard Allen, *The Cruciform Church*, 2nd ed. (Abilene Christian University Press, 1990), 27.

ciples leader in the nineteenth century, represents so many well-meaning conservatives. He did not read the Bible purely and simply (objectively)–although this was his clear intention. He read it "as a grandchild of the Puritans. He read it as an ardent disciple of John Locke and of the Scottish Common Sense philosophers who adapted Locke's thought.... Campbell was a brilliant intellectual and an intensely serious biblical scholar, but he was, like all of us, a child of his time."[55] More recently, Carl Henry, Millard Erickson, Ronald Nash, and R. C. Sproul tend toward rationalism in the service of establishing, explaining, and defending a truly transcendent God and a truly authoritative divine revelation. This rationalism, even when used as a way to establish the authority of divine revelation, is part of the problem for which solution now is being sought in the widespread quest for the "postmodern."

Moving Beyond the Modern. As the twentieth century ends, there is growing awareness that much of this Enlightenment mentality is weakening. Increasingly its adequacy is questioned. Although its modes of perception and practice are yet strong and persistent, including their control over much of the arena of conservative Christian theology, increasing numbers of interpreters now argue convincingly that "modes of certitude and domination reflected by the Enlightenment and sustained for a very long time are a spent force that no longer commands authority or allegiance."[56] Reality appears more complex than the rigid categories of human rationality. Intellectual know-how has not delivered the good life. Progress and peace obviously are not the natural followers of rational thinking and living.[57] If the Enlightenment is what typically is meant by "modern," then something "postmodern" needs to and slowly is emerging.

What has been is clear enough. That a significant cultural shift is in progress is rather clear. However, what soon will be as an alter-

---

[55] Allen, *The Cruciform Church*, 25.

[56] Walter Brueggemann, *Texts Under Negotiation* (Minneapolis: Fortress Press, 1993), 6.

[57] See Langdon Gilkey, *Society and the Sacred: Toward a Theology of Culture in Decline* (N. Y.: Crossroad, 1981), 3-14.

native is not yet clear. In the meantime, what should constitute Christian theological faithfulness? At least partial answers are available. In part, and basic to Christian theology, there should be a reversal of the "modernizing" of the Bible, so that again the Bible is seen less mechanically, less rationally precise as though it were a collection of propositions subject to scientific verification and human mastery. It should be seen more personally and mysteriously, more relationally, more as the ancient Hebrews saw it, more able to be prophetic, more the living voice of God calling people into communion with the divine.

Caution certainly is in order as Christian theology seeks to adjust to changing circumstances. Rejecting select assumptions of the Enlightenment is necessary in light of a "postmodern" awareness of their inadequacy and of their being contrary to biblical views of reality. What is not necessary or appropriate is the rejection of much that the Enlightenment properly has brought forward, things that cannot again be ignored by responsible theologians. Critical views of history, the scientific method, the processes of biblical "criticism," and the reality of cultural conditioning of all theological work are advances that carry enduring lessons, even if each has been taken to extremes.[58]

So "modernism" is under attack and Christian theology needs to react with care and courage. The baby of the Enlightenment should not be thrown out with its considerable bathwater. Nor should there be such an overreaction to rational systematizing that we become complete "deconstructionists." Language about faith issues, for instance, admittedly is itself a social construct. Even so, it goes too far to insist that religious language by its very nature is *merely* a cultural product, not tied to what is inherent in reality. Language need not be seen as only a tool of power in the hands of those who dominate

---

[58] See Bernard Ramm, *The Evangelical Heritage* (Waco, Tx.: Word Books, 1973), 70-73. In regard to biblical criticism, Walter Brueggemann, a prominent biblical scholar who honors the role of the most serious biblical study, nonetheless expresses considerable caution. With historical criticism, he says, theological interpretation "has sought validation in facticity behind the text. The outcome of such a procedure is that the texts themselves are largely dismissed, and words themselves do not count for much" (*Texts Under Negotiation*, 6).

a culture, even though it often is used this way.[59] Theology as a for-malized and authoritative language "system" is rightly suspect. On the other hand, theology that is not expressed constructively and coher-ently in language understandable today has little chance of making a difference. Reason, therefore, should remain, just not as the sole or even primary authority in the knowing and communicating process-es of Christians.[60]

Change must be faced carefully and with courage and creativ-ity. Contemporary people think increasingly in "process" terms. All appears to be changing all of the time. Parmenides long ago held that "being" is prior to "becoming," that some reality endures behind all change. Heraclitus, on the contrary, observed that one cannot even step twice into the same river. The basis of reality is constant change. The Christian tradition originally took shape in the more static con-cepts of "being" and "substance," although its Hebraic roots are not so static and restrictive.

Today human experience has been drawing common perception toward the more "process" view of things. Can Christian theology speak relevantly in this more fluid context? Is the nature of the good news of God in Christ compatible with the more dynamic thought categories of our day? Should the faith stand stubbornly with Par-menides in the face of modern perception to the contrary? Finding answers to such questions is not optional for contemporary Christian theology. Some acknowledgement of the helpfulness of "process" the-ology will be appropriate at points.[61]

---

[59] See Diogenes Allen, "The End of the Modern World," *Christian Scholar's Review* (June, 1993), 339-347.

[60] See Donald A. D. Thorsen, *The Wesleyan Quadrilateral* (Zondervan, 1990). Thorsen explains the important, although secondary role of human reason in the work of John Wesley.

[61] On the one hand, theologian Daniel Migliore insists that responsible Christian theology must be "true to the revelation of God in Jesus Christ as attested in Scripture." On the other hand, "it is necessary to reinterpret the language of Christian faith–its sto-ries, doctrines, and symbols–for our time and place if we are faithfully to serve the gospel rather than uncritically endorse the cultural forms in which it has been mediated to us" (*Faith Seeking Understanding*, 10, 12). A philosophic perspective certainly is a "cultural form." Christians see the need for translating the Bible itself into numerous human lan-guages. Each new translation is still considered the Bible, even though now appearing

This present work sees wisdom in the judgment of Ray Dunning who, in his recent systematic theology, adopted the "relational model of ontology in contrast to substantial modes of thought."[62] This adoption, while especially compatible with current cultural thinking, is not really new. Martin Luther in the sixteenth century abandoned the fixed modes of thought defining the Roman Catholic theology of his day because he intuitively grasped the fact that "the primary categories of Hebraic-Christian belief are *all* relational."[63] Dunning notes that "carnality" is always adjectival in the New Testament. Thus, carnality is not an evil *substance* to be removed from within one, but a broken *relationship* to be put right. A change in relationship will affect significantly one's attitudes, character, and actions. Christian thought and life is best conceived and fulfilled in relational terms.

Also wise is some adjustment in what has been a typical understanding of theological language. In Western culture people tend to assume a "positivistic" view of language. Language is thought to be direct, hopefully a precise reporting of the facts of experience. Such an Enlightenment view of language fits well our technological times and the prevailing mood of American pragmatism. It hardly fits Christian prayer or Christian theology in general (although it supports effectively a fundamentalism that seeks doctrinal precision at the rational and verbal levels).

As Walter Brueggemann says of the Psalms, "the use of language does not describe what is. It evokes to being what is not until it has been spoken." Special speech like this "resists discipline,

---

in a different language. While biblical translation is never an exact duplication, it is judged authoritative nonetheless, still the Bible. This says something significant about the multi-cultural nature of Christian "catholicity" (as opposed to Islam where the Koran translated out of Arabic is no longer considered the Koran by Muslims). It speaks against a "verbal inerrancy" view of biblical inspiration and for a church open to the richness that is brought to the gospel by the perspectives of various cultural communities (see Justo González, *Out of Every Tribe and Nation: Christian Theology at the Ethnic Roundtable*, Nashville: Abingdon Press, 1992, chap. 2).

[62] H. Ray Dunning, *Grace, Faith, and Holiness* (Kansas City: Beacon Hill Press, 1988), 14.

[63] Douglas Hall, *Imaging God* (Grand Rapids: Eerdmans, 1986), 99.

shuns precision, delights in ambiguity, is profoundly creative, and is itself an exercise in freedom." Such biblical language plays a double role suited to Christian theology. Concludes Brueggemann, "the language of the Psalms permits us to be boldly *anticipatory* about what may be, as well as *discerning* about what has been."[64] This more dynamic view of religious language fits well with elements of process and relational categories for theological meanings and mandates. Biblical stories often are magnificent metaphors that should not be flattened to merely descriptive and propositional language. Dealing with the divine drives one to the flexibility and expansiveness of narrative, story, metaphor, and poetry.[65] God cannot be captured by any or all of our human words!

The church should seek to address responsibly the genuine crisis in Christian identity that has emerged recently in the midst of shifting philosophies and secular societies. This identity crisis is seen in the relative silence of Scripture in today's church.[66] Unfortunately, the Bible no longer exercises anything like the authority it once did in many Christian communities. Where it does remain influential, the Bible often is used woodenly as divine justification for well-established social injustices that clearly are human in origin. There is a deep longing for certainty. Some Christians say it is not possible or necessary to attain. Others rush to claiming it prematurely, almost in blind faith.

As theologians, to some degree we are all children of our times, even while we seek to speak prophetically to our times about God and with God's authority. Theology, very much a human as well as a

---

[64] Walter Brueggemann, *Praying the Psalms* (Winona, Minn.: Saint Mary's Press, 1986), 28-29.

[65] Having affirmed, in response to Isaiah 40:1-11, that "only poetry can even attempt to speak of what happens when God comes," William Willimon poses this penetrating question: "Has the eschatological been neglected in our faith in recent centuries because many contemporary interpreters of the Christian faith are powerful, affluent and therefore content with the status quo, or because many contemporary interpreters are merely historical critics or theologians rather than poets?" (*Proclamation: Advent/Christmas*, Series B, vol. 5, Fortress Press, 1993, 16).

[66] See James Smart, *The Strange Silence of the Bible in the Church* (Philadelphia: The Westminster Press, 1970).

divine enterprise, always is in transition. Rejecting the oversimplified view that theology is a "science" of God that confidently systematizes a specific body of doctrine presumed to exist implicitly or explicitly in Scripture (the rational Enlightenment mentality), we affirm that the Christian theologian is a pilgrim thinker working on behalf of a pilgrim people.[67] There is revelation, but it is too dynamic, too personal, relating too much to a truly sovereign God for it to be put in a computer and manipulated at will.

Therapists or Theologians? The urge to manipulate the divine for personal benefit is a pervasive problem. Adding to the Bible's relative silence, possibly arising from it, is the sobering fact that many professed Christian people today do not expect or allow their own identities to be defined by Christian teachings, practices, or language. For many people, including many who are openly identified as Christian believers, there appears to be little or no direct sense of living out of the resources and authority of a specific theological tradition. Instead, there is a rootless wandering among the many truth options currently prominent. With this wandering comes an erosion of the perceived importance of theology for church life–at least a kind of Christian theology that has firm roots in a normative past and offers a prophetic power for the groping present. Even people of faith are pragmatic and self-serving regarding what they believe and how beliefs voiced in church are seen as relating or not relating to other aspects of life.

Is it legitimate or lethal to refocus the Christian faith and the church's life around the interests and felt needs of today's churchgoers? When the pews are filled with "babyboomers" returning to religion, often on their own terms, should the pulpits be filled with marketwise ministers? Is the church called to be a religious supermarket advertising a supply-side spirituality and a currently fashionable theology? Can the church prosper long and maintain its own integrity if it continues to participate in a subtle shifting of the faith's focus

---

[67] See Daniel Stevick, *Beyond Fundamentalism* (Richmond, Va.: John Knox Press, 1964), 69.

from the glorification of God to the gratification of its constituents? Are church members called to be penitents saved by grace or clients who are served well, basically in relation to their own felt needs?

What about theology? Increasingly the membership roles of the churches are filled with people not particularly "brand" conscious. Ministers commonly play the roles of program innovators, community cheerleaders, political strategists, marketing experts, and chief executive officers. Some of the most prominent religious leaders today are *therapists* more than *theologians.* Waves of Sunday School graduates are found to be almost biblically illiterate. When new congregations are planted, often by sophisticated marketing techniques aimed at selected target groups, those who comprise the new congregations tend to be attracted by things quite other than a particular theological tradition, and maybe not by theological concerns at all.

Many professed Christians today are more *belongers* than *believers.* They seek experiences that move them. Feeling fads are a bane of our day. Now is a time when prophetic voices should announce again that mindlessness is not a Christian virtue. The visceral may be tantalizing and even temporarily satisfying, but it tends to be shallow and subjective, the surface but not the substance of the faith. Spiritual experience, crucial as it is, requires the solid foundation of the truth of the faith if subjective perversions are to be avoided.

The biblical account carries a consistent warning. People find it so easy to relax in their traditions, disconnect religious practice from the values actually expressed in everyday life, and carry on lots of "worship" with little vital awareness of or obedience to God. Even people well acquainted with the God-oriented traditions of ancient Israel can grow complacent about the divine presence. So it was in the many troubled generations following the reign of King David.

Israel's worship, according to the biblical prophets, had become a mockery of God's rule. The people loved to worship (Amos 4:4-5; 5:23), but there was something about it that wearied God (Isa. 1:12-15). In the middle of all the religious activity there was a serious lack of attention being given to the person and will of the God being worshipped. The "worship experience" was not to be an end in itself.

When any people loses its sense of relationship to its personal Lord, even worship can become sin (Amos 4:4-5), something God hates (Amos 5:21-24; cf. Isa. 1:10-17). There must be a God-centeredness to true worship and the congruence of the faith expressed in worship and that lived in the streets. As Hosea 6:6 puts it, God desires "steadfast love, not sacrifice, the knowledge of God, rather than burnt offerings."

Even though an effective telling of the biblical story of God in Israel and in Christ should be styled to contemporary hearers for the sake of their understanding, a task never finished in ever-shifting times, this biblical story does carry substance beyond the contemporary setting. There is revelation from God apart from our "experiencing" of it. As Gabriel Fackre says:

> There is an out-thereness of biblical truth which is to be seen, whatever the angle of vision, and however our view of it is affected by the glasses we are wearing. There is an object with which our subjectivity deals. There is a Story which our translation seeks to communicate. There is a hard core of affirmation at the center of our perceptions and interpretations.[68]

Craig Miller, seeking to make relevant such out-thereness, summarizes the distinctive roots and attitudes of the babyboomer generation (those born in the post-war economic boom from 1946 to 1964). This generation is characterized by brokenness, loneliness, rootlessness, and self-seeking. Such people, now the North American office and wealth holders as the twentieth century closes, are seekers after something outside themselves that can provide meaning, togetherness, and healing. What they usually embrace is "unconventional, anti-institutional, emotional, experiential, and deeply personal."[69]

---

[68] Gabriel Fackre, *The Christian Story*, rev. ed. (Grand Rapids: Eerdmans, 1978, 1984), 11.

[69] Craig Miller, *BabyBoomer Spirituality* (Nashville: Discipleship Resources, 1992), 59.

This pattern tends to leave quite vulnerable the mainline denominations that are heavy on structure and tradition. It tends to place historically rooted, closely reasoned, and authoritarian sounding theological systems in the categories of perceived irrelevance and threats to personal freedom. To such a generation the biblical revelation now must be told with both intellectual sensitivity and lived authenticity.[70] This telling and living, while reaching for means of relevant communication, should not abandon the historical essence of the Christian revelation or the Christian mission. The story is not told best by erasing its script.

Clarification of the Sovereign

In loving grace, God exists and comes. Therefore, the future is open and full of positive possibility. God comes to transform and send, not primarily to make believers feel good, answer all of our human questions, and shield the faithful from the pain and death associated with being mortal. Attention should be fixed on the coming God, the potential of the divine presence, and the coming future enabled by God.

Jürgen Moltmann argues persuasively that Christian eschatology proclaims that God intends in the future to do a wonderful new thing on behalf of the world. Knowing this inspires hope that frees the believer for creative action in the meantime. The Bible, "the history book of God's promises," is to be seen as the divine revelation that reveals to us "the coming God."[71] Theology, then, is understood as an interpretation of this visionary biblical history, an interpretation that becomes the basis for the contemporary mission of the church in the

---

[70] There is good reason to believe that the young of today are ready to hear biblical proclamation when it comes clearly, courageously, and from credible Christians. See William Willimon, "Hunger in This Abandoned Generation" in Barry Callen, ed., *Sharing Heaven's Music* (Nashville: Abingdon Press, 1995), 21-32.

[71] Jürgen Moltmann, *The Experiment in Hope* (Philadelphia: Fortress Press, 1975), 45. See also Robert Cornelison, "The Reality of Hope: Moltmann's Vision for Theology," in *The Asbury Theological Journal* (Spring, 1993), 109-120. Moltmann's vision is that all Christian theology should be political, dialogical, ecumenical, and always permeated and motivated by the Christian hope.

world. Theology should be biblically rooted, mission motivated, and permeated by a hope derived from the now-coming and then-coming God of loving grace. It is to speak to both the church and the world. In its speech, however, Christian theology should seek to represent the redemptive message of the gospel and not the current "wisdom" of the world. It is to be a careful and currently understandable expression of the Word of God, not the mere words of a questing humanity. Our hope rests only in God.

Theology necessarily employs some philosophic perspective as it seeks to express its message about God in a clear and coherent form. Even so, its primary obligation is to be faithful to divine revelation rather than to what now serves as a useful rational tool. The goal of theology is to bring all human understanding into submission to the Word of God, not into the controlling domain of the methods and definitions of any particular philosophic pattern of discourse. While human reason has an important role to play, it should be preceded by faith and directed by divine grace. Again, theology evolves from a participation in the faith, the theologian being a believer working on behalf of the mission of the church. The method of Christian theology is essentially faith seeking understanding (Anselm) and not predominantly reason preparing the way for faith (Abelard).

In the midst of today's sea of human opinions, Christian theology must not deteriorate into just another idealistic anthropology, as many "liberalisms" make it appear. Theology should not be merely the verbalization of religious experience.[72] Rather, it should be an experientially informed and contextually sensitive expression of divine revelation, done by an active faith participant, in part with reliance on human reason, but always in the service of prior divine revelation. The quest is for the hearing of a word *from God* and *about God* in the midst of a sea of human opinions.

Christian theology is based on something that breaks into the realm of human experience from the beyond and offers to enlighten

---

[72] Verbalization of religious experience is the basic way that the task of theology was conceived by Friedrich Schleiermacher (1768-1834), the "father" of "liberal Protestantism."

and transform. Once made new by the God who is present to save, Christian disciples come increasingly to know God. God is revealed biblically as the One who rights relationships, is present in the relativities of the historical process, and calls to an obedient partnership in the divine plan to renew all creation. Christian theology seeks to hear the biblical story that unfolds this plan and makes known this God of loving grace. It calls believers to engage this revelation and be engaged and recreated by it.

There is good news needing to be heard in the modern marketplace of failed human dreams. Sharing this news requires a people who already have heard and been changed by the gospel of God in Israel and in Christ. Sharing as Christian disciples on mission requires a level of understanding, skill of translating, and credibility of life application that come only from actually being a new people in light of the biblical revelation of the God of loving grace. Theologians are themselves to be Christ's disciples. Their theological work is to provide a guide to participation in Christ's mission. This guidance roots in and finally is about the God who is the power of loving grace come among us lost and hurting people for our salvation.

One biblical case study will help clarify the proper path now needing to be followed. The dramatic story of the prophet Elijah on Mount Carmel (1 Kings 18-19) is "the audacious clarification of sovereignty."[73] The lack of rain had become a matter of life and death. Addressing this crisis became a contest between the God of Israel and the local gods who were said by their priests to be in charge of natural phenomena.

The dominant culture, with its kings, priests, rituals, and gods, was challenged by Elijah, prophet of Yahweh. Elijah charged that the cultural traditionalism could not deliver, could not keep its promises, could not solve this major "energy crisis." The key question was: Can the gods of the time really give life? Who really is God? Elijah believed that the God-question is crucial because everything naturally follows from it. Here we find a discussion of the relation between the *processes of life* and the *source of life*. Walter Brueggemann explains:

---

[73] Walter Brueggemann, ed. Patrick Miller, *A Social Reading of the Old Testament* (Minneapolis: Augsburg Fortress, 1994), 234.

Canaanite religion, Baalism, and indeed every civil religion, argues and presumes that the processes of life contain and are identical with the source of life. Being able to manage the process gives one control over the source. Now what this means practically is that the establishment–political, religious, or scientific–has access to the processes and can secure its own existence by mastering the processes. Baalism is a religion that believes that the mystery of life has now been put at our disposal and that we have life on the terms we might like.[74]

The Enlightenment mind-set is that humans can effectively control life. We now have the needed rational and technical *processes* and thus have virtually become the *source* of life itself. This self-seduction was challenged for all time by Elijah, who insisted that rain comes by the graciousness of the sovereign God, not by human manipulation. The best way to life's source is the process of humble prayer (1 Kings 18:36-37). God is a God of loving grace, the giver of good gifts; but God also is sovereign and not available for our "use" as desired. God is not reducible to a "technique" for our human well-being. God is not "an echo of creation...but a free agent about whom a decision must be made."[75] Such prophetic theology exposes all idols used to support the social systems of humanity by insisting on the sovereignty of God. In the midst of the many human kingdoms that seem to so dominate our earthly lives, there is urgent need today to refocus attention on the kingdom *of God*.

The dominant theme of the teaching of Jesus was the priority and fresh presence in his own coming of the kingdom of God. This theme refocused all concerns toward the gracious arrival of the sovereign God in the midst of the troubled life of God's people in this world. Such refocusing, such emphasis on the arriving God, is urgently needed again.

What exactly is the kingdom of God? At least it is the arena of time and place where the reign of God is effectively present. A "lib-

---

[74] Ibid., 235.

[75] Ibid., 237.

eral" understanding of the kingdom, one popular today, highlights a social-ethical vision. This view tends to equate the transformation of abusive economic and political structures, in the name of God's love and justice, with bringing in the kingdom.[76] A rediscovery of the prominence of the apocalyptic element in biblical materials, however, has brought a shift in perspective for many interpreters. Rather than the goal of bringing about a more just human society, the kingdom of God has come to be seen more in the context of Jesus' teaching of a dramatic intervention by God in human history. Johannes Weiss saw this inbreaking as yet future,[77] while C. H. Dodd countered with a "realized eschatology" that sees Jesus already having inaugurated the kingdom's coming.[78]

Now a mediating already-not-yet view has emerged that in varying configurations has been accepted widely.[79] God's kingdom in its fullest reality and final consummation is said to await the second advent of Christ. That is not yet. In the meantime, as the result of Christ's first advent, the kingdom now is an inaugurated reality that people are called to enter (Mk. 9:47; Matt. 21:31-32). Recognizing the kingly presence of God in our time, the kingdom of God is an invitation for all who will to live in the power of this presence, consciously deciding for this reign (Matt. 13:44-46), and doing God's will (Matt. 6:10, 7:21-23).

This mediating position gives new impetus to the kingdom of God as an integrating motif for Christian theology.[80] In view is an eschatological kingdom to be fully understood and realized only at the eschaton, the very end of time itself. Nevertheless, already this king-

---

[76] See especially Walter Rauschenbusch, *Christianity and the Social Crisis* (1907) and *A Theology for the Social Gospel* (1917). More recent is the already classic *A Theology of Liberation* by Gustavo Gutiérrez (1971, rev. 1988). This approach, worthy and appropriate so far as it goes, tends to capitalize too much on the questionable Enlightenment optimism about the socially relevant potential of human reason and action.

[77] Johannes Weiss, *Jesus' Proclamation of the Kingdom of God* (1892).

[78] C. H. Dodd, *The Parables of the Kingdom* (1935).

[79] See George Eldon Ladd, *A Theology of the New Testament,* rev. ed. (Grand Rapids: Eerdmans, 1974, 1993), 54-117.

[80] For instance, Jürgen Moltmann, *Theology of Hope* (1965) and Wolfhart Pannenberg, *Theology and the Kingdom of God* (1969).

dom's reality and power are at work, breaking into the human present from God's future. Accepting the "nowness" of the "will be" sets a distinctively divine context for the Christian understanding of all things.

The rise of a postmodern mentality at the close of the twentieth century joins biblical thought in suggesting that continued use of the kingdom theme as a focusing theological concept should be complemented with a *corporate* vision. There is to be a people, the church, who are intended to come into being as embodiment, foretaste, and agent of the kingdom of God already here and yet to come. The fact of God's present reign is to be joined by an actual people who are committed to being obedient to the divine reign.

A caution is in order. Kingdom theology, especially one poised primarily to wait for the final inbreaking of God, "easily degenerates into an individualistic theology."[81] However, the current cultural shift and the biblical vision move toward increased community focus. Noting the significant insights of Emile Durkheim (1858-1917) and George Herbert Mead (1863-1931), Stanley Grenz urges "the twin motifs" of the reign of God and the resulting community of God as forming together a proper integrating perspective for a contemporary Christian theology.[82] The God of loving grace initiates a redeemed community that seeks to reflect faithfully the nature and work of God in the world.

God is sovereign. By sheer grace the divine reign has begun to penetrate the world of sinful humanity. The resulting role of the redeemed community is crucial. The believing community "transmits from generation to generation and region to region the redemptive story, which it recounts in word and deed. In so doing it mediates to us as believers the framework for the formation of our personal identity, values and world view."[83] The story is about God, the God

---

[81] Stanley Grenz, *Revisioning Evangelical Theology* (InterVarsity Press, 1993), 148.

[82] The Believers' Church tradition has both highlighted the church as a central theological theme, consciously joined by adult decision, and been vulnerable to the invasion of an individualism that undercuts the essential corporateness of this theme. The Wesleyan theological tradition supports a resistance to individualism. See, e.g., Barry Callen, "Daniel Warner: Joining Holiness and All Truth Together," *Wesleyan Theological Journal* 30:1 (Spring 1995), 92-110.

[83] Grenz, op. cit., 159.

of loving grace, the One before and after all time, the One now reigning in the midst of our troubled world!

The Believers' Church (Anabaptist) tradition rightly maintains as central a vision of the church and its relationship to the presentness of the kingdom of God. This vision varies significantly from the relatively weak view of the church held today by the "evangelical" movement in general. J. Denny Weaver lists the three priorities of the Anabaptist consensus, identifying number two as *community*.[84] The Christian gospel includes the coming into being of a new social reality, the church, the body of Christ formed only as believers are "in Christ" and thereby have their relationships transformed and their oneness created as an alternative to the destructive patterns of our fallen world. Thus the church is viewed as "the sphere of obedience to kingdom authority. The church, in its social life and relationship to the world, is to be an anticipatory expression of the kingdom of its Lord."[85]

The church is the corporate setting where the peace, justice, and joy of the Holy Spirit are to be experienced in the world (Rom. 14:17). As Wilmer Cooper reports about the Quaker tradition: "Friends have had a deep sense that one ought to be able to live as if the kingdom of God were a reality here and now and not some golden age of the past or some blessed event of the future." This vision is not inherently individualistic since "along with a drive for Christian perfection in one's personal life, there must be a corresponding drive for Christian perfection in the corporate, social, and political world."[86]

Here the church is seen as the intended sign of the presence of the kingdom of God now arrived in a limited, but in a true and visible way. The church is to be a community of memory, the carrier of the biblical revelation of the seeking and saving Word of God in Israel and in Christ. It is to be the community of grace wherein the power of the present God works to nurture lives of faith and faithfulness. As an

---

[84] J. Denny Weaver, *Becoming Anabaptist* (Scottdale, Pa.: Herald Press, 1987), 120ff.

[85] C. Norman Kraus, "Evangelicalism: A Mennonite Critique," in Donald Dayton and Robert Johnston, eds., *The Variety of American Evangelicalism* (InterVarsity Press, 1991), 191.

[86] Wilmer Cooper, *A Living Faith* (Richmond, Ind.: Friends United Press, 1990), 102.

authentic reflection, an anticipatory expression and sign of God's will "on earth as it is in heaven," the church is to be a visible embodiment and active agent of the redemptive work of the God of loving grace.

Linking in this way the kingdom of God with its intended result, the church, provides essential biblical perspective. The kingdom may be thought of as no more than a grand abstraction, a distant memory, or a future hope. The church, however, as the kingdom's immediate expression, can and should be a living context for the exercise of faith and the processing of life within the *present* reign of God.[87] This corporate journey of faith in light of God's present reign brings a self-validating public witness to the significance of faith in Jesus Christ. The nature of truth takes on a personal and "narrative" rather than a detached and "objective" character. Theology is tied to real and ongoing history. The center is the God who *now is* as well as always was and yet will be.

This kingdom-church perspective may be viewed helpfully as the central plot of God's great drama of redemption. The full range of Christian theology is a revealing narrative of the arriving reign of God. God has come among us to recreate by grace and form by the Spirit a people who will be obedient to divine sovereignty. The church is to embody the power of the good news and gratefully spread the Word in the world that God created, still loves and forgives, and currently is re-creating by loving and patient grace.

The chapters to follow seek to explore the true nature of this sovereign, loving, re-creating, grace-full God. Our exploration will be disciplined by that which is revealed in the biblical narrative of how God has chosen to be with us in Israel, in Christ, and still today in the Spirit.[88] We will seek humbly to learn of the triune God of loving grace.

---

[87] See John Bright, *The Kingdom of God* (Abingdon Press, 1953), especially chapter eight, "Between Two Worlds: The Kingdom and the Church."

[88] According to Gerald Bray (*The Doctrine of God*, InterVarsity Press, 1993, 51): "Christian theology is the systematic exposition of a knowledge of God based on personal encounter with him in and through his revelation of himself to us. It may be possible to supplement this revelation by independent observation, but the controlling factor in any analysis of God and his works can be only his own self-disclosure."

Part One

SOVEREIGN:

The God Who Stands and Creates, the Source of Loving Grace

CHAPTER TWO

GOD THE SOVEREIGN: DIVINE BEING

—

"...the Father, the Almighty..."

—

The Nicene Creed is clear. God is one, almighty, father, creator of all that is. This Christian belief stands on the shoulders of Israel who long ago came to believe in the uniqueness of God: "Hear, O Israel, the Lord is our God, the Lord alone. You shall love the Lord your God with all your heart, and with all your soul, and with all your might" (Deut. 6:4f). Isaiah confesses that the Lord, the Creator and Redeemer, is the God not only of Israel, but of all people. All other "gods" are mere idols: "And there is no other god besides me, a righteous God and a Saviour; there is none besides me. Turn to me and be saved, all the ends of the earth! For I am God, and there is no other" (Isa. 45:21-22). A primary learning of modern theology is the realization that "in the knowing process God is *subject*, not *object*.... History has purpose and is directed to a goal–the final revelation of the glory of God."[1]

Christian theology explores the inexhaustible mystery of God. Humility on the part of humans is necessary given the divine subject. A sense of awe should surround all discussion of God. There is silence in heaven when the Lamb breaks the seventh seal

---

[1] Stanley Grenz, *Theology for the Community of God* (Nashville: Broadman & Holman, 1994), 62-66.

(Rev. 8:1). So should it always be. We proceed with the discussion of the nature of God, but with considerable caution and great gratitude.

Christians, however, speak of God in more than vague terms. They speak on the basis of very particular and defining actions of God attested by Scripture. Theology attempts to clarify human understanding of God by seeking to interpret the enduring meaning of the biblical narrative. In doing so, it never pretends full comprehension. However, because of faith in the reliability of the biblical narrative of God with us in Israel and in Jesus Christ, "orthodox" theology affirms with faithful confidence that God is one, eternal, almighty, and "Father."[2] Together these descriptions constitute at least an adequate apprehending of God. They are based on God's Self-revelation as the sovereign who comes to a lost creation as loving grace.

In the late nineteenth century and still today there is a cultural context that challenges both subtly and overtly the existence or at least real knowledge of a truly sovereign God. The central Enlightenment motifs of "modernity" include (1) scientific orientation, (2) emphasis on what is natural, experienced, and verifiable, (3) a search for the well-being of humans in this world, and (4) the assumption of the autonomy of persons and the nowness of the satisfactions they seek. So the persistent questions in recent decades have been: Is there a God? Can such a One, if existing, be experienced, known, or even spoken of meaningfully? Is such experience testable, such knowledge verifiable, and such speech free of major cultural conditioning? Or is all such experience illusory, such seeming knowledge a mere projection, such God-talk essentially empty? Many have concluded that it is empty, self-serving, even dangerous.[3]

---

[2] Note the "Limits of Gender Language" section of this chapter for consideration of contemporary concerns about the seemingly gender-specific word "Father" in the Bible, classic Christian creeds, and worship practice.

[3] Prominent names include Feuerbach in philosophy, Nietzsche in literature, Comte in social science, Marx in economics, and Lenin in politics. All sought to dethrone what they judged the needless and hurtful hypothesis of God.

These questions, typical of the modern period, clearly betray Enlightenment assumptions about reality. Addressing them appropriately will take into consideration some alternate assumptions drawn from the ancient Hebrew faith inherited by the earliest Christians. This faith includes affirmation of the one God who is the eternal and almighty Father.

Starting at the Beginning

Where does one begin in addressing the subject of God? Given the unsearchableness of God, one is almost forced to poetry and song, dynamic and celebrative forms of expression related to the ultimately inexpressible God. John and Charles Wesley, e.g., composed and published thousands of new hymns, many designed to teach a proper understanding of God. These brothers knew that Christian worship is to be informed by an emphatic and balanced trinitarianism.[4] Such a complex view of the divine reality, God somehow being both three and one, is revealed through the biblical record of divine actions. Where is the best place to begin gaining an adequate apprehension of God as understood in the Christian faith?

God always has been at the beginning. The Bible starts with "in the beginning God" (Genesis 1:1). The Nicene and Apostles' Creeds both head their classic lists of affirmations with belief in "God, the Father Almighty, Creator of heaven and earth." As known in the biblical tradition, God is the ultimate One, always prior to all time and all things. There was nothing in the beginning except God. But the question persists. Where do we limited human beings begin our quest for knowledge of the divine?

Christian faith is formed around the belief that God is known best in Jesus Christ. Therefore, a reasonable case can be made for not starting theological explorations with the eternal God. The experience of Elton Trueblood (1900-1994) explains why. Trueblood, a gifted young philosopher and traditional Quaker, was

---

[4] A discussion of the classic doctrine of the "Trinity" is found in chapter four.

influenced early in his life by what he called "the conventional liberalism of my student days."[5] He had come to suppose rather uncritically that the opponents of Christianity had a monopoly on reason, while the Christian had nothing to rely on except faith. Most modern people seem now to accept only what their senses encounter and their reasoning appears to make obvious. The dramatic rise of science has come to explain so much that used to be seen as "divine" mysteries. For many people this has left God very far off, not verifiable, apparently not relevant even if real. Then the work of C. S. Lewis came to Trueblood's attention. No longer was Christian theology to be on the defensive. Lewis has Screwtape, the arch Devil, advising his nephew on how to handle someone whose atheism is weakening. Above all, instructs the Devil, do not let this person *think*. Lewis was placing Christian faith on the offensive, hinting at the vulnerability of the reasoning of faith's opposition.

In *The Case for Christianity* (1943), Lewis settled the issue for Trueblood who now understood that the "good teacher" conception of who Jesus was is an option that Christ does not permit us to take. "We can reject Him; we can accept Him on His terms; we cannot, with intellectual honesty, impose our own terms."[6] What are Christ's terms? "No one comes to the Father except through me" and "whoever has seen me has seen the Father" (Jn. 14:6, 9). In all the relativities of our world, if Jesus is right, there is only one solid place in which faith can be rooted. With Christ at the center of human certitude,[7] one is enabled to move toward God in a dependable way. We know Jesus through the biblical narrative, and in him we are assured of the reality and Christ-likeness of God's nature and intentions.

While, then, one might reasonably begin with Jesus Christ in order to arrive dependably at the being and nature of God, these present pages take the traditional approach of beginning with dis-

---

[5] D. Elton Trueblood, *While It Is Day: An Autobiography* (Harper & Row, 1974), 100.

[6] Ibid.

[7] See Elton Trueblood, *A Place To Stand* (Harper & Row, 1969), chap. 2.

cussion of the eternal being of God. Knowledge of God is informed significantly by the biblical story of God *in Christ* (see chapter four). If the reader prefers, it would be appropriate to read chapter four first and then return to this one. Otherwise, we begin here with classic considerations of the person and work of God that eventually would become incarnationally clear in the coming of Jesus.

The "saints" of the Church of God movement[8] often sang vigorously, couching their theology in original verse and rousing melody. No song captures better the vision, the excitement, the sense of divine call and resulting human commitment of the early movement than the one titled "The Church's Jubilee."[9] By the time of its composition in 1923, the self-understanding of the movement had come to be expressed commonly in the apocalyptic and restorationist images of the biblical books of Daniel and Revelation. God was on the world's center stage and the biblical story of divine intent and action was thought to be moving toward a glorious climax. The movement humbly rejoiced, thinking it had found itself in the divine script with a mission to fulfill.

"The light of even-tide now shines," began this corporate testimony, this musical clarion call to church reform. The purpose of the shining of divine light was "the darkness to dispel." No wonder God's children were so excited, "for out of Babel God doth call his scattered saints in one, together all one church compose, the body of his Son." There was believed to have been centuries of deep darkness, of severe dividedness that had burdened, in fact, nearly had buried the church. But now God was on the move, moving the divine drama of redemption forward toward a climax, stimulating a fresh movement among people willing to be shaped by the power of the Spirit who is God with us. It was a dramatic move of God's in which God was understood to be calling together the true church. Those who "saw the church" thus began mov-

---

[8] For a theological introduction to this particular and very God-oriented Christian movement, see Barry Callen, *Contours of a Cause* (Anderson University School of Theology, 1995).

[9] Charles Naylor and Andrew Byers, in *Worship the Lord: Hymnal of the Church of God* (Anderson, Ind.: Warner Press, 1989), 312.

ing toward Christ and toward each other. It was nothing less than "the day of jubilee." The church of God was called to "rejoice, be glad!" Why? Because "thy Shepherd has begun, his long divided flock again to gather into one."

While the adequacy of the biblical and historical interpretations underlying this view of one movement's self-understanding now have been questioned widely, the dramatic sense of God's reality and present calling has not disappeared, nor has its validity been undermined.[10] A keynoting and enduring characteristic of this reformation movement of the Church of God is its consciousness of God and its radical commitment to God, and to God alone. False churchly and creedalistic allegiances of the past are seen as often so hurtful, so human, so divisive. No more! Verse two of this visionary song begins, "The Bible is our rule of faith and Christ alone is Lord." So, "no earthly master do we know, to Christ alone we bow." There was for this composer a great sense of renewed freedom because, in the fullness of God's time, "the day of sects and creeds for us forevermore is past." To God's blessed will there would be total submission, and "from the yokes of Babel's lords from henceforth we are free."

The radical commitment of this movement, then, is the same one that has been basic to the biblical story ever since Israel's deliverance by the hand of God from the darkness of Egyptian slavery. The Christian's allegiance is to be to God and God alone. This commitment is always to be enlightened by Christ, the norm of truth, guided by the Bible, the narrative medium of truth, and enabled by the Spirit, the presence and power of truth. The goal envisioned is a return to being truly submissive to the truly sovereign God known in Christ as recorded in the biblical narrative. One begins to know God by recalling humbly the sacred record of God's Self-revealing actions in the midst of human history.

---

[10] For reviews of the changing history of the interpretation of the Bible's apocalyptic literature and the relation of that interpretation to this movement's understanding of its own role in the biblical story, see John Stanley, "Unity Amid Diversity: Interpreting the Book of Revelation in the Church of God (Anderson)," *Wesleyan Theological Journal* (Fall, 1990), 74-98; and Merle Strege, *Tell Me Another Tale* (Anderson, Ind.: Warner Press, 1993), 10-14.

The origin of a proper believing is not the well-crafted, God-proving bottom line of some abstract philosophic argument about the existence of the divine. Like the Bible itself, God's existence is assumed and celebrated. At issue instead is the *who*, the identity of the Creator God, the *what* of God's intent for all that has been created, and the question of *whether* God's people are prepared to rejoice in the divine being and yield to the divine will for today.

The primary medium for coming to understand the who and what of God is the process of history itself, with pivotal events of divine Self-revelation as biblically narrated. God is known primarily by what God does, especially in Jesus Christ. One thing known is that God has been lovingly active in bringing into being a people called to covenant with God to be God's very own people on mission for the doing of God's will. Within the resulting community of grateful obedience formed by grace, the God of grace becomes known. It is "unthinkable that grace could be adequately considered abstractly, apart from the actual history in which grace is made known."[11] God is involved in human history, creating a covenant community, an interpretive community, Israel and later the church. The spiritually reborn and historically faithful believers are enabled to name God as "Father," in part by life in the community of faith as "mothering" matrix.[12]

Always affirmed anew should be the testimony central to Israel's very existence, those first words spoken at the place of covenant: "I am the Lord your God, who brought you out of the land of Egypt" (Ex. 20:2). For Israel, God was the Prior One who had entered into the flow of human history to make the divine person and purpose known. The way of Israel's thought began with the knowledge that it had been addressed. Israelites knew well that they "had not been confronted with ethical abstractions, but rather had been addressed by One who had spoken in the events of the great

---

[11] Thomas Oden, *The Transforming Power of Grace* (Nashville: Abingdon Press, 1993), 22. Compare Wolfhart Pannenberg, *Revelation As History* (N.Y.: Macmillan, 1968).

[12] Cyprian, *Letters*, in *The Ante-Nicene Fathers*, ed., A. Roberts and J. Donaldson, 1885-96, reprint, Eerdmans, 1979, vol. 5, 316-319.

tradition of which they were a part."[13] The narrative of the Hebrew Scriptures is dominated by a recounting of the activity and speaking of God about the divine intention in history, thus revealing the very nature of God. Our knowledge of the divine, then, centers in the biblical story of God's creating and redeeming actions on the human scene.

One of the loved hymns in the worship life of the church is titled "What a Mighty God We Serve!"[14] Very much in the biblical pattern, it announces with vibrant rejoicing that

> Our Father's wondrous works we see,
> In the earth and sea and sky;
> He rules o'er all in majesty,
> From His royal throne on high.

How else can one respond except with,

> What a mighty God we serve!
> What a mighty God we serve!
> Reigning now above on His throne of love,
> What a mighty God we serve!

The "above" of God's reigning indicates willing recognition by humble disciples of divine transcendence, true otherness. The "now" dramatizes the realization of the presentness of the active kingship of God. It leads to sheer joy and requires sincere commitment. Let God again reign in the church and the church will know its God!

---

[13] James Muilenburg, *The Way of Israel*, rev. ed. (Harper & Row, 1961, 1965), 15.

[14] Clara Brooks and Barney Warren, in *Worship the Lord: Hymnal of the Church of God* (Anderson, Ind.: Warner Press, 1989), 46.

Divine Embrace of Pain

A central and persistent question for Christian theology is how best to be faithful to normative Christian origins located in the past, especially known through the Hebrew Scriptures[15] and the Christ-event itself, without being captured inappropriately by philosophic categories and cultural concepts used by early theologians to report and explain these formative events. In its first centuries the Christian faith interacted with and drew upon the Greek philosophic world to articulate the new faith. The concept of God that developed was "a wholly unchanging deity, absolute in power, who is literally unrelated to the world and literally unaffected by it."[16] Such a concept of God has not proved adequate to convey the full biblical witness to the God known in the Hebrew context. Today the philosophic environment has changed to one less friendly to the ancient Greek one and more compatible in some ways to that of the ancient Hebrews. This encourages recovery of a more adequate, a more biblical view of God.

The biblical witness pictures God as the Sovereign who *stands above* and also as God the Saviour who *stoops below*. This stooping, far from being unrelated to and unaffected by the world, reveals a God who, in Jesus Christ, so utterly related to the world as to become incarnate in humanity and was so utterly affected by the world as to die on a cross. Theologians like Delwin Brown draw on "process" philosophic categories of Alfred North White-

---

[15] It is crucial that Christian understandings of God be seen in light of the background of the Hebrew Scriptures. Failure to recognize and retain the foundational "Jewishness" of Christian theology has led to serious distortions. These include a contempt for the material world, reducing the spiritual life to the private experience of the individual, and a failure to link the goals of God with social justice. The Christian God is first of all to be understood in the context of the Jewish understanding. See Marvin Wilson, *Our Father Abraham* (Eerdmans, 1989). In this work the phrase "Hebrew Scriptures" is used on occasion instead of "Old Testament." Since the Christian faith rests so significantly on the foundation of the Old Testament, there is good reason to avoid the "old" word. For too many Christians this word conveys inappropriately the negative meaning of something now outdated and theologically meaningless for Christians, the people of the "New Testament."

[16] Clark Pinnock and Delwin Brown, *Theological Crossfire* (Grand Rapids: Zondervan, 1990), 84.

head (1861-1947), categories judged more appropriate to the modern consciousness of relationships and contingencies and better reflecting the biblical emphases of God being utterly related to and affected by the world. As a result, God is seen as "always incarnate in the world, accepting the risk of that involvement, bearing the world's sorrows and sharing its joys."[17]

A view of God as static and detached from a troubled creation is not compatible with the witness of the biblical narrative. On the one hand, says Scripture, God is objectively real, prior in existence to the created world process, sovereign over all, and standing alone. God is not merely the symbol of the highest human values, some soaring heavenly expression of the loftiest human ideals. On the other hand, God chooses to be deeply related to the life of creation and willingly becomes vulnerable to being affected positively or negatively by that life. God is dramatically incarnational by sovereign choice–thus reflecting to humanity the very nature of the divine.[18]

One important qualification helps in resisting a tendency of some theologians to champion a "process" philosophic view to the point of omitting a vital aspect of the biblical understanding of the creating-relating-risking God. As Carl Henry states the concern, some process thinkers "are quite vague when it comes to isolating an act of God in history. The Bible presents a more activist God."[19] While Walter Brueggemann readily admits that there is an important sense in which even God is "in process," he joins Henry in not being convinced that "the enormous metaphysical superstructure of

---

[17] Pinnock and Brown, *Theological Crossfire,* 86.

[18] Note, for instance, the section "Incarnation and the Problem of Evil" in chapter five. Says Jürgen Moltmann: "There is a suffering which is endured not only by human beings but also by God himself in company with them. Through his covenant with Israel, God makes his name and his spirit dwell in his people. If Israel is smitten, God is smitten too. If Israel is persecuted, then God himself takes part in this through his 'indwelling' (Shekinah) and goes into captivity with Israel" (*History and the Triune God*, 27).

[19] Quoted by Bob Patterson, *Carl F. H. Henry* (Peabody, Mass.: Hendrickson Publishers, 1983), 140.

process philosophy" is useful for interpreting the Bible. It is "much simpler and more effective to deal with social/covenantal/personal metaphors on the Bible's own terms."[20]

Clark Pinnock likewise critiques the non-biblical excess of some process theologians:

> I do not think it is quite enough to assign God the role of experiencing and remembering everything, to make God the final organizer of what comes to him from the world. According to the biblical message, God takes the initiative in the history of salvation. So even though I, too, want to replace a static view of God with a dynamic view, it cannot just be any dynamic view but must be the dynamic theism of the scriptural witness.[21]

Here is the central point concerning our human knowing of God. The distinctive place where the God of the biblical witness intersected the life process of creation was at the *point of pain*. Here emerges a distinctive view of God, a dynamic theism seeing God as simultaneously sovereign over creation and suffering with creation. The divine is involved, interactive, responsive, and compassionate. Consequently, the divine can be known to a meaningful measure through human awareness of this initiative of God on our behalf. This initiative, being wholly undeserved by fallen creation, reveals a God of loving and redeeming grace.

There was a common pattern of belief found all over the ancient Near East, varying only in detail from culture to culture. Morton Smith highlights the central elements of this widespread

---

[20] Patrick Miller, ed., *Old Testament Theology* (essays by Walter Brueggemann) (Minneapolis: Fortress Press, 1992), 43.

[21] Pinnock and Brown, *Theological Crossfire*, 96. According to William Hasker: "To say, as process theism does, that God has no direct control over anything that happens in the world is to leave oneself with a picture of God's power and God's activity that is severely truncated.... God so conceived cannot create the heavens and the earth out of nothing, nor can he part the Red Sea for the people of Israel, nor can he raise Jesus from the dead as a pledge of victory over sin...." ("A Philosophical Perspective" in *The Openness of God: A Biblical Challenge to the Traditional Understanding of God*, InterVarsity Press, 1994, 140).

"contractual theology."[22] The gods in view always were supposed beings who punish any who dare offend and disobey and who reward all who please and obey. It was a theology of strict retribution. The disobedient were judged harshly and the obedient permitted to prosper.

The theology seen in the Hebrew Scriptures both participates in this common theology and, simultaneously and significantly, struggles to be free from it. So the God of Israel is characterized variously in the Bible as "the God above the fray who appears like other ancient Near Eastern gods and as a God who is exposed in the fray, who appears unlike the gods of common theology, a God peculiarly available in Israel's historical experiences."[23] For Israel, the almighty One also is a loving Father.

In the developing faith seen in the Hebrew Scriptures, God becomes known as the One above the fray, truly sovereign, the transcendent God from whom all creation has come and to whom all persons finally must answer. The world is divinely structured and operates by laws that are violated only at a high price. The Jews saw "Torah" as more than a collection of human rules for wise living. Torah reflected the way creation has been ordered and thus the way life should be lived. Jewish historians throughout the Hebrew Scriptures tend to portray the recurrent disasters of their national history as the results of Torah disobedience. The Deuteronomistic History[24] reflects this perspective strongly,[25] as does the Mosaic tradition, the wisdom literature, and even the prophets. Obedience to the covenant relationship with God yields life, prosperity, and national stability. Disobedience brings death, misery, and exile.

---

[22] Morton Smith, "The Common Theology of the Ancient Near East," *Journal of Biblical Literature* 7 (1952), 35-47.

[23] Walter Brueggemann in P. Miller, ed., *Old Testament Theology*, 1992, 5.

[24] Primarily the books of Deuteronomy, Joshua, Judges, 1 and 2 Samuel, and 1 and 2 Kings.

[25] It may be unfair, however, to read Deuteronomy wholly or even primarily through this perspective. Argue Ronald Allen and John Holbert (*Holy Root, Holy Branches*, Abingdon Press, 38-40): "On the contrary, we think that the deuteronomic historians were precisely *not* works righteousness so commonly attributed to them.

That, however, is not all. That much is similar to the theological pattern common in the Near East of the time. What is not similar is the concurrent struggle seen in the Hebrew Scriptures to *critique* this formal and fixed pattern of interpreting the relationship of God to human waywardness in history. There also is the experience of national pain and the distinctive way Israel understood God relating to its own pain. When Yuri Gagarin returned to the U.S.S.R. from his early space flight, he reported that, as his atheistic government had expected, he had not seen God out there. A Russian Orthodox priest then remarked: "If you haven't seen God on earth, you will never see him in heaven." But Israel saw God on earth. Israel came to know God in the midst of its own earthly pain and national turmoil, and thus could begin to know him "out there" in the pre-history of creation.

Israel came to recognize the inadequacy of the common, contractual theology since it tended to separate God from the harshness of life as most people experienced it and to support social and religious status-quo arrangements on earth that were highly self-serving and unjust. By contrast, God stood above the compromising dilemmas of human existence and the claimed special status of the social arrangements that pampered some and oppressed others. Unjust social arrangements, even when bringing prosperity to Israel, were judged harshly by Israel's prophetic voices who spoke on behalf of the divine perspective that favors the poor.

Israel experienced great pain and through it a distinctive discernment of the God who identified with and even shared their pain. Understanding Israel's discernment of the empathetic God is crucial for Christians. Insightful is the thinking of Hans Küng, a major twentieth-century Christian theologian who has worked carefully to avoid two false opposites, seeing God as either *apathetic* or *pathetic* (God either does not care or cares but is unable or at least persistently unprepared to help in our human pain). The first of these inadequate

---

The heart of the deuteronomic theology may be found in Deuteronomy 7:7-11.... One is not called to follow the commandment *in order to* gain the favor of God; one follows the commandment *as the result of* God's love and promise."

positions is an extreme that Christianity inherited from Greek meta-physics;[26] the second is "the error of process theology and other modern metaphysical conceptions of God that are based on the modern concept of the ultimacy of the category of change."[27]

God, according to the biblical witness, freely chose Self-limitation in dealing with fallen creation.[28] Therefore, God should not be seen either as immune to the evil and suffering of our world or trapped in an ongoing codependence with this world. The divine Other known through the biblical story stands over against the world while, at the same time, being a full participant in it (Jn. 4:24; Col. 1:15; 1 Tim. 1:17). Very wrong is the modern graffiti that sometimes appears scribbled on the sides of buildings: "God is not dead–he just doesn't want to get involved."

Israel knew God as the living, creating, calling, coming, getting-involved God. God thus known is utterly free and sovereign, underived, Self-existent; God also is responsive, vulnerable, suffering from our sin, and long-suffering on behalf of our redemption. In one sense God never changes (in being, character, and intent); in another sense the unchanging God by choice is "in process" with those of us who sin, suffer, and hope for an undeserved salvation. God exhibits loving grace in becoming known through history as both "almighty" and "Father."

---

[26] Ancient Greek thought sought to overcome the tragedies of our human existence by identifying God with timelessness. Thus the defining characteristic of God became God's exemption from time with its awkward history, constant becoming, and broken relationships. God was said to be immutable, not susceptible to being affected by the drama of our human condition and choices. Says Robert Jenson: "Whereas Yahweh was eternal by his faithfulness *through* time, the Greek gods' eternity was their abstraction *from* time" ("The Triune God," in *Christian Dogmatics*, Philadelphia: Fortress Press, 1984, I:116).

[27] Stanley Grenz and Roger Olson, *20th Century Theology* (InterVarsity Press, 1992), 266.

[28] A key aspect of God's supreme reign is the evidence of Self-imposed restraint that allows to become real possibilities both human free will and the potential of mature human faith that is freely chosen. John Wesley noted: "If, therefore, God were thus to exert his power, there would certainly be no more vice: but it is equally certain, neither could there be any virtue in the world" ("The Unity of Divine Being," in *The Works of John Wesley*, vol. 7, 1872, reprint ed., Zondervan, 1958-59, 318).

As Israel languished in its Babylonian exile, sometimes it saw itself as abandoned by God (Isa. 40:27). The prophet Isaiah refutes the peoples' charge that God is faithless (40:21-31). There is hope for a vanquished and disheartened Israel. Why? Because of the nature of God. The exiles may be faint and powerless; God, however, is said to be neither exhausted nor helpless in any set of circumstances. Isaiah asks four rhetorical questions (40:21) and answers with five verbs (40:22-23). These verbs report actions always characteristic of God, even when evil seems to dominate and paralyze all else. God sits, stretches, spreads, brings, and makes. Sitting in transcendent glory, God proceeds in compassion to create, to be present and involved when the creation sins and suffers, to offer re-creation as a substitute for Israel's doubt and self-pity, to bring oppressive rulers to nothing.

God is a genuine covenant partner with Israel and the church. The concept of covenant forces a break with the typical alternatives to Israel's distinctive understanding of God. Much is at stake as we review this issue in the midst of our contemporary consumer culture that prefers an irrelevant God, indifferent, immune, not in the road of our human agendas. The radical alternative to this self-serving preference is the biblical understanding of God as willingly impinged upon and exposed. Walter Brueggemann warns: "If our mistaken notion leads us to an impassive, self-sufficient God in heaven, then the model for humanity, for Western culture, for ourselves, is that we should also be self-sufficient, impassive, beyond need, not to be imposed on."[29] To know God rightly is to be open to sharp critique of ourselves and our societies.

The manner of the divine working in our world is distinctive and sometimes disturbing. It offers hope and then leads to responsibility. God's sovereign status was known by Israel to express its theoretically unlimited capacity in a characteristically restrained way. That way allows, acknowledges, even shares real pain. It also enables human recovery from the scourge of sin. What follows is the privilege and burden of covenant partnership with God. Thus, John Wesley rightly understood God's power

---

[29] Walter Brueggemann (Patrick Miller, ed.), *A Social Reading of the Old Testament* (Minneapolis: Fortress Press, 1994), 46.

...fundamentally in terms of *empowerment*, rather than control or *overpowerment*. This is not to weaken God's power, but to determine its character! As Wesley was fond of saying, God works "strongly and sweetly." That is, God's *grace* works powerfully, but not irresistibly, in matters of human life and salvation; thereby empowering our *response-ability*, without overriding our *responsibility*.[30]

The biblical God is Subject, the sovereign ruler of all history, and also in a sense object, a victim by choice of that history in all its evil. If being a minority person means being victim of forces not in one's control, there is a sense in which God is a minority. This is not to deny God's sovereignty and power; it is to recognize God's love and way with the world. What is denied is "an easy jump from creation to resurrection, with no cross."[31] God's way with the world, as experienced by Israel and seen in Jesus, features a divine love that chooses a cross. Love suffers, bears, is patient (1 Cor. 13). We know God best as loving grace; this view comes from our recognition of God's willing and healing embrace of our human pain. It is indeed an amazing grace!

---

[30] Randy Maddox, *Responsible Grace: John Wesley's Practical Theology* (Nashville: Kingswood Books, Abingdon Press, 1994), 55.

[31] Justo González, *Mañana: Christian Theology from a Hispanic Perspective* (Nashville: Abingdon Press, 1990), 93.

Metaphors of the Divine

Popular thought has it that the world of today seems closed, the heavens shut tight. Either God does not exist, is only the best in humans, or at least seems not involved helpfully in the harsh realities of modern life. We people, now supposedly "come of age," are on our own to be active in the achievement of whatever salvation proves possible. Even many Christians seem to function almost autonomously as though God is not or cannot. If we are church people, it often is said, we can be forgiven for an understandable although unjustified leaning on religious traditions and comforting "God" vocabulary.

This secularization process grew rapidly in the nineteenth century. The emergence of a "scientific" worldview (and its Enlightenment assumptions) inevitably brought theological crisis and revision. How, asked so many, can people continue to believe in the biblical concept of a transcendent God who also is personal and intervenes relevantly and riskingly in the shifting turmoil of the historical process? We live in a world widely thought to be controlled by natural law and increasingly explained by modern science. Don't we now realize that, in principle at least, all can be known and finally manipulated by the scientific method and its dramatic technical applications–including finally an elimination of the "gods" and "miracles" left over from our more primitive past?

Schleiermacher, the influential German theologian (1768-1834), handled this potentially faith-damaging question by seeing the Christian faith primarily as a quality of life. God, rather than being conceived as an objective, transcendent reality, is seen more as immanent in the human soul as it rises into perfect self-consciousness. Mystical experience, the feeling of being absolutely dependent on God, becomes the centerpiece of faith. Spiritual experience rather than the cosmic, majestic being of God is made the focus of Christian faith. The seeker is instructed to look inward for the divine. God is said to be indescribable, although there can be the discovery of an inner light that allows immediate apprehension of God in the soul. The way to God tends to be through the "feelings" within more than through a historically narrated revelation from without. In such a theology the facts of history tend to become seen as mere symbols and stimulants for such inward experience, not revealing realities themselves.

The prophets of ancient Israel, however, saw things differently. Revelation for them is the external Word of a transcendent God. They were more concerned with God's righteous character and authority than with speculation about God's metaphysical essence or human apprehension of God in the depths of some mystical experience. Biblically understood, God is known as the One who confronts humans as Divine Subject and enters into covenant with them. The "Word of the Lord" is a word of promise and command that is to be acknowledged and obeyed. The nature of the prophet's knowing about God is narrative, leading Hans Conzelmann to conclude: "Israel has experienced God's guidance (leading, punishment, reacceptance) in its history and can draw the appropriate conclusions for the present."[32]

The chief source of knowledge of God, according to the Bible, is divinely inspired interpretations of the events of God's activity in the outer world rather than rationally analyzed "feelings" of human introspection. God is understood to have chosen to be Self-revealing within the historical process, and thus by divine grace can be described meaningfully and actually "known," although never captured, controlled, or fully comprehended. Neither the inward, experiential quest for spiritual insight nor the rational examination of reality is the primary path to knowledge of the divine. Reliance on such paths has varied widely in Christian history, including being dominant in the theological method of some leading thinkers.

Theologians like Thomas Aquinas (1225-1274) express considerable confidence in the ability of human reason to demon-

---

[32] Hans Conzelmann, *An Outline of the Theology of the New Testament* (Harper & Row, 1969), 13. Note, however, the caution from the Wisdom literature of the Hebrew Scriptures that all of God's historical actions are not easily discernable (Ecc. 8:16-17). "Orthodoxy" is no license for arrogance. Faith both offers assurance of divine activity and faces inevitable tests of doubt and even despair as elements of this activity remain unclear.

strate logically the existence if not the nature, will, and actions of God. Generally, however, theologians in more recent times have given less credence to speculative reason and more to empirical methodology. It is assumed that we can know little about God beyond our ability to observe and experience (a "modern" Enlightenment approach to religious faith). Neither of these approaches, however, fits well the knowing style of the biblical story.

God remains "hidden," said Martin Luther, even in the midst of God's historical Self-revelation. In the Bible one comes to know God only in part and primarily through the narrated flow of historical situations. God becomes known as the mysterious, loving power who moves history toward its divinely appointed destiny. There is confidence in God's presence, but without removal of a reverent respect for the unknowns of God's being. The paradoxes are not probed analytically by biblical writers in an attempt to uncover the nature of God through rational inquiry. Instead, there is a patient waiting for mysteries to be resolved in the outcome of the historical process, in the coming of Messiah, and in the final consummation (1 Cor. 13:12). The nature of God emerges slowly in human awareness as the narrative of God's presence with us proceeds and we personally accept and represent God's lordship over us and all else.

There are limits beyond which we humans are unable to go in analyzing and describing a truly transcendent God. Excessive analysis and then a systematic cataloging of God's "attributes" can quickly reflect arrogance on our part that goes beyond what revelation makes available. On the other hand, we should not be satisfied with unnecessarily shallow generalizations that know God only as an unfocused "oblong blur."[33] God has chosen to be known to us, at least to the degree that we need to know and are capable of knowing. Our knowledge is not all, but it is enough.

---

[33] J. B. Phillips, *Your God Is Too Small* (London: The Epworth Press, 1952), 63-66.

The biblical treatment of God's attributes is more practical than speculative. The narrative perspective of the Bible avoids philosophic speculation about the qualities of God's essence, focusing our attention instead on what can be known by faith through the agency of God's Self-revealing action.[34] The elements of the biblical picture of God arise in the midst of divinely-assisted human observations about God's chosen ways of being with us and for us. In our living and especially in our pain, we frail and fallen people come to know God as Father, Mother,[35] Shepherd, Judge, and Friend. There is a vital connection between what God is as eternal being and how we come to know God through the revealing specifics of divine action.

Thus, while we never can know God *fully*, we are enabled through the unfolding plot of the biblical story to know God *truly*.[36] The intended purpose of this knowing is practical, enabling the present integrity and relevancy of faith. The primary focus is "not on God's being in itself, for that is not what the [biblical] text is about, but on how life is to be lived and reality construed in the light of God's character as an agent as this is depicted in the stories of Israel and of Jesus."[37]

---

[34] Unfortunately, the Christian theological tradition frequently has been "ambiguous and confused in speaking of the attributes of God. It has tried to synthesize the confession that God is compassionate, suffering, victorious love revealed decisively in Jesus Christ with a number of speculative ideas about what constitutes true divinity, such as immutability, impassibility, and apathy" (Daniel Migliore, *Faith Seeking Understanding*, 1991, 72). Staying with the biblical revelation avoids many problems of such speculation.

[35] The "Mother" image of God, while de-emphasized in much of biblical literature and Christian church history, certainly is appropriate and not lacking in biblical rootage. God is reported to be the One who has writhed in labor to give birth (Deut. 32:18), who is a midwife who takes from the womb and keeps safe at the mother's breasts (Ps. 22:9), and who "mothers" by providing suck, carrying on her hip, and dandling on her knees (Isa. 66:12). For caution about identification of God as "Mother," see in this chapter the section "Limits of Gender Language."

[36] Thomas Finger, *Christian Theology: An Eschatological Approach*, vol. 2 (Scottdale, Pa.: Herald Press, 1989), 484.

[37] George Lindbeck, *The Nature of Doctrine* (Philadelphia: Westminster Press, 1984), 121.

Reviewing the Hebrew Scriptures, we see that God had become known within that ancient believing community as the One who is *living, holy, jealous, righteous, gracious,* and *purposeful.* Granted, all of these descriptions are limited human understandings of the divine. They are analogies employed to describe what is finally indescribable. Nonetheless, "they are *meaningful* metaphors which carry within them crucial, albeit not exhaustive, cognitive implications."[38] They speak of the One who really is in these particular ways and they point to the ways we who believe are to be God's people in today's world.

In the unfolding narration of how God related to Israel, especially in its periods of national pain, vital pictures of God emerged, or better, were revealed. These pictures are represented by the key words living, holy, jealous, righteous, gracious, and purposeful. Together these adjectives constitute a balanced understanding of the divine being who, especially later in Jesus Christ, would also feature *gracious love* as a culminating Self-definition.

1. Living. God is known in the biblical story to be present and active in our world. Who is God? "I am the Lord thy God, who brought you out of the land of Egypt" (Ex. 20:2). God is the One who acted historically on Israel's behalf, made of them a people who were no people. God is the alive One, the One who is and who acts to deliver, who manifests power directed by purpose. In contrast to dead idols, "the Lord is the true God; he is the living God and the everlasting King" (Jer. 10:10). God is a living reality, not an inert idea. God is and will be vitally present, "and they shall name him Emmanuel (which means 'God is with us')" (Matt. 1:23b). As known biblically, God is a Subject, not an object, an initiator and thus a Self-revealer to be known by the nature of divine actions.

God is free, aware, Self-directing, a chooser, and a purposer. God is living, a willing Spirit, a personal God (Ex. 3:14; Eph. 1:9, 11), the creative power in the universe. God is the life-giving Wind that originally swept over the face of the chaos of the waters (Gen.

---

[38] Gabriel Fackre, *The Christian Story*, rev. ed. (Eerdmans: 1978, 1984), 252-53.

1:2; Isa. 40:12-14). For each of us humans, God is the agent of conception (Ps. 139:7, 13ff; Lk. 1:35) and the sustainer of the breath of life in our bodies (Job 27:3; 33:4). The Spirit of God raised Jesus from the dead and also will "give life to our mortal bodies" (Rom. 8:11).

Process theology helpfully emphasizes the *dynamism* of God. God is relational in character and persuasive in presence. But God, in this way of thinking, is not always recognized as the Creator, the fully sovereign One who is truly transcendent from the creation, the Alpha and Omega, the source and end of all things. The primary deficiency of some process thought is "its failure to direct its adherents back to Scripture's story of God–to the Lord of the prophets and the Father of Jesus, to the risen Lord Jesus Christ, and to the Lord the Spirit, who gathers believers in pentecostal power."[39] God lives, creates life, and initiates on behalf of life's redemption.

2. Holy. God also is known in the biblical story to be apart from us humans, different from us. As God is immanent, living and presently engaged in redemptive activity among us, God also is transcendent in otherness from us. God is singular. There is none like God and no other than God. God's being is without comparison and stands alone. The golden text of Hebrew faith affirms: "Hear, O Israel: The Lord is our God, the Lord alone" (Deut. 6:4). This Lord is called "the Holy One" (Isa. 40:25; Prov. 9:10). The holiness of God speaks of divine mystery, glory, purity, all that fills humans with awe, wonder, and reverence. In fact, God's name is reported to be "holy and awesome" (Ps. 111:9).

Isaiah saw the Lord "sitting upon a throne, high and lifted up." The seraphim cried out, "Holy, holy, holy is the Lord of hosts" (Isa. 6:1-4). The Hebrew word for holy is *qadosh*, meaning something withdrawn from common use. So God is separate from all else, holy. God also is different from all else, pure and good, unstained if not unaffected by the evil that has come to spoil creation. God

---

[39] James McClendon, *Systematic Theology: Doctrine* (Nashville: Abingdon Press, 1994), II:314.

expects that those who accept new life will become God-like, i. e., holy as God is holy, separated from common to divine use (Lev. 11:44-45; Matt. 5:48; 2 Cor. 6:14-7:1; Eph. 5:27)[40]. For this ultimate challenge there is narrated to us in the New Testament a model, guide, and resource, "the way." There we are privileged to learn of the glory of God's holiness in the face of Jesus Christ (2 Cor. 4:6).

3. Jealous. God is known in the biblical story to be intolerant of false alternatives to the divine being. "You shall not make for yourself an idol...for I the Lord your God am a jealous God" (Ex. 20:4-5). If God really is God, any supposed alternative is in fact a perversion of reality, falsehood, loss of true perspective, defective religion. Elijah cried out to the people: "How long will you go limping with different opinions? If the Lord is God, follow him; but if Baal, then follow him" (1 Kings 18:21).

Baal, which means "lord," and his consort, Astarte, were area fertility gods. To the Canaanites they represented security for the good life. They were treasured idols, personalized images of human desires that in fact had only whatever power the creating humans granted them. Little has changed except the names. The "good life" still is projected as our favorite god. Automated industrialism and advertising, which Norman Kraus says "have given birth to a favorite daughter, consumerism," still rule the highly developed nations.[41] Self-seeking societies act like these are lords. We grant them what considerable power they have. We bow daily, but hardly in humility.

The biblical prophets insist on a stark contrast between idols and the living God. Idolatry, which often comes in the form of seeking security through political alliances and military hardware, is not just pictured in the Hebrew Scriptures as covenant faithlessness. It also is said to be practical stupidity (Hab. 2:18-20). There is no sure

---

[40] See a discussion of the call to holiness with reference to individual believers in chapter six.

[41] C. Norman Kraus, *God Our Saviour* (Scottdale, Pa.: Herald Press, 1991), 71.

hope except in the living God who creates rather than being created. "Not by might, nor by power, but by my Spirit, says the Lord of hosts" (Zech. 4:6).[42]

Shared allegiance is no allegiance at all. The vigorous biblical witness is that serving God is to repudiate all idolatrous alternatives, "be they the philosopher's deifying of the elemental forces of the cosmos (Gal. 4:8ff.), the political tyrant's imposition of obligations that God disallows (Acts 4:19, 5:29), the secularist's idolatry of mammon (Matt. 6:24), the glutton's capitulation to appetite (Phil. 3:19), or even the Western tourists' tolerant curiosity about ancient temple idols (2 Cor. 6:16; 1 Thess. 1:9)."[43]

4. Righteous. God is known in the biblical story to exhibit, define, and reveal what is right, to expect what is right, and to assist with bringing about what is right and just. God is righteous because God is the living source of what is good and is always faithful in fulfilling promises made to a covenant people. All people are called to be righteous as God is righteous, just, faithful, and holy. Since, however, we are failures, sinners, unrighteous, God also is known to be the One who renders judgment whenever deserved. God surely is righteous, faithful, even wrathful in judgment when necessary, but fortunately there is more. In the Hebrew Scriptures contract theology yields to covenant theology that carries unmerited promises of *grace* even for those who have been unfaithful.

No divine promises are to be separated from God's commitment to justice. Justice and salvation are interlocked (Isa. 46:12-13). Human beings are to "do justice" because God is just. God's throne stands on justice and judgment (Ps. 89:14, 97:2), with particular concern expressed for the poor. To do what is right is more pleasing to the Lord than sacrifice (Hos. 6:6). The prophets of Israel were preoccupied with the significance of social justice because of their understanding of the nature and agenda of God.[44]

---

[42] See Walter Brueggemann, *Israel's Praise: Doxology Against Idolatry and Ideology* (Philadelphia: Fortress Press, 1988).

[43] Carl Henry, *God, Revelation and Authority* (Waco, Tx.: Word, 1982), V:79.

[44] See Alan Kreider, *Journey Towards Holiness: A Way of Living for God's Nation* (Scottdale, Pa.: Herald Press, 1987).

This concern is seen in Nathan's rebuke of David for his lack of pity and his theft of Bathsheba from Uriah (2 Sam. 12:1-15). On the other hand, David as king administered justice to the people (2 Sam. 8:15), the ideal of true kingship after God's own heart (Ps. 45:4, 72:1-3).

5. Gracious. God is known to be active in the crises of life, often bringing good where evil otherwise abounds. God is grace-full, exhibiting a redemptive kindness wholly unmerited. Grace precedes law.[45] Divine intervention on our behalf comes before any final judgment that is based on our violation of the divine expectations of us. The confession about the Lord in Exodus 34:6 points to the very heart of God: "The Lord, the Lord, a God merciful and gracious, slow to anger, and abounding in steadfast love and faithfulness." While God always is holy, other than us, the prophets of Israel make clear that God is "the Holy One *in your midst*" (Hos. 11:9; Isa. 12:6; Ezek. 20:41). The Holy One is present with loving and saving intention.

God comes vulnerably near to the chosen people, loving them, longing for them in their waywardness, seeking renewed relationship with them, all because of an intense love for them. God, the Almighty Creator, comes to Israel to rescue from slavery and to form a new people. Throughout its history this people of the covenant came to know God as its gracious Redeemer (Isa. 43:1-7). There was even an emerging realization that those graciously chosen by God were chosen not for privilege, but for a mission, to be a light to the nations. God's redemptive intention knows no ethnic or geographic boundaries (Isa. 49:6).

The story of the healing of Naaman through the ministry of the prophet Elisha (2 Kings 5) is a narrative presentation about the activity of God beyond the boundaries of Israel. It is a story rich in irony. The request for healing is inspired by a nobody, an Israelite prisoner of war working as a slave girl. The request is handled through the official channels of power, from king to king–even

---

[45] Contrary to the assumption of many Christians, this is true in the Hebrew Scriptures as well as in New Testament teaching.

though both were powerless to act in this case. The king of Israel, assuming that God acts only within the boundaries of Israel, wrongly interprets the request as a political ruse.

The healing is blocked at first by Naaman's ethnic arrogance—his home rivers are better than a muddy one in Israel. After the healing, Naaman appears to have accepted a quasi-magical view of God's actions. Since God's healing power probably was restricted to God's geographic territory, he takes home a quantity of Israelite soil and thus, he thought, the effective presence of Israel's God. This healing account both highlights the power of God to act in the face of a dreaded disease and the freedom of God from humanly imposed particularities like political pride, national boundaries, ethnic prejudice, and the premature exclusivity of the chosen people of God. God embraces and relieves the pain of the fallen without being limited by or legitimating their human narrowness. God's graciousness knows no such bounds.

6. Purposeful. God is known in the biblical story as the One on mission with a purpose. That purpose moves through and beyond the Jews to all people and all creation. God called Abraham and promised to bless his descendants. But the Hebrew Scriptures begin with Adam and not Abraham. Yahweh, the God of Israel, is no petty tribal god, no local lord of an ethnic enclave, but Lord of the nations, "the God of the spirits of all flesh" (Nu. 16:22; 27:16). Why did God call Abraham? The divine purpose was that "all the families of the earth shall be blessed through you" (Gen. 12:1-4). Paul later wrote: "If you belong to Christ, then you are Abraham's offspring, heirs according to the promise" (Gal. 3:29). The God of Israel is a missionary God with a redeeming purpose for all the earth. The *standing* God also is the *stooping* God, reaching for the lost, first through Israel, finally in Christ, and always with the full creation in view.

The story of Jonah (3:1-10) makes the point of God's universal caring, a caring that balances divine judgment with the divine purpose of redemption. In this dramatic narrative the king of Nineveh becomes the good Yahwistic theologian. He was unwilling to accept Jonah's ominous message of impending judgment as God's last word. Instead, he entertained the daring theological option that God might relent in the face of true repentance (even if Yahweh's prophet was more rigid than that). Maybe human action can influence God, potentially causing God, in light of God's sovereign freedom and redemptive purpose, to abandon the terrible decree of coming destruction. The king assumed that God is no prisoner of the initial divine decree of judgment. There may be potential in the process. God's purpose is to restore, not destroy. There surely would be compassion and restoring love if there were proper human response to God's redeeming initiatives.

7. Love. The central Christian affirmation about God gathers up all of these qualities, attributes, metaphors, and caps them with the affirmation that God is *love*. Love, wrote John Wesley, is God's "reigning attribute, the attribute that sheds an amiable glory on all his other perfections."[46] Similarly, "as holiness is the starting point, so love is the high point in the biblical unfolding of the nature of God."[47] This unfolding is reported from the very first chapters of Genesis. Throughout this primeval history one finds that, for each act of God's judgment on human rebellion, there is a corresponding act of unmerited divine mercy. Finally, about the eighteenth century before Christ, God actively entered human history by calling a man named Abraham. From the Garden of Eden to the Tower of Babel, humankind is pictured as running away from God. God responded by launching a pattern of actions, loving grace actions, to bring creation home again. Here is the source of the long drama of the acting out of God's amazing love.

The Johannine statement is definitive. "God is love" (1 John 4:8). Love is defined properly as active concern for the highest well-being of others. The whole Bible is a dramatic narrative revealing the history of God's acted-out concern for the well-being of the whole human family and of all creation. This love, of course, is based

---

[46] John Wesley, commenting on 1 John 4:8, *Explanatory Notes on the New Testament* (London: The Epworth Press, 1754, 1950 ed.), 914.

[47] Dale Moody, *The Word of Truth* (Eerdmans, 1981), 104.

on the New Testament assumption that the character of God is defined decisively by the life and work of Jesus Christ who is "the image of the invisible God" (Col. 1:15). This life and work pulls together, lives out, and dramatizes in Self-giving love all the attributes of God.[48]

What would happen if, in the midst of our troubled world, all the attributes of this biblically revealed God were focused in one place at one time? Note the words of Psalm 85:10– "Mercy and truth are met together; righteousness and peace have kissed each other" (KJV). When they met and kissed, there was the cross of Christ. There, in that tragic and glorious event on a hill outside Jerusalem, we see best the *living* God, so present in our world, the *holy* and *jealous* God, so singular and different from us, the *righteous* God, so committed to what is right and just despite the high cost, and especially the *gracious* God with a clear *purpose* being realized by a redeeming love beyond compare. The death of the godly for the ungodly "reveals the source of love in the subject rather than the object. God loved us not because of what we are but because of what he is."[49]

Augustine stated well the wonderful simplicity and yet delicate complexity of our human understanding of God as conveyed through the biblical account:

> You, my God, are supreme, utmost in goodness, mightiest and all-powerful, most merciful and most just. You are the most hidden from us and yet the most present amongst us, the most beautiful and yet the most strong, ever enduring and yet we cannot comprehend you. You are unchangeable and yet you change all things. You are never new, never old, and yet all things have new life from you. You are the unseen power that brings decline upon the proud. You are ever active, yet always at rest. You gather all things to yourself, though you suffer no need.[50]

---

[48] See chapter five of this book.

[49] Dale Moody, *The Word of Truth* (Eerdmans, 1981), 114.

[50] Augustine, *Confessions* I:4.

Herein is love, the holy God of redeeming grace. The biblical revelation of God's nature is seen even in the form of one key text. Psalm 25 is an acrostic poem, each line starting with a successive letter of the Hebrew alphabet. The middle letter of this alphabet begins verse ten. Orienting all else as the physical and theological center, here is the comprehensive affirmation: "All the paths of the Lord are steadfast love and faithfulness." This is artistic and eloquent testimony to the character of God. God is so committed to even sinful people because the very essence of God's being is steadfast love, mercy, and grace (Ps. 25:16; see Ex. 34:6). We all are debtors to the God of great grace!

Recovery of True Transcendence

Instead of a divine Sovereign being defined by such a wondrous complex of biblically narrated attributes, we moderns have sought subtly to make God subservient to ourselves. Like the earlier Jewish tradition, the Christian faith often has been trivialized by limiting God to given times and places, shaping God in human images, and focusing the view of God's will on the satisfaction of "our needs." The role given to God is that of being useful to what we feel we need or, worse yet, what we just want. This preoccupation with selfish pragmatism is the church's current slavery in Egypt, its voluntary exile in Babylon, its persistent temptation in the wilderness of today's rootless anxiety, loss of community, and material grasping.

Such selfish preoccupation sits in many pews and absorbs vast resources through a wide range of church programs that go under the names of "being relevant" and "speaking to where I am." For many people today theological convictions have been replaced by a hedonistic pragmatism that seeks only "religious experiences" as self-satisfactions that presumably are God related. God's people and God's cause in the world are under attack by the "utility principle." According to this principle, if religion proves useful in securing human happiness and fulfillment, then and only then is it to be seen as important and true.[51]

---

[51] Resisting the trend to domesticate God within the boundaries of human needs

Various modern concepts of God appear to reduce God to little more than an expression of the world itself. Such accommodation to the world does little justice to divine transcendence as biblically narrated. While unfortunately such excessive accommodation does occur, "conservatives" share the guilt. Without doubt, reductionism is everybody's problem. It is difficult to imagine "a more worrisome attempt to exploit the Christian God than one finds in current equations of God's will with American foreign policy, capitalist economics, patriarchal social policies, racist illusions, and a few other favorite themes of conservative sermonizing."[52]

The Reformed tradition maintains strong commitment to the centrality of the being and work of God in relation to all of human life. B. B. Warfield (1851-1921) defines a Calvinist as one who "sees God behind all phenomena and, in all that occurs, recognizes the hand of God working out His will; who makes the attitude of the soul to God in prayer its permanent attitude in all its life-activities; and who casts himself on the grace of God alone, excluding every trace of dependence on self from the whole work of his salvation."[53] While this tradition needs certain qualifications,[54] it surely is a good place to begin.

Israel did not discover and then adopt God as its own, as though it were in charge of the process. God introduced the divine presence to Israel and offered a covenant relationship as an act of sovereign grace. Seen as central to the thrust of Scripture is the humble confession that "from him and through him and to him are all things. To him be the glory forever. Amen" (Rom. 11:36).

---

and desires, Leonard Allen, Richard Hughes, and Michael Weed insist that the God Christians are to proclaim is the One "who shatters our little illusions of self-sufficiency," the One who wishes "to wean us from our frantic quest for happiness and success and from the ever-multiplying 'needs' that keep us enslaved to things" (*The Worldly Church*, 2nd ed., 1991, Abilene Christian University Press, 90-91).

[52] Pinnock and Brown, *Theological Crossfire*, 93.

[53] B. B. Warfield, *Calvin as a Theologian and Calvinism Today* (Philadelphia: Presbyterian Board of Publications, 1909), 23-24.

[54] One key qualification is John Wesley's concern that *human responsibility* not be undercut by our conception of God. Affirming a place for uncoerced human choice does not necessarily detract from the glory of God. God's grace is *resistible*. There is genuine human choice and also a truly sovereign God.

Glorifying God is an important biblical theme. It should not, however, be made an absolute as in much of the theology that is based on the teaching of John Calvin. Calvinism views the glory of God as the primary cause for God's creation, "whereby for his own glory he hath foreordained whatsoever comes to pass."[55] But, concluding that a major portion of all human creation will be eternally lost by divine choice as just penalty for sin is an inappropriate understanding of how a suffering, loving, forgiving God would choose to bring glory to the divine being. God's insistence on justice would have to be presumed the primary divine attribute. Human salvation, however, is a primary concern of God according to the biblical story. This concern suggests a meaningful freedom for humans to choose for or against the divine offer of reconciliation. In fact, it can be argued that love in search of renewed life in covenant relationship with fallen humanity is seen biblically as the primary divine attribute.

Nonetheless, drawing any attention away from the glory of God can lead to serious error. Much theology appears to be inverted today so that the faith is stated primarily in terms of meeting human needs rather than glorifying and reestablishing right relationship with a truly sovereign God. Ministry too often is understood as satisfying "needs" as individuals perceive them. God becomes a servant loved for what can be done for us needy humans. The prayer of Samuel (1 Sam. 3:9-10) is switched from "Speak, Lord, for your servant is listening" to "Listen, Lord, for your valuable creation has needs anxiously waiting to be met."

The marketplace is now full of books by Christian authors on "how to" everything (have a good marriage, invest money to the best advantage, know all about the future, be healthy, wealthy, and wise). It is not surprising that Millard Erickson finds it difficult to understand "how some people can simultaneously express great concern for the plight of the poor (a clear preoccupation of the sovereign God) and pursue the lifestyle of the rich and famous."[56]

---

[55] Charles Hodge, "The Decrees of God," in Millard Erickson, ed., *Readings in Christian Theology* (Grand Rapids: Baker Book House, 1973), I:433.

[56] Millard Erickson, *The Evangelical Mind & Heart* (Grand Rapids: Baker Book House, 1993), 47.

The church is in danger of being reduced to the utilitarian. The two central virtues of a technological society are utility and efficiency. A demand for achieving desired results governs much of life. In such settings religion is valued "mainly for the service it renders to society. The people most highly regarded are producers, not thinkers, and much less pray-ers."[57] This secularistic reductionism is as present in many Christian sanctuaries as it is in the public media and shopping malls. As Karl Marx said, religion is easily used in selfish pursuits.

Worship for many people has become "a quasi-entertaining event providing an 'emotional outlet' and promoting self-esteem and conviviality ('fellowship')."[58] Put in economic terms, God is thought of as available "capital" for our careful investing. The interest is said to be good and the yield longterm! Biblically understood, however, God is not to be worshipped because we self-serving believers find the process useful. God is God, and God's ways are not our ways. God is not the guaranteed answer to all of our fondest prayers or a heavenly bank account to be drawn on freely when our own reserves run low.

Tiresome and disturbing are some of the mass-media evangelists who seem to have yielded their ministries to the pragmatic questions, Will it work? Will it pay? Will it sell? Will it feel good? Will it protect the status quo that assures traditional values and current comforts? Instead, being loyal to the Creator of heaven and earth usually will set covenant partners sharply against the way things presently are. Our existence as true believers "must be a sign in the world of the overcoming of these powers of division and domination." Our loyalty "must clearly entail a renunciation of the ways in which we are engaged in 'unmaking' the earth."[59]

What of the call to self-restraint and selflessness? What of the humble awareness of transcendence, the sense that God is great, beyond, other, demanding of change and obedience, even if it means our discomfort? What of the reverence, the awe, the quieting and

---

[57] Donald Bloesch, *The Struggle of Prayer* (Colorado Springs: Helmers & Howard, 1988), 148.

[58] C. Allen, R. Hughes, M. Weed, 2nd ed., *The Worldly Church* (Abilene Christian University Press, 1991), 19.

[59] Theodore Jennings, *Loyalty To God* (Nashville: Abingdon Press, 1992), 57.

cleansing of the mystery and majesty of God? What of radical discipleship, even in the face of some "orthodoxies" that have become status-quo and sterile? Biblical answers are absent for the most part in the noisy and busy halls of the typical congregation that is scrambling to be "relevant," even "big-time." The prophetic voice calls for a return to a present integrity of faith in God. Believers should abandon the trivial and piously self-serving and dare to abandon the business of trying to domesticate the divine.

A movement toward the recovery of true divine transcendence can begin by going back to the Bible. Such return will reintroduce God's "shattering and unpredictable incursions into human history." To admit again "unfathomable mystery and incalculable majesty" would remind all self-seeking religionists that God's ways are not our ways. It would insist that God is worshipped "not because he is useful, but because he is God; that he is not the guarantor of our hopes for something else, but he himself is the ultimate goal of all our hopes."[60]

William Hordern, in describing the nature of God's transcendence and immanence, recognizes that difficulties related to this complex identification of God comprise one of the central theological struggles of the twentieth century.[61] The turmoil over this identification is key to the controversy in recent decades between fundamentalists and liberals. Hordern builds a case for theology in a "new reformation" perspective typically called neo-orthodoxy. The concern is "to attack the tendency to make man's life, religion, moral experience, etc., the center of theology. In place of this it has asserted the absolute centrality of God for Christian faith."[62] God is truly transcendent, but in an amazing way that risks immanence in our time and place, being in them without being of them, all because of divine love and for the sake of human salvation.

---

[60] Allen, Hughes, Weed, op. cit., 21.

[61] William Hordern, *The Case for a New Reformation Theology* (Philadelphia: The Westminster Press, 1959). Also see Stanley Grenz and Roger Olson, *20th Century Theology*, a major theological review that understands the severe swings of recent theology as various attempts to redefine and rebalance divine transcendence and immanence.

[62] Hordern, op. cit., 111.

Some theologians, usually classed as liberals, have taken the concept of divine immanence too far, tending to lose sight of the difference between the divine and the human, the eternal and the historical. God comes to be seen primarily in the human self. The kingdom of God comes close to being understood as a human system that could be built on earth if believers were at their moral and organizational best. In this way the biblical faith loses its uniqueness, its divine orientation, becoming less the story of God and more the stories of human abilities and initiatives. The Bible comes to be seen only as one crucial stage in the ongoing human search for God, rather than being recognized as the definitive place where God has told of the divine search for lost humankind and the redemptive provision made available in Christ.

God has gotten blurred and reduced in our eyes to being only the rational order of the universe or the absolute of idealist philosophy or the principle of concretion as in the thought of Alfred North Whitehead. A needful response to any such imbalance is a clear reaffirmation of the transcendence of God. God is before, beyond, and other than all creation. Nothing short of such transcendence can be true to the biblical revelation and can satisfy the persistent human questions about meaning and destiny, questions not answered successfully by the secularism of our time.

Caution, however, should bracket any vigorous reassertion of divine transcendence. Carl Henry assesses the situation:

> If Christianity is to win intellectual respectability in the modern world, the reality of the transcendent God must indeed be proclaimed by the theologians–and proclaimed on the basis of man's rational competence to know the transempirical realm. Apart from recognition of the self-revealed Redeemer of a fallen humanity, who vouchsafes valid knowledge of the transempirical world, the modern Athenians are left to munch the husks of the religious vagabonds.[63]

---

[63] Carl Henry, *Frontiers of Modern Theology* (Chicago: Moody Press, 1965), 154-155. Note, however, that "man's rational competence" and seeking to win "intel-

God not only exists transcendently and acts historically. God also speaks definitively to our human understanding. This speaking, however, contrary to Henry, may not assume the form of units of revealed information designed to allow human rationality to comprehend truths about the divine and demonstrate the intellectual respectability of the faith in ways acceptable to the secular arena.

Bernard Ramm, while affirming Henry's general concern, nonetheless is critical of a Christian fundamentalism that is overly confident of its ability to comprehend God and affirm propositionally any extensive knowledge of the divine. Rational categories and precise theological statements, rooted as they may be in divine revelation, are themselves culturally conditioned and thus always shifting and tentative. Theology has its limits as it seeks to apprehend and then articulate rational conclusions about the being of God, the most profound of all mysteries.

Because of revelation, limited but significant apprehension of the divine is graciously possible. Because of the nature of God, of fallen humanity, and of cultural conditioning, however, some unreachable mystery always remains beyond our thoughts and words. Ramm, in trying to move beyond fundamentalism, warns appropriately that we not become trapped in a rigid rationalism that "reads the revelation of God as a transcript without mystery."[64] God's revelation is not a detailed script designed to be memorized. Rather, it is a vision that inspires, a presence and power that is to be received and lived. By divine revelation, we who believe are helped to find the way at least to approach knowing the "immortal, invisible, God only wise, in light inaccessible, hid from our eyes."[65] This preliminary knowing resides more in restored relationship and dedicated discipleship and less in rational prowess and cultic correctness.

---

lectual respectability" for the faith are not necessarily to be primary Christian emphases.

[64] Bernard Ramm, *Special Revelation and the Word of God* (Grand Rapids: Eerdmans, 1961), 23-24.

[65] Walter Smith, "Immortal, Invisible, God Only Wise" (1867), found in *Worship the Lord: Hymnal of the Church of God* (Anderson, Ind.: Warner Press, 1989), 34.

The biblical analogies for divine transcendence depend heavily on *spacial* imagery. God is said to be "above," "higher," "high and lifted up" (Isa. 6:1). It was natural to express superiority in terms of elevation at a time when our world was still thought to be flat and the marvel of the heavenly bodies appeared upward from the earth's surface. Such thinking is no longer viable if taken as literal science. God is not "up there" as though height is dominance, nor is God located in any given spot as though the divine were an object to be plotted by astronomical coordinates. How can we better express the transcendence of God in ways that maintain continuity with the intent of biblical teaching?[66]

The early work of Karl Barth (1886-1968) argues for a radical separation between God and humanity. God is said to be free of all limitation and hidden from all human questing, reasoning, imaging, and attempts at proving. God is known to us only because of the divine choice for Self-revelation, and that only in Jesus Christ. While this view goes too far in what it eliminates, as Barth's colleague Emil Brunner soon pointed out, it was a timely correction to the tendencies of nineteenth-century liberalism. Barth's was a challenge to those who look for God only in the depths of human spiritual or moral experience and then picture the divine only in terms of some aspect of our human selves or moral mandate.

Being "radically other" was the neo-orthodox, non-spacial approach to divine transcendence. More recently this approach has been joined by an alternate model that focuses on time. The theologies of hope (Jürgen Moltmann and Wolfhart Pannenberg, e.g.) have moved to a more historical way of thinking about God. Transcendence, as pictured often in the biblical narrative, is seen as eschatological. God is not up there, in here, or back there, but rather *ahead of us*, the future One who functions where we have not yet been, the One impacting our present with the gracious "already" of what is "not

---

[66] Biblical teaching does not naively understand God to be "up there" in spacial terms, even though such language was employed freely. The concept of God's *omnipresence* is very biblical. God is not limited to any given place, direction, or time. God is not trapped in Israel or in the Jerusalem temple and may be worshipped equally well on any mountain (Jn. 4:21-24).

yet." Knowledge of God resides in the biblical narrative of what God has done and will do, both instructing helpfully the potential for change in the present.

God's transcendence may be conceived today as "the absolute power of the future."[67] The God who continues to come to us comes from ahead of us. This God is not to be identified closely with the failures of the church. The God whom Jesus proclaimed guaranteed no comfortable accommodation with any religious establishment, but walked awkwardly among the sacred cows of those claiming God's favor but not living in accord with God's plan. Therefore, God "is the power of the future pressing for a radical conversion of the present."[68] This transcendent otherness of the future, already present with us, is our hope. It is God come to be with us in order that all things can be made new.

Limits of Gender Language

Christians now are more aware than ever before of how imperfect and inadequate, how culturally conditioned is human language about God. In recent years the Christian community has been sensitized to the need for more "gender inclusive" language about God, regardless of how divine transcendence is conceived. To associate God exclusively with a particular human gender is an archaic and often a socially oppressive practice.

At least three things are clear after all the recent debate on this subject. (1) The societies out of which the biblical materials emerged were patriarchal. Most of the biblical writers were male and much of their language about God is predominately male in orientation. (2) Language tends to reflect established social roles and can contribute to unwarranted stereotypes and even oppression. (3) Since biblical times, males often have used the Bible to legitimate their dominance over women inside and outside the church. Elizabeth Johnson is right: "While officially it is rightly and consistently said that God is spirit and so beyond identification with either male or female sex, yet

---

[67] Carl Braaten, *The Future of God* (N. Y.: Harper & Row, 1969), 68.
[68] Ibid., 69.

the daily language of preaching, worship, catechesis, and instruction conveys a different message: God is male, or at least more like a man than a woman, or at least more fittingly addressed as male than as female."[69]

This being the case, there is an important issue to be addressed at both the theological and practical levels. Jürgen Moltmann puts the issue in question form:

> Is the God of the Bible only a further manifestation of the age-old deity of patriarchy, or is "the Father of Jesus Christ" another God: a God who leads women and men into the shared freedom of the messianic time in which there will no longer be matriarchy and patriarchy, because the rule of one human being over another has come to an end?[70]

The Bible, despite its patriarchal setting, teaches that female and male are made equally in the image of God (Gen. 1:27) and that wife and husband are to be one flesh in a union of mutual helpfulness (Gen. 2:18). The subservience of women to men and enmity between the sexes is not pictured as God's intention, but a direct result of sin (Gen. 3), a result finally overcome by the death and resurrection of Jesus Christ (Gal. 3:28).

Masculine terminology for the Hebrew God chiefly indicated "not patriarchy, but transcendence."[71] Israel believed that the God it worshipped was different from the gods and goddesses of the nations. Those supposed other divine beings were but manufactured things that reflected and hopefully maintained the cycles of nature and agricultural fertility, as well as being the presumed providers of power,

---

[69] Elizabeth Johnson, *She Who Is: The Mystery of God in Feminist Theological Discourse* (New York: Crossroad, 1992), 4-5.

[70] Jürgen Moltmann, *History and the Triune God* (1992), 1. "Patriarchy" is described by Moltmann as "a male order covering authority, possessions, and right of inheritance...represented by male images, usually of the father, and communicated through male kings and princes" (4).

[71] Thomas Finger, *Christian Theology: An Eschatological Approach* (Scottdale, Pa.: Herald Press), II:485.

prosperity, and legitimacy to the families, tribes, or nations with which they had become associated. These humanly created gods emerged from, embodied, and were intended to insure the well-being of their contexts of origin. The prophets of Israel called this idolatry.

God was believed by Israel to stand apart from the creation. Sometimes God actually altered nature's rhythms and upset social establishments, calling for and enabling their transformation in the name of justice and righteousness. The God of Israel and of all existence would not support a secure status quo, even for Israel, not when faithfulness and justice were absent. God was known to have sovereign freedom from and over all cultural claims. G. Ernest Wright insists on the classic and distinctive faith of Israel, summarized concisely in a series of belief statements:

> The belief in the existence of only one God, who is Creator of the world and giver of all life; the belief that God is holy and just, without sexuality or mythology; the belief that God is invisible to man except under special conditions and that no graphic nor plastic representation of Him is permissible; the belief that God is not restricted to any part of His creation, but is equally at home in heaven, in the desert, or in Palestine; the belief that God is so far superior to all created beings, whether heavenly bodies, angelic messengers, demons or false gods, that He remains absolutely unique....[72]

In the ancient polytheistic setting of Israel's life, how might this distinctive deity (Yahweh) be described effectively? Given the strong identification in the surrounding cultures of the feminine with the processes of the natural world (fertility, reproduction, etc.), "goddess imagery would not likely suggest a Power above nature and society."[73]

The language that would serve the purpose in that setting would be masculine images, God imaged as male and lacking a female

---

[72] G. Ernest Wright, *The Old Testament and Theology* (New York: Harper and Row, 1969), 29.

[73] Ibid., 486.

consort (most ancient "gods" came as couples). Such imagery was "almost unique, and well suited to the God who had begun transforming nature and society–including its patriarchal structures."[74] Consequently, in that setting, the Hebrew prophets were understandably cautious about feminine language for God. They assumed that female-oriented language for the deity results in "a basic distortion of the nature of God and of his relation to his creation."[75] It tends to lead to the deification of nature and a pantheistic religion.[76]

It also is the case that the character of Israel, derived from the perceived character of God, stood as a challenge to Canaanite politics as well as Canaanite religion. Therefore, the issue is not whether God is masculine or feminine. The issue is "whether this God works in *sexual* ways so that God is continuous with the normal social and natural processes, or whether this God works in *covenantal* ways and is discontinuous both from natural processes and the social apparatus."[77]

The God of loving grace is not at home in the established structures of human societies, with their typical preference for the powerful, but persists in expressing solidarity with the poor and disenfranchised. There is a crucial connection between the *character* of God and what God considers the *legitimate character* of institutions in human societies. Since the God of loving grace does not choose typically to function with patterns of coercive power, though all such power is readily available, God's people are to reflect the God-like patterns of

[74] G. Ernest Wright, *The Old Testament and Theology* (New York: Harper and Row, 1969), 486.

[75] Elizabeth Achtemeier, in D. Miller, ed., *The Hermeneutical Quest* (Allison Park, Pa.: Pickwick, 1986), 109.

[76] It is equally plain today that male language for the divine often distorts in other ways the common perception of the nature of God and God's relation to creation. Feminists frequently and rightly have pointed this out. Power and dominance, associated with the divine through traditional male language, get confused with the world's use of force and control, typical male images. Different cultures and ages have different ideas about which roles are proper to the mother and which to the father. God is not confined to the cultural assumptions of any society, including that of ancient Israel. Virginia Ramey Mollenkott offers the provocative observation that "one reason so few men attend church regularly is that they are unconsciously repelled by being called toward intimacy with an exclusively masculine God" (*The Divine Feminine*, Crossroad, 1993, 11).

[77] Walter Brueggemann, ed. by Patrick Miller, *A Social Reading of the Old Testament* (Minneapolis: Augsburg Fortress Press, 1994), 159.

non-violent, redemptive justice in its public life. What finally is at issue is less the sexuality of God and more "the way in which *different gods* are understood to sanction *different social visions*."[78]

If one takes seriously the historical character of revelation and the cultural conditioning of all metaphors for God, it becomes obvious that it would have been unthinkable in first-century Judaism for the Messiah to appear as a "Daughter of God" who called God her "Mother." The Messiah in fact was male, Jesus of Nazareth, and frequently referred to God as his "Father." The key to proper understanding lies in the attitudes and actions of Jesus, not merely in his characteristic metaphors for the divine.

What is the substance behind the surface language of Jesus? What kind of a male Messiah was Jesus in reference to the dignity, equality, and prerogatives of women? Jesus personally highlighted, embodied, and encouraged in all disciples of whatever sex the so-called feminine virtues of meekness, forgiveness, and love. He treated women as equals and gave priority to the poor, sometimes at considerable risk to his own reputation and safety. He reflected a God who stands outside culturally conditioned national, racial, gender, and commercial stereotypes, divisions, and agendas.

Jesus is reported in the New Testament to have addressed God as "my Father" some 170 times. He used the word "Abba," an intimate and tender word used by children like "papa" and "mama" to address someone trusted profoundly. When Jesus addressed God this way, however, the accent was not on the masculinity of the divine, but "on the unprecedented intimacy of Jesus' own relationship to God's divine mystery." Jesus' distinctive view of God related closely to the drawing near of the kingdom of God. This Abba-nearness in Jesus signaled a new messianic community breaking free from "the archaic powers of origin in family, class, and culture."[79] This sense of security in intimacy with the God of loving grace was also a declaration of freedom from all human dominations.

Why, then, not eliminate the near exclusiveness of male language for God so traditional in the Christian community until recent-

---

[78] Ibid., 162.

[79] Jürgen Moltmann, *History and the Triune God* (1992), 11, 13.

ly? In principle, such elimination is appropriate, but only after a key task is undertaken. This task is to appreciate the *theological burden* of a given biblical metaphor in its original historical and literary context. The full biblical witness to God should not be compromised by any premature change of metaphors for current cultural reasons. Some Christian feminists, understandably anxious to correct past wrongs regarding the status of women, have insisted on alternative language for God, even at the expense of continuity with the substance of orthodox theology. That is, they alter traditional language for God in ways that fling open theological doors that thoughtful orthodoxy has long judged lead to unorthodox and unbiblical conclusions.[80]

Such potential distortion comes when feminism moves from a call for gender fairness to a preoccupation with gender ideology.[81] Some attempts to justify an abandonment of the traditional male language for God, replacing it with "she," "mother," and "goddess" language, risk exchanging the true God for false deities who are no gods (Jer. 2:11).[82] Israelite religion, while on occasion mentioning maternal characteristics of God (e.g., Isaiah 42:14), strongly opposed

---

[80] This is not to say that being orthodox commits one forever to exclusive use of male imagery and language for God just because it was theologically strategic in an earlier setting and because some alternatives are theologically distorted in today's setting. After all, insisting that male gender best conveys divine transcendence, while the female most appropriately relates to creative activity, reinforces gender stereotypes so long held. Even so, we now live in a "new age" time when nature-oriented mysticisms and pantheisms again are common distortions of the Hebrew-Christian worldview. Carefully chosen theological language remains important in such a setting.

[81] Says Frederick Norris: "Certainly God as male has no place in Christian faith. If, however, we inject female gender into deity because of grossly chauvinistic societal and religious practices, we compound one mistake with another. God is neither male nor female. The Old Testament stands firm against a doctrine of God which proposes characteristics for God taken from nature and goddess religions. The struggle for the equality of women, for fairness and love in the ways they are thought of, talked about, and treated does not demand that the Canaanite religions be reinstituted as substitutes for Christian faith" (*The Apostolic Faith*, Liturgical Press, 1992, 62). See Elizabeth Achtemeier, "Renewed Appreciation for an Unchanging Story," *Christian Century* (June 13-20, 1990), 596-599.

[82] Elizabeth Achtemeier, "Why God Is Not Mother," *Christianity Today* (August 16, 1993), 17.

goddess worship.[83] Hebrew society rejected such worship for reasons other than the prevailing patriarchalism. The reasons were its awareness of God's genuine transcendence of creation and its deep desire to make clear in its language about God that distinctness from the created order.[84] The continuing theological concern is that language for God not encourage a too-close identification of God with the creation, subtly encouraging human beings to worship the creation and not the Creator (Rom. 1:25).

Even so, as subsequent history has made painfully clear, male images of the divine also are subject to distortions as great as pantheism. Today the cultural context appears to have changed adequately to allow, even call for a reconsideration of the nearly exclusive use of male imagery for God. The only caution is that there be a strict avoidance of the easy implication that nature and the divine are one.[85] The limits of at least the English language force us into fragile gender categories since it would be inappropriate to settle for a depersonalization of God. While neither female nor male language alone grasps adequately the essence and activity of God, use of "it" misses the mark completely. Neuter terms like Liberator, Maker, and

---

[83] Virginia Ramey Mollenkott shows, however, that, despite this caution and surprisingly for a patriarchal setting, "the biblical authors did indeed move the feminine principle into the godhead." Having reviewed biblical references to God as "nursing mother," "midwife," "female homemaker," "mother eagle," etc., she concludes: "We think it shortcircuits our full humanity to ignore the pluriform images of God that the Bible offers us, and therefore the multiple aspects of relating to that God" (*The Divine Feminine*, Crossroad, 1993, 4).

[84] Significantly, there was such awe concerning God that there was reluctance to speak God's name at all. Relying on historical narrative, often Israel referred to God's identity by redemptive function instead of by a name. God is the liberating trailblazer of destiny. When Moses at the burning bush sought the name of God, he received a cryptic response. "I will be what I will be" (Ex. 3:14), or, as James McClendon paraphrases, "I will always be ahead of you. Find Me as you follow the journey" (*Systematic Theology: Doctrine*, 1994, 285). The Exodus experience itself provided the narrative context for knowing (naming) God in this way.

[85] Unfortunately, this implication comes so easily. In Rosemary Radford Ruether's book *Women-Church* (Harper & Row, 1988) she presents fresh liturgies for women at worship. These liturgies include celebrations of the cycles of the moon and the seasons and the cycles of menstruation and menopause. Such worship appears to lean toward the world view of the Canaanites (so tempting and troubling to the Israelites) and away from worship of the transcendent "Father Almighty, Creator of heaven and earth" (Apostles' and Nicene Creeds).

Wisdom are meaningful in what they affirm about God and deficient because of the personal dimension they fail to affirm. The biblical addressing of God is primarily personal. God is known as Some*one*, not some*thing*; God is the purposeful initiator of all creation, a Self-conscious, redemptively relating reality.

This distinctive nature of God, in fact, led one Hebrew prophet to use language about God that is easily misperceived as having Canaanite overtones. Hosea deliberately used it in order to affirm that God is not a detached, invulnerable sovereignty, but a risking, faithful, Self-giving God of loving grace. He boldly used relational-sexual imagery to express a distinctive kind of sovereignty that (who) exhibits persistent caring in the face of pain and infidelity. God is like a faithful husband, so full of loving grace even in relation to a very wayward wife. A reversal of the roles of husband and wife in this story would not change the story's intended meaning, its characterization of God in relation to the covenant people. What is at issue is not the sexuality of God, but God's *covenantal faithfulness* as contrasted with the *fickleness* of Baal and the frequent inconsistency of God's people.

There are theological reasons that argue for continuing to designate the God of the Bible as "Father."[86] Such continuation, however, should be intentional in not violating the proper status and dignity of women. After all, God "was not ashamed of the male nature, for He took it upon Himself; or of the female, for He was born of a woman," thus liberating us "by the agency of both sexes."[87] The Christian faith draws its understanding of God from the acts of God, with the determining, interpreting center point of these acts being Jesus Christ.[88] Embodied in Christ is the view that, among believers and in relation

---

[86] See Theodore Jennings, Jr., *Loyalty to God* (Nashville: Abingdon Press, 1992), chapter two. See also the series of essays in Alvin Kimel, Jr., ed., *Speaking the Christian God: The Holy Trinity and the Challenge of Feminism* (Eerdmans, 1992).

[87] St. Augustine, as quoted in Thomas Oden, *The Transforming Power of Grace* (Nashville: Abingdon Press, 1993), 28-29.

[88] The biblical narrative of how God is with us shapes how we conceive of and properly refer to God. Says Daniel Migliore: "All of our images of God, old and new, masculine and feminine, personal and impersonal, receive a new and deeper meaning from the gospel story beyond the meanings that they have in the contexts in which they are ordinarily used" (*Faith Seeking Understanding*, 1991, 67). The language that comes from human experience is at best only partially appropriate when assigned to

to the implications of the faith, "there is no such thing as male or female" (Gal. 3:28). God "transcends our divisions and imperialisms. The Vision of God is inclusive of our particularities and finally beyond our gender distinctions."[89]

The God of the Bible has no sexuality. Any attribution of sexuality to God is a reversion to paganism. Sexuality is a structure of creation (Gen. 1-2) and is confined within the limits of creation (Matt. 22:30). To insist on female language for God is no advance over exclusive male language if the goal is to transcend all sexual discrimination. One might attempt some language quota system, some linguistic "affirmative action" if, in our understanding, God remains truly transcendent and the result is not a paralysis of Christian worship by the dominance of our human sensitivities.

In summary, any shift from exclusively male language for God should not be paralleled by a shift away from emphasis on the transcendency of God over all creation. While theological analogies and metaphors are to be questioned in the face of their cultural captivity, there should be no freedom to conceive a new God defined differently than the one revealed in the Bible. There is no reason to abandon belief in an objectively real God who actually exists apart from ourselves and "above" the processes of nature, whether we happen to be female or male, or live hundreds of years before or after the birth of Jesus. God is not literally a "father," but in certain ways is like a father and in other ways like a mother. To speak of God as "Father" is to say that the roles of father in ancient Israel allow us key insights into the nature of God. It certainly is not to say that God *is* a male.

A fresh vision of God is what exiles of all ages need. For the Jews in Babylon, the news finally came that their penalty was paid and soon there would be a highway home. God was intervening and "the glory of the Lord shall be revealed" (Isa. 40:5). A preacher was to get to a mountaintop and shout the news, "Here is your God!" (40:9). Who is God? God is the One who "comes with might" (40:10) and who "will feed his flock like a shepherd; he will gather the lambs

---

the divine. The biblical story of God with us should elevate and refine the meanings of our best pictures and words.

[89] Gabriel Fackre, *The Christian Story*, rev. ed. (Eerdmans, 1978, 1984), 62.

in his arms, and carry them in his bosom, and gently lead the mother sheep" (40:11). The awesome creator and the gentle shepherd, the forger of futures and the nurturer of the weak, the paternal and the maternal, here is our God of loving grace!

A broader "parental" view of God surely has its place. John Wesley, long before today's sensitivities on this subject, referred to God as "Parent."[90] In fact, "loving Parent" is Wesley's defining model of God. He saw the first "Person" of the Godhead relating to humanity as Creator/Sustainer, Governor/Judge, Provider, and Physician. Of these, Physician and Provider are the functions of divine working he most valued.[91]

Ruth Duck is anxious to halt the "injustice of sexism" by complementing the traditional naming of God with "feminine and non-gendered language." She recognizes that "faithfulness to the gospel and continuity with Christian tradition are also at stake."[92] Rejected by her is the assertion of many that "Father" is a revealed identification of God that must be retained, at least in the wording of baptisms, creeds, etc.[93] Instead, Duck calls for our going "deeper than formulas to find the language of witness, thanksgiving and praise." Her example of a step forward in this language dilemma is the text of Charles Wesley's wonderful hymn, "Love Divine, All Loves Excelling." The members of the divine Trinity are named as "pure, unbounded love" (Jesus), "loving Spirit," and "Almighty." This hymn, she says, "is grounded in salvation history. It makes no use of traditional masculine language, yet it witnesses powerfully to the triune God."[94]

Such constructive efforts are worthy of note in fairness to women, so long as no new, unbiblical "god" is being introduced subtly in the service of feminist ideology (as in the past have been

---

[90] For examples, see Randy Maddox, *Responsible Grace* (Nashville: Kingswood Books, Abingdon Press, 1994), n. 119, pg. 284.

[91] Ibid., 63.

[92] Ruth Duck, "Praising the Triune God: Beyond Gender?" *Christian Century* (May 19-26, 1993), 556.

[93] See, e.g., Geoffrey Wainwright in Alvin Kimel, ed., *Speaking the Christian God* (Eerdmans, 1992), 209-221.

[94] Duck, op. cit., 556.

unbiblical gods in the service of male ideology).[95] The challenge is to remain faithful to the intent of biblical revelation and avoid the pitfalls of cultural accommodation in the service of selfish interests.

Surviving Cultural Accommodation

In recent generations there has been a distorting shift toward viewing human experience as the real grounding of Christian theological concepts. At times this has led to an excessive interiorization of faith. Christianity often has become understood as merely an ideal vision of life, a poetic expression of the highest human values, rather than faith resting on a truth claim about the one and only sovereign God who actually exists apart from the created world. The personal "stuff" of mystical experience has replaced the biblical revelation of God in the particularity of Jesus Christ. Noting how influential humanism and individualism have been on Western theology, there now is need "to get over a bad case of cultural accommodation."[96] The Christian church often has gone wrong by leaving the Hebraic thought world of the Bible in favor of alternatives like Hellenistic philosophy.[97] Somehow the church must be relevant to the times without being excessively shaped by those very times.

The Christian faith ultimately is rooted in a sound understanding of the Divine Being. All theological heresies, ancient and modern, stem from a faulty understanding of God. An important conclusion can be drawn from the pendulum-like swings in Christian thought that have been seen over the centuries. For instance, "the immanental

---

[95] Note the constructive work of Elizabeth Johnson, *She Who Is* (New York: Crossroad, 1992). She reports: "This book's choice to use mainly female symbolism for God, let me state clearly, is not intended as a strategy of subtraction, still less of reversal. Rather, it is an investigation of a suppressed world directed ultimately toward the design of a new whole" (57).

[96] Clark Pinnock in Pinnock and Delwin Brown, *Theological Crossfire* (Grand Rapids: Zondervan, 1990), 69.

[97] Marvin Wilson, *Our Father Abraham* (Grand Rapids: Eerdmans, 1989), chapter 10. Says Clark Williamson: "Because the Christian tradition de-Judaized itself...its classical doctrine of God tells us more about pre-Christian, Greek understandings of God than about the living, covenantal God of the Bible" (*A Guest in the House of Israel*, Westminster/John Knox, 1993, 202-203).

emphasis of liberalism was reacted to and replaced by the stress on transcendence by the neo-orthodox movement. Both had adverse effects on the doctrine of God and point to the necessity of formulating a theology that maintains a balanced relationship between the two."[98] The twentieth century has had to survive significant swings in the ongoing search for how best to balance the transcendence and immanence of God.[99]

God is out there, "above" all, before all, ahead of all, the creator of all, singular and sovereign, both male and female without actually being either. God also is right here, in all, very present, Self-revealing in the processes of nature and human life, and especially in the history of Israel and Jesus Christ, all conveyed through the biblical revelation. God is affected by human sin, winces at our pain, and is open to our prayer. God comes prepared to covenant with us for the transformation of the present into a wonderfully intended future.

The Hebrew word for "truth" is *emeth*. This word is made up of the three Hebrew letters aleph, mem, and tau, the first, middle, and last letters of the Hebrew alphabet. Covering the whole, then, it represents well the truth about the identity of God. *Aleph*–God is first. There is none from whom God received the kingdom. No other is responsible for creation. *Mem*–God is in the midst of the ongoing historical process. By choice, because of love, God comes, calls, suffers, saves. Only in God's coming is the kingdom drawn near. *Tau*–God is in the future and will be at the end and beyond the end of human history. There is none to whom God will ever have to turn over the kingdom. First, now, always, together they tell the whole truth, picturing and virtually naming God. God traverses the whole alphabetic range, revealing the divine being as the ultimate origin, meaning, and destiny of all that is or ever will be.

No wonder the Psalmist concludes a confession of Israel's sins with this burst of adoring affirmation: "Blessed be the Lord, the God of Israel, from everlasting to everlasting. And let all the people say, 'Amen.' Praise the Lord!" (Ps. 106:48).

---

[98] H. Ray Dunning, *Grace, Faith and Holiness* (Kansas City: Beacon Hill Press, 1988), 185.

[99] See, for instance, the excellent survey by Stanley Grenz and Roger Olson, *20th Century Theology: God and the World in a Transitional Age* (InterVarsity Press, 1992).

CHAPTER THREE

GOD THE SOVEREIGN: COVENANT MAKER

—

"...maker of heaven and earth, of all that is, seen and unseen..."

—

The first verse of the Bible is very good news. It reports that God chose to create (Gen. 1:1). In the very beginning of the biblical narrative the goodness of God is seen at work in a voluntary and gracious act of creation. This graciousness is presented biblically as natural, to be expected of God. Why? Because God essentially is Self-sharing love. God, though Self-sufficient in divine fullness, nonetheless desired to create and be open to creation in overflowing love. Under no necessity to do so, God chose. God found the creation good "because God is dynamic and open. He loves a creation that is open like this one."[1] The choosing God placed choice at the heart of creation.

The divine Sovereign, "the triune God who eternally dwells in loving community also welcomes into existence a world of creatures different from God."[2] The word "welcomes" is the good news. We humans are intended. We belong and are loved. The creation is good, even though sin soon would appear to taint. Christians, therefore, should resist the temptation to an "otherworldly" religion that seeks to give up on this world. This is the world God made, declared

---

[1] Clark Pinnock and Robert Brow, *Unbounded Love: A Good News Theology for the 21st Century* (InterVarsity Press, 1994), 47.

[2] Daniel Migliore, *Faith Seeking Understanding* (Eerdmans, 1991), 80.

good, and still loves despite the human choice of sin. It is the world we humans are privileged to enjoy and are responsible to preserve in covenant cooperation with the creating God. This world was not created to solve deficiencies in the being of God. Rather, God created and loves the creation for its own sake. God, as loving grace, chose to take the risks of honest relationships, just the way real love would have it.

Relationships are crucial to God. What is created is called. Humanity choose to break the divine-human relationship and still was called. "Where are you" asks God of ashamed sinners (Gen. 3:9). The calling persists because God wants to re-establish relationship, renew fallen creation. Soon a covenant would be offered as a context for responsible cooperation and faithfulness. All of this makes the following clear:

> God does not control us–He calls us; God does not manipulate us–He beckons to us. Before God is anything else, God is *love*–the Love who creates us, sustains us, and longingly seeks us out, all for the sake of relationship.[3]

The intended intimacy and interdependence of the divine-human relationship is the basis for the biblical understanding of prayer.

The Possibility of Prayer

Men and women are not called to "run" the church. The church of God is God's church, God's body on earth that is to be divinely constituted and controlled. Leaders who give themselves to prayer "are less likely to become *managers* and more likely to grow into *sages*" (italics added).[4] The continuing challenge is to replace human with divine control of the church. This requires a central focus on the

---

[3] Michael Lodahl, *The Story of God: Wesleyan Theology and Biblical Narrative* (Kansas City: Beacon Hill Press, 1994), 91.

[4] Merle Strege, in *Vital Christianity*, January, 1993, 19. A key reason why Strege pursues this analysis is his observation that in recent decades many Christians have absorbed from the current Western culture too much of a management orientation.

being and presence of God and a vital role for prayer. The almighty One who creates and loves also invites partnership in creation and close communication in the divine-human relationship.

God, the Creator of heaven and earth, brought into being *ex nihilo*, literally from nothing, all that now is. How God remains related to the continuation of this creation, however, is a separate and significant matter. Having set this good creation in motion, does the creation now operate independently of God's direct involvement (*deism*, extreme transcendence)? Or is every so-called natural occurrence to be seen as the immediate activity of the divine (*primitivism*, extreme immanence)? Part of the answer lies in Romans 8:28-29.

In this passage Paul affirms neither deism nor primitivism. Rather, God is presented as the transcendent One who is able and prepared to bring good out of whatever happens, with "good" identified as that which produces in the lives of God's people a conforming "to the image of his Son." God as Person[5] is assumed to relate intimately in all circumstances with faithful persons for a personal end, the Christ-likeness of human character and life.[6] The Person-to-person communication of prayer throughout this relating process is viewed as wholly natural and needful. Prayer's focus, instead of human pleasure, comfort, or profit, should be on humility, adoration, and commitment. Only within this focus emerges the natural and appropriate presence of human petition, an asking of God growing from human need and desire, but willingly disciplined by God's will instead of the human who prays.

The foundations of Christian prayer emerge from the nature of the distinctive God who was discerned early in the experience of ancient Israel. Yahweh was known to be more than the typical con-

---

[5] For a good discussion of the meaning of "person" in reference to God, see Alister McGrath, *Christian Theology: An Introduction* (Oxford, U. K.: Blackwell, 1994), 207-213.

[6] See David Mason, "Reflections on 'Prayer' from a Process Perspective," *Encounter* 45:4 (Autumn 1984), 347-357. Mason says that "God is affected by every action, every desire, every prayer of every creature.... God initiates activity in each new present experience by responding to its past, by envisioning its best possibilities in its given circumstances, and by offering to every creature the ideal aim for it to actualize in each new present context" (351).

ception of a god who sets and rigidly enforces the rules of creation and human life. Exodus 34:6-7 reflects the enduring tension of the divine being. God both takes seriously the violations of individual people and whole nations and also is merciful without condoning or ignoring the wrongdoing. Although this understanding of God is paradoxical, the witness of the Hebrew Scriptures insists that it is so. The God of the Bible "does not flinch from this incongruity." In fact, "it is this incongruity that makes human life possible and makes biblical theology endlessly problematic and promising."[7]

Israel learned through its divinely assisted liberation from Egypt that God's name is "Yahweh" (Ex. 3:13-15; 6:3). God no longer was a great "someone in the great somewhere." God was revealed as the personal and powerful Lord, a present "I" for Israel's constantly needy "thou."

God is not merely the judge who predictably issues rewards or executes punishments. God also is the One who voluntarily, because of an unfathomable compassion, embraces the pain of human sin and oppression now rampant in the creation. The Hebrew realization of this grief-absorbing God was the step essential to understanding the glorious news later to be narrated more fully in the New Testament. In Christ there would be a voluntary "divine death" in order that all we who were yet sinners might live!

The human cry of pain is heard by the ever-listening, ever-caring, even the ever-feeling God. Understanding the complexity of God's being in light of God's hearing and compassionate responding enables the possibility of human prayer to God. What an almost unthinkable privilege! Prayer is an available and intimate means of conversation between the human heart that hurts and hopes and the God who hears, absorbs, and responds with understanding and mercy. The God who called Israel to hear (Deut. 6:4) is the same One who already had heard Israel's cry of pain in Egypt and had been moved to deliver. The call for all believers to obey is a call that assumes divine mercy already extended. That is why wonder, adoration, and thanksgiving should surround and underlie all petitions in prayer.

---

[7] Patrick Miller, ed., (Walter Brueggemann essays), *Old Testament Theology* (Augsburg/Fortress Press, 1992), 43.

God seeks covenant relationships with personal depth. The emergence of self-conscious and purposive persons in this created world surely suggests the creative One who is at least Self-conscious, purposive, personal, and certainly much more. Says Elton Trueblood: "God may be more than a person and probably is, though we do not really know what that means, but unless He is at least as personal as we are, He is not One to whom we can pray. The good news is that, by the testimony of Christ, God is *completely* what we are partially."[8] So prayer, person-to-Person communication, is possible, expected, needful, divinely welcomed, consistent with the deepest reality of the whole creation.

Given the holy, incomparable, inexpressible nature of the sovereign God, the most appropriate form of prayer, at least initially, is that of adoration. Adoration has the dimensions of thanksgiving and praise. In thanksgiving the one praying gives glory to God because of the magnificence of the very being of the divine. The Psalms "reverberate with the tumult of praise."[9] "I will bless the Lord at all times; his praise shall continually be in my mouth" (Ps. 34:1). "He put a new song in my mouth, a song of praise to our God" (Ps. 40:3).

Luke ends his Gospel with the report of ongoing adoration in the early Christian community. "They were continually in the temple blessing God" (Lk. 24:53). This celebrative process was and still should be adoration by magnification. To magnify is to enlarge the apparent size of something, increasing it beyond its normal proportions for purposes of examination. Invites the Psalmist, "O magnify the Lord with me and let us exalt his name together" (Ps. 34:3). This expansive adoration is wholly appropriate because the reality of the being, goodness, and love of God exceeds any of our human attempts to magnify them—and eludes all arrogant attempts to domesticate and manipulate them.

Such prayerful adoration, giving our meager glory to God, is possible only because God's glory already has shone on us. In the biblical setting the term "glory" means brightness or radiance, that which makes God manifest to people. The glory of God is what little of

---

[8] D. Elton Trueblood, *A Place To Stand* (Harper & Row, 1969), 72.

[9] Richard Foster, *Prayer* (San Francisco: Harper, 1992), 84.

God's presence we, enabled by divine grace, can identify and apprehend. It can be seen in creation (Ps. 19:1-6). Primarily, however, it is seen in the biblical narration of God's great acts that lead to the potential of human salvation (Ex. 14:17-18; Ps. 96:1-9; Acts 7:2-53). While God is "invisible," transcending human ability to comprehend, God's glory is the accessible reflection of the divine being. The key passage is Exodus 33:18-23. There we learn that the ultimate mystery of God remains hidden, although its greatness and graciousness are disclosed in the midst of our human history, "while my [God's] glory passes by" (vs. 22).

Any glimpse of the divine glory naturally occasions an outburst of adoring human prayer. That prayer, full of thanksgiving for past appearances of God's glory-filled graciousness, also became the vehicle for Israel's highest expectations. One day the glory of God would appear as the Messiah, the ultimate incarnation of the radiance of the sovereign God. "Arise, shine; for your light has come, and the glory of the Lord has risen upon you.... Nations shall come to your light, and kings to the brightness of your dawn" (Isa. 60:1, 3). Such high hope, as the biblical record eventually unfolds, leads to Bethlehem, the New Testament, and the most wonderful, the most theologically significant claim of all. In the person of Jesus there would shine the full glory of God (2 Cor. 4:1-6). This Jesus, the awaited Messiah, would be nothing less than the climax of the whole story, the effulgence of the divine glory in human flesh (Heb. 1:1-4). In him the sovereign God, who stands astride all time, space, and existence, would stoop to show the divine glory, share the pain of human sin, and reveal the divine love.

Prayer is made possible because of the personal, loving, responsive nature of the God revealed throughout Scripture and known especially in Jesus Christ. Adoration and thanksgiving are the natural keynotes of such prayer. But, given the distinctive nature of God as loving grace and despite today's common objections,[10] the prayer of *petition* also is appropriate.

---

[10] Often it is argued that petitionary prayer is presumptuous. Since God already knows our needs, is it not pointless either to inform God of the obvious or seek to persuade the God who needs no persuasion and cannot be managed by us anyway? Is not petitionary prayer childish, egocentric, and now outdated for people "come of age"? The biblical storyline, with appropriate cautions, leads to a firm "no."

The God of the Bible is a living God, the divine Person, not the abstraction of a philosophical first principle or a mere moral ideal, not an impersonal Brahman or the arid Aristotelian concept of an unmoved mover. The biblical picture of God as the creating "Father" emphasizes a loving grace that acts in accord with its own nature. The occasional biblical likening of God to the role of a divine "Mother" focuses on the protection of children as a hen would gather the brood under her wings (Matt. 23:37). This "Parent" God is no static absolute beyond human history, but a dynamic, interactive reality who both first launched history and now chooses ongoing involvement in it by seeking the highest well-being of all creation. Thus the prayerful interaction of the wills of Creator and creature are to remain open to real relationship, even a dynamic partnership leading to communion, liberation, and mission.

In the act of prayer God and humanity are not only characterized but recharacterized, identified and changed. That is, "prayer is a constitutive act of faith that creates the potential for newness in both God and humanity."[11] What a thought! Human prayer can create new possibilities for God as well as for the one who prays. In the understanding of the Hebrews, God is open to the possibility of change in response to human prayer. Prayer is dialogical, with each partner playing a significant role, one sovereign and involved by unconditioned choice, the other human and participating by a choice conditioned by divine grace.[12] Believers who intercede with God on behalf of themselves or others, when doing so humbly in the context of adoring and thanking God, can make a difference. God is engaging in a redemptive process with the creation, and intercessory prayer can be a vital part that the believer can play in that process.

In no way does the Bible promote or condone prayer as a means of manipulating God. God, while loving grace, is no heavenly bank

---

[11] Samuel Balentine, *Prayer in the Hebrew Bible* (Minneapolis: Fortress Press, 1993), 268. Also see Walter Brueggemann, "A Shape for Old Testament Theology, II: Embrace of Pain," *Catholic Biblical Quarterly* 47 (1985), 402.

[12] Apart from divine grace the human choice would not be possible because of the devastating results of sin. See below for discussion of human *depravity* and God's *prevenient* grace.

account to be drawn upon merely by placing our faith cards in the nearest money machine. Even so, no contradiction is seen between (1) God as the sovereign Lord and (2) God being open to change in response to human prayer in light of the love and compassion inherent in the divine nature. In prayers of lament found in Jeremiah, Job, and Habakkuk, for instance, hard questions are put to God that both challenge and bring change to divine decisions. We who accept a covenant relationship with God thereby acquire an awesome responsibility. We can actually help to shape the particulars of how God will be present with us. God, so the biblical witness goes, has chosen not to exercise the divine will distantly and mechanically. By God's gracious choice, what happens on creation's stage is within the context of a living, dynamic, divine-human, covenant relationship. By definition, this is a call to the privilege and power of prayer!

Prayer, even petitionary and intercessory prayer, is vital to the life of faith because of the very nature of God and God's initiatives. Something else also is true. The act of prayer in the biblical narrative often serves to delineate divine character. Beyond what is said *to* God, it is what is said *about* God in the believer's prayer that provides insight into how the one praying understands God's identity and manner of relating to the world.

Hezekiah's urgent prayer is a good example. Assyria's siege of Jerusalem was raging in 701 B.C.E. The aggressor was boasting of having already destroyed other lands right in the faces of their helpless gods. So Judah's king prayed:

> O Lord, the God of Israel, who are enthroned above the cherubim, you are God, you alone, of all the kingdoms of the earth; you have made heaven and earth. Incline your ear, O Lord, and hear; open your eyes, O Lord, and see; hear the words of Sennacherib, which he has sent to mock the living God. Truly, O Lord, the kings of Assyria have laid waste the nations and their lands, and have hurled their gods into the fire, though they were no gods but the work of human hands—wood and stone—and so they were destroyed. So now, O Lord our God, save us, I pray you,

from his hand, so that all the kingdoms of the earth may know that you, O Lord, are God alone (2 Kings 19: 15-19).

The witness to the divine nature embedded in this prayer affirms God as the Lord, the God of Israel and of all earth's kingdoms, the Creator who listens and sees with compassion, the only God, the God capable and presumably willing to deliver from dire distress. In various biblical prayers there is witness to God's exclusive sovereignty (2 Kings 19:15, 19), God's creation of heaven and earth (2 Kings 19:15; cf. 1 Chron. 29:11), God's power (2 Chron. 14:11; 20:6, 12), and God's great faithfulness, mercy, and justice (Ezra 9:6-15; Neh. 1:5-11, 9:6-37). To such a God belongs all praise and glory! To such a God one is invited to respond, relate, pray, serve.

How then do we come to know this God? What of the impact of human sin? How does God now work in the world? To what, if anything, are we predestined by divine judgment and grace? How does God express divine almightiness in the whole process? To such major questions we now turn.

Human Sin and Divine Power

The biblical narrative illumines a massive stage on which the drama of all human history unfolds. The drama begins with a prologue that prefaces what is to follow. In the beginning was the Author of this whole story. Contrary to our modern secularisms, no doubt is left that this creating God is real and that our world is a created and dependent reality. Nothing in heaven or earth is understood properly except in light of the divine Parent who brought it into being, who is its ground and goal, who is sovereign, fully able, fully faithful, full of justice and mercy. This God summons forth prayer, prayers of adoration, thanksgiving, petition and intercession, because God created and now chooses to engage humanity and the world in a relationship of redemptive reciprocity.

We now explore briefly four crucial dimensions of this biblical drama. (1) God is at the beginning. (2) Sin has intruded to alter the story. (3) God remains constant in relation to changing circumstances.

(4) There is a special way in which God chooses to be "almighty" in the midst of sin and its tragic consequences.

1. Knowing the Creator. Knowledge of God does not originate in the rational pondering of independent and particularly insightful individuals. God is the Creator, not humans. God is the originator of history, humans, and the proper understanding of all things. According to the philosopher Descartes, the only reliable starting point in the search for truth is human self-consciousness. "I think, therefore I am." Christian logic, rooted in the biblical revelation, differs from this Cartesian logic. Instead of "I think, therefore I am" is the logic "God is, therefore we are, we think, and we can know."

The sovereign God is the seeking and Self-revealing God. Psalm 139 describes God as assuming the initiative. Human knowledge of God derives primarily, not from our own searching skills, but from God's enlightenment of and care for us. This divine initiative is intensely personal, first person singular. "O Lord, you have searched *me* and known *me* (vs. 1, emphasis added). God remains above being fully known or controlled by humans. Nonetheless, God seeks, finds, and enables knowing. The One we cannot comprehend is the very One who knows, loves, and provides for us. Astonishing. Hallelujah!

God listens and responds as well as speaks and acts. In all this involvement, God is not to be reduced in human view to merely a creative process that resides in nature and includes the totality of nature within the divine being. In this kind of "process" view, God moves the world "by the magnetic lure that he exercises upon the entities of nature."[13] The process theologies based on the work of Charles Hartshorne and Alfred North Whitehead are too naturalistic in that they posit the world of nature as the only reality, even though that nature is said to be permeated by the divine, creative presence. In opposition to such reductionism of classic Christian faith, noble and right in part as it is, the Bible portrays God as beyond and before as well as voluntarily and redemptively immersed in the life of the cre-

---

[13] Donald Bloesch, *The Struggle of Prayer* (Colorado Springs: Helmers & Howard, 1988), 27.

ation. While indeed permeating, God also predates and transcends, forms, and informs.[14]

The orthodox Christian community across the centuries has followed its Hebrew and Apostolic base in affirming that God is voluntarily present *to* the world, but not confined *within* the world. Thus human prayer to God makes sense. Answers to petitionary prayer are possible in addition to the creative, evolutionary processes resident in the world itself. While a holy God cannot be manipulated, and attempts to bend God's will to our self-centered wills are unworthy and finally self-destructive, God can be reached through prayer since being reached is consistent with God's nature and intention toward us.

A Christian theology of prayer, in fact, Christian theology in general, does not stop with its basis in God the Father. Christian prayer "rests upon the irreversible fact of the self-revelation of God in Jesus Christ and its confirmation in our hearts by the Holy Spirit."[15] Apart from the coming of Christ and the Spirit's intercession for us, we would not be able to know God adequately or communicate with God dependably.

We are getting ahead of the biblical narrative when we mention this early the Son and Spirit, although divine revelation centers in Jesus Christ and all parts of it inevitably pull toward the center and draw their fullest meaning from the center. God would act finally and fully in Christ, releasing revealing light on the purpose of all God's acting from the very time that the creation was first conceived. The

---

[14] Christian theologians of the fourth century insisted that creation is of the "will" but not the "essence" of God. On the other hand, the Word of God (Jesus Christ) is said to be "begotten, not made" and "of the essence of the Father" (phrases of the Nicene Creed). Creation of heaven and earth flows from God's imaginative love, not from God's substance like a series of emanations (Neoplatonism). The three typical models for viewing God in relation to creation are *theism* (God is transcendent Creator of the world), *pantheism* (creation is a mode of God's being), and *panentheism* (creation and God are mutually dependent). Today this third option is chosen often, with the creation described as God's body. Daniel Migliore is right in judging that "while emphasizing the intimacy of the relationship between God and the world, [panentheism] fails to depict appropriately either the freedom of God in relation to the world or the real otherness and freedom of the world" (*Faith Seeking Understanding*, Grand Rapids: Eerdmans, 1991, 94).

[15] Donald Bloesch, *The Struggle of Prayer* (1988), 26.

biblical story starts with that creation and with God who is the great Prologue to and continuing Author of what finally will be.

Before the beginning of created historical reality, God already was. God is the unbounded framer of all that is, the "foreword" of the drama that is rooted in the mists of unpenetrable eternity. But even there, by means of a divine gift emerging from the depths of distant mystery, one finds understanding because one finds the interpretive center of the story. "In the beginning was the Word, and the Word was with God, and the Word was God" (John 1:1). The Christ who later would be with us in flesh to reveal, reconcile, and explain the whole of divine revelation always was with and even always was God.

In the beginning God created. No outside necessity compelled a creation nor was there some deficiency in the divine life that made creating necessary. God is Self-existent and complete. In one sense, however, creation appears a natural and almost expected happening since such a sovereign action turns out to be consistent with God's nature as now known in Christ. To speak of God as Creator is to recognize the character of the divine as reaching love with a will-to-community. God's calling grace did not originate with the beckoning of Abraham. It expressed itself initially in creation where "God already manifests the Self-communicating, other-affirming, community-forming love that defines God's eternal triune reality and that is decisively disclosed in the ministry and sacrificial death of Jesus Christ."[16]

So the biblical story starts.[17] In the beginning was God (Gen. 1:1), and God chose to create. Deep in the being of God, well beyond the reach of unaided human understanding, God conceived a purpose, dreamed a dream, envisioned a plan. Paul spoke of it as "God's wisdom, secret and hidden, which God decreed before the ages for our glory" (1 Cor. 2:7). The biblical tale, then, the story of Israel and the church, is the record of God's pursuit of that plan and realization of that dream, all the way from the time of creation to the still-awaited

---

[16] Daniel Migliore, op. cit., 85.

[17] Israel's historical experience of "salvation" preceded its perspective on divine creation. By the Exodus and covenant, Israel became God's people. Only then did this people gather and adapt already existing creation stories, making them fit the particular nature of the God now known in Exodus, at Sinai, and in the calling of and promise to Abraham.

final consummation. We are assured by Paul that in everything God continues to work toward that good end (Rom. 8:28).

2. The Intrusion of Sin. Genesis 1-11 forms an extended telling of the early intrusion and apparent victory of sin and death over divine-human communion and life. We are shown the sad disintegration of the divine dream. The harmonious world pictured in Genesis 1-2 is thrown out of balance through a series of "falls." Human disobedience brings dismissal from the garden, a divine curse, even brother murdering brother (Gen. 4). Despite a massive divine cleansing by means of a flood (Gen. 6-9), the fallenness quickly resurfaces and spreads again the persistent infection of a now corrupted creation.

What is "sin"? Sin is the biblical way of referring to the turning inward of the human self, a deliberate and disastrous turning away from God, nature, and neighbor. Sin is idolatry. It is an intentional fouling of the divine-human relationship, with all the negatives that result. The primal sin was yielding to the temptation to "be like God, knowing good and evil" (Gen. 3:5).[18] It was the pride of "playing God," of rejecting the divine plan, of replacing God by our own megalomania (Rom. 1:18-23).

Sin is when women and men choose selfishly and become separated from the source of life, God, and from their intended destiny, harmonious relationship with God and with all of God's creation.[19] Thinking of sin in relational terms, it is human nature deprived of right relationship to God and thus acting out of itself rather than out

---

[18] An insightful review of the major thinkers who have introduced alternate secular accounts of human sin and misery (beginning with Jean-Jacques Rousseau, 1712-1778) is found in Bernard Ramm's chapter "If Adam Didn't, Who Did?" (*Offense to Reason: The Theology of Sin*, Harper & Row, 1985). Ramm argues that, while not denying that Christians can learn from other sources, the Christian doctrine of sin "is the most comprehensive and satisfying explanation of personal and social ills" (37).

[19] To acknowledge God as Creator is to recognize ourselves as radically dependent. We humans are finite, contingent beings who exist only at the pleasure of God. Life is fragile, like grass that quickly withers and dies (Isa. 40:6). Friedrich Schleiermacher defines religion as a feeling of "absolute dependence." The Psalmist warns that we should "know that the Lord is God. It is God who has made us and not we ourselves (Ps. 100:3). We are dependent on God for the gift of life, the renewal of life, and the fulfillment of life. Therefore, sin is human arrogance thinking and acting as though it were not so.

of the Spirit.[20] The sad fact is that such sin has become universal in human experience. Rooted in misuse of creaturely freedom, it now is a structural part of human existence. It is "a refusal to love, a saying no to relationship...whoring after other gods, after other lovers."[21]

As we humans choose darkness, we lose sight of the light of life. We fall into the bondage of our own wayward wills. What is required in this now universal circumstance, this sickness unto death, is a divine act of redemption. The gracious God who first created now has to recreate by making possible a loving rescue from a ruined relationship. Accomplishment of this redemption would come, but in the form of a long and often painful story. Even our own contemporary experiences, far distant from the original "fall," still yield frightening evidence of the "cosmic powers of this present darkness" (Eph. 6:12). They are powers of evil that continue to fight against the divine intention of human freedom, peace, love, and destiny.

Sin is not merely a privation of good, but an active, negative force now loose in creation (traditionally personalized as Satan). While universal, sin is not to be viewed as a substance transmitted genetically.[22] Neither should sin be viewed only as a circumstance infecting the plight of individuals. There is the social nature of human personhood. Social structures are formed by human beings, who then are formed in part by them. Humans are both producers and products of their conditions. Sin now infects the whole social fabric of human existence, giving rise to the widespread and often institutionalized idolatries of racism, classism, sexism, etc.

From the beginning of creation God's intention has been clear. This intention remains even now as God continues to be present with and recreate a troubled creation. The biblical way of identifying this enduring divine purpose is narrative in nature, observing God's way with Israel and especially God's way with all the world in Jesus Christ. Christ is the goal toward which the whole creation moves. All

---

[20] See Leon Hynson, "Original Sin as Privation," *Wesleyan Theological Journal* (Fall, 1987), 65-83.

[21] Clark Pinnock, in Pinnock and Delwin Brown, *Theological Crossfire*, 124.

[22] As affirmed above, the basic categories of Christian theology are *relational* rather than "substantive."

things "hold together" in Christ (Col. 1:17), making the world a loved cosmos and not an abandoned chaos. Christian theology has to do with a coherent story, not a twisted tale that is full of sound and fury, signifying nothing (Shakespeare). The biblical story is one of God's intended and historically unfolding re-creation in the face of human sin.

The subject of sin in modern Western societies has almost disappeared from common vocabulary in favor of concepts of ignorance and sickness that presume less moral responsibility.[23] Sin has moved to theological anthropology (humans are estranged from themselves, others, and God) and political change (the need for liberation from the oppression of unjust power arrangements). While the reality of sin is all too obvious,[24] what seems absent is talk of God's holiness and justice.

A biblical concept of sin requires the prior assumption of a holy God whose standards have been broken by a violated relationship. Note this prophetic word surely styled for today: "Clearly, the first order of business of any congregation of Christ is to proclaim the sovereignty of God, the sinfulness of humankind, and salvation through the grace of Jesus Christ. Congregations which allow aerobics, marriage therapy, counseling centers, and self-enhancement fads to preempt this first concern simply have lost their way."[25]

Sin certainly is real and serious. But it is not to be seen primarily as a legal infraction of divine law or honor now requiring punishment.[26] Sin is human refusal to accept God's love. It is a turning away from God's gracious presence and frustrating God's loving purpose. It is deliberate relationship violation. David possessed Bathsheba by getting her husband killed in battle. Yes, this was a breaking of divine commandments; but worse still, it was a rupturing

---

[23] Karl Menninger wrote *Whatever Became of Sin?* in 1973 (N. Y.: Hawthorn Books), hoping to restore the concept of sin as actual moral guilt.

[24] Sin is very real in the late twentieth century. A recent report said that in 1995 the two most lucrative businesses in the world were (1) the building and selling of military weaponry and (2) the traffic in drugs.

[25] L. Allen, R. Hughes, M. Weed, *The Worldly Church*, 2nd ed. (Abilene Christian University Press, 1991), 41.

[26] See chapter five for discussion of the meaning of the atonement of sin accomplished in Jesus Christ.

of the divine-human relationship. David confessed: "Against you [God], you alone, have I sinned" (Ps. 51:4).

Even so, in loving grace, God remains unwilling that any should perish. Rather than rejecting the sinner (the one who has reversed "live" into "evil"), God's work of judgment is intended to restore the divine-human relationship. God is concerned with restoration, not obsessed with the guilt of our sins. So the biblical narrative is witness to the long and loving work of God on behalf of the restoration of a lost creation.

3. Divine Constancy and Predestination. This biblical story of redemption begins with the crucial transition seen in Genesis 12:1-4a. Divine attention focuses on a man named Abraham and centers in a marvelous promise. Blatant human disobedience is faced with a fresh opportunity of blessed, divinely offered grace. These key verses are, in fact, more about God than about Abraham. They contain six divine "I" statements. God will be known by what God will do. God will combat the power of all sin and death, will move to meet poison with promise, will take the initiative to bless Abraham on the basis of his faith, and will graciously guide into a new land and thereby eventually bless all the nations. Originally, out of "chaos" had come creation. Now, out of corruption would come covenant, the work of the God of loving grace.

Creation's original purpose still could be fulfilled in spite of humanity's choice to break harmonious relationship with God and stray into fallenness and death. God had first created because of the overflowing of divine love. God chose not to be God without the world. The divine purpose, so the biblical narrative reads, was that another might come to exist, a humanity granted being and the capacity to freely choose entrance into a life together with God. God's love bore us. We are people who are invited to be with God so that we might find our fulfillment and realization of the meaning of all creation in right relation to God. The creation of historical reality is the playing out of this divine choice and vision. The divine vision is of the restoration of right relationship between God and creation, the coming into being again of a Divine-human covenant characterized by a shalom of peace and joy.

Fulfillment of this shalom required certain characteristics of the humans who were created. Since God was inviting the created into a loving relationship with the Creator, this relational intention made necessary in the covenant partner a real freedom to respond positively or negatively to God's invitation. Divine-human mutuality "cannot be programmed. Genuine life together can rise only out of a love born in freedom."[27] So we humans are not puppets manipulated by God, but creations invited by divine love to respond freely in love. This world and human life in it form a real drama, not a carefully controlled marionette show. There is real choice, real risk, both wonderful and frightening possibilities.

Life is not pre-programmed. Nor are all or some of us humans predestined, assured in advance of eventual eternal bliss or doomed in advance to eternal punishment by the sovereign choice of God. This kind of sordid scenario would spoil the divine plan. Augustine allowed "a dark shadow...to fall on God's character when he suggested that God actually planned the damnation of the damned...for God's greater glory."[28] To the contrary, the biblically known God is no coercive and calculating deity who determines all destinies. Human beings have been granted dignity and freedom, freedom even to choose against God–the God of loving grace. Choices have consequences. God chooses to adjust to human choices and allow the consequences.

Therefore, it is not proper to picture God as *immutable*, at least not in the sense of God being incapable of change. Since the creation is free, God responds as the historical process unfolds. The Bible tells of sin chosen by humans and then grace offered by God. It includes numerous instances of God altering plans to adjust to changing circumstances. Albert Gray, after affirming that God's nature and attributes never change (Mal. 3:6), proceeds to clarify that "the immutability of God is not to be understood as denying him the privilege of free action in accordance of his perfect nature."[29] God is not static same-

---

[27] Gabriel Fackre, *The Christian Story*, rev. ed. (Eerdmans, 1978, 1984), 69.

[28] Clark Pinnock, *Tracking the Maze* (Harper & Row, 1990), 192. See Augustine, *Enchiridion*, chapters 96-102.

[29] Albert Gray, *Christian Theology*, vols. 1-2, combined ed. (Anderson, Ind.: Gospel Trumpet Co., 1946), 100.

ness, but unchangingly known as eternal love. There is a crucial difference between having a fixed nature and exercising flexibility on behalf of fixed purposes.[30]

While the God known in Israel and in Christ is "the same yesterday, and today and forever" (Heb. 13:8), God's sameness is to be seen as the unchanging reliability of divine qualities such as love, mercy, and justice. It is "precisely because God is unchanging in the eternal purpose of self-giving love that God is so attentively answerable, so free in responding to changing historical circumstances, and so versatile in personal response."[31]

Regarding the covenant with Israel, Israel failed, but God did not. The covenant persisted only because God persisted. This is what is meant by *chesed*–the steadfast, unfailing, holy love of God. God adjusts as the creation makes its fateful choices, when the human story sometimes takes a dark turn. Regardless of these choices, God will not be deflected from the divinely chosen course. God, in fact, sometimes changes the divine plan of action because, in changing human circumstances, God's will is unchanging. The Bible tells of a stubborn God, steadfast in purpose (Ps. 102:27; James 1:17).

God is affected deeply by what happens to people and societies. Two biblical texts deny that God ever repents or changes the divine plan. But the issue really being addressed in Numbers 23:19 and 1 Samuel 15:29 is the *constancy* of God's character, not the *content* of God's experience with the creation. God does not lie, does not make promises lightly, is faithful, predictable in purpose, always the God of loving grace. So God, whose nature always is to love, changes and does not change. It is because "God's love *never* changes, God's experience *must* change."[32] It is the unchanging nature of God to change course as love may direct in shifting circumstances.

---

[30] Gerald Bray rightly warns that a dangerous imbalance arises easily when the "impassibility" of God is denied in favor of stressing the "suffering" of God in Christ. "The Christian gospel is not just a message of suffering; it is a message of victory and salvation from suffering and death.... Christ did not come to share in our sufferings as such; he came to provide the answer to them" (*The Doctrine of God*, InterVarsity Press, 1993, 249-250).

[31] Thomas Oden, *The Living God* (San Francisco: Harper, 1987), 112.

[32] Richard Rice, in Clark Pinnock, et al, *The Openness of God* (InterVarsity Press, 1994), 48. In this same volume Clark Pinnock laments in this regard the excessive

4. God's Way of Being Almighty. If there is change within God's unchangingness, in what sense then is God "omnipotent"? Often it has been claimed that God is all-powerful, and thus can do anything. Unfortunately, at some point in history almost anything imaginable has been attributed to God's powerful doing, including authorizing military crusades to recover control of "holy places" at whatever human cost and enslaving one people to another on the basis of race. But, if freedom, love, and covenant characterize humans and the relationship we are invited to allow reestablished with the creating and still sovereign God, brute force could hardly characterize the typical way God chooses to relate to the historical process. Rather, God relates out of love and in ways consistent with the dignity and freedom granted to human creation.

The revealed way of divine sovereignty refutes humanity's usual view of power. The divine victory that finally overcomes the evil of the world is pictured unforgettably in the Christ who, of all places, reigns even from the horror of an old rugged cross. God's weakness is said to be stronger than human strength (1 Cor. 1:25). In light of the biblical witness, to say that God is omnipotent is to say that, with patience and even suffering, God can and will accomplish all that is promised. Such divine power "includes the power of self-restraint; it allows a real drama of invitation, rejection and resistance to unfold; yet it also bespeaks a power of persistence that stubbornly endures until victory is won.... It manifests the power of powerlessness."[33] Such is the way of the God of loving grace.

We, of course, know the answer to "Is anything too hard for the Lord?" (Gen. 18:14). The answer is that with God "all things are possible" (Matt. 19:26). But there is divine condescension involved in God's decision to create our kind of world where power is shared with

---

influence of Greek philosophic ideas on early Christian theologians. Unfortunately, "the tradition has taken immutability far in the direction of immobility and inertness. Some have claimed that God is wholly actual and not at all potential and thus cannot change in any way.... This is a mistake from a biblical standpoint.... I do not mean that God is subject to change involuntarily, which would make God a contingent being, but that God allows the world to touch him, while being transcendent over it" (117-118).

[33] Gabriel Fackre, *Ecumenical Faith in Evangelical Perspective* (Grand Rapids: Eerdmans, 1993), 121.

the creation and freedom to choose is real. God has willingly surrendered unbridled power for the purpose of allowing loving relationship and a true partnership with humans. God chooses not to rule in an all-determining way. Theology thus should not use the abstract idea of power in a way that confuses sovereignty with tyranny.[34]

The Bible narrates through a series of actual human circumstances how God works through weakness[35] to confront strength. Abraham, called to be the pioneer of God's new people, moved out as a wandering herdsman, not even sure where he was being called to go. The "suffering servant" songs in Isaiah portray the true servant of God as the one who prevails through selfless suffering (e.g., Isaiah 53). In the terrible experience of Babylonian exile and then the new-exodus return, Israel learned that it could be God's people without functioning as an economic and military power. God was in control in God's way even when Israel lacked all control of circumstances. Rather than defining God's omnipotence as the power to determine everything, it is the power of loving grace expressing the intent of dealing redemptively with all situations that arise (Rom. 8:28).

The promise in Jeremiah 32:15 is that fields once again would be bought and sold in Judah. It seemed incredible in light of the impending fall of Jerusalem to the Babylonians. But by faith Jeremiah affirmed: "Ah Lord God! ...Nothing is too hard for you" (v. 17). When the disciples wondered about who could be saved if it is so hard for a rich person to enter the kingdom of God, Jesus made plain that "for mortals it is impossible, but for God all things are possible" (Matt. 19:26). This possibility-creating God always is defined in part by the power to persist in any circumstance brought about by the evil now so active in cre-

---

[34] See Wolfart Pannenberg, *Systematic Theology*, 1:416.

[35] Weakness, of course, is judged here from a human perspective as the surprising and voluntary avoidance by God of coercion to accomplish the divine will. Jesus on the cross endured those who sneered at him: "He saved others; let him save himself if he is the Messiah of God, the Chosen One" (Lk. 23:35). The choice of Self-sacrifice is an astonishing, an other-than-human way for God to exercise power. Such is the way of the God of loving grace whose purpose is to win our hearts in reconciliation, not dominate our wills in a demeaning power play.

ation.[36] Standing over against the transitoriness of humans, "from everlasting to everlasting you are God" (Ps. 90:2). God remains constant in capability and compassion. God is durable regardless of circumstance. God is dependably loyal to divine intention and promise.

Psalm 136 is a review of the narrative of God's activity among us to the time of that writing. Here we are reminded of God's work in creation (vv. 4-9) and in the history of Israel (vv. 10-22). The thankful congregation responds this way at the end of each verse of joyous memory: "for his steadfast love endures forever." The final book in the whole biblical drama leaves with all who will hear the same reassuring message: "'I am the Alpha and the Omega,' says the Lord God, who is and who was and who is to come, the Almighty" (Rev. 1:8).

God is almighty. God is unlimited, except for voluntary Self-limitation arising from the fact that divine actions happen only in accord with the divine nature and will (2 Tim. 2:13). There is no final dualism, no reality other than God that is able of itself to limit God's acting. God is not restricted to the causality of the so-called "natural" process of things. God's omnipotence is ample ground for what humans view as sheer "miracles." To confess with the ancient creeds that God is the "Father Almighty" in part is to affirm that God is able to fulfill all promises. In fact, it was in connection with God's covenant promise to Abraham that God's own name was revealed to be "God Almighty" (Gen. 17:1).

Looking ahead to the center of the biblical revelation, Jesus would confront his many adversaries in an almighty way, and yet non-coercively. In fact, God's supreme act in Jesus Christ would be the choice to arrive gently in the midst of the sordidness and brutality of our wayward historical process. The arrival would not be in the form of a conquering Creator coming powerfully to force things right, but in the form of a crying and helpless baby![37] God's omnipotence, therefore, is not the unlimited power to coerce, although such power is a reality in principle, but God's ability and willingness to persevere

---

[36] See Emil Brunner, *Dogmatics*, I:266-68; and Karl Barth, *Church Dogmatics*, II:1, 608-40.

[37] Note the story of the temptations of Jesus in the wilderness (Matt. 4:1-11). A key issue was the way God chooses to work in the world. Would Jesus flex divine mus-

through loving vulnerability and grace-full persuasion. The loving nature of God colors the biblical narrative with the warm glow of compassion and thereby reveals the character of the divine kingdom and the conduct appropriate for those who claim to be its citizens. The kingdom of God is "not food and drink but righteousness and peace and joy in the Holy Spirit" (Rom. 14:17). It is the "meek" who will inherit the earth (Matt. 5:5).

To be so vulnerable to evil's plotting not only reveals God's distinctive way of being powerful. It also suggests that the unchanging God is voluntarily open to change. Some interpretations of divine constancy have drawn too heavily on the Greek idea of immobility and thus have pictured God as never changing, even as inactive and uninvolved with creation. The biblical view is one of God acting in dynamic ways that adapt to shifting circumstances.

We, then, should not derive our understanding of the power and ways of God by thinking of human power increased to the ultimate degree. The proper derivation is not from who we as humans are and how we would do it if we only could, but from what the biblical narrative reveals about how God chooses and thus how we all should choose to view and do things. John Wesley conceived of God's power...

> in terms of *empowerment*, rather than control or *overpowerment*. This is not to weaken God's power but to determine its character! As Wesley was fond of saying, God works "strongly and sweetly." That is, God's *grace* works powerfully, but not irresistibly, in matters of human life and salvation; thereby empowering our *response-ability*, without overriding our *responsibility*.[38]

---

cle to accomplish his mission? No. The coming of God's kingdom would not be in a manner contrary to God's character. It would be a reign of peace, initiated by grace, at the price of major sacrifice.

[38] Randy Maddox, *Responsible Grace: John Wesley's Practical Theology* (Nashville: Kingswood Books, Abingdon Press, 1994), 55.

The point is that God always is dependable. God is omnipotent, that is, God is unlimited so far as having the capacity to act decisively in accord with the divine nature and will, regardless of human rebellion or any other circumstance. God can and will act as promised, fulfill commitments, is always to be trusted, all because God's nature and intent do not change (Lam. 3:22-23; 1 John 1:9). Omnipotence, according to the biblical witness, is not characterized as God's instant control of all things at all times. God is relational. God is love and God chooses to function with a responsive and adapting compassion toward those loved. While not dependent on or defined by the processes of this world (a view of some "process" theologians today), God functions both freely, dependably, and contingently in relation to this shifting and often evil world. The paradox is that God "has the power to be without becoming, yet he has the power to become in his sovereign freedom and grace. God is neither static immutability nor dynamic event when viewed alone. He is the Eternal Being who acts in freedom and is constant through all change."[39]

Given the assumed authority for Christians of the biblical revelation, there is to be no doubt that, working persistently, powerfully, vulnerably, dependably, God has a dream, a plan, and the ability to bring it to eventual reality. The Maker of heaven and earth stands by the plan and chooses to be the ever-present Sustainer and Redeemer of even a fallen creation. "Time is in holy keeping," affirms Gabriel Fackre of the patient providence of God. "Neither fate nor chance, neither the stars nor the cycles of nature and history determine what shall be, but the implacable love of God moving toward its goal."[40] As put in the Gospel of Luke, God "has brought down the powerful from their thrones, and lifted up the lowly" (1:52).

So the divine nature determines the distinctive way that God relates to creation. God's way is not a mere projection of the human way of conceiving power. God chooses to function "neither as an autocratic regent or a take-charge Western sheriff."[41] This same divine nature

---

[39] Dale Moody, *The Word of Truth* (Grand Rapids: Eerdmans, 1981), 99.

[40] Gabriel Fackre, *The Christian Story*, 1984, 87.

[41] Ibid., 259.

also defines what is good. When God created, it was Goodness generating goodness. The evil in the creation is not original with the creation, for, when God created, all was judged good (Gen. 1:25).

In fact, in humans God invested the divine image (Gen. 1:26; 1 Cor. 12:7). In significant ways God mirrored aspects of the divine nature in us humans, the crown of creation. This divine image consists at least of the gift of vision to see God's covenant intention and the freedom to respond in love to the offered relationship of peace and joy. We are enabled by the gift of God's creation to know who God is and who we should and can be in relation to God (Gen. 2:15-18). Thus, rising above our fallen selves and finding fulfillment in covenant relationship with God, we are *spirit,* made in the image of God, who also is *Spirit* (Job 27:3; 33:4).

In light of the sin that has contaminated the whole creation (Rom. 1:18-3:20), the wonder of the reality of God's very nature has surfaced ever more clearly. As the Islamic affirmation states so simply and correctly, God is one! But, as the biblical revelation further reveals, this divine oneness has a rich texture, a triune complexity.[42] In part, the truth of this rich singleness is protected and conveyed by the ancient belief in creation "ex nihilo," literally the divine initiating of something out of nothing.

This belief intends to avoid two unacceptable alternatives. First, creation is not merely an historical extension of divinity itself. There is no biblical basis for confusing ourselves or our world with God, a confusion that often has become a playground for idolatry. The source of creation is distinct from the creation. Second, the evil now in creation is not the historical presence of some perverted being or negative substance that existed alongside God prior to creation. To affirm any such dualism denies the singularity of God, who is the only ultimate and eternal One.

John Cobb and David Griffin argue that God does not create out of absolute nothing. Rather, "process theology affirms...a doctrine of creation out of chaos."[43] God is said to be creating constantly by

---

[42] See chapter four for a discussion of the "trinity."

[43] John Cobb and David Griffin, *Process Theology: An Interpretative Exposition* (Westminster, 1976), 65.

contributing to an infinite variety of developmental occasions. Surely, they insist, this is so since God chooses to relate dynamically to the creation that once was not and now and always is changing. While there are positives in this process view, in it also is an incipient dualism that should be resisted because it pulls against key elements of the biblical revelation.

John 1:3 affirms that "all things came into being through him, and without him not one thing came into being." Prior to creation nothing existed alongside God. Because God is prior to and the cause of all that is, even the potential for though not the actuality of evil, no part of creation is devoid of spiritual significance. Human sin cannot be blamed on the evil realm of the material, which becomes evil only by human choice, not inherently. Only God deserves worship. The creation is not an emanation from God and thus not one with God in a way inviting worship of creation. Creation is *from* God's hand, not *one with* God's hand. We exist at all only because God is a creating, relating, and restoring God. The divine-human relationship now is ruptured by our choice. So the only human hope lies in the God who calls to the brokenness and invites to a reconciled return.

The God Who Calls

Genesis is the book placed first among the library of biblical materials. This placement is appropriate since its contents lay out the beginnings of all biblical believing. It is genesis, the launching of the story of God among us and for our salvation. It is the place to start in understanding our lives, our world, and the God who first created and now calls for the purpose of re-creation. The rich theological meanings available in Genesis are found only as one takes seriously the form and content of this book, an epic narrative of how God chooses to be with us in our created glory and even in our sinful misery.

This first book of the Bible features *four callings* from God.[44] Knowing these callings is to know much about God's will and ways

---

[44] See Walter Brueggemann, *Genesis*, in the *Interpretation* commentary series (John Knox Press, 1982). The content of this section is organized around the outline of Brueggemann's presentation.

in our world. Hearing and responding in faith to these callings is to approach knowing God through God's revealing presence with us. It is to take the divine initiative seriously and to reach by faith for the opportunity to again become joyful and fruitful expressions of the divine likeness, even agents of the divine intention for this world.

God is a calling God. God creates, calls, and finally comes. In Genesis we are told that God called the world into being (Gen. 1-11) and then, in the face of its chosen fallenness, called a special people to be faithful agents of the divine in accomplishing the world's reconciliation (Gen. 12-50). We learn much of God's ways with this world and with this special people (Israel and later the church) by the nature both of God's callings and the varieties of human responding. The series of stories in Genesis 12-50 grow out of God's initial promise to Abraham, a promise subsequently renewed for Isaac (Gen. 26) and Jacob (Gen. 28:1-17). The central character in all these stories is not the patriarchs and their families, but God. The plot revolves around how God keeps divine promises in the midst of the convulsions of human history. God is known by what God does for and through us humans, often in spite of ourselves and outside our immediate awareness.

The persistent issue is faithfulness. Will God remain faithful to the promise to preserve and reconcile creation despite all the waywardness and tragedy that now intervenes? Will God's chosen people remain faithful in being God's redemptive body on behalf of the world? We will follow the Genesis narrative for answers since, as Walter Brueggemann puts it, "the *mode* of the story matches the *substance of the promise* in a peculiar way." The biblical presentation in Genesis is not interested in "deep structures," "abiding truths," or "exact proofs."[45] What is presented in narrative form is a distinctive pattern of God's relating to a divinely chosen people, even in the midst of their faithlessness. Since this pattern reflects God's very nature and long range intention, we should follow this presentation with care, for it is the story of God with us. God still calls; how will we respond?

---

[45] Brueggemann, *Genesis* (John Knox Press, 1982), 4

God's call is (1) *sovereign*, bringing worlds, including Adam and Eve, into being. God's call to a new future beyond human fallenness must be (2) *embraced*, as did Abraham and Sarah and as we yet must. God's call, once embraced, inevitably will be (3) *conflicted* as it encounters the active darkness such as is seen in the life of Jacob and in us and our world. Finally, God's call, though sure, somehow always remains (4) *hidden*, not fully clear or controllable, just as once it quietly worked through the surprising turns in Joseph's life. In all these events and lives reported in Genesis, God's marvelous and mysterious ways are to be seen. These four features of the divine calling continue, beckoning us with loving grace and inviting our faithful response.

First, God's call is *sovereign.* The key theological issue is the relation of Creator and creature. In the biblical narrative we encounter neither the "mythological" view that sees all the action with the gods, creation in itself having little significance, nor the "scientific" view that assumes that the creation can be understood adequately by reference only to itself. The Genesis account tells of sovereign Creator and fallen creation having to do with each other decisively, neither being understood except in relation to the other. God's speech is neither subject to debate nor coercive in its nature.

Can this world of mixed response again become a creation of doxology (cf. Rev. 11:15-19)? Although this world clearly is fallen, it is just as clear that there remains a deep resolve on the part of the Creator. Will God's sovereign, persistent, redemptive call prevail? The Genesis narrative lives in hope since God is sovereign. In fact, hope, rooted in the nature of the divine, is basic to the life of faith and essential for any contemporary commitment to the mission of God's people in our fractured world.

Second, God's sovereign call is *embraced.* By reading Genesis 11:35-25:18 in the context of Genesis 1:1-11:29, a central truth emerges. The witness to God lovingly remaining with the creation reveals that the One who first called the whole creation into being, and had remained in loving tension with its subsequent disobedience, is the same One who chose to call again. This second call is intended to initiate a special community of obedience through which God wishes to function on behalf of the eventual redemption of all the disobedient. So this second call, once embraced by Abraham and Sarah, would form Israel, with the divine intent of eventually transforming all the families of the earth. This call was one of promise. To be effective, it had to be embraced by faith.

Will God keep this promise of redemption? Can Abraham and those after him continue to live by faith in this promise? Genesis answers both questions affirmatively. Faith, however, is never easy, as seen in Abraham's deception to save his own skin (12:10-20; 20:1-18) or his choice of an alternate wife just in case (16:1-16). But faith still managed over time to focus on a God who is able and had promised to violate religious conventions (18:16-32), shatter normal definitions of reality (18:14), and bring about genuine newness (21:1-7). What was thought impossible because of sin becomes possible by the promise and power of God (18:14; Mark 10:27). The divine call invites people to embrace God's promise by faith against all apparent odds.

Third, embracing the sovereign call of God leads unfortunately to a *conflicting* of the call. The Genesis story about Jacob shows the troubled and scandalous side of the working out of God's purpose in the face of fragile human faith in a fallen setting. We hear tales that present a tangling of God's purposes in a web of human self-seeking and shady intrigue. God chose Jacob and the divine promise prevailed, but only in the midst of trouble that reveals the treacherous dimension of fallen humans and the loving and patient resilience of God. This God, so the Genesis narrative shows, journeys with the unworthy until finally they are brought home safely by grace.

This sojourning God is the One who is faithful even to the faithless. God is the One who one day, contrary to common expectation, would send and be the Crucified Jesus as the means of making all things new. To the faithful hearers of God's call, conflict inevitably comes since God challenges the very ways in which the world wants to understand itself and operate. Jacob may have known trouble all his days, often of his own making, but God still called, chose, promised, and finally fulfilled.

Fourth, God's call, sovereign, embraced, and conflicted, remains *hidden*, working itself out quietly and surprisingly amidst the conflict and faithlessness of this world. Joseph is crucial to the Genesis narrative, functioning as a literary means of conveying through a chain of dramatic stories a crucial theological affirmation. God's ways in this broken world are reliable and sure, even though often they work almost unnoticed. Regardless of contrary human attitudes and actions, God works on. God manages the triumph of the promise, even without the conscious assistance of any faithful human and in spite of Egypt, Joseph and all his brothers, and us.

A pivotal truth is disclosed in Genesis 45:4-8 and 50:19-20. Joseph, like all the faithful, lived between the hint of promise (37:5) and the joy of promise fulfilled (50:20). God's ways are as sure as they often are inscrutable. God will accomplish the divine purpose through faithful persons or in spite of them (Isa. 55:8-9). Regardless, God calls and God will work! This is seen clearly in the revealing course of the biblical narrative, the story of God with us for our salvation. The New Testament announcement centers in the claim that salvation was *immediately present* in Jesus. God had come visiting and seeking the lost. The three parables in Luke 15, for instance, tell of a lost sheep, coin, and "prodigal" son. In each case there was divine initiative, love, and grace.

God's work involves more than creating and being faithful to a specially called people. The whole of creation is valued, judged good, and to be preserved and redeemed. Many debate the relation of divine creation to the modern theories of evolution.[46] Creation, understood within the larger movement of the biblical witness to the creating God, is not merely a one-time event in some distant past (six

---

[46] See David Ray Griffin, *God and Religion in the Postmodern World* (State University of New York Press, 1989), chapter five titled "Evolution and Postmodern Theism." Griffin notes the widespread conviction that God and evolution are incompatible. "Creationists" deny evolution and Darwinians deny God. What is needed, he says, is a theistic approach holding "that the direction of the evolutionary process [whatever its degree of reality] is rooted in a cosmic purposive agent" (70). He sees in the emerging postmodern worldview some significant intellectual changes that give real credibility to belief in a cosmic purposive agent, the biblical God who is "a supreme power that is personal, just, loving, and works by persuasion alone" (82). Griffin, however, also argues for some limitations of God not characteristic of the biblical narrative as classically interpreted.

thousand or several billion years ago). Justo González is right: "Creation subsists, even now, because God has called it and continues calling it out of nothingness into being.... The doctrine of creation, therefore, is not merely a statement about origins; it is also and foremost a statement about present reality and present responsibility."[47] Also, in whatever way and over however much time God originally created and continues to create, it is unbiblical to suggest that the primary principle of creation is "the survival of the fittest." God is Creator and remains sovereign. The primary principle is "whosoever will."

We humans have been granted the freedom and sacred obligation of participating in God's ongoing creation by our stewardship of the earth (Gen. 1:28). Out of deep concern, however, John Cobb reports the sadly obvious: "Too often, Christians have read the biblical creation story as if it told us that the earth existed only for human benefit.... But the text does not say that. Before and quite apart from the arrival of human beings, God rejoices in the creation."[48]

Genesis 2 narrates the divine plan for co-creation, a partnership plan for preserving the creation so loved by God. Men and women are to "name" the animals, that is, decide their place and meaning in the scheme of things. The ongoing creation is not "a paint-by-numbers process." While as Christians we believe that this work is preeminently the artistry of God, "we are called to be God's artisans." Delwin Brown concludes that "our task is sensitively to explore the evolving pattern of life, and to take responsibility for helping to create in our own time and place those particular life forms that will best serve God's general aims for the world."[49]

---

[47] Justo González, *Mañana: Christian Theology from a Hispanic Perspective* (Nashville: Abingdon Press, 1990), 122-123.

[48] John Cobb, *Can Christ Become Good News Again?* (St. Louis: Chalice Press, 1991), 180.

[49] Delwin Brown, in Clark Pinnock and Brown, *Theological Crossfire*, 102. Gabriel Fackre warns that one serious distraction from this co-creating responsibility is failure to recognize that the Bible's intent is to "tell the tale of its [creation's] meaning and destiny" (*The Christian Story*, 1984 ed., 74). The Bible drew on the science of its day and does not intend to be used as a textbook of geology or astrophysics. Christians often ask the wrong questions of the biblical text, inadvertently sidetracking the story and initiating needless battles with science.

Surely God's general aims for the world do not include an ugly raping of the earth and its resources in the quest for a material prosperity for privileged and greedy humans.[50] Unfortunately, even the Christian community has contributed to the present shameful and potentially disastrous ecological crisis. Four reasons for this are obvious, especially in relation to some expressions of "evangelical" Christianity:

1. The call to have dominion (Gen. 1:28) is claimed to entail treating the earth as intended solely for the good of humans; the result has been the virtual rape of creation;

2. Modern science and technology's exploitation of the earth too often has been condoned by Christianity in the name of "progress";

3. Christianity sometimes has promoted a dualism that regards the natural, the physical, and the "secular" as of less value than the spiritual and the otherworldly;

4. Belief in the second coming of Christ, which will usher in the complete and perfect reign of God, has tended to remove the sense of need for ecological concern.[51]

In seeking to resist a domesticating or even elimination of God in the minds of "sophisticated" modern people, too many Christians react defensively by stressing God's transcendence to a fault. The fault is a deemphasis on divine immanence that leads to neglect of the divine-human partnership in caring for the creation. The ancient

---

[50] Impending ecological disaster, now being caused largely by human selfishness, is the opposite of acknowledging humbly that God lovingly created all that is (Gen. 1:1). It is the shameful reverse of Psalm 19 where Hebrew believers glorify, praise, and thank God for having brought into being this wonderful creation. The goal of Christian life is not a frantic accumulation of material things, but contentment with simplicity and disciplined stewardship of what one has (Matt. 6:20; 19:21; Lk. 12:15; Heb. 13:5).

[51] These are listed by Millard Erickson, *The Evangelical Mind and Heart* (Baker Book House, 1993), 52.

creeds focus on God as the "Creator of heaven and earth." All who now would covenant with the Creator, therefore, should be committed to self-discipline and the search for peace. Justifying violence in the modern world has reached the level of threatening the very survival of life on the earth. Huge inventories of rapid-delivery multiple warheads raise the specter of the whole earth being reduced to a barren landscape in a matter of minutes.

The biblical proclamation of redemption applies both to humans and to the whole creation (Isa. 11:6-9; Hos. 2:18-20; Rom. 8:22-23; Col. 1:20). Delwin Brown thus speaks of creation and salvation as "biocentric," not merely "anthropocentric." Jesus has transformed the meaning of "lordship" into stewardship and servanthood (Mark 9:33-37 and 10:42-45), so that "the call to be the 'lord' of nature is the command to serve nature's well-being."[52] God creates, calls, grants dominion, and invests the exercise of this dominion with great responsibility.

Beyond preservation of the earth's environment, a biblical concept of God's nature and will necessarily interacts with all aspects of public life. A recent referring to God with the metaphor "Economist"[53] makes clear that there are no limits to the spheres for which God cares and in which God works. The Greek language origin of "economy" literally means "management of the household." In the public household of a society, the economy refers to the production, distribution, and consumption of the basics that sustain human life. This is so fundamental to the well-being of humans, God's crowning creation, that God never should be thought of as "non-economic."

---

[52] Delwin Brown, "Respect for the Rocks: Toward a Christian Process Theology of Nature," *Encounter* (Autumn, 1989), 312.

[53] M. Douglas Meeks, *God the Economist: The Doctrine of God and Political Economy* (Minneapolis: Fortress Press, 1989).

Election and Prevenient Grace

All of creation now is fallen. Humans by choice have become marred, totally "depraved" at least in the sense of being unable to regain right relationship with God apart from divine assistance. That is the bad news. The good news is that God is the God of loving grace. God's grace is active in opening a way of return. God calls, enlightens, invites, enables.

At the core of the biblical witness to Israel's faith is the assurance of its having been summoned into being by God. We learn best about the nature of God and of God's intent in the world by "following the narrative of the community (Israel) as it chooses and finds itself being chosen."[54] Who is God? The Hebrew response was that God is "the Lord your God, who brought you out of the land of Egypt, out of the house of bondage (Exodus 20:2 and throughout the Hebrew Scriptures). God had become historically Self-defined for human awareness through centuries of acting, speaking, and calling.

An important caution is in order. Christians should cease thinking of their faith as one of divine grace in contrast to a presumed Jewish faith of rigid law. In fact, Israel understood God's redeeming it from Egypt as an historical revelation of the marvelous love of the divine. God acted as the One who exhibits loving grace, the mighty One prepared to take an insignificant group of slave laborers, single them out from among all the earth's peoples in order to dwell with them (Ex. 29:46). God made them "a people of his own possession" (Deut. 4:20). In remembrance of this gracious possession, Israel confessed that God had acted out of sheer love. It was not because Israel was more numerous than any other people, just the opposite. It was because the Lord loved Israel and kept a divine promise that Israel became a people by its liberation from Egypt. Such liberation by the hand of God was the creation of a new community, the gracious act of a loving God.

Israel was called out of Egypt to be a people with a distinctive destiny. This new people was to be an instrument of the divine, a redemptive reflection of God in the world, not merely a people bask-

---

[54] Walter Brueggemann, *Hope Within History* (John Knox, 1987), 3.

ing in God's privilege. Israel came to know God as the One who had brought it into existence, who often called it to new being, who in fact initially had called the whole world into being, and who promised an eventual new heaven and earth. The heart of it all was divine grace, a redemptive plan, the amazing fact of election. Such gracious election is the very fabric out of which the biblical revelation is woven.

Election is the doctrine that seeks to highlight "the gracious aim and intention of God initiated in creation, realized in Jesus Christ, consummated in the new heaven and new earth."[55] God chose a people, and through them all peoples, to be potential recipients of and witnesses to God's unfailing and forgiving love. Consequently, despite much Christian teaching to the contrary, it is a serious misconception to presume that God wills destruction for some and salvation for others.[56] As Karl Barth makes clear, God's single will for all people is salvation. God elects all humanity in Christ. This is a gracious act freely chosen, a sovereign decision emerging from the character of the divine.[57] Therefore, "no conception of foreordination that empties Christian teaching of movement, tension, or purpose fits the saga." The biblical story reveals a God who does not mark out some for salvation and others for damnation. Any such "double predestination" is ruled out because "the dynamic interplay of narrative character and events is therein rendered a charade."[58]

The biblical witness to divine election is a matter of good news that inspires human joy. It is not news of an unalterable divine decree

---

[55] Theodore Jennings, *Loyalty To God* (Nashville: Abingdon Press, 1992), 61.

[56] The Reformed tradition, rooted in the teachings of John Calvin, has tended to view such a "predestination" as the logical outcome of an appropriate stress on the absolute sovereignty of God. If such absolute sovereignty is the foundation of the "system" of Calvinism, predestination is its keystone. When once you have adopted the view that God shall be God in the full sweep of all the many relationships with creation, argues H. Henry Meeter, "you will arrive at predestination as a very logical conclusion. All limitations of God's decree regarding man restrict God's supremacy and infringe upon his majesty" (*The Basic Ideas of Calvinism*, 6th ed., Baker Book House, 1990, 21). Daniel Migliore reads Calvin himself more generously than he does later Calvinists since Calvin located his discussion of the doctrine of election with the life of faith and not in an abstract consideration of the decrees of God (*Faith Seeking Understanding*, 1991, 78).

[57] Karl Barth, *Church Dogmatics*, II:2 (Edinburgh: T. & T. Clark, 1936-1969)), 3-194.

[58] Gabriel Fackre, *The Christian Story*, 1984, 260.

that leads to the fatalistic dread of some people being chosen for salvation and others left to inevitable damnation. God is a God of free grace. The Hebrew Scriptures witness to Israel being chosen as God's people solely on the basis of God's freely given love (Deut. 7:7-8). The favor of God is extended to sinners, outcasts, the poor, those with no evident merit. In Jesus Christ, God chooses to be gracious to both Jew and Gentile (Rom. 11:25-36). A narration of this pattern of grace leads to a praising of God who "chose us in Christ before the foundation of the world to be holy and blameless before him in love" (Eph. 1:4). God created and keeps on creating out of love.

This ongoing creation is not a mechanical arranging in advance of how things must be for puppet beings. There is divine foreknowledge. God does see the end from the beginning. "Even before a word is on my tongue, O Lord, you know it completely" (Ps. 139:4). To know in advance of coming sin brings great pain to the God who loves, seeks to persuade, but refuses to coerce. The paradox is that God foreknows how free agents will choose, and yet does not determine their choice. It cannot be argued that one necessarily forced past events to have happened just because one now remembers that they did happen. Likewise, the God of loving grace, committed to human freedom, does not compel future events to happen just because it is known that they will. Events are known by God because they exist; they do not exist merely because God knows them. The Spirit's redemptive call to lost humanity intends to be effective for all, but it is not irresistible.

Often the Bible refers to those who hear and respond gratefully to God's invitation as the "elect" (2 Tim. 2:10; Titus 1:1). By responding obediently to God's call, personal freedom is enhanced rather than diminished. Concludes Thomas Oden: "God knows in advance those who will respond in faith to saving grace, who by the right use of their will and knowledge of revealed truth, trust in it, and who thereby will be justified. But this does not imply that God decides for them...."[59] Here is a paradox of profound proportions. God truly is sovereign; human beings truly are free and responsible. God functions by choice as the One who extends loving grace.

---

[59] Thomas Oden, *The Transforming Power of Grace* (Nashville: Abingdon Press, 1993), 132.

The word "providence" often is used to identify the pattern of God's oversight of creation. Providence *pro*vides, sees beforehand; providence also pro*vides*, makes provision for the possibility of what is foreseen. God preserves and guides the creation toward what is meant to be its rightful end. Creation is not self-sufficient, but is held together by God (Col. 1:17). According to Psalm 104, God set the earth on its foundations (v. 5), sends streams into the valleys (v. 10), and provides food for all creatures (vss. 24-30). Contrary to a mechanical "deism," God did not create and then depart the immediate scene, leaving all things to function automatically by the "laws of nature." God remains in the historical process, actively preserves the beloved creation, and thus becomes known narratively by the recorded human awareness of such divine remaining and preserving. This preservation moves toward a particular end since "we know that all things work together for good for those who love God, who are called according to his purpose" (Rom. 8:28).

The divine purpose, of course, forms the very center of the biblical revelation. We all are "elected" to God's loving purpose, called to participate in God's redemptive vision. The problem is the deliberate fallenness of humankind. There now is no true knowledge of God available to the "natural man," John Wesley's term for the fallen human condition apart from divine grace. The "image of God" in the creation has been sufficiently spoiled by the fall that we humans have become unable to regain on our own a true vision of and relationship with God. And yet, all of us still possess a created capacity for God, a longing and potential receptivity for divine relationship, a "conscience" that desires the right even if the content of the right has become clouded and its realization beyond unaided reach.

This present fact of positive possession is the result of "prevenient grace."[60] John Wesley understood prevenient grace to be:

---

[60] The Protestant Reformers (Luther, Calvin, etc.) "placed powerful emphasis on man's total depravity in order to underline the absolute necessity of God's sovereign grace in salvation. The move led them practically to deny the image of God in sinners. Wesley began to move in a better direction.... He taught that the grace of God is available to all sinners and that the natural propensity to sin can be conquered by God's grace, which is at hand" (Clark Pinnock, in Pinnock and Delwin Brown, *Theological Crossfire*, 127-128). For an excellent discussion of prevenient grace, see H. Ray Dunning, *Grace,*

God's initial move toward restored relationship with fallen humanity. As a first dimension, this involved God's merciful removal of any inherited guilt, by virtue of Christ. A second dimension...is a partial healing of our debilitated human faculties, sufficient for us to sense and respond to God. The final dimension is God's specific overtures to individuals, inviting closer relationship. If these overtures are welcomed, a grace-empowered relationship of cooperative and progressive transformation sets forth. Since God's grace is universal, so is the possibility of such relationship. Since God's grace is resistible, no individual's participation is inevitable.[61]

Universal human waywardness necessitates a divinely initiated drawing toward God. Jesus said that "no one can come to me unless drawn by the Father who sent me" (Jn. 6:44). Any inclination we now have toward God has been stimulated by the gracious activity of God. This is prevenient grace, the work of the Spirit, the grace that makes clear our human inability to save ourselves without prior divine intervention (2 Cor. 4:4; Eph. 4:18). We love God because God first loved us (1 Jn. 4:19). Such grace is available, allowing and urging us to respond, to cooperate with grace. Without God we cannot, and without us God will not. The biblical tension affirms both "without me [God] you can do nothing" (Jn. 15:5) and "I can do all things through Christ strengthening me" (Phil. 4:13).

Prevenient grace is God stirring sinful men and women out of spiritual slumber and igniting their eyes to see, their desire to respond, their ability to become new creations in Christ (Ezek. 11:19; 2 Cor. 5:17). This grace, consistent with God's nature, is resistible. It is an opportunity provided by love.

Faith and Holiness (1988), 161-170, 338-339. He calls it "God's activity prior to any human movement toward God" (338). It is offered universally, can be resisted, and makes all people responsible before God.

[61] Randy Maddox, *Responsible Grace: John Wesley's Practical Theology* (Nashville: Kingswood Books, Abingdon Press, 1994), 90.

Grateful Christians reflect on the God who comes first and creates new potential for salvation. Often they sing these words in joy:

> 'Twas grace that taught my heart to fear,
> And grace my fears relieved;
> How precious did that grace appear
> The hour I first believed.[62]

The God who calls is the God who seeks preveniently to reclaim through loving grace. Note this typical narrative testimony:

> I sought the Lord, and afterward I knew
> He moved my soul to seek him, seeking me.
> It was not I that found, O Savior true;
> No, I was found of thee.[63]

God has shed light on all persons so that none sins helplessly because of lack of grace, but in the face of the grace that is available and not embraced. Though "deprived" by sin, grace renews our response-*ability* and thus our responsibility. John Wesley instructs us here. At its heart his theology features a combination of three emphases, each of which is crucial. They are the primacy of divine grace, the inability of fallen human nature to do anything that would merit salvation, and the full responsibility of the person to respond appropriately to God's gift of prevenient grace and salvation in Christ.

All truth gained without awareness of the biblical story of Israel and Jesus Christ, whether derived from culture, mystical experience, or philosophic inquiry, comes by the enablement of the same prevenient grace of God. On the one hand, creation has fallen and now is perverted beyond having redeeming qualities in God's eyes. On the other hand, God has a plan of redemption and chooses to brighten our dark paths enough that our choosing the right path is again a possibility and a responsibility.

---

[62] Hymn "Amazing Grace," words by John Newton, in *The United Methodist Hymnal* (Nashville: The United Methodist Pub. House, 1989), 378.

[63] Hymn "I Sought the Lord," words anon., in *The United Methodist Hymnal,* 341.

John Wesley had a pervasive optimism about divine grace that formed a foundation for his emphases on the potential of all people being saved, the faithful witness of the Spirit, and the call to human transformation from the sinful state. The so-called Wesleyan synthesis, reflecting well the multiple dimensions of the biblical story of God-with-us, holds in balance the sovereignty of God and human freedom. The balancing factor is prevenient grace, the loving choice of God to go before any faith response so that all people at least are placed in a savable position. This grace is God's first step in the plan of human redemption. It reveals much about the very heart of God.

By contrast, the teaching of scholastic Calvinism on common or general grace grants it no meaningful part in the redemptive plan. It is replaced by an absolute divine sovereignty that is said to be unqualified by human freedom and expresses itself by an unconditional election of some, and only some, to salvation. It should be noted that Wesley himself came to the edge of Calvinism in (1) ascribing all good to the free grace of God, (2) denying any concept of a natural free will, any human power to effect salvation antecedent to grace, and (3) insisting that there never is any human merit justifying salvation since all that humans ever have or do is by the grace of God.[64] In this way Wesley maintained a careful synthesis that opens to all people the potential of salvation through the initial agency of prevenient grace. He elevated the operation of God's wonderful love, but not by domesticating divinity or divinizing humanity.

In one sense, elevating God's wonderful, initiating, electing, risking love is to "domesticate" the usual view of God (and the gods). The gods typically are said to be preoccupied with their own majesty and invulnerability in the safe sacredness of their heavens. The biblical God, however, chooses to covenant with the fallen creation. To covenant redemptively, riskingly, is to recharacterize God against "a theology that knows too much, a God who is too strong, a church that is too allied with triumphalist culture, and a ministry that moves too

---

[64] See Thomas Jackson, ed., *The Works of John Wesley* (London: John Mason, 1829-31), VIII:285, noting the minutes of the 1745 Conference.

much from strength."[65] The choice to embrace lovingly an unworthy partner is definitional for God, the God of loving grace. It also should be definitional for the church of God that is to continue God's servant mission in this world.

The light of this prevenient grace shines on all people (Ps. 19: 1-6; Rom. 1:18-32). In the pluralistic world of our times, and in our social context of radical tolerance for almost anything, the wonder, and yet the limits of this universal shining need careful clarification.

Pluralism and Particularity

Christians today are living on a globe where a large percentage of humanity does not share belief in Jesus Christ as the universal Redeemer. The world of religious scholarship is inclined generally to discredit the traditional Christian claim that there is a revelation of God that is normative for all human cultures and religious systems. The recommended back-up position usually is to study the various phenomena of religion in a comparative manner. Instead of overt evangelism, the preference is for a process of interfaith dialogue. Rather than trying to convert, Christians are encouraged to listen and learn as well as share. Learning and sharing, of course, are always appropriate. The hard question is the one of Christian "particularity." Is the revelation of God in Israel and in Jesus Christ the final, the only fully adequate revelation which others finally should recognize if they are to know *the* truth?

A careful study of the evangelistic assumptions and practices of the earliest Christian church reveals strong commitment to the certainty of belief in a given and exclusive gospel content. The goal of any dialogue with the hearers of the gospel apparently was limited to correcting misunderstandings rather than negotiating and then reformulating the content of the gospel itself. While the church seen in the New Testament did speak in terms intelligible to its hearers, addressing them in their different situations, there is not "the slightest sug-

---

[65] Walter Brueggemann, edited by Patrick Miller, *A Social Reading of the Old Testament* (Minneapolis: Fortress Augsburg Press, 1994), 43.

gestion that the church and the world conversed as equal partners in the search for truth."[66] This view of biblical precedent should not eliminate Christian involvement in today's inter-faith dialogue.[67] It should, however, encourage a clear highlighting of the Christian good news in any dialogue.

The tension of particularity is basic to the central Christian announcement in John 1:1-18. The witness in this passage is to having seen God's glory in Jesus. This man Jesus is proclaimed to be the very Word of God who has become flesh and lived among us. Of course, there were then and always are many people who disagree, or at least claim to see the same glory elsewhere (1:11). The scandal of Christian faith, the stumbling block to those who view differently, is that the New Testament makes a definitive declaration. In Jesus, it insists, like in no one and nowhere else, we see the fullness of divine light and experience the direct presence of God. Apostolic Christian faith insists that God is known best in a particular Person through a particular narrative, the New Testament story of a specific life, the man Jesus who was born in Bethlehem and yet also is identified with God before time began.[68]

The examples found in Acts 11 and 15 and in Galatians 2 show how the early church grew in its own understanding of the exclusive Jesus Story through dialogue inside the believing community. The early preachers entered into dialogue with the world they faced in order to understand it and thus to be able to present meaningfully the life-changing message of Jesus. Their primary intent was to *proclaim*, not to *discover* truth. The truth in Christ, they believed, already

---

[66] I. Howard Marshall, "Dialogue with Non-Christians in the New Testament," *Evangelical Review of Theology* 16:1 (January, 1992), 45-46.

[67] Terry Muck, "Evangelicals and Interreligious Dialogue," *Journal of the Evangelical Theological Society* (December 1993), 525, suggests that the view of Marshall may be influenced excessively by this scholar's strong reaction against much inter-faith dialogue that today is judged to be only a common search for truth, and not a sharing of strongly held convictions.

[68] Christian particularism does not imply that there is no rightful place for the presence of some expressions of "pluralism." Reports Donald Thorsen of the approach of John Wesley: "His willingness to bring Scripture into relationship with tradition, reason, and experience relieved Wesley of the dangers of an absolutism resistant to a healthy pluralism" (*The Wesleyan Quadrilateral*, Zondervan, 1990, 235).

had discovered them! Their belief was that finally there is no salvation apart from faithful response to God's coming in Jesus Christ. That
coming is the preached good news for those with opportunity to hear
and is available in a less direct way to those without a hearing opportunity (Rom. 10:10-15; Heb. 11:4-10).[69]

Suggesting an indirect way of appropriating the gospel of Christ
means that, while there is no salvation outside Christ, there is, by
God's loving grace, salvation outside the institutional confines of the
Christian church. Many people never hear the Christian gospel, at least
not in a convincing manner from credible witnesses. But God is not
bound to dispensing the grace in Christ only through the structures and
people of the Christian community. The Westminster Confession says
that there is no *ordinary* possibility of salvation outside the church
(XXV.2), leaving in God's hands any and all extra-ordinary means. In
fact, "God is pleased to cooperate with human beings *where they
are*–in all their humanity, in all their social and historical particularity–as He begins to move them to *where they ought to be*."[70]

Concludes Thomas Oden: "All who desire saving grace must
avail themselves insofar as is possible of the means of grace, which
ordinarily means placing themselves within the orbit of the believing
community."[71] It remains true that "no one comes to the Father
except through me [Jesus Christ]" (Jn. 14:6). "There is salvation in no
one else, for there is no other name under heaven given among mortals by which we must be saved" (Acts 4:12). Nevertheless, salvation
may not come through the Christian proclamation as such. Nor will
all who seek to respond ever find their way to the visible Christian

---

[69] In reflecting on those people never exposed to Christian revelation, John Wesley rejected one approach often espoused throughout the history of the church, namely
that God will provide them another chance after death. He could not believe that people
who lacked knowledge through no fault of their own would be excluded automatically
from heaven by a fair and loving God. Their fate is left in the hands of a merciful God,
the God of loving grace who presumably will judge in accord with the light people had.
See Randy Maddox, *Responsible Grace: John Wesley's Practical Theology* (Nashville:
Abingdon, Kingswood Books, 1994), 32-34. Also see Maddox, "Wesley and the Question of Truth or Salvation Through Other Religions," *Wesleyan Theological Journal*
(Spring/Fall, 1992, 27:7-29) and Dean Flemming, "Foundations for Responding to
Religious Pluralism," *Wesleyan Theological Journal* 31:1(Spring 1996).

[70] Michael Lodahl, *The Story of God* (Kansas City: Beacon Hill Press, 1994), 46.

[71] Thomas Oden, *Life in the Spirit* (San Francisco: Harper, 1992), 329.

community. Saying this is to recognize the sovereignty and graciousness of God in circumstances far less than ideal.[72] It is not to limit the importance of the Christian proclamation or the community of Christ, the church. It is to limit any unwarranted human arrogance in relation to the grace of God.[73]

The truth of divine revelation, believed to be centered first in Israel and then in Christ, traditionally has led Christians to the assumption that a saving knowledge of God is not found in non-Christian religions. Jesus Christ is seen as the sole mediator between God and humankind (1 Tim. 2:5; cf. Jn. 14:6, Acts 4:12). A prominent exponent of such radical discontinuity between the Christian faith and other faiths was the Dutch layperson Hendrik Kraemer (1888-1965). He resisted the assumption that the Bible is one of many expressions of a general transcendental religion. True, awareness of God is present in non-Christian religions, but not in a way that leads directly to Christ. So the church is called to be the necessary bearer of the good news.[74]

More recent times, however, have seen increased emphasis on some continuity between Christianity and the world's other religious faith communities. The change is seen clearly in Roman Catholicism. Vatican Council II (1962-1965) altered this church's longstanding thesis that there is "no salvation outside the church" (meaning the Roman Catholic Church). The revised view is that salvation is attainable by those who "through no fault of their own do not know the gospel of

---

[72] Philip Rosato, S.J., suggests four complementary biblical designations of the Spirit of God that help provide a theological base for viewing the regenerating mission of the Spirit inside and outside the Christian church. They are Teacher, Unifier, Liberator, and Vivifier. Regarding the Spirit as Teacher, he says: "Although expressly acknowledged and announced only by Christians, the 'two hands' of the Father, the equally glorious Persons of the Son and the Spirit, extend and bestow elements of divine truth to all human beings in ways conducive to their salvation.... Since the Word and the Spirit of the Father are present and active in real, even if hidden, ways beyond the church wherever human beings earnestly search for truth, it is proper that Christians pray that this search be blessed and fulfilled" ("The Mission of the Spirit Within and Beyond the Church," in *To the Wind of God's Spirit*, Geneva, WCC Publications, 1990, 22-23).

[73] See John Wesley's sermon "A Caution Against Bigotry" (*Works*, Abingdon Press), 2:63-78.

[74] For similar views, see Stephen Neill, *Christian Faith and Other Faiths* (N. Y.: Oxford, 1970), 1-19, and Lesslie Newbigin, *The Open Secret* (Grand Rapids: Eerdmans, 1978), 181-214.

Christ or His Church, yet sincerely seek God and, moved by grace, strive by their deeds to do His will as it is known to them through the dictates of conscience."[75] Therefore, the world's religions are to be viewed as *pre-Christian* rather than *non-Christian*. This approach may be called developmentalist since other faiths are seen as stages toward, but themselves falling short of the full revelation in Christ. A prominent example is Judaism, with the "Old" Testament often viewed by Christians as a necessary preparation that now is superceded by a new and better way.

A more dialogical view of the relation of Christ to other faiths assumes that all participants in the inter-faith dialogue take their own faith commitments seriously, conversing from real and particularized faiths, not ready to compromise faith for some easy peace. Paul Tillich, for example, was not a mere relativist in calling for Christians to engage in inter-faith dialogue. After all, he insisted, intense exchange about deeply held beliefs can assist all participants to discover latent dimensions of their own faiths. This includes the potential of Christians seeing more clearly the fullness of God's revelation in Jesus Christ.[76] If God as known in Christ functions as community builder through non-coercive and vulnerable love, then the finality of Christ is as much a promise we humbly pursue as it is a possession we confidently preach. Christians are to be "for others" in Christ rather than aggressively "out to get" others by Christ. While surely not ruling out evangelism, this approach brings caution about motives and methods often associated with overly aggressive Christian witnessing.

The picture is complex. On the one hand, God unceasingly reveals to all humankind the general character of the divine being (Rom. 1:19-20; 1:32; 2:14-15; 14:17; Acts 17:26-28). On the other

---

[75] *Dogmatic Constitution on the Church*, 2:16. Note the concept of "anonymous Christians" taught by Karl Rahner. This means that, while Christ is affirmed as the ontological basis for all human salvation, it is possible for people to share in this salvation without explicit knowledge of Jesus and while remaining a faithful adherent of a non-Christian religion. Rahner draws on the assumption that all persons are aware of and reaching for infinite Being. He uses this assumption as a way to balance the Catholic teaching that there is no salvation apart from Christ and that God intends for salvation to be made available to all people.

[76] Paul Tillich, *Christianity and the Encounter of the World Religions* (N. Y.: Columbia University Press, 1963).

hand, people continue to pervert what they know into rebellious idolatry (Rom. 1:21-28).[77] Salvation by "works" clearly is an unacceptable view, with or without direct awareness of God's revelation in Christ. Still, there is justification for recognizing both the continuity and discontinuity between the human quest for God in faiths other than Christianity and the fullness and finality of the knowledge of God "in the face of Jesus Christ."[78] One need not belittle the religious insights and experiences of anyone in order to exalt Christ "as the One through whom all religious beliefs, practices, and experiences are to be sifted and judged."[79]

What about Christian mission in our pluralistic times when tolerance of nearly anything seems the public standard? Elton Trueblood judges the following to be the best reason for being committed to spreading faith in Jesus Christ: "the conviction that this faith conforms to reality as does no other alternative of which we are aware."[80] We choose to be Christian in the belief that the center of the Christian faith is true. If one is gripped by the conviction that there is definite good news in this bewildering world of numerous faith claims, an ultimate

---

[77] The Lausanne Covenant (1974) affirms that all people "have some knowledge of God through his general revelation in nature." It moves quickly, however, to deny that this can save, "for men suppress the truth by their unrighteousness." Denied also is "every kind of syncretism and dialogue which implies that Christ speaks equally through all religions and ideologies. Jesus Christ...is the only mediator between God and man."

[78] This affirmation of some continuity or "general" revelation is in opposition to Karl Barth's overreaction to the liberalism of the nineteenth century. That liberalism attempted to build a whole "natural" theology on the base of general revelation. For Barth, saving revelation is always and only the revelation of God in Jesus Christ. Emil Brunner separated from Barth at this point. John Wesley focused on the universal working of God's *prevenient grace* that enables those who have never heard of Christ to enter into God's saving work. Of course, cautions Randy Maddox, "while such salvation would be apart from explicit acquaintance with Christ, Wesley would always maintain that it too was 'through Christ,' since any human response to God is possible only because of the universal Prevenient Grace of God, which is rooted in the atoning work of Christ ("Wesley and the Question of Truth or Salvation Through Other Religions," *Wesleyan Theological Journal*, Spring/Fall, 1992, 18).

[79] Lodahl, op. cit., 47. Direct knowledge of Christ's work of redemption is not absolutely necessary. "No one will be saved without Christ's atonement, but one need not be aware of that work of grace in order to benefit from it" (John Sanders, "Evangelical Responses to Salvation Outside the Church," *Christian Scholar's Review* 24:1(Sept. 1994), 52.)

[80] Elton Trueblood, *The Validity of the Christian Mission* (Harper & Row, 1972), 56.

truth among all the untruths and partial truths, then the burden of witness is upon us. Stephen Neill says that "whereas there should hardly be any limits to our tolerance of people as people, the moment we raise the question of truth, we are faced by the painful issue of the intolerance of truth."[81]

The truth, whatever it is, surely is worthy of our diligent search and then full commitment. In the modern global-village world of high mobility and nearly instant communication, the traditional faith communities are mingling as never before. The hearing and comparing of truth claims happens nearly every day and almost everywhere.[82] Should Christians be apathetic, relying on the common assumption that all truth is relative, culturally conditioned, merely a matter of individual perception and community tradition? No, responds traditional Christian faith. By divine initiative there has come the opportunity of glimpsing beyond the heavy cloud of human conditioning and relativity. Our gaze into the depth of reality always will be partially blinded, but there is light to be seen and, by the divine grace in Jesus Christ, we can have eyes that truly see God.

Having reviewed the common claims to an essential unity of the world's religions, Thomas Finger rightly concludes that the lordship of Jesus sets him in opposition to other claims to ultimate truth. The essential task of Christian mission is to witness to this lordship and actualize its redemptive implications. "Jesus and his claims are not merely *relevant* to all people, but also *normative* for their lives.... In other words, a central task of mission will be evangelism: the explicit presentation of the kerygma, including the call to repentance, forgiveness, and the gift of the Spirit."[83]

From the point of view of traditional Christian faith, four central issues are at stake as Christians dialogue with persons of other faiths. They are:

---

[81] Stephen Neill, *Call To Mission* (Philadelphia: Fortress, 1970), 9.

[82] One example is Christianity and Islam, especially in contemporary Europe. See an analysis of this difficult relationship as presented by Barry Callen to the European Conference of the Church of God convened in Germany in 1992 (appearing in three parts, *Church of God Missions*, September, October, and November, 1993 issues).

[83] Thomas Finger, *Christian Theology: An Eschatological Approach* (Scottdale, Pa.: Herald Press, 1989), II:314, 317.

1. *Truth.* Dialogue cannot manufacture truth. God is truth. Dialogue can discover forgotten truth and sharpen perceptions of known truth. Dialogue assumes the existence of a single, unified truth;

2. *Commitment.* Dialogue does not demand tentative commitment. Dialogue does demand honest expressions of commitment to one another. The best dialogue takes place between people committed to the absolute truth of their religious traditions;

3. *Attitude.* Dialogue does not demand acceptance of all the dialogue partner's ideas. Dialogue does demand acceptance of the dialogue partner as a person deserving respect and love. No dialogue can take place if the integrity, good will, and personhood of the other is in any way compromised;

4. *Evangelism.* Dialogue does not demand that either side eschew evangelism. Dialogue does demand nonmanipulative, chaste evangelism. Dialogue must be seen in some kind of relationship to evangelism.[84]

A witness to Jesus Christ as the full and final truth concerning the meaning and hope of human beings and of all creation does not suggest that other religious traditions are totally lacking in truth and therefore to be denounced. One must accept truth wherever it is found. Since God is not without a witness among the nations (Acts 14:16-17), one should expect to encounter echoes of God's activity in the maze of the world's religions.[85] What is being suggested here, and

---

[84] Terry Muck, "Evangelicals and Interreligious Dialogue," *Journal of the Evangelical Theological Society* (December, 1993), 529.

[85] In Romans 1:18-32 Paul affirms clearly that there is divine revelation prior to and apart from the gospel of salvation in Jesus Christ. John Wesley was not prepared to condemn to hell all who, for whatever reason, were outside of Christ. He once wrote: "Nor do I conceive that any man living has a right to sentence all the heathen...to damnation. It is far better to leave them to Him that made them..." (*Explanatory Notes Upon the New Testament,* reprint, Salem, O.: Schmul, 1976, 7:353).

what leads to the necessary exclusiveness of truth, is the belief that anything true anywhere is already in Christ, is best understood in light of Christ, and finally will be consummated with Christ.

An alternative view popular today is the "unitive pluralism" position of John Hick and Paul Knitter. They argue that all the major religions have an approximately equal salvation value since all are in touch with the same transcendent Reality.[86] Hick focuses on the presumed shared essence of the great religious traditions (Judaism, Christianity, Islam, Hinduism, and Buddhism), arguing that they all effect in their devoted followers a shift from self-centeredness to a centeredness on "the Real."[87] Knitter is criticized for viewing salvation "solely in existential/anthropological terms, to the utter neglect of the objective/cosmically redemptive emphasis found in the Christian Scriptures."[88] A neglect of this kind disregards the New Testament claim that, whatever "general" revelation of God is available to all humanity apart from Jesus Christ, God is now Self-revealed in an unparalleled manner in and through Christ.[89]

Here is the heart of the biblical revelation, the base of Christian faith, the keynote of Christian theology. In Jesus of Nazareth has appeared once-for-all a unique event with universal salvation significance. The significance is that salvation now is available to, although not received by, all people. Any compromise of this witness to finality, in order to accommodate today's religious diversity or to promote a friendly tolerance of neighboring alternatives, is a misguided shift

---

[86] Such a non-exclusive view is common among contemporary theologians who emphasize the conditionedness of all faith systems and are anxious for the presumed mutual learning available in interfaith dialogues. Shubert Ogden sees Paul's christology implying "that authentic existence can be realized apart from faith in Jesus Christ or in the Christian proclamation" (*Christ Without Myth*, 1961, 144). Rosemary Ruether says "the cross and resurrection are contextual to a particular historical community," implying that other revelations are also valid in their contextualizations (*To Change the World: Christology and Cultural Criticism*, 1981, 43). Christ, then, is seen as decisive *for us*, but not necessarily for all others.

[87] See part four of John Hick's Gifford Lectures, *An Interpretation of Religion: Human Responses to the Transcendent* (Macmillan Press, 1989).

[88] Paul Eddy, "Paul Knitter's Theology of Religions: A Survey and Evangelical Response," *Evangelical Quarterly* 65:3 (1993).

[89] See Clark Pinnock, *A Wideness in God's Mercy* (Zondervan, 1992) and John Sanders, *No Other Name* (Eerdmans, 1992).

to a different gospel than the one promoted by the New Testament. Warns Carl Braaten: "The church of the twenty-first century will be called upon to escape the deluge of neo-Gnosticism that places Jesus reverently into a pantheon of spiritual heroes."[90] The biblical revelation focuses on one truth, the fullness of truth, the one divine Actor on the human scene. This Actor, God, is known best in Jesus Christ, the Son revealed by the Spirit.

Three understandings of the world's religions and the doctrines they hold are outlined by George Lindbeck.[91] The approach of John Hick illustrates the "experiential-expressivism" model that assumes the underlying unity of all religious experience. An approach closer to Lindbeck's "cognitive-propositionalist" model is one assuming that doctrines embody truth claims that genuinely inform believers about the nature of God. However one judges Lindbeck's own choice of the third model, "cultural-linguistic", he is attempting to accomplish an important and difficult task. He seeks to balance salvation found only in Christ and the potential salvation of those not explicitly Christian, while avoiding the syncretistic ideology of religious pluralism.[92]

Copernicus finally was proven correct. The sun and not the earth is the center of our solar system. While this new perception was a dramatic overturning of the old Ptolemaic astronomy, it does not justify, as John Hick would have it, "a Copernican revolution in our thinking about Christianity and the religions."[93] Hick wants an end to the old theology that sees Christ at the truth center of all the religions. Instead, he would put God at the center, relativising Jesus Christ so that Jesus is not truth itself, but only the one through whom Christians have come to know God. Christianity and the other faith communities are seen as revolving around the ultimate One whom each has

---

[90] Carl Braaten, *No Other Gospel!* (Fortress Press, 1992), 13.

[91] George Lindbeck, *The Nature of Doctrine* (Philadelphia: Westminster Press, 1984).

[92] For helpful analysis, see Kenneth Surin, "Many Religions and the One True Faith," *Modern Theology* 4:2 (January, 1988), 187-209.

[93] As quoted by Braaten, *No Other Gospel!*, 66.

come to know only in part (a theocentric, not christocentric approach).[94]

The New Testament, contradicting the inclusive spirit of our times, assumes the exclusive particularity of the proclaimed truth about Jesus Christ. Christ is said to be unique, universal, final, and normative, the Son of God, the "sun" of truth around whom all alternatives must revolve and finally be judged. Of course, God is central; but God was *in Christ*, making Christ central without at all diminishing the priority of God. As Braaten reports for Lutherans, so it is for traditional Christian belief: "Christ is not merely *expressive* of a divine salvation equally available in the plurality of religions; salvation is *constituted* by the coming of God in the concrete history of Jesus of Nazareth."[95]

This commitment to definitive truth resident in Jesus does not, of course, suggest that any believer fully comprehends it or that there is no more need for pursuit of honest dialogue with anyone serious about the ultimate questions of life. Christians have much to learn as well as proclaim. The mystery of God that is revealed in Jesus Christ is yet to be plumbed in its depths or lived out in all its implications. Listening as well as speaking is required of believers. Christians are to be in the midst of the marketplace of faiths and of no faith, not defensively, not arrogantly, yet confident that all that can be learned there will only brighten the light of God that shines from the face of Jesus Christ.

---

[94] Daniel Migliore warns: "This approach is reminiscent of the Enlightenment rationalism that sought to identify the natural or universal religion behind all historical religions. Neither then nor now does such abstraction from the concrete understandings of God in the world religions seem very helpful. For Christians, it is not a Supreme or Transcendent Being as such who is spoken of as God, but the One who freely became a humble servant in Jesus Christ" (*Faith Seeking Understanding*, 1991, 163-164).

[95] Carl Braaten, op. cit., 74.

From Creator to Redeemer

Christian theology and preaching centers in retelling the biblical revelation of the God of loving grace and applying its implications to each new setting. Settings change; the historical narrative of God with us does not. The good news always focuses on the God who is and who has acted, first in creation, then in Israel, and especially in Jesus Christ. The God who created and called finally came. As Gabriel Fackre puts it: "In a play the characters are fully developed only when the action is completed. So too in the divine drama, God's final Self-disclosure comes when humanity meets its Maker face-to-face."[96] Thus we move from the first article of the ancient creeds, having to do with the almighty, creating God, to the second article that speaks of the God who comes in Jesus Christ.

A key passage is Romans 4:13-25. The pressing question often is less "does God exist?" and more "what kind of God does exist?" Throughout Romans Paul wrestles with how God can be a truly moral deity and still justify ungodly people. With Abraham, God is said to have set three precedents for judging the divine character.

First, God is the One who "gives life to the dead and calls into existence the things that do not exist" (4:17). The miracle-working God made the difference for Abraham and Sarah (Gen. 17:1-7, 15-16). Second, God is the One who is faithful to do what is promised (4:21). Abraham and Sarah had to live between the times of almost unbelievable divine promise and its later fulfillment. Third, God is the One who "raised Jesus our Lord from the dead" (4:24).

In the whole Christ-event, God was the primary Actor. So, following the biblical trail of God's actions, and thereby gaining vital understanding of God's character, we arrive in the streets of Bethlehem. There we learn that "God the creator and God the promise-keeper finds fullest expression in God the redeemer. We now turn, therefore, to the person (chapter four) and the mission (chapter five) of Jesus Christ.

---

[96] Gabriel Fackre, *Ecumenical Faith in Evangelical Perspective* (Grand Rapids: Eerdmans, 1993), 117.

Part Two

SAVIOUR:

*The God Who Stoops and Saves,
the Christ Initiative of Loving Grace*

CHRIST THE SAVIOUR: IDENTITY

—

"One Lord, Jesus Christ, the only Son of God, eternally begotten of the Father, Light from Light, true God from true God, begotten, not made, of one Being with the Father... By (the power of) the Holy Spirit he became incarnate from the Virgin Mary and was made man."

—

To this point we have been following the biblical story as it moves from creation to human sin, to covenant, and finally to the expectation of the Christ. God created out of love. Following the tragic rebellion of humans, rupturing their relationship with God, the story tells of the grace-full persistence of divine love. There was a process by which the broken relationship was restored through a covenant, an agreed partnership between God and a special people chosen to bring God's light and love back to all the world. But the covenant was violated repeatedly by privileged humans.

So we encounter a dramatic turn in the biblical story. It is a decisive development that focuses on a renewed covenant made in a person, Jesus of Nazareth. As noted above, God may be conceived helpfully today as the absolute power of the future, the One who presses for radical conversion of the present. This is our hope as sinners. The transcendent otherness of the future, God, already is present with us, especially in the historic person of Jesus the Christ.

Following the lead of John Wesley, our concern with the Godhead is not abstract curiosity. The creation now is in turmoil and needs a Saviour. Like the classic Christian creeds, Wesley focused on the second and third "Persons" of the Trinity in order to address the twofold need of alienated humanity. In Christ we are graciously reconciled to God (justified); by the Spirit we are graciously gifted and

167

empowered to become what God intends (sanctified). We will focus on Jesus the Christ in chapters four and five and on the Spirit of Jesus the Christ in chapters six and seven. This focus explores the possibility of and the path to human salvation (reconciliation with God) and mission (discipleship in the world).

Jesus as the Jewish Lord

Christians soon came to identify Jesus as "truly God" and "truly human" (see below). But, as context, it is first important to recognize that Jesus was a continuation of the biblical story begun with Abraham. He was "truly Jewish." The biblical revelation through Israel is of God graciously among us humans for our salvation. It is first the Jew's story, for initially it was about God with the Jews as God's chosen. It was they who faithfully told it across the generations. It is the story that, now through the coming of Christ, has become the salvation story for non-Jews as well. Note, however, that Christian faith, while more comprehensive than its Jewish foundation, nonetheless is dependent on that foundation.

Paul warned early Gentile Christians not to be arrogant toward Jews who had not yet accepted Jesus as their Christ (Rom. 11:17-18, 24). All is by God's grace. The Jewish root supports all who are graciously grafted in.[1] In the second century, Christians wisely condemned as heretical the view of Marcion that the faith of Jews and Christians are so different that Christians should tear out of their Bibles the Hebrew Scriptures. The fact is that the Bible is all one story. The God of Abraham and Moses, Miriam and Deborah, is the God and Father of Jesus the Christ. To receive all but Jesus is to fail to understand fully any of the story, including the identity of Jesus.

The Gospel of Matthew can be seen as narrative christology, i.e., a telling of the story of the true identity of Jesus in the context of his being an extension of the story of God's preparation for Christ in the history of the Jewish people. Matthew begins with a Jewish geneal-

---

[1] See Ronald Allen and John Holbert, *Holy Root, Holy Branches* (Nashville: Abingdon Press, 1995), and Brad Young, *Jesus the Jewish Theologian* (Peabody, Mass.: Hendrickson Publishers, 1995).

ogy that leads to Jesus. Jesus is presented as "Israel's new David, as the fulfillment and zenith of God's history with His people Israel."[2] The one all-important difference between Saul the Jewish Pharisee and Paul the Christian apostle was his new evaluation of the person of Jesus. Rooted in the Jewish past, this Jesus also came to be seen as the very presence of God's future.

The Sovereign God, reports the biblical story, chose to come among us in incarnate form. In the course of human history, one man,[3] who was really a man, also somehow was God among us in flesh, the full revelation of the divine nature and intent. This chapter reviews the content and earliest development of such a stunning affirmation about Jesus, the Christ. It explores the increasingly complex path by which this affirmation, rooted in the actual experience of the first believers, was reflected on by the maturing Christian community and finally was stated in terms of the "Trinity" doctrine, Hellenistic philosophy (Chalcedon), and then in more recent philosophies.

What a story! The main theme is that a Palestinian preacher was actually God among us for our salvation. By following the narrative of the story of Jesus, the New Testament affirms, we can come to understand the way of God with a fallen creation, and thus ever more of the nature of God's eternal essence and forgiving love. With one text we come to the center of the biblical revelation of God with us. The decisive divine deed on which the whole sacred narrative turns is that "the Word became flesh and lived among us, and we have seen his glory, the glory as of the Father's only Son, full of grace and truth" (Jn. 1:14).

The approach to "christology" (study of Jesus as God's Christ) is crucial. The significance of the biblical narrative is stressed here. Jesus was a Jew and first must be understood and appreciated in that

---

[2] Michael Lodahl, *The Story of God* (Kansas City: Beacon Hill Press, 1994), 129.

[3] The genuine humanity of Jesus is emphasized in the face of perennial "gnostic" tendencies to assume that he was God only *appearing* to be present as flesh and blood. Note that the Apostles' and Nicene Creeds, when read carefully, contain several very human details about Jesus obviously intended to highlight his real humanity.

specific context. Intellectualized concepts about the identity of Jesus, while inevitable and crucial, nonetheless are to remain responsible to the historical foundations of the biblical revelation. Great leaders of church history capture our attention and tend to hold our loyalties through various theological perspectives and denominational traditions. What should happen, however, is closer to what Stephen Seamands recommends to United Methodists about their theological mentor, John Wesley: "Wesley is of secondary value to us. He is useful only when he serves as a pointer beyond himself to our primary source–Scripture itself, which in turn points beyond itself to the living Christ."[4] The center is Jesus, the Christ, the fulfillment of the biblical narrative of God with the chosen people for the sake of the whole world.

We now reach the highpoint of biblical revelation, the very center of the story of God with us needy humans. Christian theology begins with the conviction that Jesus Christ is the normative revelation of God to us. In Christ, God actually was with us. Jesus was quite other than just another great religious leader of history, someone who grew especially close to God and then started a new religion to conserve and pass on the findings. He was the "Word become flesh" (Jn. 1:14).

Christian believing about Jesus as the Christ of God, a man "of one being with the Father" according to the Nicene Creed, did not begin with refined doctrinal confessions.[5] It began as a small community of believers who lived through a series of amazing events and came to find great meaning in the story that these events told. What was there about Jesus that convinced the earliest Christians that this lowly man from Nazareth is the Self-disclosure of God? At least it is

---

[4] Stephen Seamands, *Holiness of Heart and Life* (Nashville: Abingdon Press, 1990), 17.

[5] Good perspective is offered by Frederick W. Norris, "Wonder, Worship and Writ: Patristic Christology," in *Ex Auditu: An International Journal of Theological Interpretation of Scripture*, 7 (1991): "Mature patristic views of Trinity and Christology, the attempts to explain the incarnation, are actually hermeneutical models; their original intent in the writings of many early Christian theologians was to make sense of those leaders' deep, living and worshipful memory of scripture.... In a significant and yet secondary way those models also were framed to answer specific

not the usual things defining religious leaders. Summarizes Norman Kraus:

> Certainly it is not some philosophical argument offered by Jesus or one of his apostles. Jesus and Socrates represent two very different approaches to knowledge of the truth. Jesus said, "I am the truth," not "I have a truth to teach you." Neither is it Jesus' mystical sainthood. He was no "Mahadevi" who achieved divinity through mystical visions. Nor was he a Guatama in search for enlightenment who achieved Buddhahood through ascetic discipline and meditation.[6]

The dramatic assertion is there nonetheless. Jesus is Lord! This bold belief is the clear and unwavering conviction of the New Testament witness. Central to a belief in Jesus as the Christ, the Son of God, are the dramatic biblical reports, the history-based story. The first believers had become convinced by their own experience that Jesus was no ordinary person. What he said and did led them to statements like "You are the Messiah, the Son of the living God" (Matt. 16:16) and "My Lord and my God!" (Jn. 20:28). Clearly Jesus was a human being. What is startling is that these earliest witnesses, despite close association with Jesus in all his humanness, and in spite of their staunch Jewish monotheism, came to believe that Jesus also was God with them. Sometimes at the risk of their own lives, they insisted publically that Jesus was a man deserving of their worship and devotion just like the eternal, sovereign God.

In the book of Colossians this conviction is defended in the face of the beguiling of a syncretistic alternative that bears striking resemblance to the cultic and "new age" emphases of our own day. People in ancient Colosse were hungry to rise above their frail selves and

---

cultural questions. As models they could be talked about on their own, but their adequacy always depended upon their ability to bring together what was said variously and widely in scripture, to understand it within the church and to make it clear to specific audiences" (59).

[6] C. Norman Kraus, *God Our Savior* (Scottdale, Pa.: Herald Press, 1991), 21-22.

faulty society and tap into the supposed resources of "divine powers." That hunger endures. A resource adequate to meet the deepest of human needs still is being sought, often in the most irrational, bizarre, and fruitless places, even by wealthy, highly educated, and "scientific" professional people.

Paul's warning and testimony to the Colossian Christians represent spiritual wisdom crucial then and essential now. The sovereign God will not be manipulated toward the selfish ends of superstitious humans. Spiritual alternatives to God in Christ really are no alternatives at all. Only Jesus is Lord! God indeed can be known because the divine nature and will have been revealed in the Jewish Christ now known also to Gentiles. The ultimate conceivable is declared confidently to have become fact. In Jesus Christ are "hidden all the treasures of wisdom and knowledge" (Col. 2:3). In him "all the fullness of God was pleased to dwell," and through him God has acted "to reconcile to himself all things" (Col. 1:19-20). In Jesus of Nazareth, God is said to have intersected grace-fully, lovingly and decisively, human history and culture, and continues to do so, never being locked in any past.

No more extensive claim could be made concerning Jesus than the one recorded in the Gospel of John. This man Jesus, who appeared on the human scene in a very humble way, is said to have been in some profound sense the Word of God who always has been! (Jn. 1:1, 14). John affirms an unparalleled identity for Jesus in direct light of the life Jesus lived among us (including, of course, his dramatic death and even more his dramatic resurrection). Divine glory was seen in him. Later the New Testament speaks about "what we have heard, what we have seen with our eyes, what we have looked at and touched with our hands, concerning the word of life...the eternal life that was with the Father and was revealed to us (1 John 1:1-2). The impact of the life, death, and resurrection of Jesus convinced his first followers that Jesus was more than another prophet. He was the Word, the Self-expression of God embodied in human existence (Phil. 2:7-8).

This divine disclosure brought two rather surprising, immediate, and quite status-quo disrupting insights to the first Jewish believers.

First, the revelation of God in Jesus showed again how God chooses to be present and work in the world. Jesus came not as a revolutionary with military prowess to vindicate his people and rule the earth. He came not as a stern religious judge anxious to gather the righteous and damn all others. Rather, he came washing the feet of those who walked with him along life's dusty paths and shedding tears over those who chose to walk away in unrepentant arrogance. Here was God, coming in a surprising way, revealing the divine nature and goal through an actual life lived in the midst of chaotic human history. The power of redeeming love, made clear by the narrative of Jesus' life, lies in patience and sacrifice instead of in coercion and manipulation.

The second insight is that the Jesus-revelation of God brought salvation for all the world. God comes not to condemn, but to save (Jn. 3:16-17), not to vindicate limited human expectations, but to redeem all creation in God's time and way. Many Jews had built exclusionary walls of identity and protection for themselves over the centuries in light of having experienced frequent struggle and persecution. They tended to think that God sanctioned their walls and that God was comfortable staying inside them. Then came Jesus, a faithful Jew, who questioned even the walls seeking to protect God's own covenant people. The religious and cultural barriers needed abolished (Eph. 2:14-15). Salvation would be available to all people on the basis of faith, not birth (Gal. 2:15-17). It was "a totally non-imperialistic announcement that at long last God's salvation has been manifested in a universal Savior. Indeed, an explicit part of the good news was that Gentiles did not have to convert to religious Judaism in order to be disciples of Jesus."[7]

Such disruptive stances are not usually spawned by an established faith community. It is not the story that many in the Jewish community of the first century expected or would have written (or afterwards did write, except for the many Jews who gladly followed Jesus). Where did such radical stances come from, including the view that Jesus was the Christ? These life-changing and world-

---

[7] C. Norman Kraus, op. cit., 24-25.

changing convictions grew in stages, a natural process in light of an historical revelation. The truth emerged in the process of a sequence of happenings associated with Jesus and in a corresponding sequence of Spirit-inspired insights into the real meaning of these happenings. Some who had seen and touched were assisted by the Spirit to remember and really understand (John 14:26, 16:13).

The inspired perception of the whole biblical story of God, now culminating in Christ, made all things new for believers. Narrative-based insights into Jesus as the Christ soon would be analyzed, theorized, and philosophized in attempts to explain and defend them in widening circles. First, however, the faith was not a *proposition* but a *Person.* The confession concerning the Christ initially was historical narrative, autobiographical testimony, the story of divine reality as experienced in the life, teachings, death, and resurrection of Jesus. Explaining this reality philosophically and theologically would come later in the process of struggle with competing claims and the challenges involved in engaging in world mission.[8] But first comes the foundational witness of the New Testament.

The Virginal Conception

The very appearance of Jesus among us, so the biblical witness reads, was dramatic and full of meaning. Mary was the mother, but it is reported by Matthew and Luke that neither Joseph nor any other human male was the biological father. Probably it is not helpful for us to press our "Western" questions about exactly how this all happened. If God is as the Bible says, such a thing is possible. The biblical narrative reports simply that the conception occurred because of the Spirit's overshadowing, without the assistance of a human father. This miraculous happening is full of theological meaning, especially in regard to the basis of human salvation. The virginal conception

---

[8] The Believers' Church tradition joins John Wesley in having limited interest in *explaining* Christ's nature as God-incarnate, a process often speculative, politically influenced (see the discussion later in this chapter), and an "unwarranted imposition of philosophical conceptions on the simply-expressed teachings of Scripture and the earliest Church" (Randy Maddox, *Responsible Grace: John Wesley's Practical Theology*, 1994, 94-95).

"shows, as Catholics have stressed, that human acts do play a part in God's saving work. And, as Protestants have insisted, even these depend on a grace which far transcends our capacities."[9]

Drawing enduring theological implications from the ancient world's designation of gender roles, Karl Barth writes: "When we look at the beginning of the existence of Jesus, we are meant to be looking into the ultimate depth of the Godhead.... The male, as the specific agent of human action and history...must retire into the background, as the powerless figure of Joseph."[10] God chose Mary, the woman who responded to God with only these words: "Here am I, the servant of the Lord; let it be with me according to your word" (Lk. 1:38).[11]

Matthew and Luke are the only New Testament writers who report the virginal conception of Jesus. Their primary emphasis in this regard appears to be stress on this conception as an eschatological event. The point of the biblical story is that, from the very beginning of the earthly existence of Jesus, the Holy Spirit was the active agent in the dawning of a new age. The narrative begins with the blessed mystery of the origin of life in God and by God, and then sets in motion a series of events that will culminate in the final judgment of the world and the salvation of the faithful children of God. What one

---

[9] Thomas Finger, *Christian Theology*, vol. 2, 1989, 478. Ray Dunning says that the primary emphasis of Matthew and Luke is on this conception as an eschatological event. God set in motion with Mary's conception a chain of events leading finally to salvation, judgment, and the age to come. Dunning stresses the truth of "discontinuity" in relation to the incarnation. Commenting on the messianic expectation of "a root out of a dry ground" (Isa. 53:2, KJV), he says: "Jesus cannot be explained as a product of natural causes, the apex of an evolutionary development, but only as the inbreaking of God into human history" (*Grace, Faith and Holiness*, 406).

[10] Karl Barth, *Dogmatics in Outline* (Harper & Row, 1959), 99.

[11] Considerable caution is appropriate in relation to a teaching sometimes found among Christians that Jesus had to be born of a virgin or he could not have been divine. Says Millard Erickson about this assumption: "The transmission of Adam's sin is believed to have been broken by removing the human father. This seems to imply either that women do not have original sin, or at least that they do not transmit it to the next generation. This idea, however, seems to be without any firm biblical support..." (*The Word Became Flesh*, 546). It also implies a definition of the nature of sin that is substantive, not relational, and perpetuates a negative view of human sexuality also not rooted in biblical revelation.

day will be already is in Jesus. It was so from the moment and even by the means of his very conception.

The virginal conception of Jesus also ties his resurrection and destiny to his true origin.[12] The life of Jesus is an extension of the biblical story of God's initiative for human salvation. The virginal conception emphasizes, as did the burden of John Wesley's teaching about Christ, that

> God is the one who takes initiative in our salvation: it is God who died in Christ to make possible our pardon; it is God who awakens us to our need of grace in Christ the Prophet and drives us to Christ the Priest; it is God who initiates our restored relationship in Christ the Priest; and, it is God who guides us as Christ the King, leading us into all holiness and happiness.[13]

The New Testament affirmations of the distinctive origin of Jesus do not say that he was divine and sinless *by virtue* of this special kind of conception. The virginal conception, however, does signify "the full presence of God in the full story of Jesus."[14] Christology does not rise or fall with the historicity of the virginal conception as it does with the historical resurrection. The early apostolic proclamation of faith in Jesus Christ never appealed to a special physical conception as the necessary foundation for the declaration that Jesus is divine. The virginal conception is not the *ground* of faith, but an *object* of faith. We join the classic witness of the church in believing the simple witness of the Gospel writers in this regard.[15]

Two major theological questions readily present themselves

---

[12] Jürgen Moltmann, *The Way of Jesus Christ* (Fortress Press ed., 1993), 82.

[13] Randy Maddox, *Responsible Grace*, 117-118.

[14] James McClendon, *Systematic Theology: Doctrine* (Nashville: Abingdon Press, 1994), 270.

[15] For an excellent discussion of the issues related to the virginal conception of Jesus and the history of their handling in the church, see Stanley Grenz, *Theology for the Community of God*, 1994, 409-423.

when one accepts by faith the biblical report that the Jesus event from its very beginning was the initiating God of loving grace. (1) Who is Jesus Christ? This is the question of identity and leads from the earliest narration of the Jesus Story to the central but difficult Christian concept of the "Trinity" (see below). (2) What has God through Jesus Christ accomplished for sinful human beings and for all creation? This is the question of the mission of Jesus, the meaning of atonement, of reconciliation between God, humanity, and all creation (see chapter five). Answering these two questions establishes the very heart of the biblical revelation and the foundation of Christian faith. The answers should never be separated from those early and formative historical experiences of the first disciples, the pivotal and experience-based perceptions of the apostolic eye-witnesses.

Theological metaphors are fragile carriers of meaning as they migrate from culture to culture. What persists is the biblical witness, the actual pattern of historical events in which God was present and active. Reality lay *in life*, something prior to and more basic than the conceiving in available language and the formalizing into doctrines that necessarily follow.

Inspired by the biblical narrative and later expressed in the church's historic confessions of faith lies a *triple affirmation* about the identity of Jesus Christ and a *triple office* approach to understanding Christ's accomplished mission on our behalf. To these crucial triads we now turn attention, with the affirmations addressed in this chapter and the offices in the next.

The Triple Affirmation

The Nicene Creed (381) is formed around the "Trinity," God known as Father, Son, and Holy Spirit. Always at the center of these three is the Son, Jesus Christ. Belief in "Jesus Christ, His Only Son, Our Lord" determines from a human perspective the interpretation of what goes before, the character of God the Father, and what follows after, the nature and role of God the Holy Spirit.

Elton Trueblood refers to Jesus as the Christian's "center of certitude."[16] Theodore Jennings agrees: "For the Christian there is no secure knowledge of God apart from a consideration of the preaching and action, the life and death, the fate and destiny of this Jesus."[17] God the Father, the transcendent One who stands as Sovereign, comes to be known to us humans through the story of God the Son, the immanent, the incarnate One. In Jesus Christ, God stoops as Saviour to make the divine being and love known, accessible, and effective.

The best way to inform our understanding of God is to give attention to the earthly story of Jesus in the New Testament. Christian theology is based on narrated and interpreted history (kerygma), real history understood in its divine depths. The range of experienced meanings found in the biblical narrative soon came to be expressed by the church in the distinctive doctrine of the "Trinity." Historically, long before the *dogma* of the Trinity was the *experience* of the Trinity.

It must be admitted that if ever something looked as though it were designed to confuse even the most perceptive of seekers after truth, here it is. God is one, although in some essential and inevitable sense the one God is said to also be three. No wonder many Christians generally avoid theology. After bowing in humble contrition and sometimes weeping their way into new life in Christ, babes in the faith are faced with the awesome task of thinking seriously about the truths that are the very constitution of their new citizenship in the Kingdom of God. As classically defined, point one of the Christian constitution reads like a riddle. It certainly can leave one spiritually chilled if all that gets communicated is a cold, intellectual formulation, the apparent enigma of an excessively abstract idea. Our hearts cry out for God, not for a perplexing three-in-one theological formula!

While the doctrine of the Trinity is a post-biblical Christian development emerging from a particular philosophical and political context in a particular era of the church's history, it remains a classic way of expressing the ultimate meaning of the Jesus Story. Granted,

---

[16] See Elton Trueblood, *A Place To Stand* (N. Y.: Harper & Row, 1969), chapter 2.

[17] Theodore Jennings, *Loyalty to God* (Nashville: Abingdon Press, 1992), 63.

the Trinity as a doctrine is taught only by implication in the New Testament. Nonetheless, it clearly is implied by the very structure of the biblical revelation about God and therefore is not to be dismissed lightly.[18] This complex concept has come to be judged theologically foundational for Christians (not necessarily the last word, but without question a very important word). It dramatizes and holds in balance the creative tension always existing in an adequate Christian understanding of the God revealed in the Bible.[19] The Father is divine transcendence emphasized. The Spirit is divine immanence emphasized. The Son, Jesus Christ, is where and when and in whom the transcendence and immanence are experienced jointly and understood simultaneously, wholistically, historically, redemptively.

We humans are painfully aware that our minds are so small and God's being is so vast. We reach out for the ultimate, hoping that the divine reality will be available, understandable, clarifying and not confusing. Many of us are nearly deafened by the noise of church business operations and occasionally disgusted by the constant attraction we have to our own self-serving and culturally bound ideas. What we need is good news about God, news that is *from* God and not from ourselves. However, it takes some precision and patience if we are to keep any such good news free from distortion.

---

[18] The concept of Trinity is present implicity in the New Testament. Paul begins what probably was his earliest epistle (therefore the earliest writing in the New Testament) with: "We always give thanks to God...remembering before our God and Father your work...in our Lord Jesus Christ. For we know [that] our message of the gospel came to you...in power and in the Holy Spirit" (1 Thess. 1:2-5). See also Matthew 28:19 and 2 Cor. 13:14.

[19] Stanley Grenz and Roger Olson's *20th Century Theology* (InterVarsity, 1992) is an extensive study of the struggle of a wide range of Christian theologians to maintain this delicate balance in the face of the challenges of "modernity." Much innovation and many unbalanced attempts are reviewed, thus emphasizing the importance of the historic balance maintained by the Trinity doctrine. Announces Alister McGrath: "Happily, the ultimate grounds of the doctrine of the Trinity are to be found in the pervasive pattern of divine activity to which the New Testament bears witness. The Father is revealed in Christ through the Spirit.... The doctrine of the Trinity can be regarded as the outcome of a process of sustained and critical reflection on the pattern of divine activity revealed in Scripture, and continued in Christian experience. This is not to say that Scripture contains a doctrine of the Trinity; rather, Scripture bears witness to a God who demands to be understood in a Trinitarian manner" (*Christian Theology: An Introduction*, Blackwell, 1994, 248-249). Doctrine derives from the Bible's narrative structure of truth presentation.

A corrupting simplification is tempting. We are dealing with God–or, better, God has taken the initiative by stooping to deal with us. The task is to be open to whatever has been made known. Instead of opting for the simplistic, we should follow the biblical story wherever it leads. It leads to "Trinity" talk, talk that is "not basically an attempt to foist upon Christian credulity an unintelligible and incredible speculation regarding Ultimate Reality; it is the effort to discover what must be true of Ultimate Reality because of what our experience of that Reality tells us."[20]

What does the whole of the biblical narrative suggest? The fullness of the divine being, as God has made it known to us in Jesus Christ, leads to what the Christian doctrine of "Trinity" seeks to express. This traditional centerpiece of theology is not trying to complicate a straightforward truth; rather it is a useful way of holding together a series of coordinate truths that, only in their togetherness, bring into focus the full truth about God. Again, Jesus is the center. The biblical narrative about him prompts the quest for an adequate way to express the profound implications of who he is, what he did, and thus who God is and how we then should live. The quest for the identity and mission of Jesus as God-with-us is called christology. It is undertaken for the purpose of truly knowing God, being renewed by God's loving grace, and being sent on God's mission. To *know* rightly is "orthodox."

At least a hint of this complex Trinity teaching is found in Paul's benediction to the church in Corinth (2 Cor. 13:14). Apparently Paul's perspective took its rise from the richness of lived stories of early Christian saints. Such people had been privileged to encounter God and they had found that no descriptive words or concepts about God were adequate unless, at a minimum, they included "Father, Son, and Holy Spirit." What they had come to know of God, through the historical events associated with Jesus and subsequent personal expe-

---

[20] Laurence Wood, *Truly Ourselves, Truly the Spirit's* (Zondervan, Francis Asbury Press, 1989), 151. This approach relies on the method of human analogy by assuming that humanity is made in the "image of God." Jesus used this method often ("If you, being evil, know how to give good gifts to your children, how much more your Father in heaven"). The very center of the faith is the assumption that the experience of knowing Jesus in the flesh is to know truly God in heaven.

rience associated with Christ's Spirit, combined and demanded such a breadth of affirmation.[21]

It is important to begin with the biblical narrative that tells the whole story of God's redemptive involvement with humanity. A proper reading proceeds in light of the life of Jesus as that light is inspired by our own experience of grace through the Spirit. Theological reflection evolves best out of our own redemption as that is informed by the story of Jesus that originally was inspired by the Spirit and again is inspired as we remember and open ourselves in faith and obedience to its perspective and power.

Significantly, Paul's reference in 2 Corinthians to the triune God begins with "the grace of the Lord Jesus Christ." The dynamic of the Christian movement and its understanding of God originated in the life of a real man. The impact of Jesus' teachings, death, and resurrected life on the re-born lives of his amazed, forgiven, changed, and commissioned disciples spawned then and spawns now a triune vision of God.

The bare facts are straightforward enough. A long time ago Jesus was born in one little town and grew up in another. They both were mere dots on the map of a marginal Roman province called Palestine. Jesus started out following his father's[22] manual trade. Soon gripped by some powerful convictions, however, Jesus moved from settled obscurity to roving notoriety. But, shortly after his popularity with the area's masses skyrocketed, it all went sour. He ended up hanging on a Roman cross in apparent disgrace, executed on false, politically inflammatory charges. Why, then, has this man's relatively brief life and especially horrible death become the greatest story ever told in the entire history of humankind? How does the

---

[21] Beginning with human experience of God in Christ sometimes is called approaching the Trinity "from below" or even "eschatologically." This approach starts with the presently experienced work of the Spirit "who brings the *eschaton* alive and hastens all things towards the consummation" (Thomas Finger, vol. 2, *Christian Theology*, Herald Press, 1989, 234). From the biblically narrated story of Jesus, including the dramatic presentness of the eschaton, human reflection circles back to seek understanding of the work of Christ and the foundation of all theology, God.

[22] This reference, of course, is to Joseph. Theologically, a key New Testament emphasis is that God is the "Father" of Jesus. See above for discussion of the "virgin birth."

apparent tragedy of one man's life relate to the eternal being and activities of God?

The answer conveyed by the biblical story is a dramatic one. It fits all the facts as we can know them and calls only for a step of reasonable faith. The sharp turn in the story of Jesus is the report of his bodily resurrection from the dead. Numerous eyewitnesses were forced by unexpected circumstances to declare that the grave of Jesus had failed to hold him for more than three brief days. Faced with this stunning fact, the opened eyes of faith led early disciples to the conclusion that Jesus was more than another spiritually sensitive man seeking after the ultimate truth of God and rejected by a spiritually insensitive world. In some mysterious and marvelous way, through the birth, life, death, and now resurrection of this Jesus, God was seeking to be revealed and to redeem a lost creation. Jesus indeed was the Christ, the anointed One, the Self-revelation of God on the human scene.[23] Here is the highpoint of the whole biblical story.

The Christian faith makes a particular claim to truth. It centers in a belief that the salvation of humankind and of all creation already has arrived in Jesus of Nazareth. This claim is so central that Carl Braaten concludes: "Any church that either ceases to affirm the ultimacy of this event in the history of salvation or attempts to place alongside it other events of equal validity will fall into idolatry and apostasy."[24] Rather than lining up in the pantheon of the world's spiritual heroes, this Jesus is said to be the embodied presence of the sovereign God, the God who voluntarily chose, in Jesus the Christ, to assume incarnate form and suffer among us humans for our salvation. What a story!

---

[23] Says Archibald Hunter in reference to the Gospel of Mark: "Mark's story is not that of 'one more unfortunate gone to his death,' or even of the supreme prophet sealing his testimony to the truth with his life's blood. Mark's purpose is to record how God's saving rule was inaugurated on earth in his only Son Jesus the Messiah and realized 'with power' (9:1) by his resurrection from the dead: in short, to tell the story of Jesus as the great act of God which enables those who believe to do his will, receive the forgiveness of their sins, and lay hold on eternal life" (*Introducing the New Testament*, 3rd rev. ed., Philadelphia: Westminster Press, 1945, 1957, 1972, 44).

[24] Carl Braaten, *No Other Gospel!* (Minneapolis: Fortress Press, 1992), 13.

This historical, Christ-centered biblical story is prior to all doctrines that now claim to be derived from it. Doctrines are to be evaluated by how faithful they are in representing the substance and intent of the biblical revelation. The Bible narrates what is claimed to be the historical embodiment of the redeeming activity of God. It tells about a distinctive way of knowing God and of being God's people in this world. Jesus Christ is said to be that moment in the historical process in which the part reveals the whole. Through Christ we are enabled to know the One who is eternal and unsurpassably good, the One who is the ground of our being, who gives life, and in whom all things cohere (Col. 1:3-20). It is through participation in Christ that our human stories get caught up and transformed in the divine story. Only in Christ does the Christian community continue to come alive.

A key thrust of Paul's teaching in found in Colossians 2:9-10. There the apostle makes clear that Jesus is the source of Christian truth, the divine good news from and about the divine. Jesus alone is the crown of God's Self-revelation. In Jesus "the whole fullness of deity dwells bodily" (2:9). This fullness does not mean that Jesus merely *reflects* divine qualities to an unusual degree, but that he actually is the incarnate presentation of the divine essence, the earthly appearance of the very presence of God. As portrayed in the New Testament, Jesus is not a divine being masquerading in human form (Docetism). Nor is he a mere man who has touched God and been elevated to a special status by God (Adoptionism). For centuries, both of these characterizations of Jesus have been judged by the mainstream of the Christian community to be wholly inadequate ways of conveying the dramatic New Testament declaration. In fact, they have been judged heretical, dangerous because they distort the biblical story by missing so much of its marvelous truth.

What the biblical narrative reveals is that, in Jesus, God actually was with us,[25] so much so that there is a necessary and intimate oneness of the being of God and the being of Jesus. The Son, a theological designation of Jesus in relation to God, is not only the servant or

---

[25] The Bible goes on to affirm that God in Christ *still is with us* as the Spirit of Jesus, the resurrected Christ (see chapter six).

supreme earthly manifestation of God. The Son is God with us.[26]

Today many Christians view Jesus more narratively than philosophically. Often their approach is "functional," meaning that the "divinity" of Jesus is seen primarily in the activity of God in and through him. Viewed this way, the person of Christ is not initially identified in philosophic categories of the fifth or twentieth centuries. More functionally and relationally than that, functional christology is the theological way of saying that God was with us in the life, teachings, death, and resurrection of Jesus. Avoiding speculative doctrines that highlight metaphysics over existential impact, *christology* may be identified as the contention that God is with us. Whatever else they do, "the cross manifests the radicality of God's entry into our humanity, God's solidarity with our suffering and brokenness; and the resurrection manifests the permanence, indefeasible even by death, of that radical presence in our lives."[27]

Charles Brown presents a form of this view of Jesus. He says that Christian doctrine is not "a miscellaneous bundle of theories about many debatable subjects." Rather, it is "an organic body of truth rooted in the person of Jesus Christ."[28] Says a loved prayer chorus:

---

[26] The classic confessional statements that developed in the early centuries of the church use then-current philosophic categories to express the relation of Jesus to God. These statements became ecumenical orthodoxy, maintaining that Christ is truly human, truly God, one person. Each of these two natures of Christ remains whole and distinct, yet without confusion. While such Greek thought forms as these are not native to the biblical story, the apparently paradoxical affirmations being expressed are. Jesus as the Christ is described in the New Testament as before Abraham, yet born in a manger, upholding all things by the word of his power, yet growing dependently in the womb of Mary, knowing all from the foundation of the world without knowing the time of final judgment, creating all things without having a place to lay his own head, unlimited in power while dying the horrible death of a cross, dead and buried, yet the resurrected One in whom the eternal life of God resides and works forever. Such contrasting affirmations either are absurdities, inherently contradictory, or they are the elements of the amazing grace of God that later were formalized as the logic of the divine-human personal union.

[27] Delwin Brown, in Clark Pinnock and Brown, *Theological Crossfire* (Zondervan, 1990), 179.

[28] Charles Brown, *We Preach Christ* (Anderson, Ind.: Gospel Trumpet Co., 1957), 14. This centrality of Christ is seen clearly in the stained glass window featured in the chapel of Anderson University's School of Theology. Using the image of the vine and branches, the resurrected Christ dominates, with the branches moving out-

Come, Lord Jesus, be among us;
Fill our lives with hope and power;
Now receive our loving service,
Make us one with Thee this hour.[29]

Christian faith is founded on a story, the greatest ever told. This story is the epic recital of human redemption resulting from divine initiative. It is a narrative conveying to us God's promises and actions for human reconciliation to God. The highlight of the story, the key that unlocks the whole plot that stretches from the beginning to the end of time, is the story's chief character, the risen and exalted Lord, Jesus Christ.

This story is not reducible to law, dogma, theory, or philosophic system, although constant efforts are made in this direction. Even the classic doctrine of the trinity is an after-the-story philosophic construct that in itself is not authoritative or necessarily final. Instead, authority lies with the biblical narrative that is a moving picture, a cosmic drama of the creating and recreating God who comes in Christ to reveal and reclaim. It is the portrait of a promise first shared with Abraham (Gen. 12:3) and later fulfilled when God sent the divine Son (Gal. 4:4-7). The central scene of this whole salvation script is the event of God's personal coming when "the Word became flesh and lived among us" (Jn. 1:14).

The Story of Christ unfolds in the New Testament. Paul proclaims that the time of salvation promised by the prophets is now inaugurated by the Christ event. Jesus' advent is said to be the turning point in the history of redemption, the climax that, at least in principle, set-

---

ward from him to encircle the full range of the key elements of the biblical story. All find their fulfillment and fullest meaning in Jesus Christ. For a color reproduction of this window and its theological intentions, see Barry Callen, *Contours of a Cause* (Anderson University School of Theology, 1995), 218-221. In 1988 the General Assembly of the Church of God movement (U. S. and Canada) stated guidelines for the movement's national agencies to follow in relating to interdenominational bodies like the National Council of Churches (U.S.A.). One guideline is: "Any interchurch body involved in a relationship should be committed publicly to the divinity and lordship of Jesus Christ. He is central to the meaning and mission of the church!" (see Barry Callen, *Thinking and Acting Together*, Warner Press, 1992, 27-30).

[29] Verse one of "Come, Lord Jesus, Be Among Us" by James Edwards and Lloyd Larson, in *Worship the Lord* (Warner Press, 1989), 98.

tled everything for all time. In Jesus, God's kingdom dawned over humanity's horizon. What once was mystery now is disclosed. The day of salvation is at hand (2 Cor. 6:2), a day in which "everything old has passed away, see, everything has become new!" (2 Cor. 5:17).

What is the good news in the biblical story? According to Romans 6:23, "the wages of sin is death, but the free gift of God is eternal life in Christ Jesus our Lord." Clearly the intended emphasis here is on the "in Christ Jesus our Lord." Why? Because "in him every one of God's promises is a 'Yes.' For this reason it is through him that we say the 'Amen,' to the glory of God" (2 Cor. 1:20).

Revealed in Christ are the true nature of God and the true condition of humanity. Accomplished in Christ is human reconciliation to God (see chapter five). Becoming a Christian is to believe this story by faith, be changed by grace through the Spirit in light of this story, and live life anew as a grateful witness to this wonderful story of redemption. Christianity is "not rooted in speculative philosophy or in nature mysticism but in this story, which constitutes the community and gives it its identity."[30] God in Christ is the fundamental Christian reality, "for no one can lay any foundation other than the one that has been laid; that foundation is Jesus Christ" (1 Cor. 3:11).

This good news roots in a triple affirmation. Father, Son, and Spirit are the active agents as we humans perceive the biblical story of salvation. That which originated with the Father has been established by the Son and activated by the Spirit in our own experience. So the story reads. This multiple affirmation is not a subtle polytheism (three gods), but a comprehensive way of affirming how the one God stands, stoops, and stays, is at once Sovereign, Saviour, and Sustainer. This one God provides our salvation by originating, expressing, and actualizing it.[31]

---

[30] Clark Pinnock, *Tracking the Maze* (Harper & Row, 1990), 160.

[31] Thomas Finger uses these three words, originate, express, and actualize. He cautions, however, that no one Person of the Trinity should be limited to one of these functions (the biblical narrative presents a far more interactive pattern than this). What we have is a "dynamic divine unity" (*Christian Theology*, vol. 2, 1989, 449), an ongoing circular flow. The being of God is one. The Trinity should not be thought of as a hierarchy with the Father at the top, the Son in the middle, and the Spirit at the bottom. The Son is God for us. The Spirit is God with us.

To assert the deity of Jesus Christ, then, is to claim that God (not merely some representative) has come among us, taught, healed, suffered, served, and saved. God is the suffering servant, expressing in Jesus the loving and forgiving divine nature for the purpose of human understanding and salvation. To affirm that the Son and the Father are one is to say in part that God is like Jesus. It also is to say that the church as Christ's body is called to reflect the Christ by discovering the same divine presence and embodying the same divine power to live with humility, for service, even with suffering. In this way the theology of the trinity offers an essential key to the nature of Christian life and mission. Christian discipleship means "commitment to the social radicalism of a nonconformist Christ; it required (and requires) not inner torments or guilty consciences but entire reorientation to a life with Jesus that will necessarily collide again and again with the powers, with the world's No, that is, with a cross (Mk. 8:34f)."[32]

Christ is the center of all Christian theology. God saves, redeems, and restores, not by accrediting as adequate any human works of righteousness, but by extending mercy to us in Christ. Salvation is through divine grace and by faith alone. Therefore, we preach the unsearchable riches of Christ and announce "good news of great joy for all people: to you is born this day in the city of David a Saviour, who is the Messiah, the Lord" (Lk. 2:10-11). God *in* Christ, *as* Christ, stooped to painful participation in our evil-ridden life and thereby, through the ongoing ministry of the Spirit, acts to overcome the raging evil and to extend an "amazing grace." God acts in loving grace because the character of God *is* loving grace.

The fact that God not only acts in three relatively distinguishable ways, but exhibits such tri-unity in the inmost divine being is not theological hairsplitting. Such insight grows directly out of the biblical story, is basic to the story, and provides the grounding for many themes of Christian theology.[33] To affirm God as trinity is to affirm

---

[32] James McClendon, *Systematic Theology: Doctrine* (Nashville: Abingdon Press, 1994), 279.

[33] Thomas Finger has suggested six such themes. They are: (1) agape—the universe is created and sustained by a love that overflows toward others who are not

that God came, comes, and will come to us as God truly is. Specifically, "Jesus' sufferings, the Spirit's groaning, the Lord's glorious return–these are not mere 'modes' of God's presence but the very activities of God's own self."[34]

We, then, should imitate the Wesleys in their concern to form a truly trinitarian balance in their Methodist followers. It is a balance of "(1) reverence for the God of Holy Love and for God/Father's original design for human life, (2) gratitude for the unmerited Divine Initiative in Christ that frees us from the guilt and enslavement of our sin, and (3) responsiveness to the Presence of the Holy Spirit that empowers our recovery of the Divine Image in our lives."[35] In summary, the words of Laurence Wood serve us well:

> **God the Father** stresses the *ultimacy* of the Divine… Ultimacy affirms the transcendence of God. It reminds us of the mystery, the ineffability, as well as the primacy and finality of Deity. Here, we think of God primarily in His relation to the whole of His Creation… **Jesus Christ** defines the *character* of God and of His Holy Spirit… That mighty, limitless Ultimate Power is not mere undifferentiated Might; but the life-transforming, life-redeeming Energy of the character of Jesus of Nazareth… Here, we have in view primarily God's relation to mankind… The **Holy Spirit** affirms the *intimacy* of omnipotent Power discerned as to His character in Jesus Christ… Here, we

---

deserving; (2) personal salvation–becoming a disciple is a participatory process requiring intimate relationship with God; (3) sacramental presence–God truly is present in the life of creation and especially in the life of the church, placing us "in Christ" and sending us out as companions in Christ's sufferings, enabled through the dynamism of the Spirit; (4) corporate salvation–participation in the style of the Trinitarian fellowship opens one to others, upbuilds the church, and issues in works of love; (5) image of God–since people are created in God's Trinitarian image, they are to exist in community and are destined to fulfillment through our redemptive relationships; and (6) society–seeing God in other than hierarchical terms, with the Father not isolated as an exalted monarch, questions the ordering of human societies in impersonal and authoritarian ways (*Christian Theology*, vol. 2, 1989, 454-455).

[34] Ibid., 457.

[35] Randy Maddox, *Responsible Grace: John Wesley's Practical Theology* (Abingdon Press, Kingswood Books, 1994), 140.

think especially of God-near and God-at-work in the souls
of those ready and eager to receive Him.[36]

Yes, three, yet always one! The ultimate One, God, is before and
above all, has the graceful character and loving intention of Jesus, and
remains by our sides to shape and empower the lives of believers.
Ultimate, incarnate, and intimate is the God of loving grace.

God As Palestinian Preacher

At Caesarea Philippi Jesus asked the greatest of his questions
and offered a ringing challenge to his closest circle of friends. Here
was a strange set of circumstances. First, a wandering Galilean
preacher was addressing a little company of uneducated men while
the religious authorities were successfully scheming to bring about his
death as a dangerous heretic and disturber of the establishment's
peace. Next was the setting itself, filled with the memories of the
ancient gods of Canaan, a place where persons had worshipped the
gods of Greece and now where the white splendor of a magnificent
temple marked the majesty of imperial Rome. Finally, there was the
apparent awkwardness of Jesus asking a question that invited an
answer nothing short of identifying him as God, sovereign of all
people and time, currently present and active on earth!

It all sounds unlikely, a misguided man with an overextended ego
and a set of mesmerized friends whose unbounded view of this man's
identity suggested to many that they had lost touch with reality. But
those pagan gods of Canaan, Greece, and Rome are now gone, those
kingdoms are only the stuff of ancient history, while this Jesus continues as nothing less than a 2,000-year-old contemporary phenome-
non! The question that Jesus posed about his true identity still echoes
loudly in our "postmodern" ears. Could it be? Could God indeed
have been present and ministering as a Palestinian preacher?

Whatever may be thought about the reported miracles of Jesus,
he himself surely deserves consideration as the greatest miracle of all.

---

[36] Laurence Wood, op. cit., 175-176.

Some explanation must be found for the fact that Jesus managed to move from being a peasant woman's "illegitimate" child[37] in an out-of-the-way corner of the ancient world to being the holder of a foremost place in the massive stream of human history. This striking fact alone demands attention and invites our admiration, and potentially even our worship.

Jesus must have had amazing personal charm. People with real prejudice against him, like the woman of Samaria or the officers sent by the priests to arrest him, listened to him in spite of themselves. A woman told him all about herself and rushed to tell others of the integrity, perception, and gentleness of this man. Some officers fell under his spell and went back to Jerusalem flatly refusing to carry out orders against him.

For a time Jesus was a popular dinner guest in Jerusalem. Children apparently delighted in him and even some "sinners" seemed so comfortable around him that the resulting rumors were scandalous in the eyes of the Jewish religious authorities. It probably was the case that many of the first disciples of Jesus did not begin to follow him because he was the Messiah (some were not sure of that after three years of being with him, or at least seriously misperceived the true meaning of his Messiahship). They tended to follow initially because he was an attractive and compelling person who talked sense, had courage, taught with an apparent authority not present in other teachers, and was thought able to accomplish that for which they longed–liberation from the oppression of Rome.

Jesus could and still can be misunderstood easily–just an eccentric Palestinian preacher, a clever revolutionary who finally was not clever enough, the founder of another of the world's many religions, a noble soul whose idealism did not and still will not work in our cruel kind of world. Jesus often seemed to wrap himself in an evasive cloak of secrecy concerning his real identity, almost as though he wanted to remain ambiguous to avoid being misunderstood.[38] For

---

[37] Note above the discussion of the "virginal conception" of Jesus.

[38] The issue of the "Messianic secret" is speculated on often. In the Gospel of Mark, Jesus is quoted frequently as cautioning people not to tell what they had seen done by his hand. Jesus apparently was seeking to distance himself from the politi-

some reason he called upon persons to search for him. His real identity cannot be had cheaply. It usually turns out to be in contrast to popular expectations of who he is supposed to be.

Recognition of the full reality of the identity of Jesus costs each potential disciple a certain agony and obedience, mixed with persistence in knocking, believing, and yielding of oneself to the radical claims of this man. It always has taken faith to grasp the real person of Jesus. Faith becomes effective only when it is supplemented with the enlightening initiative of God and the wisdom that comes from spending time with this still-present Jesus on the road of life. Who is Jesus? Christians know who he is by faith in the historic witness of inspired Scripture, informed by the classic creedal affirmations of the church, and in the pivotal historic events upon which the Scripture and creeds are based. But knowledge of his real identity comes only as we ourselves choose to walk in his way. *Orthodoxies* from the church's theological history need supplemented by commitment to *radical discipleship*, itself an avenue of wisdom.

Perception and persistence are inseparable, as are doctrine and discipleship. As Albert Schweitzer said in those famous sentences about the Christ of faith:

> He comes to us as One unknown, without a name, as of old by the lakeside He came to those who knew Him not. He speaks to us the same word, "Follow thou Me," and sets us to the task which He has to fulfill for our time. He commands. And to those who obey Him, whether they be wise or simple, He will reveal Himself in the toils, the conflicts, the sufferings which they shall pass through in His fellowship, and, as an ineffable mystery, they shall learn in their own experience who He is.[39]

---

cally dominated messianic hopes of Judaism that had become common under the Roman occupation of Palestine.

[39] Albert Schweitzer, *The Quest of the Historical Jesus*, German ed., 1906 (London: Adam & Charles Black, 1910), 401.

Hans Küng writes at length about Jesus' relationship to the four main social groupings in the Jewish society of his time (groups that by differing names are found in all times).[40] The Sadducees were allied with those in religious and political power. They were the clever accommodationists. Jesus was not one of them, not a priest, scribe, elder, or power broker. The Zealots sought to overturn the oppressive status-quo by violence if necessary. Jesus had plenty of opportunity, but was not one of them, choosing poverty and passing by the violence option. The Essenes sought escape from an impure world by a spiritual retreat from all public compromise. Jesus was not one of them. He ate with the impure and sought out the compromised, saying that is why he had come. Finally, the Pharisees were religiously elite conservatives, doggedly devoted, the proud protectors of received tradition. Jesus was not one of them, although he loved his heritage and intended to fulfill rather than separate from it.

The sad fact is that people try to "domesticate" Jesus, this mysterious figure who lived outside the usual religious groupings. They evolve a mountain of laws, doctrines, attitudes, and institutions to sanction in Jesus' name almost everything in synagogue, church, and society! But Jesus did not and does not belong to the establishment, religious or social. He loved and provoked all parties, championing none. Jesus was not "brought up at court as Moses apparently was, nor a king's son like Buddha. But neither was he a scholar and politician like Confucius nor a rich merchant like Muhammad. The very fact that his origins were so insignificant makes his enduring significance all the more amazing."[41]

When Peter confessed that he knew who Jesus really was, Jesus replied that "flesh and blood has not revealed this to you, but my Father in heaven" (Matt. 16:17). The lesson is clear. The human search succeeds only by the grace of God. "When you search for me you will find me; if you seek me with all your heart, I will let you find me" says God (Jer. 29:13-14). According to Christian faith, the most fruitful place to begin an honest search for God is with the

---

[40] Hans Küng, *On Being a Christian* (Garden City, N. Y.: Doubleday & Co., 1976).

[41] Küng, op. cit., 212.

grace-inspired, biblically-narrated story of the historical person of Jesus.

There it is! The central teaching of the Christian faith is that recognizing the true identity of Jesus is finally knowing God. Discovering the identity of Jesus is actually being found by God. The Gospels are laden with references to disciples who were filled with awe as they looked at Jesus through the grace-enabled eyes of faith and became convinced that they were seeing nothing less than God's Self-revelation in a uniquely revealing and saving way.

Surely one of the most remarkable facts in the whole history of religious thought is that, when the early Christians reflected after Jesus' resurrection on the dreadful realities of the crucifixion, it made them think of the redeeming love of God. They now saw not the worst deed of humanity, but the best gift of divinity. Seen in that old rugged cross was not merely the sacrifice and compassion of the man Jesus; it was the eternal love of God in action on their behalf. Where Jesus was, God was. What Jesus did was God in action. What happened to Jesus happened to God. In Jesus the Kingdom of God had arrived, as Jesus had said all along. Jesus and his Father in heaven functioned as one and somehow actually were one!

The Nicene Creed affirms that "on the third day he [Jesus] rose again from the dead." This resurrection is of central importance in the New Testament.[42] For Paul, belief that God raised Jesus from the dead is what comes to distinguish Christians from other people: "If you confess with your lips that Jesus is Lord and believe in your heart that God raised him from the dead, you will be saved" (Rom. 10:9). For the Christian, the resurrection is God's seal on Jesus' work on the cross. It is the proleptic anticipation of the reality yet to come, making Jesus the ground of human hope. What will be has begun in this man and this historical event.

The resurrection is the dramatic present instance of God's coming future. It transformed the first disciples of Jesus. It set the func-

---

[42] In his *The Apostles' Creed: A Faith to Live By* (Eerdmans, 1993, 37-42), C. E. B. Cranfield reviews the typical arguments used to resist belief in the resurrection and then notes six considerations that argue persuasively for the truth of the resurrection as a literal, historical event.

tion of the church as pioneer of God's future. It determined that the Christian life should be characterized by a new life issuing in present actions of forgiveness, justice, and peace, all empowered by the divine reign of God already arrived in Jesus and yet to come in its full-ness. It also makes even clearer the real relationship of Jesus to God. The resurrection of Jesus

> ...was an act of God in time, reversing history's judg-ment as represented by the authorities, by the opponents, even by the hapless friends of Jesus. All these read histo-ry's judgment to be: death to this one. The resurrection opposed that judgment by entering God's own judgment: life, life to this same one. God reversed all human judg-ment by identifying the life of Jesus of Nazareth afresh with God's own life, so that from that time, and in accor-dance with an eternal purpose of God, the history of this man, Jesus of Nazareth, was to be counted identical with God's inner history, in such a way that in the knowing of Jesus Christ God could be truly known.[43]

Only after the resurrection event did the disciples come to the belief that Jesus, in spite of the apparent tragedy and shame of the cross, indeed was God's Messiah. With the additional enlightenment and empowerment experienced at Pentecost (Acts 2), they also realized that the Spirit was authenticating all that Jesus was, said, and did, and was thrusting faithful believers on a mission to the whole world. Increas-ingly Jesus was seen in retrospect as related intimately and centrally to the whole drama of God at work in fallen creation. The disciples came to believe that the authority, power, judgment, and love known in Jesus were God's own. The road to Emmaus is a symbol of what happened

---

[43] James McClendon, *Systematic Theology: Doctrine* (Nashville: Abingdon Press, 1994), 247. So the resurrection is God's vindication of Jesus as the Christ and of God as Lord of human history. It also provides a glimpse at the coming end of the biblical drama, the ultimate end of all creation. Says McClendon, without the resur-rection "we might at best revere a memory or idolize a phantom. Since it has taken place, faith in Christ is anchored in history, exactly in the history of God's own Israel" (250).

(Lk. 24:13-35). Sympathetic but disheartened witnesses to Jesus' life, teachings, and death searched the Scriptures looking for answers to what appeared to be a terrible turn of events. Only in light of an encounter with the *risen* Christ did real answers come.

To believe this makes all things new. St. Paul is a prominent example. Through faith in Jesus, now risen from the grave, he acquired the ability to endure threats and tragedies of many kinds. He had concluded that nothing "will be be able to separate us from the love of God in Christ Jesus our Lord" (Rom. 8:39). Paul taught the Corinthian believers that "Jesus Christ...was not 'Yes and No'; but in him it is always 'Yes.' For in him every one of God's promises is a 'Yes'" (2 Cor. 1:19-20).

By faith in the crucified and resurrected Jesus, guilty and fretful women and men finally are privileged to come to know with confidence that the sovereign God is present as forgiving love. The evidence generally observed in human experience is yes and no, God exists and does not exist, is love and is not love, actively cares for the creation and yet may have abandoned the creation to its deserved fate. But in Jesus we see by faith the ultimate "yes" beyond the constant paralysis of our yes-no human conclusions. We finally are enabled to see because, in Jesus Christ, God has chosen to be seen in a manner intelligible by our human ways of experiencing and understanding. The need for faith is not removed. Divine grace nurtures by persuasion rather than pressures by coercion. Since we are speaking of God, we are helped to apprehend, never fully to comprehend. We can begin, however, to approach knowing the great Unknowable by knowing God *in the person of Jesus Christ*.

What has been provided at God's initiative is a concrete focus of the divine, a man who offers the definitive reference point in the human search for God and in God's reaching out for lost humanity. That reference point is the man Jesus. Note the testimony of Lesslie Newbigin after a lifetime of world-wide involvements in multiple religious circles:

> I still see the cross of Jesus as the one place in all the history of human culture where there is a final dealing with the

ultimate mysteries of sin and forgiveness, of bondage and freedom, of conflict and peace, of death and life…. I find here… a point from which one can take one's bearings and a light in which one can walk, however stumblingly. I know that that guiding star will remain and that that light will shine till death and in the end. And that is enough.[44]

The question of the true identity of Jesus is not exhausted by inquiries into his psychological development, how his mind worked, when and to what extent he was conscious of an "otherness" about himself and his mission. The real question is whether you and I can accept his biblically-reported claims about himself, claims seemingly substantiated by the amazing facts that surrounded him from virginal conception to resurrection from the dead. Our faith is called upon to receive him as (1) the climax of humankind's age-long quest for the reality of God and (2) the apex of God's enduring quest to reclaim a lost creation. Jesus, the Palestinian preacher, was and is to be received as none other than God come among us for our salvation!

Edward Scribner Ames is right, but only partially right. He confesses, "I believe that Jesus Christ is the proper object of faith because his words and example inspire men to the highest spiritual life."[45] The basis of this faith for Ames is the personality, teaching, vision, and life example of Jesus. By his living a life so faithful to God, Jesus showed God in a new way and showed us the way to God. This portrayal of Jesus as the highpoint of human spiritual aspirations and accomplishments, true as far as it goes, runs the danger that Albert Schweitzer pointed out in his classic *The Quest of the Historical Jesus* (1906). Interpreters tend to see Jesus through the lens of their own cultural perspectives, picturing him as the fulfillment of their own ideals. Rather than being recreated by the Christ, we create him.

---

[44] Lesslie Newbigin, *Unfinished Agenda: An Autobiography* (Grand Rapids, Mich.: Eerdmans, 1985), 254-255.

[45] Edward Scribner Ames, *Beyond Theology* (University of Chicago, 1959), 76. Ames represents the more liberal tendency among the Disciples of Christ movement early in the twentieth century. He taught for years at the University of Chicago and served as dean of the Disciples Divinity House there.

Another position of partial rightness is that of Frederick Kershner. Especially appreciative of the theology of Albrecht Ritschl (1822-1889), Kershner approaches christology from an ethical concern. In Jesus, he taught, we see a shift from the externals of religion to its meaning for moral life. Jesus effects a "moral revolution" and raises humanity to a new moral maturity.[46] True, but is this all?

According to mainstream Christian tradition, Jesus was more than a pioneer of human faith, the supreme spiritual pathfinder, the greatest of all believers, the ultimate discoverer of the true and living God, the example whose words and deeds inspire us to the highest in spiritual life and ethical maturity. If he were only these things in his own elevated humanity, he would deserve our imitation, but hardly our worship. But, according to the biblical witness, there is more. God, whose true nature Jesus has made known, is the One who has been seeking us and who has reached us fully and finally, having come to be with us and for us *in this man Jesus*. Thus the mainstream Christian tradition rightly goes beyond the *humanity* to affirm the actual *divinity* of Jesus.

Galilee to Chalcedon

Were theological thieves encountered by the Christian community as it traveled the road from Bethlehem and Jerusalem to the famous church councils at Nicea (325), Constantinople (381), and Chalcedon (451). That is, was something of the New Testament's narrative witness to God's action in Jesus sadly lost or inappropriately added by the time the church formalized its classic christological statements in the fourth and fifth centuries? Was the Jesus of history unjustifiably transformed by zealous followers into the Christ of faith? Was the adoption of the church by the establishment of the Roman Empire[47] in effect a domestication of the church by the political interests of the world? Were the church's creeds about the nature

---

[46] Frederick Kershner, *The Religion of Christ* (N. Y.: Fleming Revell, 1911), 18. Kershner, another representative of the liberal tendency within the Disciples of Christ movement, taught for years at Butler University in Indianapolis.

[47] Emperor Constantine, Edict of Milan, 313.

of Jesus Christ, emerging after the "Constantinian shift," a worldly as much as a churchly product? Is classic christology only dated abstraction fitted to the philosophic environment of another time–and thus archaic in ours?

Within today's Believers' Church community,[48] such questions spawn lively debate. This is a particular Christian tradition in which the actual person of Christ rather than establishment theological positions about Christ is central (at some points, of course, there is no difference). The concern is to minimize abstractions, stay with the basics of the biblical revelation, and maximize current discipleship. There is special sensitivity to the importance of the separation of church and state and the necessity of a distinctive, Christ-like lifestyle in contrast to the world.

In recent years leading Mennonite and other theologians have addressed the question of whether the creeds of Nicea and Chalcedon are adequate and definitive representations of New Testament teaching. Are these creeds the continuing basis for the church's belief as it maintains its biblical stance as an alternative to the world's social order? Or are these creeds examples of the church of the past accommodating itself to the social order of the Roman Empire and Hellenistic thought?[49] Which is authoritative, these classic creeds as fixed definitions of biblical teaching or the biblical revelation and the Christ in relation to all creeds and any other church authority systems? Does this choice have to be made?

Extensive research and seemingly endless scholarly speculation have been expended in recent generations to explore and propound one particular hypothesis. The simple and noble Jesus presented in the Synoptic Gospels may have been transformed by the early church into

---

[48] Brethren, Baptists, Quakers, Mennonites, etc. See Donald Durnbaugh, *The Believers' Church*, 1985 ed. (Scottdale, Pa.: Herald Press) and J. Denny Weaver, *Becoming Anabaptist* (Scottdale, Pa.: Herald Press, 1987).

[49] As sensitive as Justo González is to the tyranny of dominant cultures that often use religion to perpetuate their privileges, in this case he thinks the best about the church leaders that gathered long ago at Nicea. No matter "how difficult their task may have been by the manner in which the issues were posed, they were trying to articulate what had been the faith of the church for centuries" (*Mañana*, Abingdon Press, 1990, 103).

someone he actually had not known himself to be. Did the proclaimer inappropriately become the proclaimed?[50] From the rustic paths of Galilee to the sophisticated creed of Chalcedon, so this hypothesis goes, there evolved an elaborate, theoretical interpretation of Jesus that may have been influenced more by Greek philosophy than by historical reality and divine initiative. The obviously interpretive character of all the Gospel writings makes it "difficult to discriminate between those things that are straightforwardly true of Jesus of Nazareth and those things ascribed to him as a result of the imaginative creativity of the evangelist or the corporate experience of his community."[51] For generations scholars have raised questions at this point.

There is a metaphysical problem rooted in the fact that the classic christological formulation of Chalcedon is stated in the "person" and "nature" categories of Greek philosophy. The heart of this formulation conceives the human-divine nature of Jesus in a particular way not compatible with much of today's philosophic environment. Here is a test case for examining theology's comprehensive task of stating the enduring gospel in ways currently comprehensible and compelling, with the result still being the original and not some new gospel.

In the earliest centuries of the Christian church the perplexing question was how to relate in the one "person" the historical Jesus, a fully divine and a fully human "nature." The Council of Chalcedon judged its conclusion an adequate way of expressing all that the biblical narrative affirms or clearly implies about God incarnate among us. This Council spoke of the two "natures" of Jesus Christ. Christ was said to be of the same essence as God the Father in his divinity and of the same essence as us in his humanity. These two natures are said to be united "without any commingling or change or division or separation," so that by their union "the specific character of each

---

[50] For a detailed discussion of the many answers given to this critical question, see Thomas Oden, *The Word of Life*, systematic theology, vol. 2 (Harper, 1989), chapter 7.

[51] Maurice Wiles, "Can We Still Do Christology?," in A. Malherbre and W. Meeks, eds., *The Future of Christology* (Fortress Press, 1993), 234.

nature is preserved."[52] This formulation became Christian orthodoxy. It reflects the prologue of John 1, the confession of Thomas in John 20, and the emphases in Hebrews 1:8, 1 John 5:20, Romans 9:5, Colossians 1, and Philippians 2.

There is a problem with this two-natures approach, at least as judged by many today. On the one hand, it is argued that the two-natures doctrine is not true to the original biblical witness. Since the Hebrews thought historically and functionally rather than abstractly and ontologically, surely the identity of Jesus should be approached more in terms of what he did and how he fit the divine plan and less in terms of what he was in some abstract philosophic sense. Either the Chalcedonian two-natures view of Jesus' identity (1) makes explicit what really was implicit in biblical thought or (2) is post-biblical doctrinal work that is both different from and to some degree alien to the thrust of the biblical narrative.

On the other hand, whatever the relationship between fifth century and biblical thinking, the real concern is said to lie with the relationship of fifth century to current thinking. It is argued by many that the "substance" metaphysics of the past is not as appropriate as the more current "process" metaphysics that sees reality as spontaneous, not static. This shifting worldview can lead to a significant reshaping of who we understand Jesus to be.[53]

One form of the metaphysical objection is the contention by scholars like Oscar Cullmann that New Testament teachings do not

---

[52] Thomas Finger (*Christian Theology*, vol. 2, 1989, 460-65) notes that many modern theologians are troubled by the philosophic appropriateness of the Hellenistic meaning of "person." They judge the Chalcedonian formulation warped by its overemphasizing of the divine side of the being of Jesus. They prefer to emphasize the human side in order to bring biblical balance. Finger reviews two prominent examples, the christologies of Karl Rahner and Wolfhart Pannenberg, noting both their critiques of and alternatives to Chalcedon and the weaknesses that also trouble their own positions. Finger concludes that Christian theology should not originate from prevailing philosophic notions (fifth or twentieth century), but "from below," from the narrative, the witness found in the biblical data itself. Even so, he sees value in holding to the language of Chalcedon.

[53] See, e.g., John Cobb, Jr., and David Griffin, *Process Theology: An Introductory Exposition* (Philadelphia: The Westminster Press, 1976). These authors work in insightful ways with biblical materials, but out of a different philosophic framework not typical of Christianity as defined doctrinally by the classic creeds.

include an ontological, but only a functional deity of Christ (the divine dimension residing in his *doing* rather than in his *being*). Contemporary "evangelical" scholars dispute this contention.[54] Some have criticized "process" christology in particular.[55] They are certain that the Chalcedonian formulation expresses something vital that needs preserved, something about the eternal *being* of Jesus Christ, not just his historical *doing*, something not fundamentally flawed by its use of categories from ancient Greek philosophy.

Chalcedon, while thought indispensible by conservative scholars, is judged even by them to be not fully adequate for today's philosophic setting. While properly honoring the classic formulation and maintaining the New Testament base, something both new and apostolically authentic seems needed today and has not yet emerged. Noting the increased membership of conservative Christian theologians in organizations like the Society of Christian Philosophers and the American Philosophic Association, Millard Erickson ventures the hope that soon there will come a "supply of useful conceptual tools for relevant and competent expression of incarnational Christology."[56]

Economic and Immanent

In the meantime, certain insights already are available for immediate use by the church. They lie in reflection on the distinction theologians often make between the *economic* Trinity (the differentiated roles of Father, Son, and Spirit observed narratively in the "economy" of salvation) and the *immanent* Trinity (the differentiated Father-Son-Spirit life affirmed to be true within the eternal being of God apart from the immediate biblical story of human salvation). The Believers' Church tradition, of course, prefers the economic which relies on the biblical narrative to illumine human understand-

---

[54] See, e.g., I. Howard Marshall, "Incarnational Christology in the New Testament," and R. T. France, "The Worship of Jesus: A Neglected Factor in the Christological Debate?" in H. Rowdon, ed., *Christ the Lord* (InterVarsity, 1982).

[55] See, e.g., Royce Gruenler, *The Inexhaustible God: Biblical Faith and the Challenge of Process Theism* (Grand Rapids: Baker, 1983).

[56] Millard Erickson, *The Evangelical Mind and Heart* (Grand Rapids: Baker, 1993), 105.

ing of God through awareness of divine action. John Wesley likewise had limited interest in metaphysical speculation, but keen concern for the God known *in Christ for human salvation.*[57]

Some argue that necessarily we are limited to the economic approach. We humans know about what we experience or learn from the experience of others, with any more being only speculation. Of course, humans know God at all only because of prevenient grace and the biblical salvation story with its shaping of our own lives as disciples by the Spirit's power. Whatever we venture to presume about the complex richness of God's own being and life, in and of itself apart from creation, admittedly is an extension of our "economic" knowledge of the Trinity (doing theology "from below"). Even so, surely God's own life is consistent with what is seen in how God relates to the world. God acts in character with who God is.[58] So, by God's *actions* narrated in the biblical story, especially the part about Jesus Christ, we get significant and accurate glimpses into who God eternally is (and thus why God acts and what God expects of us who learn from divine actions). James McClendon summarizes well:

> This "economic versus immanent" question can be expressed thus in our terms: Is the God we know in the story–the One who called Abraham, knew Moses, spoke through the prophets, lived and died and rose again in Jesus Christ, descends upon the church in pentecostal power, demanding our conversion–is this "economic" God the real God, or is there some other, secret God beyond God? The answer of faith is that this is "the true

---

[57] While Wesley's focus tends to be immediate, practical, and soteriological, he nonetheless affirms the traditional position of the historic church on christology. In fact, his *A Letter to a Roman Catholic* sounds like a rehearsal of the Nicene-Constantinopolitan Creed. Even so, such affirmation for Wesley related more to "the Eastern Orthodox stress on the full coinherence of the three distinct and equal Divine 'Persons' than with the Western tendency toward One God who is revealed to be Father, Son, and (often, subtly subordinate) Spirit" (Randy Maddox, *Responsible Grace*, 1994, 139).

[58] See Karl Barth, *Church Dogmatics* I:1 (2nd ed., 1975), 384-489.

God" (1 Jn. 5:20); the "economic" doctrine is the "immanent" doctrine–this is the identity of God.[59]

The technical trinitarian language is carefully conceived by
Christian theologians not to form a strange riddle, but to proclaim an
enlightening link between being and action, both God's and ours.
Knowing God through Christ by the Spirit eliminates many distortions
found in human perceptions of the true nature and expectations of God.
The trinitarian doctrine "wants to say that God is sovereign, costly love
that liberates and renews life. It wants to say that God's love for the
world, in Christ now at work by the power of the Spirit, is nothing acci-
dental or capricious or temporary. It wants to say that there is no sin-
ister side of God altogether different from what we know in the story
of Jesus who befriended the poor and forgave sinners. God *is* self-
expending, other-affirming, community-building love."[60] God is lovingly graceful and God thus *acts* in loving and graceful ways.

Tanzanian bishop Christopher Mwoleka speaks with a prophetic and practical voice. Christians go wrong when they think the trinity is a puzzle to be solved instead of a model to be lived. We have not
received a riddle to guess about or discard as outdated, but an example to imitate because it reflects the very being of God. God says,
"You shall be holy to me; for I the Lord am holy, and I have separated you from the other peoples to be mine" (Lev. 20:26). Here are two
obviously important evidences of valid Christian life arising directly from a trinitarian vision of God's own way of being. To be holy as
God is holy includes (1) true community, a special way of being united together in love as are Father, Son, and Spirit (Jn. 17:21), and (2)
rich shalom, a harmony of existence and action that is a special way
of being in the world on mission as God's representatives.[61]

---

[59] James McClendon, *Systematic Theology: Doctrine* (Nashville: Abingdon
Press, 1994), 322.

[60] Daniel Migliore, *Faith Seeking Understanding* (Eerdmans, 1991), 63.
Migliore concludes (67-71) that the trinity of God affirms that (1) the eternal life of
God is personal life in relationship, that (2) God exists in community, and that (3) the
life of God is essentially self-giving love.

[61] Christopher Mwoleka, as in G. H. Anderson and T. F. Stransky, eds., *Mission Trends No. 3: Third World Theologies* (N. Y.: Paulist Press, 1976), 151-152.

Justo González goes further. God is love, so for us "life without love is life without God; and if this is a sharing love, such as we see in the Trinity, then life without sharing is life without God; and if this sharing is such that in God the three persons are equal in power, then life without such power sharing is life without God."[62] Implications for Christian life today are many. To live is to love sacrificially. The church is to be an enabling environment of transforming love being shared. To proceed coercively is to leave God's way. To oppress others for reasons of gender, race, or personal greed, grasping for and holding privilege in God's name, is to blaspheme the triune God known in Jesus Christ.

All of these "immanent" insights and implications come from our "economic" awareness of God. This awareness of God in action is dependent on the reliability of our primary source, the Bible. Perception of biblical reliability, particularly with reference to Jesus, has taken significant strides of a positive nature since the distressing vacuum that was left by the shattering assessment of Albert Schweitzer in 1906. Nineteenth-century scholars, he concluded, had lost the reality of Jesus by misrepresenting him in their own images as the ideal man of the modern world. They had been sure that we could not have confidence in the biblical narrative to provide a real picture of the actual Jesus separated from the church's later interpretations of him. So, unconsciously, they had made him in their own image.[63] Is this the sad lot of us all?

Rudolf Bultmann (1884-1976), e.g., accepted such historical skepticism, arguing however that it was no major problem since the central question is not who Jesus was, but who Jesus is for each individual in the existential reality of today. Here is retreat from the necessity of the historical base of the biblical narrative in favor of a radical inwardness. Now, however, there is an extensive reaction to this retreat from history, a "new quest" for the historical Jesus. Ernst Käsemann, a student of Bultmann, realized the significance in the early church of not separating the risen Christ from the humiliated

---

[62] Justo González, *Mañana: Christian Theology from a Hispanic Perspective* (Nashville: Abingdon Press, 1990), 115.

[63] Albert Schweitzer, *The Quest of the Historical Jesus* (1906).

Messiah as he was in the days of his flesh.[64] There is an accurately reported history in the Gospels that takes us directly to the earthly figure of Jesus.[65] The "early believers understood themselves to be conserving a tradition and not to be creating one. They certainly believed that the living Jesus was still in their midst."[66]

Conservative theologians today insist that a "critical" biblical scholarship, minus any anti-supernatural bias, leads to a traditional, incarnational christology linked closely to the historical Jesus. Some of these scholars now see themselves, not pre-critical or un-critical in their approach to biblical studies, but post-critical. They judge themselves "more critical than the radical critics, being willing to submit the methodology itself to critical evaluation and modification."[67] The Gospels, contrary to the conclusions of radical form and redaction critics like Rudolf Bultmann and Norman Perrin, are not full of views of the early church read back to and falsely applied to Jesus. Rather, they are reliable reports of what Jesus said and did and so can be used to build a fair picture of the historical Jesus, and from that an incarnational christology. The New Testament story, in other words, is historically based and accessible in authentic form.

Carl Henry recently sampled the many scholars who have tackled the core issue at hand. Is there a clear congruence, he asks, between the self-understanding of Jesus, the New Testament witness about him, and the influence of a Greek philosophy that supposedly soon transformed a noble teacher into a metaphysical "logos" and then into the Chalcedonian formulation? Henry concludes that the congruence is clear and crucial.[68] Jesus was not inappropriately

---

[64] Käsemann gave his famous lecture on the problem of the historical Jesus in 1953. While agreeing that the Gospels are primarily theological documents (an assumption of the Bultmannian school), he insisted that the writers based their work on historical information about Jesus of Nazareth, so that the Gospels are both *kerygma* (theologically interpreted proclamation) and *historical* narrative.

[65] See Günther Bornkamm's *Jesus of Nazareth* (N. Y.: Harper & Row, 1960).

[66] Stephen Neill, *Jesus Through Many Eyes* (Philadelphia: Fortress Press, 1976), 171.

[67] Ibid., 90. See, e.g., R. T. France, *The Evidence for Jesus* (InterVarsity, 1986), 103.

[68] Carl Henry, *The Identity of Jesus of Nazareth* (Nashville: Broadman Press, 1992), 49.

reconceived into a presumed oneness with the very essence of God by later, speculative, politically controlled theologians. He always was such according to the reliable witness of the New Testament. To know the true identity of Jesus, one should begin with the biblical narrative of his historical life, the base on which theologizing should proceed and Christian life should be modeled.

A Narrative Approach

Focusing then on a narrative approach to determining the true identity of Jesus Christ, we begin by looking within the unfolding biblical narrative.[69] Incarnation means that God is "Emmanuel," God with us. As the prologue to the Gospel of John makes clear, whatever Jesus seemed to the natural eye, in fact he was one with the pinnacle of God's long pursuit of the divine purpose of human redemption. One needs the whole perspective of this biblical narrative to know the Christ.

The biblical narrative originates in the Hebrew Scriptures. There one finds an extended and often frustrating chronicle of divine-human covenant established and broken. Too often Israel regarded the divine promise as belonging exclusively to itself. It was assumed, especially at times when things were going well, that the promise finally had come to realization. After the exodus from Egypt and first settlement in Canaan, then when the Davidic monarchy flourished as a "worldly" power, and again when an end came to the tragic Babylonian exile, Israel rejoiced in the faithfulness of God on its behalf. But increasingly the prophetic voices emphasized that mere national well-being was not the whole of the promise. All the families of the earth were to be included in the scope of any true fulfillment of the promise.

---

[69] Some christologies are developed *from above*, drawing their substance directly from the presumed doctrinal propositions of divine revelation. Some are developed *from below* by featuring the insights gained from human experience. The narrative approach is developing christology *from before* in the sense that meaning is sought first in the unfolding context of the biblical drama of salvation, not in pre-formed theological propositions. That drama speaks both of the reality of revelation and of the significance of an experiential involvement with that revelation if it is to be understood and lived today.

In its earliest form the divine promise to Abraham had said that its intended blessing eventually would be for all the nations (Gen. 12:1-3). Then, in light of Israel's repeated covenant failures, the evolving biblical story-line is that resistance to God's goal is so deep in the human heart that somehow God would make a "new covenant" written on the very hearts of those who would be the people of the divine promise (Jer. 31:31-33). Though such an expectation took various forms by New Testament times, including violent revolution against Rome, the biblical story guides the reader through the maze of expectations and straight to the little town of Bethlehem. Here was the humble place of the birth of the child Jesus. This child would grow, teach, heal, suffer, die, and experience resurrection, an amazing story that forms the historical basis of Jesus becoming known by disciples then and now as the saving Christ of God, the fulfillment of the promise, the hope of the world.

John's Gospel records the "I am" statements as direct claims of Jesus concerning his own nature and mission. Jesus exercised the right to forgive sins (Mk. 2:1-12; cf. Lk. 23:34) and the prerogative of final judgment of all humankind (Jn. 5:22f). He taught that eternal life lay within himself (Jn. 5:26) and assigned to his own teaching the enduring validity of the Word of God (Mk. 13:31). To accept or reject Jesus was to accept or reject God (Matt. 10:40; Lk. 10:16).

In addition, prominent scholars now contend that the substance of the main christological titles–Son of man, Son of God, Christ, the Lord–is present already in the thought and teachings of Jesus himself, and that his claims in this regard are not merely functional. That is, Jesus was not only playing a key salvation role on behalf of the divine; in his very being there was oneness with the divine.[70] Therefore, "the weight of evidence is that Jesus believed he was God's incomparable Son, standing in God's place with divine authority and right and determining the destiny of human beings according to their response to his life and work."[71]

---

[70] See, e.g., C. F. D. Moule, *The Origin of Christology* (Cambridge: University Press, 1977) and I. Howard Marshall, *The Origins of New Testament Christology* (Downers Grove, Ill.: InterVarsity, 1976).

[71] Carl Henry, op. cit., 50. This stress on New Testament unity is, of course, not to deny that there is considerable diversity and theological development within the

The point is that there is no significant discrepancy between the pre-Easter self-understanding of Jesus and the post-Easter christology of the early church. The church in its theological enthusiasm did not "invent" the Jesus of faith; instead, in its faithfulness, it developed theological reflections based solidly on the Jesus of history. The christological outlook of these reflections no doubt discloses some development. The key point is that such development remained in essential continuity with the real Jesus known by the lakeside, on the dusty paths, on that "old rugged cross," and in dramatic encounters after the resurrection. The later theological unfolding was a refinement of what Jesus and his followers had affirmed from the beginning.

The church's later high christology seems to build on four observations: (1) that Jesus operated with divine power and authority; (2) that he was able to bestow such divine power and authority on some of his followers during his ministry; (3) that he believed a rejection of his ministry meant a judgment of that person at the eschaton; and (4) by contrast, that an acceptance of Jesus and his mission got one into God's *malkut* and secured a resurrection at the messianic banquet.[72] The New Testament evidence suggests that Jesus saw himself as God's royal Son and that throughout his ministry he acted in light of his belief that "he was called to a messianic mission, and that he had been endowed with the necessary divine knowledge, power, and authority by God's Spirit to carry out that mission to Israel."[73] The seeds of later christological development really are found in the actual relationships, deeds, and words of the historical Jesus.

The church did not create the good news about Jesus, but over time evolved more sophisticated expressions of its meaning in changing circumstances. What later was unfolded theologically was the original New Testament witness that in Jesus Christ dwelt "all the fullness of the Godhead bodily" (Col. 2:9). Carl Henry insists with the

---

New Testament itself. Rather, it is to affirm an essential unity and a pattern of complementarity instead of confusion, contradiction, or outright invention.

[72] Ben Witherington, *The Christology of Jesus* (Minneapolis: Fortress Press, 1990), 274.

[73] Ibid., 268.

church across the centuries that "the truth of the Christian religion is, in the first and last analysis, tied to the affirmation of Jesus Christ as the one incarnate divine Savior."[74]

Even so, some scholars judge as diverse indeed the evidence of the New Testament regarding the relation of Jesus to God, so much so that we are said to be left to choose what appears best to our modern sensitivities. A better view is to recognize a significant unity among a range of surface differences in the biblical narrative. The the real identity of Jesus emerges first in his human particularity rather than in an abstract concept of his divine nature. The New Testament approach also begins with an historical narrative about Jesus that then leads to christological reflections. A formalized christology developed especially when the missionary impulse of the early church required translations of the Jewish Messiah. The real and resurrected Jesus was rethought and reproclaimed in categories of the Hellenistic world. The resulting categories are timely, but not necessarily timeless.

Paul's first epistles focus much on Christ's death, resurrection, and eventual return. Soon the early church realized that it was crucial to ground these marvelous events and expectations in the earthly history of Jesus (cf. Lk. 1:1-4). The motivation for writing the Gospels was largely to connect the risen Christ with the earthly Jesus. Likewise, the theological formulations about Christ emerging in the fourth and fifth centuries left an important practical vacuum. These creeds included ontological definitions of Jesus as "wholly God" and "wholly man," a person with two natures interacting in a carefully defined manner. Monotheism was preserved while high claims were made for Jesus, without any denial of his incarnate existence as a real human being. This has become the widely accepted *orthodox* base of Christians. But a *radical* dimension also is needed. The goal is Christ-likeness, serious discipleship.

---

[74] Carl Henry, op. cit., 58.

Guided by Deep Structure

We should resist seeing any creedal statement as the absolute word, the final way of saying something best for all time. J. Denny Weaver points out that the fourth/fifth century statements about Christ "are the end product of one kind of translation of the Jesus narratives into another worldview. However, as a conclusion specific to a worldview, this christology should not be awarded the status of an absolute norm to which all other statements must conform."[75] One thing they lack, for instance, is any focus on the life and teachings of Jesus. That focus would tie theology to ethics, doctrine to discipleship. Back to the Bible one should go to recover the narrative beginning for a truly biblical christology. This norming base then is to be translated freshly into each current setting as theological reflection. Dedicated Christian discipleship is always to be directed by the historical life of Jesus.[76]

A return to the Gospels and the earthly life of Jesus opens the practical door to the special way of life belonging to the Kingdom of God, the way that was inaugurated among us with the coming of Jesus. The rudiments of theology should become the motives for mission. They allow for fresh ways of conceptualizing the person and work of Jesus without a loss of the biblical foundation. The goal is never merely to get just right an abstract doctrine about Jesus as the

---

[75] J. Denny Weaver, "Perspectives on a Mennonite Theology," *Conrad Grebel Review* (Fall, 1984), 200.

[76] A clear example of tying together the historical Jesus, the contemporary setting, and the call to practical discipleship was set forth in Howard Thurman's *Jesus and the Disinherited* (Abingdon Press, 1949). As an African-American seeking to shape christology in a way relevant to the experience of this people, Thurman recalls that the biblical narrative identifies Jesus as a poor Jew, a member of an oppressed minority. Who, then, is Jesus for today's downtrodden? Thurman sees Jesus avoiding the options of active violence and passive withdrawal and instead offering to the Jews of his day a form of resistance based on the Kingdom of God understood as an internal reality that nonetheless is relevant to outward circumstances. James Evans (*We Have Been Believers*, Fortress Press, 1992) notes two biblical references of Thurman that became "central motifs in the subsequent development of christology in black theology" (85). They are "the Kingdom of God is in us" and "the Spirit of the Lord is upon me [Jesus], because he hath anointed me to preach the gospel to the poor." These themes emerge directly from the biblical narrative of Jesus and lead to the demand for current discipleship.

Christ (although some doctrines clearly are more faithful to the biblical witness than others!). God wants disciples of Jesus to get just right *a special way of life*, the Jesus way, modeled in Galilee and Jerusalem before it was expressed in classic creeds.

Within the New Testament itself one sees several interpretations of the Jesus Story made by early Christians in relation to differing worldviews already being faced. In chapter one of Colossians, for example, Jesus is presented as superior to the presumed network of superterrestrial powers. In chapter one of John, Jesus is said to be prior to a kind of gnostic hierarchy. The book of Hebrews views Jesus in relation to an elaborate Jewish sacrificial system. These worldviews tend not to be our own today. Therefore, it follows that twentieth-century theologians can and should exercise the same kind of discretion in christological interpretation exercised by the biblical theologians and those of the following centuries.

This discretion begins by reestablishing the uniqueness of Jesus and his visible representation of the Kingdom of God on earth, based mostly on the Gospel accounts. Then modern theologians "will develop christologies which account for the biblical materials and the modern cosmology."[77] Biblical materials are basic, all language about God is metaphorical, and theological concepts, to be helpful, should be shaped to the times. Always, discipleship in the context of our times is the immediate, practical goal. Therefore, the task now is "to make another translation of 'Jesus is Lord' from the narratives about Jesus to our worldview."[78]

To illustrate, John Howard Yoder surveys the christologies found in John 1, Hebrews, Colossians 1, and Revelation 5.[79] They are diverse. Each was an affirmation of Jesus the Christ in response to a prevailing thought system seeking to absorb Jesus as a new footnote to itself. Each of these New Testament christologies brings the story

---

[77] Weaver, ibid., 198-99.

[78] Ibid., 205. Weaver notes particularly "process" philosophy as a shaping worldview in our times, saying that it can serve well the theologian's cause, but with qualifications (207).

[79] Yoder's presentation was at the Believers' Church conference at Bluffton College (Ohio), October, 1980. A revised version is found in his *The Priestly Kingdom: Social Ethics as Gospel* (University of Notre Dame Press, 1984, rev. ed., 1994).

of Jesus to a competing system and demonstrates in that system's thought environment that Jesus is superior to the limits of that world-view. Each New Testament christology, observes Yoder, shares a common "deep structure" as it faces a given challenge in its distinctive way. That structure: (1) places Jesus above and in charge of the cosmos; (2) identifies the lordship of Christ by focus on the rejection and suffering of Jesus in human form; (3) affirms the pre-existence of Christ, co-essential with the Father and participating in creation and providence; and (4) teaches that writer and readers can share by faith in the victory of Jesus.

No one New Testament christology, then, is the ultimate or exclusive one, although they share a common historical base, set of themes, and discipleship implications. So, when developing christology in a worldview setting different from those glimpsed in the New Testament, "one cannot simply repeat one of these christologies developed for another worldview, but rather must begin anew with the Jewish Messiah and make a fresh translation for the different cosmology."[80] The Apostles', Nicene, and Chalcedonian creeds are three such translations, very important and instructive ones for the thought worlds of their times. But they are not the last word, the ultimate translation for all settings and times. Instead, "what is authoritative is the process of developing christology from the Jewish Messiah to the new cosmology on the basis of the deep structure which Yoder demonstrated to stand behind the four [New Testament] christologies on which he commented."[81]

Consequently, a narrative approach to christology is crucial. One begins with the stories of the historical Jesus that report as christological raw material his Jewishness, teaching, deeds, death, and resurrection, all together making present the Kingdom of God and making inevitable certain conclusions about God's nature, will, ways, and relation to Jesus. The narrative of this real history, with its inspired "deep structure," provides the enduring model from which emerges

---

[80] J. Denny Weaver, "A Believers' Church Christology," *Mennonite Quarterly Review* (April, 1983), 115.

[81] Ibid., 116.

understandings of the deity of Jesus, as well as the model and motive for the mission of his disciples in all times and places.[82]

The conclusion is that "even an orthodox formula like Chalcedon is the beginning and not the end of the discussion...."[83] The discussion shifts with settings and times, while remaining anchored to "the astounding claim of the Christian story," namely that "through this man, Jesus of Nazareth, God has definitively manifested himself. In Jesus Christ, the God of the universe is uniquely present and working in history among us, as validated by the resurrection from the dead.[84] Why, after all, did anyone ever come to regard the crucified Jesus as the incarnate Son of God and ever-living Lord? Because, according to the biblical narrative, after the cross came the resurrection.

Jesus came preaching the arrival of the Kingdom of God and presented himself as the appointed instrument and pivotal personification of God's gracious rule. None other than this Jesus is human existence as God intends. Only this Jesus is the fullness of God's loving and sacrificing presence, enabling again the intended existence for all those who would repent and enter by faith. Clark Pinnock's words are concise and yet comprehensive: Jesus "is all that we are meant to be; he is all that God is for us."[85]

Note the logic that leads to discipleship. God is as Jesus was, meaning that there now is to be a body of disciples, the church, sharing the image of God as in Christ through the Spirit. By being aware of and believing in the historical reality of Jesus as narrated in the biblical story, we now are privileged to know the very heart of God and

---

[82] Weaver emphasizes the "way of life" concerns of the Mennonite tradition. He is sensitive to the lack in the Chalcedonian formula of any reference to the historical life of Jesus or the ethical implications inherent in his deity. This ancient creed addresses the issue in a way appropriate to its setting, but does not represent the full New Testament witness (nor did it claim to do so). For that fullness, Weaver concludes that "christology from a narrative perspective best serves the tradition which sees the church as an extension of Christ and which takes Christ as its model for life as well as the agent of that new life" (ibid., 126).

[83] Clark Pinnock, *Tracking the Maze* (Harper & Row, 1990), 198.

[84] Ibid., 197-198.

[85] Pinnock, in Pinnock and Delwin Brown, *Theological Crossfire* (Grand Rapids: Zondervan, 1990), 144.

thus we are empowered for restoration in God's image in order to become God's community on earth. At the center of a refocusing of Christian theology should always be the Christ, in whom the Kingdom now is inaugurated. Such refocusing is to result in a visible church representing that Kingdom in the world.

Christ Jesus, says the New Testament, "was in the form of God" and he "emptied himself, taking the form of a slave, being born in human likeness. And being found in human form, he humbled himself and became obedient to the point of death, even death on a cross" (Phil. 2:6-8). This emphasis on "emptying" has helped some theologians to conceive how the eternal Son actually could assume humanity without losing his divine personal identity. They argue that the Son temporarily surrendered certain of the divine attributes (omnipotence, omniscience, and omnipresence) and retained others (holiness, truth, and love). Such an argument, while easy to follow, has many problems.[86] Instead of dividing God so that only selected attributes of the divine being remained in Jesus, we propose that a better approach retains more wholeness for the divine in the incarnation.

In fact, if the divine incarnation in Jesus, and especially in the cross and resurrection of Jesus, truly reveals God's nature and will, then the emptying of God was less a setting aside of aspects of divinity to make incarnation possible and more a revelation of who God actually and always is in the fullness of the divine being and intention. God is the serving, loving, Self-giving One, the One who can risk to redeem without ceasing to be wholly God in the process. Jesus was the arrival of God among us in human form, truly human and truly God.

The human form of Jesus, lacking sin and lived in full obedience to God, reveals both the essence of God and the basic design of how we as responding humans also ought to be in this world. To say that Jesus Christ is God with us is to confess belief that God has entered our world, become all that we are, yet without sin, while remaining truly of the essence of God. The God who said "Let light shine out of

---

[86] For a critical discussion of this, see Wolfhart Pannenberg, *Jesus: God and Man* (Philadelphia: Westminster, 1968), 307-323.

darkness" in the process of the original creation is the same God who now, for the sake of re-creation, has shone in our hearts and in our history to give the light of the knowledge of the glory of God. Where is that marvelous light to be seen? In the face of Jesus Christ (2 Cor. 4:6). Where should it lead? To right thinking about God in Christ, of course. But beyond careful theological thought, there is to be dedicated discipleship.

Creeds and Discipleship

Christian creeds often are claimed by "sectarian" Christians to have been conceived and worded in ways that are fully dependable, and thus are still to be used for judging, controlling, and dividing from any who deviate from them. The doctrine of the "two natures" of Christ, for example, took shape in a particular time and intellectual, political, and ecclesiastical setting. Nonetheless, while most dogmatic formulations did come later than the experience of the first disciples and the writing of the New Testament, the major ones, the Apostles', Nicene, Chalcedonian, etc., certainly were intended to state with care essential ideas assumed to be resident in the New Testament witness. There is a normative foundation, the biblical, but a developing and always fragile conceptualizing and creedal articulating of that foundation.

Creeds have their place and their limitations in the church's current life, even the Chalcedonian statement about Jesus Christ. William Barr's caution is valid: "Christian faith is commitment finally not to a christological theory or doctrine, but to a person. And it is in discipleship to and with him that we are led in faith into new and fuller understanding of the truth, including the truth concerning him."[87] This important caution should be disciplined, however, by an equally important observation of Clark Pinnock. He expresses concern that "liberal" theologies, rather than seeking appropriate new translations of the biblical foundation, in fact tend to propose its denial and

---

[87] William Barr, "Christology in Disciples Tradition," in K. Lawrence, ed., *Classic Themes of Disciples Theology* (Fort Worth: Texas Christian University Press, 1986), 25.

replacement by modern presuppositions and perspectives.[88] Being overly fluid theologically, disconnecting from the norming role of the biblical narrative, can open one to almost anything. Valid Christian theology, while always dynamic in one sense, is never disconnected from the control of its biblical foundation.

In response to Pinnock, Delwin Brown emphasizes the datedness of classic creeds. He suggests carrying the doctrine of the incarnation to what he sees as its logical conclusion by now seeking to speak of God and God's activities in terms of "our modern knowledge."[89] Noting always the continuing frailty of our theological speaking, we do speak of God the best we can, and in terms of the best philosophical perspective and historical evidence we now know. For Brown, "God is incarnate in Jesus. Jesus is a sacrament making present the power of God to transform life in ways that we do not manage on our own."[90]

Pinnock is happy to champion Brown's affirmation that "God is incarnate in Jesus." But, as in the tradition of the historic church, he offers significant objection to an inference included in Brown's use of these words. Rather than seeing Jesus as the *decisive* and *necessary* event of God's redemptive incarnation for humankind, a "process theist,"[91] warns Pinnock, sees "redemptive grace everywhere in the world in principle quite independent of Jesus, though evoked for us by him."[92] If the cross of Christ had not happened, runs such process thinking, nothing would have been lost concerning the suffering and saving God in our world except that Jesus would not have been the vehicle for evoking that "Christ pattern" for the Christian community.[93]

---

[88] Clark Pinnock, in Pinnock and Delwin Brown, *Theological Crossfire* (Grand Rapids: Zondervan, 1990), 151.

[89] Ibid., 158.

[90] Ibid., 163.

[91] By process theist is meant one who draws upon the process categories of the philosophy of Alfred North Whitehead and Charles Hartshorne to conceive and word understandings of God, Christ, human salvation, historical process, etc. For example, see John Cobb, Jr., and David Griffin, *Process Theology: An Introductory Exposition* (Philadelphia: The Westminster Press, 1976).

[92] Clark Pinnock, in Pinnock and Brown, op. cit., 173.

[93] Even so, process thought brings valuable insights and effectively counters some weaknesses of many expressions of classic theology. Note, for instance, its cen-

To the contrary, the New Testament witness is one of particularity. The classic christological creeds of Nicea and Chalcedon still enjoy an ecumenical consensus that declares Jesus Christ to be truly God, truly human, truly one. Here is an enduring attempt of the church to be faithful to the figure it sees in the biblical pages and experiences in its own life. Chalcedon may not be the final formulation of christology, but it has proven durable as a signpost that keeps attempts at fresh formulation from straying outside the limits of basic biblical revelation.

To summarize, the Christian confession of God is triune in nature because of Christian commitment to the authority of the biblical revelation of God's salvation initiative in the real life of Jesus. A doctrine of "trinity" as such is not revealed biblically in so many words as a finished doctrinal statement (a narrative theology does not function that way). But a summary description of the Scripture's witness to God's unfathomable love rests upon such love being known in the incarnate Jesus as experienced and celebrated in the community of faith by the witness of the Spirit. The good news is about God's love, revealed in Jesus the Christ, through the Spirit, as reported in the biblical witness and now seen in the church that is formed by this news.

The goal is discipleship, being with Jesus, knowing Jesus, coming to live like Jesus in the power of the Spirit of Jesus. Before such discipleship can become reality, would-be disciples must know who Jesus is and what he has *done* to enable new life and provide good news for the world. The difficulties of determining the *person* of Jesus are resolved in part by exploring the biblical narrative that also speaks of the *work* he accomplished. A consideration of the mission of Jesus is the task of the next chapter.

---

tral critiques of what it considers typical distortions of the true nature of God (Cobb and Griffin, op. cit., 8-10).

CHAPTER FIVE

CHRIST THE SAVIOUR: MISSION

—

"For us all and for our salvation he [Jesus] came down from heaven....
For our sake he was crucified under Pontius Pilate; he suffered and was buried.
On the third day he rose from the dead in accordance with the scriptures;
he ascended into heaven and is seated at the right hand of the Father.
We believe in...the forgiveness of sins."

—

It was important in the last chapter to examine the identity of Jesus so that in this one we might understand better his saving mission. We are told that Jesus the Christ came to save humanity from sin (Matt. 1:21), that for our sake he was crucified under Pontius Pilate (Nicene Creed). Only God-with-us could save. In fact, none other than God *was* with us in Jesus of Nazareth, the Christ of God. God was with us to make possible our reconciliation to God and to restore our true partnership with God in the renewing of all creation. Such reconciliation and restoration was the work of Jesus.

Reflection on the meaning of Jesus Christ as the Saviour of humanity began in the narrative context of the lives of the earliest disciples of Jesus. The reality that gave rise to the whole New Testament was this dramatic testimony: Christ is risen! Given the resurrection, new perspectives and relationships arose. It was necessary and now possible to reconsider the real meaning of the cross of Jesus. How did the death of a man condemned as a criminal relate to, even account for the wonderful new realities the disciples had come to know? How was the pain of the cross tied to the tidings of salvation? The resurrection of Jesus finally opened doors of understanding.

Since its earliest years, the Christian community has witnessed gladly that "Christ died for our sins in accordance with the scriptures" (1 Cor. 15:3). Variations on this central affirmation appear in what may be excerpts of early Christian hymns (Eph. 1:7; Phil. 2:7-8; Col. 1:20; 1 Pet. 2:21). The Apostles' and Nicene creeds recall the historical events believed essential to the work of Christ. Their focus is on the main features of what happened, events bringing fresh potential for all people to be reconciled with God. Speculative explanations of the "how" of such reconciliation are avoided in these classic creeds, although theologians have sought for centuries to explain the means of Christ's salvation work. Their explanations have tended to feature one of several patterns (see below), with no consensus on any one of them being a final explanation apart from the others.

Confessing that "Jesus is Lord!" in response to the gospel story and experiencing a reconciliation with God made possible in Christ are more important than rational attempts at explanation. This priority, believing and actually being reconciled to God before seeking any Enlightenment-like explanations of the how of it all, is what we see in the New Testament. The earliest Christians "saw and experienced this [reconciling] reality personally in Jesus' ministry to Judaism's outcasts, in the community-creating experience of Pentecost, and in the missionary ingathering of Gentiles in Palestine, Samaria, Syria, and finally in Asia Minor and Greece. From the earliest days of the primitive community in Jerusalem, the apostles began to find and use images to communicate and to explain the reality which they had experienced."[1] The early believers received, experienced, and proclaimed saving grace in Christ while they remained in the process of seeking to understand. There was immediate joy in the fact of it; there was ongoing process in probing the how of it.

Attempts at explanation are inevitable. The first ones were more celebration images than creedal formulas. These images, the biblical alternatives to literal definitions and formalized doctrines, at first came from the Hebrew Scriptures. They include sacrifice, vicarious suffering, ransom, redemption, liberation, justification, etc. These all are provocative pictures that point to, illuminate, and hope to communicate a reality which is bigger than the terms themselves. The fact is that "no single term (or combination of terms, for that mat-

---

[1] John Driver, *Understanding the Atonement for the Mission of the Church* (Scottdale, Pa.: Herald Press, 1986), 15.

ter) is capable of wholly containing the meaning of the atoning work of Christ."[2] Nevertheless, they surely set the scene and inspire crucial insights that guide us aright as we seek to receive and share the most wonderful of all realities.[3]

The New Israel

Since Jesus was a Jew claiming to fulfill in his own ministry the intent and expectations of the Jewish law and prophets (Matt. 5:17), we begin consideration of the mission of Christ by looking at the church. Jesus inspired into being a new community of believers, both continuous and discontinuous with ancient Israel.

If "people of God," "body of Christ" and "chosen race" are prominent New Testament metaphors for the church, another metaphor presents equally dramatic and demanding results, as well as difficult questions. The church is said to be the "new Israel." The language of Paul indicates that the terminology used for Israel in the Hebrew Scriptures is now to be applied to the church of Jesus Christ. The church is "the elect of God" (1 Thess. 1:4; 2 Thess. 2:13), the offspring of Abraham (Gal. 3:7, 14, 28-29), thus the "Israel of God" (Gal. 6:16). The writer of Hebrews uses the priesthood of Israel as an analogy of the greater priesthood of Christ. Peter declares the church "God's own people" (1 Pet. 2:9) by drawing on Exodus 19:5-6. What is to be avoided, however, is any inference that the Jewish and Christian communities should now be separated sharply. Such a gulf evolved only after about the year 135, the original "fall of the church" when its tie to Judaism was virtually severed.[4]

---

[2] Ibid., 16.

[3] Driver shares a significant concern. While it is true that "metaphorical language generally carries the ability to communicate more powerfully (and more imaginatively) than purely prosaic language," that power is lost when authentic experience fades. Once separated from their experience base, the images tend to lose their power and become merely "a yardstick to measure orthodoxy" (op. cit., 18-19). Driver describes his own view of the atonement as a "radical evangelical" approach. Real understanding of reconciliation with God always lies close to the actual experience of being so reconciled.

[4] John Howard Yoder identifies the "fall" this way, as quoted in James McClendon, *Systematic Theology: Doctrine* (Nashville: Abingdon Press, 1994), 351-354.

The church of Christ is an outgrowth, a flowering of what God began in Israel. It exists in continuity with a historical movement stretching back to Abraham and carries forward the memory of God's mighty deeds and faithfulness through the centuries. Christian claims can be established only by narrating this long story of God's redemptive presence with fallen creation. The church fulfills rather than replaces God's intentions for Israel,[5] meaning at least that the church continues to have a significant relationship to its Hebrew heritage, even while it embodies a new and multi-ethnic form of the covenant community through which all peoples will be blessed (Jer. 31:31-34; Acts 2:36; Eph. 3:6; Heb. 8:8).[6] The very structuring of the narrative of the life of Jesus as reported in the Gospels is influenced significantly by key themes of the Hebrew Scriptures.[7]

Few issues have been more complex and controversial in the twentieth century than the current status of the Jewish people in the ongoing work of God. Have the Jews been removed from the script of the later chapters of the biblical story because they failed to receive their Messiah in the coming of Jesus? Is the Christian church now the true Israel, eliminating the former Israel in God's eyes and plans? Is salvation available within contemporary Judaism apart from specific faith in Jesus Christ? Is the modern nation of Israel central to or unrelated to the sequence of events that will bring human history to a close? Was the tragic Holocaust of Nazi Germany the deserved judgment on those who "killed Jesus" or a horrible inhumanity driven mostly by a lethal mixture of ethnic prejudice and political imperialism on the part of those guilty of this travesty?

---

[5] The replacement or "suppressionist" view has become common in many Christian circles. Such, however, is not necessarily the clear teaching of the New Testament. See, e.g., David Efroymson, et. al., eds., *Within Context: Essays on Jews and Judaism in the New Testament* (Collegeville, Minn.: The Liturgical Press, 1993).

[6] For one of many excellent expositions of the features of this continuing relationship between the Jewish heritage and the church, see Marvin Wilson, *Our Father Abraham* (Eerdmans, 1989). For a brief review of the way the Christian church has viewed and related to the Jewish community, see Clark Williamson, "The Teaching and Practice of Contempt" in Williamson, ed., *The Church and the Jewish people* (St. Louis: Christian Board of Education--Disciples, 1994). Much in church history has been unChristlike, often tragic for Jews.

[7] Willard Swartley, *Israel's Scripture Traditions and the Synoptic Gospels: Story Shaping Story* (Peabody, MA.: Hendrickson Publishers, 1994).

How should such a holocaust influence Christian theology?[8] Should we agree with Markus Barth that "after Auschwitz and the early church-supporting pogroms our [the Christians'] only task is to be penitent and let ourselves be converted?"[9] Since World War II many Christian bodies have taken the paradoxical view that God's special covenant with the Jewish people remains in force, calling into question for many Christians any direct attempt to convert Jews to Christianity.[10] Christians believe God has acted definitively in Jesus Christ, requiring the church to proclaim this good news to all persons. But, are the Jews to be seen as a significant exception?

Originally God elected Israel. The Abrahamic covenant, reads the biblical story, reached a point of climactic crisis when a new covenant came into being with Christ. But how are old and new covenants now related? One view is that the church now is the true Israel in a way implying that God's former covenant with Israel has ended. Another is that, parallel to the new covenant, God still is faithful to the "old" covenant, that salvation is possible even apart from Jesus Christ, and that sharing the Christian good news with today's Jews verges on arrogance and may even be a subtle form of anti-Semitism.

What is appropriate in this special circumstance of Christians and Jews? Clearly appropriate is at least: (1) Christian recognition of the crucial role played by the Hebrew Scriptures in Christian faith; (2) encouragement of "completed" Jews (Jewish converts to Christianity) to draw upon their Hebrew heritage as enrichment to their faith in Christ; and (3) commitment to resist the continuing scourge of anti-

---

[8] See Clark Williamson, *A Guest in the House of Israel: Post-Holocaust Church Theology* (Louisville: Westminster/John Knox, 1993). Williamson writes: "If we ask what Christianity is, the anti-Jewish answer is: everything new, good, spiritual, and universal that the old, bad, carnal, and ethnocentric Jews can never be. Every Christian doctrine can be and was interpreted through the lens of this anti-Jewish hermeneutic" (5).

[9] Markus Barth, *Jesus the Jew*, trans. by Frederick Prussner (Atlanta: John Knox, 1978), 94.

[10] For many such statements, see *The Theology of the Churches and the Jewish People* (Geneva, Switz.: World Council of Churches Pub., 1988). Michael McGarry refers to Judaism as "a viable, integrated and fully adequate response to God's call for faithfulness as found in the Hebrew Scriptures" (*Christology After Auschwitz*, Paulist Press, 1977), 7-8.

Semitism. Regarding the core question about whether or not the church now has replaced Israel in the drama of human redemption, careful biblical interpretation is required.

New Testament books like Luke and Acts reflect a trend in the early church for the gospel to take hold in the Gentile world. This led to fresh ways for the young church to give expression to its faith in the person and work of Jesus Christ. Very early there was the issue of how to conceive the Christian gospel in its traditional Jewish setting. Five New Testament books appear especially written to work on the theological task of thinking through how the Christian faith relates to its Hebrew heritage (Matthew, Romans, James, Hebrews, and Revelation).

In Matthew, Jesus is seen as King of the Jews and the fulfillment of earlier prophecy (5:17). He is Lord of the Covenant (chaps. 5-7), functioning as the new Moses; he is Lord of the disciples (chap. 10), the kingdom of God (chap. 13), the church (chap. 18), and the future (chaps. 24-25), a future extending far beyond the bounds of Judaism. If not displacement of Israel, there certainly is in Matthew an implied enlargement beyond Israel. The Gospel of Mark, especially harsh in characterizing the Jews, clearly pictures the church as having superseded Judaism (12:6-9).[11] Several highly judgmental references to "the Jews" found in John's Gospel need to be interpreted in the historical context of their writing.[12]

Chapters 9-11 of Romans are crucial. Paul both deplores the failure of some of his Jewish contemporaries to receive God's good news in Jesus and warns believers in Jesus not to be arrogant since God has not abandoned Israel. He identifies the Israel who receives the Christ as the remnant (Rom. 9:27). Not all Israelites actually are such merely because they are descendants of Abraham (9:6-7). Those Jews who failed to embrace Jesus as their Christ are said to have incit-

---

[11] It is likely that the four Gospels tend to portray Jesus and Jewish people, practices, and institutions in reference to their own times (70-95 C.E.). Several sources of church acrimony toward Judaism had arisen by then. See Ronald Allen, "Judaism and Early Christianity in the New Testament," in Clark Williamson, ed., *The Church and the Jewish People* (St. Louis: Christian [Disciples] Board of Education, 1994), 15-23.

[12] See David Efroymson, et. al., eds., *Within Context: Essays on Jews and Judaism in the New Testament* (Collegeville, Minn.: The Liturgical Press, 1993).

ed God's displeasure, so that "through their stumbling salvation has come to the Gentiles" (11:11). But there seems to be some level at which God's rejection of unbelieving Israel is not the whole of the story.

In Romans 11 the original covenant made with Abraham is likened to an olive tree that does not wither and die when some of its branches become barren. The dead branches of unbelieving Israel are broken off and in their place are grafted fresh branches from a wild olive tree (Gentile believers)–although the root remains and the original but now barren branches can be regrafted if later they come to believe (11:23). Gentiles are now heirs together with Israel, members together of one body (Eph. 3:6b). Believing non-Jews have a new identity. Their story is now rooted in and an extension of Israel's story. The church, planted firmly in Hebraic soil, knows its true identity only in connection with Israel. The biblical story is one story. In the New Testament we see interactive sub-plots, story shaping story (the Hebrew tradition interacting with the revelation in Jesus the Christ).

Will the potential regrafting of the now barren branches of Israel ever happen? Certain of Paul's assumptions suggest that they will. Even if Israel is faithless, God is faithful (Rom. 3:3-4). Paul says, "as regards the gospel they are enemies of God, for your sake; but as regards election they are beloved for the sake of their ancestors" (11:28). There will be a time when "all Israel will be saved" (11:26), based finally on the only ground of salvation, faith in Jesus Christ as Lord and Savior (Rom. 10:5-17; 11:23).[13] Israel is the root that sustains the church (11:18); the church is the agent of gospel proclamation that allows Israel to appreciate the fullness of its own glorious heritage, including the person and work of Jesus Christ, and thus final-

---

[13] Gabriel Fackre explains: "Abraham is 'the father of faith,' and those who are his true children in Israel before Christ are 'saved'–albeit by the retroactive 'application of the benefits of Christ,' as the traditional teaching has it." What about the future tense of Paul's comment that "all Israel will be saved"? Fackre cautions that this "all" should be read in light of the truth that "not all Israelites truly belong to Israel" (Rom. 9:6b). True heirs are limited to those with Abrahamic faith. By implication, "those in the future (after Christ) who stand in this faithful line constitute 'all Israel.' Whoever has Abrahamic faith, then and now, has saving faith" (*Ecumenical Faith in Evangelical Perspective*, Eerdmans, 1993, 164). For this to be so, all those who will be redeemed must in some way encounter and be accountable to their Redeemer, Jesus Christ.

ly to claim its intended destiny (10:8-17; 1 Cor. 1:21-24).[14] In Romans 9-11 Paul appears to argue that "the people of God is not the Christian community *instead* of the Jewish community, but Israel and the church *together*."[15]

There seem to be two biblical non-negotiables not easily coordinated. First, the New Testament implies that the Abrahamic covenant, including the promise of salvation for "all Israel," is irrevocable. Second, the New Testament clearly teaches a christological singularity, the new covenant in Jesus Christ as the one way to salvation. Jesus said, "do not think that I have come to abolish the law and the prophets; I have come not to abolish but to fulfill" (Matt. 5:17). But how can Israel's covenant with God continue after God has come in Christ? The two non-negotiables are inseparable as promise and fulfillment. The heritage of Israel is not annulled, but has flowered to fullness in Christ. In this sense it persists forever. None has room to boast. Neither Christians nor Jews are called to be God's privileged elite. All are sinners saved only by grace.[16] The biblical story is one story, understood best in light of Jesus Christ.

Christian scholar Donald Bloesch finds common cause with Jewish scholar Franz Rosenzweig. Rosenzweig sees Judaism as "the star of redemption" and Christianity as "the rays of that star."[17] Bloesch sees the star "not as the religion of Judaism but as the

---

[14] Shirley Guthrie, "Romans 11:25-32," *Interpretation* (July, 1984), 286.

[15] There is, therefore, no irremediable curse because of the Jews' rejection of Jesus. Both the Jews and Romans, directly involved in the death of Jesus, acted out of ignorance (Luke 23:34; Acts 3:17-18; 13:27-30). "The real cause of Christ's death was God himself, who decreed that the Messiah must suffer" (Donald Bloesch, "All Israel Will Be Saved," *Interpretation*, April, 1989, 135). The New Testament narrative says that, rather than an avenging God, God in Christ has assumed the guilt and shame so that those who believe might not perish (Rom. 4:25; 2 Cor. 5:21; Gal. 3:13).

[16] Sidney Hall says that Christian theology with respect to the Jews can have credibility today only if it is defensible while standing in front of the ovens of Auschwitz and realizing the destructive results of Christianity's classic anti-Semitism. He asks: "Is it possible for Christianity to cast off its rejection and replacement theology and uphold the foundations on which Christian tradition rests? Yes! Such a theology can be accomplished and it can be demonstrated through Paul" (*Christian Anti-Semitism and Paul's Theology*, Augsburg Fortress, 1993, 21).

[17] Donald Bloesch, "All Israel Will Be Saved," *Interpretation* (April, 1989), 138-139.

covenant with Israel reaffirmed and fulfilled in Jesus Christ." The rays of the star "signify not Christianity as a religion but the proclamation of the gospel in the power of the Spirit." To shift metaphors, Bloesch says that Christianity and Judaism can be likened to "two moons that reflect the light of the Sun of righteousness (Mal. 4:2), who, in Christian perspective, is identical with the Son of God incarnate in Jesus of Nazareth. These moons do not possess any light in themselves but point to the light that resides in the living Christ." They share connected roles in the one biblical story, which finally is the Christ-Story, read best in light of the life, death, and resurrection of Jesus of Nazareth.

These two intimately related faith communities also can be compared to an orchestra that plays for the world the song of God's holiness and love. "Those instruments representing the heritage of Israel, when played by themselves, are in discord." On the other hand, there is "incompletion or imbalance in the symphonic rendition when the contribution of Israel is deleted. It is only when the orchestra functions as the Israel of God (Gal. 6:16), the eschatological unity of the two traditions, that we have a perfect and full witness of the Wisdom of God incarnate in Christ."[18] To know the truth, one must tell the whole story. The story of the God of loving grace with us in our sin is understood only in light of its climax, Jesus Christ. This climax is incomprehensible apart from the earlier chapters of the story, God in covenant with Israel.

Is witness to Jews on behalf of Christ appropriate? Yes. The biblical revelation seeks to illumine all its participants from the vantagepoint of its own fulfillment in Christ. According to Paul, the Jews actually have priority in Christian evangelism since the gospel "is the power of God for salvation to every one who has faith, to the

---

[18] Ibid., 139-140. History has shown that when Christianity separates from its Jewish roots, it either blends into a kind of Enlightenment rationalism or moves toward an ahistorical mysticism. All Scripture is judged rightly by Christians to be inspired, meaning in part that the Hebrew Scriptures, viewed in light of Christ, continue to play a significant role for Christian faith. See John Bright, *The Authority of the Old Testament* (Abingdon Press, 1967, reprint by Baker Book House, 1975). See also Ronald Allen and John Holbert, *Holy Root, Holy Branches: Christian Preaching from the Old Testament* (Nashville: Abingdon Press, 1995).

Jew first and also to the Greek" (Rom. 1:16). Jesus told his disciples that they were to be "witnesses in Jerusalem, and in all Judea and Samaria, and to the ends of the earth" (Acts 1:8). The good news is for all people, although Christian witness to Jews should include acknowledgment of special indebtedness to the Jewish tradition and confession of guilt for Christian complicity through the centuries in anti-Semitism.[19] Such complicity is utterly inappropriate to the gospel of Jesus Christ. Nonetheless, witnessing to Jews concerning the Christ, *their* Christ, is not anti-Jewish. Jesus the Jew is the full flowering of Judaism itself. He came to fulfill.

Jewish-Christian relations since about the year 135 admittedly make current Christian witness to Jews awkward and often unsuccessful. Note:

> It is not the case, as liberal sentiment would have it, that the original gospel has nothing to offer Jewish people. They, too, have needs that Jesus fulfills. They like others can be blessed by the Spirit poured out on "all flesh" at Pentecost. Yet the fateful choice of second-century Christians to isolate their communities from Jewishness, the tragic Jewish participation in this parting, and (most of all) the subsequent centuries of evil poured out upon Jews by professed Christians–all this has made it unlikely that today's informed Jew can even *hear* the good news.[20]

Is the Christian church "the new Israel"? Yes, to the degree that the Christian community faithfully represents the fullness of God in Israel and in Christ. No, if arrogance is involved through a displacement and even persecution attitude toward Jews. The church should not assume that stress on the good news of Christ is of itself an anti-Jewish act, blessed church replacing cursed synagogue.[21] The Hebrew writings are to be understood and appreciated first in their original set-

---

[19] See David Rausch, *Fundamentalist Evangelicals and Anti-Semitism* (Valley Forge, Pa.: Trinity Press International, 1993).

[20] James McClendon, *Systematic Theology: Doctrine* (1994), 361.

[21] See Daniel Spross, in *The Asbury Theological Journal* (Fall, 1990), 21, 24.

tings,[22] but also recognized as finally interpreted best from the perspective of the revelation in Christ, the Messiah of the Jews.

The church of Christ has become an inclusive designation for believing Jews and Gentiles. In this sense it is the new Israel, in full continuity with the Israel of old.[23] The church of Jesus is to be a prophetic voice to the Abrahamic heritage that in part has not yet affirmed its own Messiah. It is to be God's witness to the ends of the earth (Isa. 43:10, 12; 55:4). It is to be a new creation of God through whom all peoples can benefit from the work of Jesus Christ now raised from the dead. To a description of this work we now turn.

Prophet, Priest, and King

From the identity of Jesus as the Christ, described in chapter four, we now move to an exploration of the nature and implications of his mission. Apart from belief in the God-related identity of Jesus, one could not possibly believe in his life-changing mission as described below. Only the fullness of a classic triple affirmation of Jesus' identity, the doctrine of the trinity, allows for the fullness of a consequent affirmation of three "offices" as a way of describing his mission.

Christ's work often has been organized by reference to his embodiment and fulfillment of three "offices" common to the biblical narrative prior to the time of Jesus.[24] The Reformer John Calvin (1509-1564) gave special attention to the Christian meaning of such

---

[22] This also is true of the New Testament writings. See David Efroymson, et. al., eds., op. cit.

[23] As fulfillment of the story and prophetic expectations of the Hebrew Scriptures, Jesus himself can be said to be the new Israel, the only one who truly fulfilled God's expectations of Israel. The church, then, is the new Israel only to the degree that it truly has its being and life "in Him."

[24] Although it has been common in Protestant theology to organize the identity and mission of Jesus Christ into the offices of prophet, priest, and king (as does Karl Barth who sees Jesus fulfilling the functions of these offices as assigned originally to Israel), most emphasis has been placed on the role of priest. Albrecht Ritschl (1822-89) criticizes this as overemphasis (*Justification and Reconciliation*, 428-34). Since the arrival of the kingdom of God was at the center of Jesus' own mission and message, Thomas Finger and others explore aspects of this kingdom as an alternative organizing scheme. Finger

offices.[25] They represent the truths that (1) Jesus reveals God (prophet), (2) reconciles God and humanity (priest), and (3) rules and will rule over all creation (king). Their elaboration by John Wesley (1703-1791) is classic.[26]

Wesley's theology is built on the three offices of Jesus Christ. These offices are derived from the very name Christ, the "anointed." Prophets, priests, and kings in the Hebrew tradition were inducted into office by a ceremony of anointing with oil.[27] In his first sermon in Nazareth (Lk. 4:18) Jesus witnessed to his own anointing with the Holy Spirit on the occasion of his baptism. This brought together in Jesus the functions (offices) of prophet, priest, and king. Wesley tied these to the enabling of human salvation. He saw restored relationship with God featuring an overcoming of the power of sin and a recovering of intended holiness.

Each office is said to answer in Christ a need for salvation in the human heart. (1) We humans are in spiritual darkness and need a prophet to enlighten our minds. The fall into sin has distorted our view of God's will for human life. (2) We are alienated from God and need the mercy of a priest who can mediate a reconciliation. The fall into sin has distorted our standing before God and necessitates forgiveness. (3) We are enslaved to powers and passions that require a kingly power beyond ourselves to bring liberation and renewal. Christ, then, is the physician of our souls who seeks to heal our wounds, calls us to partake of his holiness, removes all barriers to salvation, and mediates the power needed for us to be free of all enslaving powers. He is the light, the link, the liberator.

---

identifies such aspects as the detaching of the nationalistic idea of revenge from the hope of redemption, the poor receiving significant attention, the servant-like departure from the usual notion of how a king is to wield power, in fact, the dawning of a new social reality that valued women and introduced radical new attitudes for human sharing and freedom (*Christian Theology*, vol. 1, 279ff).

[25] John Calvin, *Institutes of the Christian Religion*, Bk. 2, chapter 15.

[26] See Kenneth Collins, *A Faithful Witness: John Wesley's Homiletical Theology* (Wilmore, Ky.: Wesley Heritage Press, 1993), 44-56.

[27] Note H. Ray Dunning, *Grace, Faith and Holiness* (Kansas City: Beacon Hill Press, 1988), 366, n. 6, for an explanation of the frequent exception of the prophets.

Alexander Campbell (1788-1866) describes the priestly work of Jesus as enacting reconciliation of God and the world through his own sacrificial death. Such sacrifice, while not necessary to make God merciful, was nonetheless needed in order for the divine extending of mercy "according to law and justice."[28] Refuting predestinarian theology, Campbell joined teachers like John Wesley before him in insisting that Christ's redemptive work is unlimited in its aim (he died for all), but is limited in its effect since it must be received voluntarily by faith. Campbell notes the prophetic office by calling Christ the "oracle" of God, the one who interprets God's will for humankind. As king, Christ reigns in the life of each believer and in the church because he is "able to do all for us that our condition needs."[29]

The three offices are explained by Campbell this way. Christ as *Prophet* is the dependable revealer of divine truth. Being one with God, he is the perfect manifestation in flesh of God's eternal character (Jn. 1:14) and the essence of what it means for a human being to reflect the image of God. From the depths of the suffering love of Jesus, taught and enacted, comes light for our greatest darkness. Christ as *Priest* is the agent who intercedes, atones, and reconciles God and human sinners. On our behalf Christ suffered and died. God, in the person of the Son, bore the pain of our sin, clearing the way for our full reconciliation when we are willing to appropriate it by faith. Somehow the cruelty of the cross got transformed into our at-one-ment (reconciliation) with God. Christ as *King* is the triumphant Lord, validated by the resurrection, now ruling at the right hand of God. He is victor even over death and stands ready to give us life, releasing us to live truly and eternally.

The three offices are seen commonly as an effective way to overview the whole of Christ's saving work. For instance: "Jesus first appeared as a teacher in the prophetic office; then as high priest and lamb sacrificed in his suffering and death; and finally by his resurrection received his kingdom and remains active [as king] in his

---

[28] Alexander Campbell, *The Christian System* (Bethany, Va.: pub. privately, 1835; reprint, Nashville, Tenn: Gospel Advocate Co., 1964), 23.

[29] Ibid., 36.

office of cosmic governance, as eschatological ruler in this king-dom."[30] Given the diverse themes in the biblical revelation about the mediatorial role of Christ, Thomas Oden's schema,[31] based on the three offices, provides broad perspective on the offices and their related functions:

Prophet	Priest	King
To teach	To sacrifice	To empower
Christ preaches	Christ atones	Christ governs
Pedagogy	Expiation	Guidance, protection
Earthly ministry	Dying ministry	Glorified ministry
Messianic beginning	Messianic act	Messianic consummation
Mosaic type	Aaronic type	Davidic type
The Rabbi	The Lamb	End-Time Governor
God revealed	Humanity redeemed	Redemption applied

Jesus is a prophet like Moses, raised up by God from among his own people (Acts 3:22). He is "a priest forever, according to the order of Melchizadek" (Heb. 7:17). He is the incomparable "King of kings" (Rev. 17:14).

God has engaged human history in Christ, choosing personal presence amid all the fallenness. At the cross of Jesus the opposing powers were encountered and defeated (Col. 2:15). This divine vic-tory is our hope, addressing human guilt with justification, the grip on us of the evil powers with sanctification, and the need of hope beyond death with glorification. The kingdom of God now has been inaugu-rated and we who believe are privileged to live in the glow of its early light. At the second coming of Christ the victory will be complete and demonstrated visibly with the consummation of the kingdom. In the meantime, salvation by divine grace is possible and discipleship by the same grace is essential. To be "saved" by grace is necessarily to live savingly by the same grace.

Life can be redeemed and thus liberated to function redemp-tively in this yet fallen world. Thinking of the finished work of

---

[30] Thomas Oden, *The Word of Life*, systematic theology, vol. 2 (Harper, 1989), 280.

[31] Ibid.

Christ, we should be filled with thanksgiving for the victory found in Christ. We are called to "grow in the grace and knowledge of our Lord and Savior Jesus Christ" (2 Pet. 3:18). Thinking of our freedom and resulting responsibility as fresh carriers of the light of Christ: "No more do we fear the thrones and authorities that rattle their swords in this world, for they have met their match and we are empowered to resist them in the liberation and reconciliation struggles of our time, even as we meet the last enemy, death, in hope."[32]

Many people die prematurely because of the way they live. So it was with Jesus. His lethal problem was not chemical addiction or physical excess or accident of any kind. It was his being so committed to God, so representative of the kingdom of God over against the twistedness of this world, that the world in its perversity was not prepared to understand, accept, even tolerate. So the world retaliated and Jesus died early. His death, however, just as his life, was not without profound meaning. That meaning has been at the heart of his church's life and proclamation ever since. There can be no sharp separation between how and why Jesus lived and how and why he died, or between who he was in the flesh and what he did on the cross for all flesh, or between who he was as Son and what the Father was doing through him.[33]

Nor should there be any separation between the work of Christ in resolving past human alienation from God and his work of enabling the present discipleship of believers. John Wesley was concerned that Christian ministers inculcate the *pattern* of Christ's work in the Methodist people. He wanted to insure "that God's grace known in Christ as Priest was never separated from the response of discipleship

---

[32] Gabriel Fackre, *The Christian Story*, rev. ed. (Eerdmans, 1978, 1984), 154.

[33] Note, however, the observation of Theodore Jennings. The phrase "was crucified" is pivotal in the Apostles' Creed and St. Paul decided "to know nothing among you except Jesus Christ and him crucified" (1 Cor. 2:2). "There can be no Christian theology which is not at every point a theology of the cross," insists Jennings. But this fact is ignored often by contemporary Christians who isolate consideration of the cross to Holy Week. Even then, "the majority of Christians pass directly from Palm Sunday, with its triumphal entry into Jerusalem, to Easter and its celebration of the resurrection of Jesus. This move from victory to victory without passing through the contradiction of the cross produces the anti-gospel of success and 'positive thinking'" (Jennings, *Loyalty To God*, Abingdon Press, 1992, 105-06).

that Christ modeled as Prophet and calls for from his followers as King."[34] While Christ died *for* us, he also is to reign *in* us, carrying on his present mission in large part *through* us. Being prophet, priest, and king, Jesus Christ has revealed, reconciled, and reigns, all in order that we who believe might know, relate rightly, rejoice, and work to restore others.

Maze of Reconciliation Metaphors

The New Testament narrative places great emphasis on the event of the death of Jesus on the cross. Somehow what happened there links Jesus Christ, in the function of all his offices, to the salvation of humankind. Note these classic hymn lines of Charles Wesley (1738), lines that reflect the amazement, the celebration, the questions about "how" before any answers are attempted:

> And can it be that I should gain
> An interest in the Savior's blood?
> Died He for me, who caused His pain?
> For me, who Him to death pursued?
> Amazing love! how can it be
> That Thou, my God, shouldst die for me?

Much recent theological literature addresses the question of whether the cross event can be said to be *illustrative* or *constitutive*. That is, did Jesus on the cross vividly illustrate to the world the saving nature and will of God, making known more clearly a significant insight into an unchangeable situation, or did he constitute by the cross event a new situation, dramatically changing the circumstance that previously had made human salvation impossible?

The illustrative approach treats the work of the cross as an historical symbol of a timeless truth. Christ reveals rather than activates the saving will of God.[35] By contrast, much of the theology of

---

[34] Randy Maddox, *Responsible Grace: John Wesley's Practical Theology* (Kingswood Books, Abingdon Press, 1994), 113.

[35] Rudolph Bultmann and Paul Tillich argue such a general position.

human salvation written before the Enlightenment was constitutive in nature. It was assumed that something new had been brought about because of what Jesus did on the cross. There he made possible the reconciliation of humanity with God. Christ did not merely reveal to us something of eternal significance; he accomplished something new that was essential for salvation to be possible for us.[36]

Given these broad illustrative and constitutive perspectives on the meaning of the mission of Jesus, three basic explanations of Christ's accomplishment on behalf of human salvation have been prominent at different times in the church's life. Each draws support from the Bible, focusing on differing biblical metaphors. Recall that metaphors are not simple "facts" or rigid definitions. They are more picture windows in front of which one stands to ponder the beauty and depth of meaning. The New Testament uses a series of metaphors for picturing the meaning of Christ's life and death. No one of them should be taken as the whole in isolation from the others.

There are financial, legal, military, sacrificial, and other metaphors in the New Testament. Some have been developed into major theories or models of the atonement (seeking to explain the "how" of the reconciling accomplishment of Christ that restores human at-one-ment with God). No one metaphor appears to carry all the meaning alone, nor has any one received exclusive ecumenical approval as the "official" manner of the church's understanding of the work of God in Christ. Three are most prominent in the history of Christian interpretation.

1. Substitution/Satisfaction. First is the *substitutionary* model of the meaning of the death of Jesus. Christ on the cross is understood to have turned aside God's wrath toward all humanity. Anselm of Canterbury (1033-1109) taught in his famous book *Cur Deus Homo* (Why God Became Man) that sin demands a price, humans cannot pay the price, so only God can satisfy God's demand in the sin circumstance. But because humanity originally was supposed to obey God and resist Satan, it is humanity who should have avoided the

---

[36] The constitutive approach remains central for most of "evangelical" Christianity. Colin Gunton, e.g., argues this way (*Actuality of Atonement*, 1988).

need for satisfaction. Thus a God-man (Jesus) came to carry out the task. Such a One would have the ability (as God) and the obligation (as a human being). The incarnation, therefore, took place. Jesus' death paid the penalty, provided the required satisfaction for human sin, and thus merits eternal life as we humans never could.[37] Offended honor was satisfied.[38]

Anselm's development of this constitutive approach rose in part out of a medieval thought world (God and humans are related as feudal lord to serf, with any dishonor of the lord requiring satisfaction). Even so, and with this cultural conditioning rather obvious, a substitution/satisfaction approach to atonement goes beyond medieval culture by also having significant biblical rootage. The "suffering servant" highlighted in Isaiah (42:1-9; 49:1-6; 52:13-53:12) was "wounded for our transgressions" (53:5). Matthew interprets the healing ministry of Jesus by reference to such a servant song (8:16-17). There are references like Mark 10:45, 14:24; Heb. 10:6, 8; 1 Jn. 2:2; and 2 Cor. 5:21.

This atonement model remains in common use in the Christian community. The Lausanne Covenant[39] (1974) says that Jesus "gave himself as the only ransom for sinners" (satisfaction). The Junaluska Affirmation[40] (1975) states that "by His [Jesus] death on the cross the sinless Son propitiated the holy wrath of the Father, a righteous anger occasioned by sin." Such focus on propitiation (appeasement) of God is unacceptable to some who prefer to avoid a theological affir-

---

[37] Theories of the atonement often reflect the culture at the time of their origin. Sacrificial language was natural for early Jewish Christians. The images of rescue and redemption were familiar to those with experience of the laws regarding slaves and prisoners in the Roman Empire. In the Middle Ages, Anselm's time, drawing upon the feudal categories of honor and satisfaction would have been understood readily. A major problem today is that none of these cultural settings is shared by secularized societies, thus obscuring any ready appreciation of the meaning of the cross.

[38] For Anselm, "God's concern is not with his own honor, for that cannot be diminished by anything outside God. Rather, God is concerned with the 'universal order and beauty' of the universe, his creature" (James McClendon, *Systematic Theology: Doctrine*, vol. 2, Abingdon Press, 1994, 205).

[39] Congress on World Evangelization, Lausanne, Switzerland, 1974, sponsored by the Billy Graham Evangelistic Association.

[40] This statement of faith represents the contemporary "Good News" movement among United Methodists.

mation presuming God's wrath and anger. However, comments Paul Mickey on this affirmation, "to avert one's face from this scriptural truth is to hide in the enormity and pervasiveness of sin and to refuse to face the theological reality of sin.... God's wrath is a holy and right-eous anger. It is brought about by our willful violation of God's pur-pose in creation, not by a distempered spirit in God. Christ did not come nor die to appease the ill temper of a tribal, vindictive god."[41]

In the satisfaction (substitution) model of atonement, the priest-ly role of Jesus is pictured as paramount, with little necessary refer-ence to his life or resurrection being crucial to the substitution-satis-faction process. The cross is central. Jesus is viewed as the needed sacrifice for human sin. This emphasis was accepted widely by Protestantism in the late sixteenth and seventeenth centuries and remains so in many conservative circles. It, however, troubled Anabaptists who had concerns similar to those of the earliest church, concerns hardly arising from a culturally dominant, "magisterial"[42] church. They were concerned by a Protestant perspective that subtly implies comfortable passivity. Since Christ has done it all, many Christians act like they do not have to do anything at all! Jesus "paid it all," so we need only receive and rejoice. But, is not Christ's work to be *shared* by true disciples? Did Paul not say, "I fill out in my body what was lacking in the afflictions of Christ?" (Col. 1:24)? Are we not, in some real sense, to "work out our own salvation in fear and trembling," including facing in this evil world the likelihood of suf-fering for the Lord's sake? Does not the One who reconciles us also give us our own ministry of reconciliation (2 Cor. 5:19)?

While several New Testament references clearly employ the metaphor of substitution or satisfaction, much in the New Testament can be seen as resisting any overemphasis on this metaphor since it hardly pictures the Father of our Lord Jesus as bringing "good news of great joy" when the news centers in God's justice needing to be pla-

---

[40] Paul Mickey, *Essentials of Wesleyan Theology* (Zondervan, 1980), 128-129.

[42] "Magisterial" means the church as officially sanctioned and supported by the state. For instance, the Lutheran branch of the Protestant Reformation became established by the governments of several nations, including Germany. Nations that sanction and sup-port usually also seek to define and control.

cated with a literal human sacrifice.[43] If grace is made conditional on required satisfaction, is it really grace? The New Testament message is that humanity and not God needs to be reconciled. It was *God* who was in Christ reconciling us (2 Cor. 5:18). It is *we* who need reconciled, not God. The suffering of Christ on the cross, says Jürgen Moltmann, "is human sin transformed into the atoning suffering of God." So he concludes:

> If we understand sin and atonement in personal and relational terms, then we are parting company with the inadequate images of the sacrificial theories–ransom, atoning sacrifice, satisfaction, and so on. It is not the case that our objectified sins have to be made good by objective acts of atonement. We ourselves have to be justified as sinners because of the way in which we contradict life, and have to be restored to life. That happens through the atoning love of God.[44]

God's redemptive acts often are pictured in the Bible less as commercial transactions, payments of ransom, or satisfactions of honor offended, and more as free yet costly acts of divine grace (Isa. 45:13; 52:3). When Paul reports that "you were bought with a price" (1 Cor. 6:20; 7:23), he does not mean that some previous owner has been paid off. His point is that God's gift of grace, the reaching and suffering love of God, is costly to God.

---

[43] To resist the view of God's placated justice is not necessarily to reject the scandal of the cross of Jesus. John Stott refers to 1 Cor. 2:1-5 as central to all Christian proclamation. Paul resolved to know nothing except Jesus Christ and him crucified. Stott explores five contemporary objections leveled against Christ and the cross, ones Paul anticipated facing at Corinth. "He knew that his message of Christ crucified would be regarded as intellectually foolish (incompatible with wisdom), religiously exclusive (incompatible with tolerance), personally humiliating (incompatible with self-esteem), morally demanding (incompatible with freedom), and politically subversive (incompatible with patriotism)" (*The Contemporary Christian*, InterVaristy Press, 1992, 61-67). To accept this multi-faceted scandal of the cross, however, does not commit one to all dimensions of the several related atonement theories formalized in the church over the centuries.

[44] Jürgen Moltmann, *History and the Triune God*, 52.

2. Moral Influence. A second approach is the *moral influence* model of the meaning of the reconciliation accomplished by Jesus. This is an *illustrative* rather than a *constitutive* approach. The focus here is on a dramatic demonstration by Christ on the cross of the love of God for humanity. Surely the first thing to be said about the death of Jesus is that it is the supreme revelation of the amazing love of God. Christ is understood to have bridged the gap between God and humanity by enhancing humanity's religious understanding and moral development.

Peter Abelard (1079-1142), for instance, set forth a position in reaction to both the satisfaction-to-God's-honor and ransom-to-Satan views. He judged:

> How cruel and unjust it appears, that anyone should demand the blood of the innocent as any kind of ransom, or be in any way delighted with the death of the innocent, let alone that God should find the death of His Son so acceptable, that through it He should be reconciled to the world![45]

Abelard taught to the contrary that the work of Jesus is more a redemptive demonstration of God's love than a satisfying of God's wrath or some bill that had to be paid by God to God, the devil, or someone else. To Abelard, the central purpose of the incarnation was for Christ to illuminate the world by his wisdom and to inspire it to a responding, selfless love like that of God.

The shift seen here is from the objective, constitutive view of Anselm to a movingly subjective, illustrative view that features the existential impact of the biblical story, an impact revealing the forgiving heart of the God of loving grace. Similarly, Schleiermacher said that the sufferings and cross of Jesus impress and draw us and vividly show the way in which God was in Christ reconciling the world. The sacrificial theme is thought of as a lower stage of Old Testament faith, with the social aspects of the covenant and the moral

---

[45] Abelard, *Commentary on Romans*, quoted by Robert Franks, *The Work of Christ: A Historical Study of Christian Doctrine* (London: Nelson), 145.

emphases of the Hebrew prophets the higher stage. "Expiation" language is said to be much less frequent in the New Testament than "love" language. Redemption, then, is essentially the process of the stimulation of God-consciousness of alienated humans through the moving influence of the loving Christ.

It is readily understandable how the showing of God's amazing love to us in such a compelling way as the cross of Jesus can lead to our wonder and gratitude, and thus to our repentance and reconciliation. Christ's love for us, even unto death, tends to evoke in us a like love, allowing us to be restored and appropriately forgiven. Reported Jesus in one instance, "Her sins, which were many, are forgiven; for she loved much" (Lk. 7:47 KJV). Sin tends to be viewed in this atonement model as human ignorance regarding the true nature of things. Salvation, therefore, can be achieved by Christ sharing vital information about God with a confused and ignorant (sin-blinded) humanity. The idea of sin as ignorance, of the Enlightenment belief in the fundamental goodness of human nature once properly enlightened, has been shocked by the repeated atrocities of brutal warfare and death camps in the twentieth century. Is the human problem more profound than mere ignorance?

The strength of this more subjective view of atonement is that it emphasizes God's love as great and unconditional, although sinners must respond in repentance, faith, and a like love to make it effectual. How easily, however, supporters of this approach limit themselves to the subjective, underestimate the power of evil, and thus sentimentalize the love of God and the work of Christ. Too much popular piety reduces Jesus to "my personal buddy," the dear Jesus with the children, while hardly accounting adequately for the treacherous and tenacious evil in our world.

3. Christus Victor. Third is the *Christus Victor* model of the meaning of the reconciliation accomplished in Jesus. The difference here from the substitutionary model is that in view is not deliverance from God's wrath by satisfaction of divine honor and justice, but deliverance from the bondage of evil powers. This model was common in the early Christian community until Anselm, whose thinking then dominated until the popularity of the moral influence model rose in the nineteenth century. In the face of the dramatic evils of the twentieth century, many Christian theologians have begun taking with renewed seriousness the demonic dimension of life, something not to be dismissed lightly as mere "mythology" of biblical times.[46]

Swedish theologian Gustav Aulén (1879-1977) revived the Christus Victor model.[47] Aulén's view of Christ's work emphasizes the military metaphor (e.g., Col. 2:15). Christ liberates humanity from binding powers and himself emerges victorious in the resurrection. The issue highlighted is not only release from the guilt of sin by some process of justification before God. Human sin is recognized as having resulted in humans being released by God into the control of satanic forces, working in personal and institutionalized forms. A divinely enabled liberation is needed.

While the substitutionary model tends to focus on the death of Jesus and the moral influence model on the life and death of Jesus, the Christus Victor model calls special attention also to the resurrection, that glorious event that completed Jesus' triumph over the powers, rescuing believers from the *control* of sin.[48] It views Christ's achievement in relation to evil (or its personified head, the devil), and thus may be characterized as an *evilward* or *devilward* atonement view. By contrast, the more *Godward* view (Anselm) develops primarily in relation to God (satisfaction of God's honor or justice)[49].

According to most traditions of the Western church, the atonement that releases from sin is grounded exclusively in the death of Jesus and not in his resurrection. The resurrection, while crucial, is

---

[46] The Enlightenment mentality tended to regard the "Christus Victor" view of Christ's work as primitive. Dismissed as premodern superstition was all belief in a personal devil and the domination of human existence by satanic forces of sin and evil.

[47] Gustav Aulén, *Christus Victor*, Eng. trans. 1931 (reprinted by Macmillan, 1969, with a foreword by Jaroslav Pelikan). See also Aulén's *The Faith of the Christian Church*, 2nd Eng. ed. (Philadelphia: Fortress, 1960), 196-213. Several contemporary Mennonite theologians champion this atonement model as biblically faithful and directly compatible with traditional concerns of the Believers' Church tradition (John Howard Yoder, J. Denny Weaver, John Driver, Thomas Finger, and C. Norman Kraus).

[48] Release from the controlling power of sin ("sanctification") was a central concern of John Wesley.

[49] See James McClendon, 1994, 208-209.

understood only as divine authentication of the work of Christ. But Christ both died and rose for us (Rom. 5:10). Beyond forgiveness for past guilt, the goal of God in Jesus is to create anew in place of the "old that has passed away" (2 Cor. 5:17). The resurrection of Christ from the dead is the beginning of the new creation. This is why the Orthodox Church of the East has proclaimed forgiveness at the Easter festival and celebrated Easter as the feast of atonement.

The triumph over sinful forces featured in the Christus Victor view is intended to be seen eschatologically. That is, the war between good and evil already is won in principle, but with real battles still going on and yet to be fought–although there is a liberating present awareness of future victory. The evil powers are still active and very influential. Paul says that we are enslaved to the "elemental spirits of the universe" (Gal. 4:3-9; Col. 2:8, 20). These spirits apparently include the law (can become deceiving and enslaving) and sin that takes us captive (Rom. 7:11, 23). While the moral influence model of Christ's atonement sees the church on the frontier of social changes that are to be reducing the rule of evil, the Christus Victor model admits that the church still is engaged in a hostile conflict. This conflict may persist stubbornly, probably until the end of time. Even so, eventual victory is already known. Christ's grave is empty!

The New Testament teaches that Jesus struggled constantly to overcome Satan (Matt. 4:1-11, 12:22-32, 27:37-44). Liberation from evil powers is a pervasive theme (Gal. 1:3; Acts 10:38), with all powers finally to be subordinated to Christ (1 Pet. 3:22; 1 Tim. 3:16). A classic statement of the Christus Victor atonement model is Hebrews 2:14-15: "Since, therefore, the children share flesh and blood, he himself likewise shared the same things, so that through death he might destroy the one who has the power of death, that is, the devil, and free those who all their lives were held in slavery by the fear of death." Early Christians rejoiced that, in the cross and resurrection of Jesus, God somehow "disarmed the rulers and authorities...triumphing over them in it" (Col. 2:15). The victory motif captures well the biblical story of God's long conflict with enslaving evil powers, beginning with the dramatic exodus from Egypt, a primary paradigm of faith and salvation throughout the Hebrew Scriptures. Christ's victory over the rulers and authorities is at the heart of one of the earliest Christian confessions of faith (Phil. 2:9-11).

The battle goes on and is not limited to "otherworldly" evil powers that function only in the spiritual realm. The crucifixion, death, and resurrection victory of Jesus occurred in the physical, historical world in which we live. God's victorious kingdom continues to have both reality and visibility wherever and whenever God's people live according to the example of Jesus, giving present visibility and reality to the kingdom of God. The biblical revelation views the work of Christ as establishing "a new social order which stands over against–in confrontation with–the structures of the world."[50] Such standing against is possible only because of the liberating victory of Christ on our behalf.

This view of Christ's work probably was so popular in the post-apostolic period because it spoke forcefully to Christians of both Jewish and Gentile origin, many of whom knew much about oppressive military and spiritual powers. Justo González calls this the "classic" atonement model. He judges that the human problem is not fundamentally that we owe a debt to God (satisfaction) or lack necessary knowledge or inspiration to love God (moral influence), theories related closely to socio-political issues prominent in church life long after biblical times.[51] Such theories often have functioned to support the control of ruling classes in many cultures. Rather, the primary human problem is enslavement to evil, "and it is no coincidence that the 'classical' view of atonement began to recede into the background when the church became powerful."[52]

---

[50] J. Denny Weaver, "Atonement for the Non-Constantinian Church," in *Modern Theology* 6:4 (July, 1990), 309. This new social order is the church, the minority ecclesiology as emphasized in the Believers' Church tradition. Note that this atonement model has been subjectivized in ways that Weaver finds abortive of the full biblical intent for a visible, social demonstration of the victory of God. Rudolf Bultmann and Paul Tillich used the theme of victory by focusing on existential forces that deprive modern humans of "authentic existence." In this way the atonement of Christ tends to be reduced to a subjective victory within human consciousness only. American revivalism often has encouraged a similar reductionism. The biblical narrative is far more outward and historical than this.

[51] See Justo González, *Christian Thought Revisited: Three Types of Theology* (Nashville: Abingdon Press, 1989).

[52] Justo González, *Mañana: Christian Theology from a Hispanic Perspective* (Nashville: Abingdon Press, 1990), 154.

Work of Atonement

What, then, is the primary meaning of the atonement accomplished by Jesus Christ? What are the prominent aspects of the at-one-ment, the reuniting now made possible between God and all creation? From the maze of models with their varying emphases, we learn at least that somehow the life, death, and resurrection of Jesus all are involved and crucial to a broad understanding. We observe that there is not one comprehensive theory that is fully adequate, although viewing the substitution and moral influence models in light of the Christus Victor model follows faithfully the biblical revelation and addresses with special effectiveness the church's redeemed and redeeming role in the world.

Returning to the three offices of Christ, we find a helpful way to keep our understanding of Christ's atonement open and inclusive of the various New Testament models, metaphors, and emphases. Daniel Migliore helpfully restates Calvin's teaching about these offices, relating each to a major atonement model: "Christ as prophet proclaims the coming reign of God and instructs us in the form of life appropriate to that reign (moral influence); Christ as priest renders to God the perfect sacrifice of love and obedience on our behalf (satisfaction); Christ as designated king rules the world despite the recalcitrance of evil and promises the ultimate victory of God's reign of righteousness and peace (Christ the victor)."[53] The particular relevance today of the Christus Victor model appears clear. It is based solidly in the whole biblical narrative about Jesus and provides a compelling eschatological framework within which all Christian theology and life should be viewed.

The dawning among us of the kingdom of God surely was central in the mission of Jesus and thus is central to understanding the meaning of his life, death, and resurrection. Jesus taught and acted out the kingdom's present reality, God's unobstructed reign over all dimensions of our lives. The eschaton has come, the already of the not yet that soon will fully be. Jesus successfully (in God's distinctive way) opposed all forces that fight this divine dawning. In the resurrection of Jesus, God demonstrated victory and liberation from all evil forces that bind and oppose the coming kingdom.

---

[53] Daniel Migliore, *Faith Seeking Understanding* (Eerdmans, 1991), 155.

Humanity, because of its sin, is unable to liberate and reconcile itself. Therefore, God stepped in, acted on behalf of us in love, accomplished whatever is necessary to clear the path to fully restored relationship. Christ did and still does for us what we cannot do for ourselves. Christ identified with us in love and to the death, representing us to the Father as victorious over all evil so that we might be freed to become reconciled and reconciling children of God. Such freedom to again stand in right relationship with God is available only at a high price to God and ourselves. It comes only as we share in Christ's death and resurrection (Rom. 6:4), have a part in God's suffering on our behalf (Phil. 3:9-10), follow Jesus by the sacrifice of our own arrogant egos, and take up our own cross in his service (Mk. 8:34). When we have so shared, suffered, and sacrificed, when we begin to act in the world as though Christ was victorious, then we have solidarity with Christ and thus real reconciliation with God.

The substitutionary and moral influence atonement theories complement each other. The one stresses the redeeming action of God on our behalf in the face of the crippling horror of sin, a cosmic "legal" transaction apart from us. The other highlights the historical dimension of Jesus entering our fleshly life, drawing us by his life and death, and sharing the consequences of living a loving way in this fallen world. The one view sees salvation through satisfying God's wrath and justice with Christ's sacrifice; the other view sees salvation through Jesus penetrating our rebellion with the allurement of God's amazing love. Both views are part of the biblical way of imaging and explaining the atonement. They both feature the loving grace of God.

But, if sin is understood relationally and not substantively, then a satisfaction theory needs careful qualifying. God does not keep quantitative records of sin, with a corresponding price to be paid before forgiveness is possible. The familiar phrase "Jesus paid it all" can be misleading. As Ray Dunning says, "the idea that Jesus bears the punishment for man's sins is totally foreign to the New Testament. The language it uses is 'suffering,' not 'punishment.'"[54] Jesus fulfilled the two biblical roles of priest, *identification* and *representation.* In his full humanity

---

[54] H. Ray Dunning, *Grace, Faith and Holiness* (Kansas City: Beacon Hill Press, 1988), 372.

245

Jesus identified intimately with us. We now have a high priest genuinely able to sympathize with us in all our weakness (Heb. 4:15). This identification with us is the ground for his representing us before God.

Irenaeus of Lyon (c130-c200) taught that what we lost in Adam has been restored in Christ. Having fallen by our solidarity with Adam, we now can be reconciled by solidarity with Christ, our sympathetic representative to a merciful God. God suffers with us for our sins and in Christ gladly forgives. The reconciliation is not the result of a required substitutionary payment, but a relationship restored when we believe in the restoring initiative of God in Christ and then choose to appropriate to ourselves its benefits and dedicate ourselves to its sacrificial way of life.

The focus lies in a *restoration* to be achieved more than a *payment* to be made. Many of the early Greek and later Eastern Orthodox theologians have judged wisely. The essential human need is "therapeutic" in nature. We sinful humans need healed, restored to the original divine image within us, freed from our slavery to sin, and re-related to God by the power of divine presence. Athanasius (c.296-373), for example, said that in the incarnation "God became like us so that we might become like God."[55]

The third atonement model, Christus Victor, relates in many ways to the first two (substitutionary and moral influence), while focusing on the deliverance of God that frees sinners from the dominion of all evil forces. This way of viewing sin and salvation, deliverance from dominating forces that rule us with divine permission because of our sin, corresponds closely with the narrative structure of the biblical story and thus appears especially significant.

This model has an objective quality, highlighting something Christ has accomplished apart from our responding faith. This something is not a legal or commercial transaction between God and Christ or God and the Devil (assuming our punishment or paying a required price). The substitutionary theory "abandons the New Testament affirmation that God is the agent, not the object, of reconciliation."[56]

---

[55] Athanasius, *On the Incarnation of the Lord*, no. 54.

[56] John Howard Yoder, *Preface To Theology* (Elkhart: Goshen Biblical Seminary, 1981), 221-22.

Summarizes Ray Dunning: "On the stage of history, where the human problem of sin must be met, Jesus Christ came into mortal combat with Satan in his own sphere (this present age) and overcame him, thus making available to men the same victory over sin in the here and now."[57]

The victory of the cross and resurrection of Jesus[58] addresses the guilt as justification, provides the power as sanctification, and assures the consequences as eventual glorification. The kingdom of God has been inaugurated in Christ on our historical scene and its firstfruits are to be the liberation, reconciliation, restoration, and commissioning of kingdom citizens for new life in the world. Our human understanding of the proper focus of Christ's atonement should not be limited to a resolution of the guilt of our past sin. It also is our being set free for life now, life dedicated to God's mission in this world.

Judges 2:11-19 is a key passage summarizing the witness of the Hebrew Scriptures about sin's consequences and how God restores. Idolatry was a characteristic temptation of the Israelites. How was such sin punished? It is said that Yahweh usually judged by handing over faithless Israel to its enemies. People were allowed to reap what they had sown. Yahweh had saved Israel from Egyptian slavery; but when the covenant was broken God "gave them over to plunderers, who plundered them." When, however, from time to time the Israelites cried out in repentance and sought mercy, God responded graciously and "raised up judges who delivered them out of the power of those who plundered them."

Similarly, Jesus bore God's judgment for us by suffering innocently with God's guilty people at the hands of the religious, political, and demonic forces, agents of God's judgment in that day. The wrath which Jesus bore on the cross is not pictured best as being poured out by the angry Father on the innocent Son for the sake of sat-

---

[57] H. Ray Dunning, *Grace, Faith and Holiness* (Kansas City: Beacon Hill Press, 1988), 388.

[58] Says Clark Pinnock: "We must keep the cross and resurrection together and jointly prominent. Evangelical theology has been biblically deficient in its treatment of the resurrection of Christ. It treats the cross soteriologically [as central to effecting human salvation] but seldom the resurrection. It is a remarkable omission in evangelical theology" (in Pinnock and Delwin Brown, *Theological Crossfire*, 148).

isfying divine justice. Instead, the Son chose to be handed over to the cruel forces of evil, functioning as our priest, fully identifying with and willingly suffering the results of human sin. Throughout the ordeal, God always loved and deeply grieved, demanded no revenge, delivered no ransom. God, who had judged by means of permission given to evil powers in response to sin, now willingly saves by Christ's victory over these very powers as our representative.

Why was Jesus crucified? For our sins, we immediately and rightly respond. Note, however, that the evil powers to which Jesus was handed over and which Jesus conquered on our behalf included political forces. The penalty for various violations of religious laws among the Jews was stoning. The stoning symbol of our salvation is a cross. The cross was Rome's method of executing those guilty of political crimes. Jesus was accused of "forbidding us to pay taxes to the emperor, and saying that he himself is the Messiah, a king" (Lk. 23:2). He was killed for presumed rebellion against the ultimate authority of a human empire.

Surely an overcoming of such arrogant worldly authority is included in the Christian good news. Jesus reversed the whole arena of worldly power and offers liberation to the oppressed in the midst of their worldly oppression. By the cross, Jesus "disarmed the rulers and authorities and made a public example of them, triumphing over them" (Col. 2:15). Concludes Theodore Jennings: "If our faith has no relation to this public and political sphere, then our faith has no relation to the historical cross of Jesus."[59] Kwame Bediako of West Africa insists that the death and resurrection of Jesus have enthroned Jesus on the "stool of power" with God. Kings of the earth may still reign, but now they are "desacralized" by Christ's rule. Christian loyalties are changed. In a culture where ancestors long deceased are still claimed to have significant reality, Bediako says that "once Christ has come the ancestors are cut off as the means of blessing for we lay our power lines differently."[60] Says the Nicene Creed: Jesus now "is seated at the right hand of the Father." When a believer

---

[59] Theodore Jennings, *Loyalty To God* (Nashville: Abingdon Press, 1992), 109.

[60] As quoted by William Dyrness, *Learning About Theology from the Third World* (Grand Rapids: Zondervan, 1990), 169.

chooses to be "in him," that person belongs to a new kingdom, and King Jesus is Lord of all!

Christ's Atonement for Today's World

The meaning of the Cross centers in God coming near to us, suffering with and for us in Jesus the Christ, conquering in a non-worldly way all that opposes divine presence and sovereignty. It is a solution to our sin and a challenge to religious and political powers that seek to usurp the place of God. It is the divinely provided potential of human freedom and a clear call to Christian mission of a cross-like kind.

The cross of Jesus is even more. It is a verdict against an exclusive view of the identity of Israel as God's only chosen ones. On Golgatha God nullified all such exclusiveness, introducing "the revocation of the frontiers of election. By means of the cross, the gospel 'crosses' these frontiers to reach the whole earth."[61] Paul uses the first eleven chapters of his letter to the Romans to clarify how the rejection of Jesus by the Jews opened the gospel to the whole world. The gospel of the crucified Jesus has escaped the restrictive boundaries of all ethnic and national identities and loyalties to become the good news for all humanity. Human divisions melt before the warming love of God in Christ. The church of Christ should be free of parochial barriers so that, as representatives of the cross and resurrection, it can be a healing and reconciling witness to the world.

Images of Christ and understandings of the atonement accomplished by him vary within the New Testament and certainly among Christians from the many cultures of today's world. As broad generalizations, Westerners think in individualistic terms, often separating religion from public life (Jesus saves me from my personal sin and prepares me for heaven).[62] Africans think of Christ as reigning over

---

[61] Jennings, op. cit., 113-14.

[62] An overemphasis on a substitution view of the atonement gives the impression that significance lies only with individual sinners being *justified*, and not also with the *sanctification* of believers, the church, and even the structures of the world through the transforming power of God.

the world of spirits. Asians seek biblical images relating to Christ's reign over the entire cosmos. Latins ask how the reign of Christ will manage to alter oppressive political structures. This also is true of Christian African-American theologians in relation to racial oppression and feminist theologians in relation to gender oppression. It is important, according to the biblical revelation of Jesus, not to limit the implications of Christ's accomplishment, and certainly not to construe redemption only in futuristic and other-worldly terms. Focus instead should be on the biblical affirmations that Christ already has conquered evil, making deliverance possible in this world and making Christians responsible as agents of liberation.[63]

William Dyrness reminds us that "a proper reading of Scripture must be made by the whole body of Christ."[64] Here is one of several reasons for the importance of unity (not uniformity) in the church. Christians need each other in order to fully know their Christ and Christ's accomplished and ongoing work. A diversity of perspectives in the church can be threatening and confusing. Still, when being faithful to the biblical narrative rather than merely acting as an apologist for some traditional and possibly self-serving ideology, differing perspectives can illumine aspects of the work of Christ usually overlooked by others.[65]

---

[63] See, e.g., Letty Russell, *Human Liberation in a Feminist Perspective* (Philadelphia: Westminster, 1974).

[64] William Dyrness, op. cit., 184.

[65] For instance, typically overlooked by the Western church is the distinctive Eastern view of the faith. The Western understanding of the human condition focuses on the guilt of sin, the human inability to atone, thus the juridical approach of Christ's cross and shed blood satisfying the penalty. Eastern Orthodoxy emphasizes more the human need for divine assistance in attaining to the likeness of God. So the incarnation itself is the center of attention (more than the cross). God condescended to human flesh, subject as it is to suffering and death. With Christ now the resurrected and ascended King, "the transformation and exaltation of human nature (is) made possible by Christ" or, to say it differently, "God became like us so that we might become like God" (see Randy Maddox, "John Wesley and Eastern Orthodoxy," *The Asbury Theological Journal* 45:2, Fall, 1990, 36). Justo González affirms this Eastern view and cautions that "become like God" not be misunderstood. He explains: "God's very being is love, for-otherness. This is the Trinitarian God. This is the God revealed in Jesus Christ. What Jesus has done is precisely to open for us the way of love, to free us so that we too can begin to be for others. In being for others we are most truly human. And in being most truly human we are most Godlike. Indeed, God did become human so that we could become divine!" (*Mañana*, 1990, 155).

This concern for not viewing the work of Christ through self-serving ideologies has been promoted vigorously in recent decades by a range of "liberation" theologies. Salvation in Christ is said to have freed believers in both personal and political ways (reliance on the Christus Victor model of reconciliation). Clearly the reconciling work of Jesus extends to human relationships, since on the cross Jesus destroyed the barriers dividing human beings (Eph. 2:11-22). Salvation has a corporate and public dimension. This dimension means that Jesus exposed and is defeating the ideologies and structures of sin and society that work to destroy human life. As Jesus died voluntarily and sacrificially and rose by the power of God in victory over evil and death, so Christians are called to carry such a cross and live such a life. Knowing and living are inseparable. Jon Sobrino insists that "only through Christian praxis is it possible for us to draw close to Jesus. Following Jesus is the precondition for knowing Jesus."[66] Knowing Jesus is to be free and freeing.

Ours is a world of violence. God in Jesus Christ faced all such violence and suffered terribly at its hands. God's boundless, non-coercive love clashed with the evil way of the world and voluntarily became a victim of its worst. Love is like that. It reaches and risks. Jesus lived and died that we might live in the power of this forgiving and freeing love of God. Love reverses the way of violence (1 Cor. 13) and opens a path of peace. God "raised the crucified Jesus and made him the chief cornerstone of a new humanity that no longer espouses the way of violence, that no longer needs scapegoats, that no longer wills to live at the expense of victims, that no longer imagines or worships a bloodthirsty God, that is no longer interested in legitimations of violence, but that follows Jesus in the power of a new Spirit."[67] The resurrection of Jesus signals the beginning of what one day will be the full victory of God over all rulers and authorities.

The cross of Jesus is the distinctively Christian lens for viewing all of reality. When we look through it, all becomes cross-shaped, "cruciform." Three things become clear. First, "through the cross

---

[66] Jon Sobrino, *Christology at the Crossroads* (Maryknoll, N.Y.: Orbis Books, 1978), xiii.

[67] Daniel Migliore, *Faith Seeking Understanding*, 1991, 159.

we see the heart of God revealed most clearly." Second, "only through the cross can we see the true nature of human sin and the depths of divine grace." Finally, "the cross provides the model for God's new social order, the messianic community."[68]

The Anabaptist (Believers' Church) and "liberationist" traditions especially underscore this third point. The salvation gained is not to be limited to a private transaction of personal guilt forgiven. God's goal is a *new people* in this world, a visible, cross-shaped church. Jesus "opens the way for us to participate in true fellowship...[and] authors among us the divine design for human life."[69] The Servant (Jesus) suffered in part to model, inspire, and empower a suffering community of disciples who are enabled to become liberated people living for others and for whom servanthood replaces dominion over others (Mk. 10:42-44). Cross-bearing liberates to lives of peace and reconciliation. Atonement intends to lead to life in the Spirit and the reality of a Spirit-filled church.

It is in regard to the person and work of Jesus Christ that one senses most the inadequacy of common language and simple logic to capture full meaning. These are subjects of profound complexity and paramount importance. Models and theories about them abound as the church moves through the centuries and the cultures of the world. Some views are better than others based on the degree of their rootage in the biblical narrative. But none are final and fully adequate. We "cannot understand the full meaning of the cross of Christ. We can only stand in silence before it, acknowledge its wonder, and submit to its power."[70] This circumstance should lead the wise theologian and humble Christian of today to the language of worship, a language less precise, though more profound and thus more adequate than rational formulas and arid arguments. Standing before God inspires song more readily than academic dissertations.

---

[68] C. Leonard Allen, *The Cruciform Church* (Abilene Christian University Press, 1990), 133.

[69] Stanley Grenz, *Theology for the Community of God* (Nashville: Broadman and Holman Publishers, 1994), 457.

[70] Ibid., 443.

The satisfaction model of Christ's atonement is seen clearly in the hymn "O Sacred Head Now Wounded":

What thou, my lord, hast suffered
  was all for sinner's gain;
    mine, mine was the transgression,
    but thine the deadly pain.[71]

Echoes of the moral influence theory of Christ's work ring in this grateful testimony:

I've found my Lord and He is mine,
  He won me by His love;
    I'll serve Him all my years of time,
    And dwell with Him above.[72]

Elements of the Christus Victor model are heard clearly in:

Mercy there was great and grace was free,
  Pardon there was multiplied to me;
    There my burdened soul found liberty,
    At Calvary.[73]

The cry of every human heart is addressed by two verses of another great Christian hymn. The narrative of its origin is instructive. A highpoint for insight into the human quest for deliverance and freedom came soon after Charles Wesley concluded a disappointing five months in the colony of Georgia. He traveled to Charleston to catch a ship bound for England and home. But in Charleston his dejection only worsened as he encountered firsthand the horrible, government-sanctioned treatment of human slaves. His heart cried out for all people to

---

[71] As in the *United Methodist Hymnal* (Nashville: United Methodist Publishing House, 1989), 286, vs. 2.

[72] Daniel Warner, "His Yoke Is Easy," in *Worship the Lord: Hymnal of the Church of God* (Anderson, Ind.: Warner Press, 1989), 599, vs. 1.

[73] William Newell, "At Calvary," in *Worship the Lord: Hymnal of the Church of God*, 573, chorus. Note also the beloved hymn "A Mighty Fortress Is Our God."

be released from such terror. Then his mind turned to Jesus, the hope of all who suffer in bondage of whatever kind. He wrote:

> Come, thou long-expected Jesus,
>   Born to set thy people free;
> From our fears and sins release us;
>   Let us find our rest in thee.
> Israel's strength and consolation,
>   Hope of all the earth thou art;
> Dear desire of every nation,
>   Joy of every longing heart.
>
> Born thy people to deliver,
>   Born a child and yet a King,
> Born to reign in us forever,
>   Now thy gracious kingdom bring.
> By thine own eternal spirit
>   Rule in all our hearts alone;
> By thine all-sufficient merit,
>   Raise us to thy glorious throne.[74]

The familiar hymn "Joy to the World" reflects the triple office of Christ by announcing that "He rules the world with truth and grace...." He *rules* as God's appointed King over all things. He rules *with truth* as the dependable prophet of God. He rules with truth *and grace* as the divinely anointed priest who brings mediation between loving Creator and fallen creation. No wonder, given the comprehensiveness of this mission of Christ on our behalf, this hymn calls on us to "repeat the sounding joy!"

What about all the "theories" of the atonement accomplished by Jesus Christ? The right stance is to recognize that "none are ours, since the setting has changed–and all are ours for the light they shed on the one story of Jesus and God."[75] What is this multi-faceted light reflect-

---

[74] In Charles Wesley, *Nativity Hymns* (1754), as quoted by S. T. Kimbrough, Jr., *Lost In Wonder* (Nashville: The Upper Room, 1987), 53.

[75] James McClendon, *Systematic Theology: Doctrine* (Nashville: Abingdon Press, 1994), 232.

ed from the various biblical metaphors? Comparing complimentary vantagepoints to ancient Rabbinic midrash (biblical interpretations emphasizing contemporary relevance):

> From the ancient *Christus-victor* midrash we gain the theme of cosmic conflict fought out on earthly terms as many a witness endured demonic evil and held fast to Christ, who (once for all) has overcome. From the medieval (and later) satisfaction *midrashim* comes awe at the divine righteousness working in Jesus and at work still. In the modern subjective *midrashim* (with their Anabaptist antecedents) we recognize the self-involving character of the cross.... Yet none of these narratives was meant to replace, but only to illuminate, the story Scripture tells.[76]

God in loving grace is a covenant maker. The central paradigm of the divine-human saving relationship is the covenant motif. Being brought back to right relationship with God is an interpersonal issue not to be hindered by attempts to "explain" it. Indeed, we should "stress the covenant relationship between God and His people while minimizing the insertion of theological constructs which are external to the canonical text or which are *occasional* rather than *universal* paradigms for atonement."[77] The Christian teaching on atonement comes in the form of a *story*, not a *theory*. A beloved gospel song speaks about "the old, old story, of Jesus and His love." The point is that God, in the life, death, and resurrection of Jesus, loves, suffers from our sin, provides opportunity for new life, and expects that we move in faith from being *observers* of the cross of Jesus to being *participants* in his resurrected life! To fully and finally explain the *how* of the atonement accomplished by God in Jesus Christ is beyond us humans; but to celebrate and participate in the atonement is our privilege and calling.

---

[76] Ibid.

[77] R. Larry Shelton, "A Covenant Concept of Atonement," in *Wesleyan Theological Journal* 19:1 (Spring 1984), 91. Emphasis added.

Incarnation and the Problem of Evil

Martin Luther is right: "The cross alone is our theology." The cross of Jesus is the center of Christian faith. In fact, "the haunting image of the crucified Christ is the crucible in which all our thinking about God is forged."[78] Here is God at work in our world, shattering human wisdom, contradicting what the world calls foolish, weak, ineffective. What appeared to the Golgatha onlookers as God's tragic absence turned out, in light of the resurrection, to be the dramatic presence of the suffering and saving God. God really was there, powerfully and peacefully there, in the worst horrors of human existence. God so remains with all those who believe. Christian existence is "life under the cross, life spent in its shadow while we await the dawn of the resurrection light."[79] Waiting requires great patience since evil yet remains.

The meaning of the cross of Jesus Christ is central in approaching one of the more difficult problems faced by all people of faith. It is the problem of evil that remains rampant in our world. Why do the wicked prosper and the treacherous thrive? (Jer. 12:1). Why do the wicked live and reach old age and the mighty grow in power? (Job 21:7). These persistent questions are reviewed here by (1) admitting the dilemma caused in relation to belief in a God who cares and is capable of eliminating evil, (2) affirming the voluntary vulnerability of God, and (3) calling for our patience and protest.

1. Theodicy. David Hume stated clearly the problem confronted by anyone believing in the God revealed in the Bible and thoughtfully observing the sordid drama of ongoing historical existence. Is God willing to prevent evil, but not able? Then God is impotent. Is God able, but not willing? Then God is malevolent. Is God both able and willing? How then is continuing evil to be explained?[80] Biblical faith affirms that God is aware, willing, and

---

[78] Alister McGrath, *Spirituality in an Age of Change* (Grand Rapids: Zondervan, 1994), 76.

[79] Ibid., 81.

[80] See David Hume, *Dialogues Concerning Natural Religion*, part X, 8-9.

able, thus the problem. If a good, all-knowing, and all-powerful God exists alongside the obvious presence of evil, particularly gross and seemingly relentless in the twentieth century, then one faces what has been called the most intractable of theological problems. C. S. Lewis translates this way a couplet from Lucretius: "Had God designed the world, it would not be, a world so frail and faulty as we see."[81]

The effort to understand and vindicate the justice of God in permitting natural and moral evil is known as "theodicy." The notion of theodicy combines the issues of God *(theos)* and justice *(dike)*. Probably the earliest mature theodicy is the biblical book of Job, a narrative tale that explores in considerable depth the trouble experienced by a man of real faith and the many explanations of the origin of this evil that were pressed on him by his "friends." Recalling the major biblical prophets, it can be argued that social evil, unjust power arrangements for which God is claimed as the legitimator and guarantor, is at the center of Israel's thought. For ancient Israel, theodicy "is not an interesting speculative question, but is a practice of social criticism of social systems that do or do not work humanely and of the gods who sponsor and guarantee systems that are or are not just. A god is known by the system it sanctions."[82]

Elton Trueblood admits that "the problem of evil cannot, so far as we know, be wholly solved, but it likewise cannot be avoided with intellectual self-respect."[83] Having reviewed classic ways of solving the problem of evil,[84] he concludes with a confident faith which knows that "the fellowship of perplexity is a goodly fellowship, far superior to the fellowship of easy answers."[85]

Even when we turn to the biblical revelation for answers, we find complexity. The Bible as a whole yields no simplistic answers,

---

[81] C. S. Lewis, *Surprised by Joy* (N. Y.: Harcourt Brace, 1955), 65.

[82] Walter Brueggemann (Patrick Miller, ed.), *A Social Reading of the Old Testament* (Minneapolis: Fortress Press, 1994), 178.

[83] D. Elton Trueblood, *Philosophy of Religion* (Harper & Row, 1957), 235.

[84] These classic ways are: (1) that suffering is a direct result of sin; (2) that evil is really illusory; (3) that evil is a necessary defect in a good plan; (4) that God's power is limited (E. S. Brightman and Peter Bertocci's theory of "the given" in God's mind); and (5) that a childlike faith is the best approach.

[85] Trueblood, op. cit., 244.

but appears to address this perennial dilemma with "a roundtable discussion...chaired by the master, Jesus."[86] The highlight of the conclusion reached involves going to Calvary, gazing at the broken Son of God, and contemplating suffering in light of this amazing act of God on our behalf. God is one with us in our suffering and can use suffering to achieve the highest good. If the cross of Jesus is suffering and injustice at its worst, through this very cross we can discover best the true heart of God.

We humans often learn best through story, reflection on real historical experience. Evil can be radical, irrational, horrible. Ancient Israel knew evil as slavery and exile. A more recent moment of such horror is captured by Elie Wiesel. Here is a story worth engaging. The scene is the Nazi death camp of Auschwitz. A young Jewish man is hanged cruelly and senselessly for some minor infraction of a camp rule. Now his body dangles limply, deliberately displayed for all other prisoners to stare at as an object lesson. Millions of other Jews would meet similar fates. Someone asked prisoner Wiesel in response to this sickening scene: "Where is God now?" Wiesel reflected to himself in profound remorse: "Where is He? Here He is–He is hanging here on this gallows."[87] A God traditionally thought to be both good and almighty seemed in as much difficulty as the dead man. What of belief in God after an Auschwitz?

A testimony comes from the tradition of the Church of God movement (Anderson).[88] Many early movement leaders taught that physical healing was included in Christ's atonement. Therefore, medicine was rejected in favor of faith in God when the evil of illness plagued a believer. Enoch Byrum traveled widely around the United States, called by sickly saints because of his reputation of having the gift of healing.[89] But cases like that of Charles Naylor (1874-1950)

---

[86] David Thompson, "Job at the Biblical Roundtable on Suffering and Divine Justice," *The Asbury Herald* 106:3 (Summer 1995), 6-7.

[87] Elie Wiesel, *Night* (New York: Bantam Books, 1982), 62.

[88] To review the theological tradition of this contemporary Christian reform movement, see Barry Callen, *Contours of a Cause: Theological Vision of the Church of God Movement* (Anderson University School of Theology, 1995).

[89] See Enoch Byrum's *Divine Healing of Soul and Body* (Moundsville, W. Va.:

proved a difficult theological challenge. Naylor was prolific, writing beloved songs like "The Church's Jubilee," "Once Again We Come," and "More Like Christ." He also was crippled by an accident while helping set up a large tent for a gospel meeting. He remained bedfast for many years with unrelieved pain and no physical healing, despite much prayer on his behalf. The lesson of such experiences helped enlarge this movement's theology of healing. Naylor put into words the mystery that embraces suffering people of faith.[90]

At some points theology reaches its limits. The fact that all theology is "broken thought" (Barth) is nowhere clearer than when seeking to relate the providence of God to the radical evil of our fallen world. A young saint is dying of incurable cancer, a drunken driver kills a small child at play, Nazi Germany, a society that represented the best of Western culture, a "Christian" and highly educated nation, annihilates millions of its own citizens out of patriotic arrogance. Bombs capable of almost instant destruction of massive metropolitan areas are stockpiled by the thousands. The sheer scale of such evil numbs thought and threatens to derail traditional Christian theology.

Christian theologians, of course, always have known the problem. They usually have concluded that solutions attempted without the assumption of the biblical God are more problematic than with it. Augustine's classic *City of God* tried to explain the providential role of God as the Roman empire disintegrated. God was said to allow people to misuse their freedom. While not the cause of evil, God is permissive and uses evil to eventually work toward the divine purpose. John Calvin was even more direct in affirming God's control over all that happens. God is said to "decree" what occurs, although God still is not to be considered the author of evil.

Gospel Trumpet Co., 1892), and *Life Experiences* (Anderson, Ind.: Gospel Trumpet Co., 1928).

[90] Some of these words are found in Naylor's book *The Secret of the Singing Heart* (Anderson, Ind.: Warner Press, 1954, rev. 1974). His hymn "I Am the Lord's, I Know" (in *Worship the Lord*, Warner Press, 1989, 639) speaks eloquently. It is theology learned narratively by life experience. Affirms verse one: "Whether I live or die, Whether I wake or sleep, Whether upon the land, Or on the stormy deep; When 'tis serene and calm, Or when the wild winds blow, I shall not be afraid, I am the Lord's, I know."

How can this be? How can God be in full control, with love as the divine motive, while evil appears to run rampant? Three answers have been heard most often. (1) We must trust and be patient when things are beyond our understanding. (2) God must be punishing the wicked or disciplining the people of God. (3) Whatever the reason, suffering is an opportunity to learn and grow spiritually. There is some truth in such partial answers, all having elements of biblical rootage. Daniel Migliore, however, elaborates helpfully on these attempted answers and concludes that "they are all marked by a lack of sustained attention to the gospel story."[91] Brutal evil is to be seen by Christians in light of the narrated love of God seen so vividly in the crucified Christ.

2. Voluntary Vulnerability. While an adequate approach still will be "broken thought," at least its general direction has been shown by the divine incarnation in Christ. "God is limited," says Elton Trueblood, "but limited in a special way.... He is limited by the conditions of goodness." Assuming that God has a good purpose in creation and providence, "God's purpose would be defeated if goodness were compelled." Therefore, "if the possibility of goodness involves choice, it also involves the possibility of evil; and, if the possibility is genuine, it will sometimes by realized."[92] Evil is the high price paid for moral freedom. God's Self-limitation in relation to evil derives not from the nature of reality (as though evil had equal status with God, an unbiblical dualism), but from the nature of goodness which is the nature of God seen throughout the biblical story. The God of loving grace grants freedom, risks rebellion, chooses vulnerability to the emergence of evil. Such is the way of real love.

Remaining acquainted with the "fellowship of the perplexed" in a fallen and evil world like ours, there nonetheless is in the biblical revelation a way to begin addressing the problem of evil. That way holds together the love of God, the power of God, and the reality of evil. This way does not solve the difficult problem by bringing into question any one of these non-negotiables. The way is the revelation itself, the faith understood in narrative terms so that evil is given its

---

[91] Daniel Migliore, *Faith Seeking Understanding* (Eerdmans, 1991), 106-108.
[92] D. Elton Trueblood, op. cit., 249-250.

deserved due in the tension-filled and Bible-illumined drama of real historical existence. Assyria, Exile, Holocaust, Viet Nam, and AIDS happen, and the painful questions they raise must be heard. Our hearing, however, is not deafened by a theological vacuum.

In the beginning of history, reports the biblical revelation, the love of God expressed itself as God's voluntary vulnerability to the potential for evil. This divine risk was taken for the sake of human freedom, required by the nature of love and authentic covenant relationship. In the central chapter of the biblical story, when the actual presence of sin came to require divine confrontation, the power of God is revealed as other than the mere ability to exercise brute force to accomplish the divine intention. In the life, cross, and resurrection of Jesus, the "weakness" of God proves stronger than the misdirected muscle of evildoers. In reality, almost like Wiesel reflected in Auschwitz, God is the One hanging horribly for all to see. This hanging is not God's tragic absence, however, but God's distinctive and saving presence.

Such divine sovereignty being expressed through vulnerable servanthood, so the biblical narrative relates, relentlessly, though not coercively, pursues its redemptive goal along the tortured trail of human history, from the first sin all the way to the end of time. God is patient, often pained, but never defeated. The overarching fact is that one day every knee shall bow in recognition of the One who has the last word (Phil. 2:10). History moves from divine beginning to divine ending. An evil-filled tension lies between. Sometimes the pain of the present is best endured by looking ahead and reading again about the assured ending.[93]

That ending of the biblical story, however, is predicated upon and already inaugurated in the middle of the story, the event of Jesus Christ. In this event can be seen the beginnings of the answer to evil. To view evil appropriately, one is encouraged by the biblical revelation to see evil in relation to the divine incarnation in Christ. Here divine goodness itself entered the realm of temporarily prevailing evil, appeared conquered by that evil on the cross, then turned and in its own patient way conquered evil for us and for all creation. The crea-

---

[93] See Gabriel Fackre, "Almighty God and the Problem of Evil," *Pacific Theological Review* 15 (Fall 1980), 11-16.

ture is not a marionette on the strings of the Creator. God "rules in and over a world of freedom."[94] God is sovereign, freedom and evil are real, and God suffers even while reigning. It is all revealed dramatically in Jesus Christ.

The New Testament speaks jointly of God incarnate in Christ and the reality of evil that we often experience in our lives in the flesh. Following a survey of the presence of evil and its negative effects (Rom. 8:18-39), Paul asks, "who will separate us from the love of Christ?" (v. 35). The answer affirms that no form of evil, nothing in all creation can bring such separation (vv. 38-39). Focusing on the love of God seen in Christ may not solve all theoretical dimensions of the problem of evil (not even atheism does that); but it does bring significant perspective and offers hope and a way of life that can proceed triumphantly in the face of whatever may come.

It is understandable how one might assume that a transcendent God is either indifferent to or at least not really understanding of the evil that humans face. Can God really empathize with the pain of starving children or terminal cancer when God lacks a physical body prone to pain and exists above the possibility of death? Can God really understand the trauma of human temptation when God cannot be tempted (James 1:13)?

The answer, lying deep in the mystery of the triune God, focuses for us in the incarnate Christ. God actually came to be with us in the frailty of real flesh! Reports Hebrews 4:15: "For we do not have a high priest who is unable to sympathize with our weaknesses, but we have one who in every respect has been tested as we are, yet without sin." In Jesus, the triune God identifies, suffers, is tempted, knows evil firsthand. Thomas Aquinas, using the thought of Aristotle, mistakenly insisted that God is incapable of suffering. Millard Erickson rightly counters: "Orthodox doctrine holds that God does indeed choose to permit evil to occur and continue, but that he does so with full knowledge of its consequences, for he himself is victimized by the force of evil."[95] Real acceptance of incarnation leads to acceptance of

---

[94] Karl Barth, *Church Dogmatics*, III:3, 90, 93.

[95] Millard Erickson, *The Word Became Flesh* (Baker Book House, 1991), 608.

divine suffering.

Of central importance is the fact that all evil endured by God is a result of its voluntary acceptance because of divine love. From the initial decision to create humans with free wills, God chose a degree of subjection to creation. Entering into covenant with the Hebrew people involved God's acceptance of the obligations of that relationship (Heb. 6:13-20). To become incarnate among us in Christ meant God was open to what would follow, even the cross. Incarnation was a costly choice. It was an act of loving grace. Jesus laid down his life freely, voluntarily (Jn. 10:17-18). In that laying down on our behalf, God absorbed the momentous pain of evil at its worst. God suffers at the hands of human sin in order that we might be restored by the divine grace in Christ.

Beyond addressing the guilt of sin by means of the incarnation and death of Jesus, God also worked through the life of Jesus to counter the consequences of sin. Jesus saw himself as engaging the forces of evil as he went about healing the sick, casting out demons, even raising the dead. This he did by the active power of God, not by the opposite as some accused (Matt. 12:22-37). He chose the path of self-sacrificing love as the means to heal the deepest hurts of humanity. The last and greatest enemy is death itself (1 Cor. 15:26). Here is evil in its starkest reality. The victim of death this time was Jesus, the One who had done no wrong, the divine agent of selfless love, the one who nonetheless became the object of the wrath of evil until he was dead. It was God's own holocaust.

The key to a Christian understanding of evil goes beyond what the world did to Jesus on the cross. It goes on to some very good news. It proceeds in surprised joy to what God did in the resurrection of Jesus. Death does not have the last word. There is no real solution to the problem of evil if this earthly existence is all there is. Many lives end with justice not done. This is one reason why theories of "reincarnation" are so popular. Surely, people surmise, there will be another time, another chance, a place where wrong things finally will get put right.

Jesus spoke clearly of the often unresolved evil of this life and the reality of life beyond the grave. He warned that we should not lay up our treasures on earth, for all manner of evil can befall them here.

There is a heaven with God where goodness truly reigns, where our treasures belong and will be free of evil corruption (Matt. 6:19-21). We learn from the parable of the rich man and Lazarus that later on justice will bring some great reversals of present circumstances.

We are told by Jesus that all necessary reversals and rewards are part of his own work as the incarnated, crucified, and resurrected Christ who has gone on to prepare a better place (Jn. 14:2). The One who has come to suffer with and for us is the same One who now has gone to prepare for us a place of justice and eternal peace. Jesus will be the One to come again to receive us and separate us finally from the arena of evil. Therefore, Paul could live in hope knowing that "the sufferings of this present time are not worth comparing with the glory about to be revealed to us" (Rom. 8:18).

Why does God not act now to counter evil decisively? God has so acted, out of divine goodness and grace, and within the limits involved in the initial divine choice to grant freedom to human moral agents. A major biblical theme is that God works to bring good out of evil. Joseph discovered a divinely enabled good emerging from what evil had sought to do (Gen. 45:5, 8; 50:20). The worst that the world could do to Jesus was to kill him. Once that was done, brutally, God used that frightful evil as the very means to bring redemptive hope to the world. Christians now "cherish that old rugged cross," clearly an "emblem of suffering and shame," because it was "on that old cross, Jesus suffered and died, to pardon and sanctify me."[96]

3. Patience and Protest. Modern theologians have worked hard on the problem of evil, testing to the limit the boundaries of the biblical revelation. One frontier commonly crossed today is the move from passivity to protest of social injustice.

The protest form of theodicy,[97] while understandable, proves biblically inappropriate. Elie Wiesel and many other sufferers have

---

[96] George Bennard, "The Old Rugged Cross," in *Worship the Lord: Hymnal of the Church of God* (Anderson, Ind.: Warner Press, 1989), 195, vv. 1, 3.

[97] Again, "theodicy" is an attempt to justify the ways of God in relation to humanity and creation, despite disturbing appearances to the contrary. Theodicy seeks to explain how one can believe in a God who is both sovereign and good when there is evil still in the world.

come to question the total goodness of God.[98]   Since evil seems overwhelming, they feel justified in quarreling with any assumption about the love and providence of a supposedly sovereign God.

On the other hand, theologians like John Cobb question the power rather than the goodness of God. They often employ process metaphysics (Whitehead) to face the dilemma.[99] God, while good, is said to function with a significant restriction of power, working in the historical process by persuasion only, thus not able to prevent a Holocaust. God intends good and shares the suffering caused by evil, but is limited metaphysically. This kind of theodicy departs from the biblical revelation by employing a speculative philosophic system that reduces the full sovereignty and transcendence of God in a way that God has not chosen as Self-limitation. What we actually face is the paradox of a truly sovereign God who remains truly sovereign even while functioning in an evil world with voluntary Self-limitation, all because of loving grace.

The biblical story focuses on rather than denying this present, historically real and largely evil world. Thus the typical theodicy of the "liberation" theologians today stays with the challenges of the here and now. It struggles with how to relate the continuing oppressiveness of moral and social evils on marginalized people to belief that a truly good and all-powerful God is at work to liberate them. Karl Barth, though departing from the acquiescence characteristic of Calvinism in the face of evil (God is sovereign, so wait and believe), is criticized for not introducing a balance between *patience* and *protest*. Liberationists like James Cone stress the importance of human participation in God's current struggle against evil. God is said to provide "power to the powerless to fight here and now for the freedom they know to be theirs in Jesus' cross and resurrection."[100] Christian faith enables patience, but should not encourage inactivity. We are to be partners

---

[98] Clark Williamson argues that the whole of Christian theology needs careful reconsideration following the Holocaust suffered by the Jews and others at Nazi hands (see his *A Guest in the House of Israel: Post-Holocaust Church Theology*, Westminster/John Knox Press, 1993).

[99] John Cobb, Jr., *God and the World* (Philadelphia: Westminster Press, 1969), 87-102.

[100] James Cone, *God of the Oppressed* (N. Y.: Seabury Press, 1974), 183.

of God in overcoming evil.

Christian faith that is instructed by the biblical revelation is aware that God reaches out to express love and form community. Being vulnerable by gracious choice, not aloof and immutable, God overcomes the evil now in creation "by a costly history of divine love in which the suffering of the world is really experienced and overcome by God."[101] Faith requires insight and then calls for action. The insight is to know "the crucified God"[102] through the story of the cross and the suffering and death of the Son of God in the service of love. The Bible "directs us to God's powerlessness and suffering; only the suffering God can help," wrote Dietrich Bonhoeffer.[103]

Stanley Hauerwas challenges the arguments of most books about the "problem of evil" since they seldom raise the question of who has the right to ask the question and from what set of presuppositions. The modern project of self-mastery and self-fulfillment, launched by the Enlightenment, assumes that we humans are in control of life. If something goes wrong, there must be a reason and we can find it. Hauerwas thinks it more Christian to face evil honestly in a way that enables us to move on, even without a rational explanation.[104] Suffering needs a voice within the context of a supportive community at worship. That voice may lack explanations, but it nonetheless assists hurting people to move from despair and stunned passivity to a vision of hope that allows courageous action. Walter Brueggemann observes that "any 'world' that is 'made' in liturgy which does not include honest elements of pain is a false world that leads to death."[105] But to know pain in the midst of a community of faith is to find a way to move through and beyond it without denial of its reality.

---

[101] Daniel Migliore, op. cit., 115.

[102] Jürgen Moltmann, *The Crucified God* (N. Y.: Harper, 1974).

[103] Dietrich Bonhoeffer, *Letters and Papers from Prison* (N. Y.: Macmillan, 1972), 361.

[104] Stanley Hauerwas, *Naming the Silences: God, Medicine and the Problem of Suffering* (Eerdmans, 1990). This approach also cautions that Christians not insist on a rational explanation of the atonement accomplished in Christ. Rather, a believer should (1) absorb the marvelous reality as it comes in its many biblical metaphors and (2) move on in this evil world as a new person saved by grace!

[105] Walter Brueggemann, *Israel's Praise: Doxology Against Idolatry and Ideology* (Fortress Press, 1988), 133.

To know that all evil has been experienced and absorbed by God inspires the call to action, to work for peace and justice, to join the One whose love is at work from creation to completion–a love that will prevail in the face of all evil. God works not through coercive omnipotence, so as to avoid the presence of any evil, but by the power of suffering and redeeming love (Isa. 53). In the face of the destructiveness of evil, one should not link too closely God's providence and either the use of raw power or a retiring patience that appears unready to act at all to counter evil. Evil, while not to be resisted with more evil, is to be resisted (Rom. 12:21)! Resistance is to be carried on "in Christ," by the power and in the manner of the Spirit, with the sure hope that the already inaugurated reign of God one day will be consummated.

God is righteous, meaning in part that loving justice now is or at least one day will be fully realized. We have been promised that God "will wipe every tear from their eyes. Death will be no more; mourning and crying and pain will be no more" (Rev. 21:4). All Christian efforts to cope with evil should begin with consideration of the crucified Christ. There one learns about a suffering and redeeming love that rests in divine grace and is liberated to hope for the "glory, as yet unrevealed, which is in store for us" (Rom. 8:18).

Beloved hymn lyrics recognize the abundance of evil, pray for freedom from paralyzing fear, and speak of the journey of faith:

> Lo! the hosts of evil round us,
>> Scorn Thy Christ, assail His ways!
> From the fears that long have bound us,
>> Free our hearts to faith and praise.
>
> Save us from weak resignation
>> to the evils we deplore;
> Let the search for Thy salvation
>> Be our glory evermore.[106]

---

[106] Harry Emerson Fosdick, "God of Grace and God of Glory" (vss. 2 and 4).

To live life in this hopeful, fear-less, faith-full way, based on the biblically narrated identity and mission of Jesus Christ, is dependent on the ongoing ministry of the Spirit of God. To a consideration of this Spirit and this ministry we now turn.

Part Three

SPIRIT:

The God Who Stays and Sustains,
the Presence of Loving Grace

CHAPTER SIX

SPIRIT: WITNESS AND ENABLER

—

"We believe in the Holy Spirit, the Lord, the giver of life"
who proceeds from the Father, who, with the Father and
the Son, is worshipped and glorified."

—

We said in the last chapter that the atonement accomplished
by Jesus Christ intends to lead to life in the Spirit and to the
reality of a Spirit-filled church on mission in the world.
The church is to live in hope as it continues to remember and benefit from the crucified and resurrected Christ, all by the present power
of the Spirit of God. Summarizes Jürgen Moltmann:

> The present power of this remembrance and this hope is
> called "the power of the Spirit," for it is not of their own
> strength, reason, and will that people believe in Jesus as the
> Christ and hope for the future as God's future.... Faith in
> Christ and hope for the kingdom are due to the presence of
> God in the Spirit.[1]

Paul refers to the Spirit of God as the "first fruits" or "downpayment" of the final resurrection (Rom. 8:23; 2 Cor. 1:22; 5:5; Eph.
1:13-14). Into our present has broken God's future! What then of the
resurrection of Jesus Christ? It was more than an isolated event in
which one individual overcame death. It was "the death of the old
aeon and the birth of the new aeon. Hence to be in Christ or in the

---

[1] Jürgen Moltmann, *The Church in the Power of the Spirit* (N.Y.: Harper &
Row, 1977), 197.

Spirit (which we have seen to be synonymous) is to be in the age to come and to participate in its power."[2]

The present experience of the Spirit of God features the resurrection power of Jesus, the risen Christ. Jesus' disciples, once aware of his resurrection, knew that it was really just the beginning. However rich their Jewish heritage and however dramatic the saving events of God in Christ, God also was propelling them into the future. They were learning that "to be a Christian was [is] to be a risk-taker. Every day they could expect that God's Spirit would do creative things in making Jesus' presence real."[3] To live in Christ is to live by God's loving grace, through the Spirit of God, as an extension of the emerging post-resurrection life of Jesus. To do so together as the body of Christ is to be the church, the community of the Spirit.

Community of the Spirit

The Apostles' and Nicene Creeds have three major articles. The first two affirm God the creator and reconciler. If not for the third article, however, Christians would be left to live with abstraction, knowing only about a distant deity who long ago created and then once came near in Israel's history and supremely in Jesus Christ. According to John Calvin: "As long as Christ remains outside us, and we are separated from him, all that he has done and suffered for the salvation of the human race remains useless and of no value to us."[4] But there is a third article in the ancient creeds. In fact, John Wesley's contribution to the Western theological tradition has been identified as his "pursuit of what can be termed a theology of the third article of the creed, a theology of the transforming consummation of creation in and through the Holy Spirit."[5]

---

[2] H. Ray Dunning, *Grace, Faith and Holiness: A Wesleyan Systematic Theology* (Kansas City: Beacon Hill Press, 1988), 476.

[3] Alan Kreider, *Journey Towards Holiness: A Way of Living for God's Nation* (Scottdale, Pa.: Herald Press, 1987), 204.

[4] John Calvin, *Institutes of the Christian Religion*, 3.1.1.

[5] D. Lyle Dabney, "Jürgen Moltmann and John Wesley's Third Article Theology," *Wesleyan Theological Journal* 29:1-2 (Spring/Fall, 1994), 144.

The God who is *over* and *for* us (God the Father and the Son) is available to be *in* and *through* us (God the Spirit). The biblical story of God-with-us moves from the risen Christ to the present Spirit. The divine purpose remains redemptive, intending to intersect and infuse our personal and corporate life stories. The present God is a missionary God working to flow through our new lives in Christ so that the Spirit may impact the world. The Holy Spirit is the theological way of speaking about God's active relatedness to creation and especially to human beings. The Spirit is divine immanence, distinguishable from the incarnate immanence in Christ, but intimately related to it. There is only one God. God was in Christ and now is with us as the Spirit of that Christ.

When speaking of God as Father, Son, and Spirit, we limited human beings are speaking narratively of how we experience God's presence historically and personally. Enlightened by the biblical story, we have become aware of God as the creative source and sustainer (Creator-Parent). We have come to know God as Savior in the historical Jesus Christ. Since the resurrection of Jesus, believers also have continued to experience God's presence and power. This is God still with us, the Holy Spirit. The Spirit does not supercede, but enhances the divine Self-revelation known as Father and Son. Charles Wesley, "the songster of the Spirit, an Orpheus among the theologians," knew that "the Spirit of God is God in action" so that "when the Spirit acts, the entire Godhead is in action."[6]

Such continuity, in fact co-identity of the Divine, requires that the Spirit be understood in the context of the Hebrew Bible, just as the messiahship of Jesus can only be understood in the context of Hebrew history. To fail to recognize this biblical narrative as foundational to Christian belief is to strip theology down to no more than a sterile scholasticism or a fleeting subjectivism. The Spirit is God-with-us in Israel, in Christ, and in the now of our lives.

The Spirit originally is said to have set the whole creation in motion and now nurtures it toward its final liberation. God the Spirit is creative "wind" sweeping over what yet was only a formless void

---

[6] T. Crichton Mitchell, *Charles Wesley: Man with the Dancing Heart* (Kansas City: Beacon Hill Press, 1994), 131-132.

(Gen. 1:2). The divine wind blows where it chooses (Jn. 3:8), bringing life, wisdom, and peace (Jn. 14:26-27). She[7] brings the eschaton
alive, directing us toward Jesus, the Lord who inaugurated the kingdom of God among us at his first coming and will consummate it at
his second coming. The Spirit brings believers into the Son's own intimate relationship with the Father and liberates the yearnings of our
hearts toward the future (Rom. 8:22-27; cf. Gal. 4:6, 5:5). The Spirit
is the divine presence, the sustainer who stays after the ascension of
Jesus Christ. The Spirit's work is to witness to God in Israel and Jesus
Christ, transform believers into the image of Jesus, and initiate them
into the church, so that at Christ's return "we will be like him, for we
will see him as he is" (1 Jn. 3:2). Believers are to be a remembering
community, the church, remembering Jesus in the present community
of the Spirit.[8]

If *christology* (study of Jesus as the Christ) answers the question
of how God has acted incarnationally in Jesus to provide for human
need, *pneumatology* (study of the Spirit of the Christ) deals with
how reconciling resources provided by Christ are effectively communicated to fallen humanity in each ongoing present. The Spirit of
God is "the presence of that Jesus who was crucified and raised, and
who constitutes the realization of the promises of God. Thus, the presence of the past of Jesus and the presence of the future of God characterize the action of the Spirit."[9] The very One who was and will be

---

[7] See chapter two for a discussion of gender language and the nature of God the
"Father." Because God's Spirit (*ruach*) is feminine in Hebrew, some contend that the
Spirit should be considered the "feminine principle" in God. However, God is beyond
gender. We must avoid idolizing our metaphors for the divine. Noting that theologians
often apply female language to the birthing and nurturing Spirit of God, Daniel Migliore
warns rightly that "the triune God is neither an exclusive fraternity nor a divine company of two males (the Father and Jesus) and one female (the Holy Spirit). That the triune
God is also called Spirit teaches us to think and speak of God as uniquely personal, allowing gender-specific imagery, yet far transcending all such imagery." He adds the sug-
gestion that "the Word and Spirit of God can be described respectively as the Son and
Daughter of God, working together to make us all adopted children of God" (*Faith Seeking Understanding*, 1991, 174).

[8] See C. Norman Kraus, *The Community of the Spirit: How the Church Is in the
World*, rev. ed. (Scottdale, Pa.: Herald Press, 1993).

[9] Theodore Jennings, Jr., *Loyalty To God: The Apostles' Creed in Life and Liturgy* (Nashville: Abingdon Press, 1992), 180-181.

now is present and active as the Spirit for the enablement of salvation and mission.[10]

In only five brief verses the Gospel of John (20:19-23) describes central features of the church's origin, nature, and mission. All is authorized by the resurrected Christ. The disciples rejoice in God's presence, receive the peace of Christ, and are commissioned for service, but only after they have received the Holy Spirit. The church is to be an ongoing resurrection event of community formation, the gathering of a people who were no people, a new community of the Spirit.

The resurrection of Jesus is the pivotal event as the biblical story tells of the launching of the Christian community. In 1 Corinthians 15:1-11 Paul argues vigorously for the literal reality of this resurrection. More than a key past event, however, the point being made to the Corinthians is that the divine power that raised Jesus somehow has made of his death a saving event in relation to the sinful condition of all humanity. This power transformed Paul and will bring new life to the Corinthians as they hear the good news and believe. The resurrection overturned the death of Jesus and now, through the ministry of the Spirit of Christ, can bring new life, light, and hope to the death, darkness, and despair of human sin.

There is more. The resurrection of Jesus brings into being a new community of faith, the church. It evokes, forms, and authorizes the community of the ever-alive Jesus. Jesus comes unexpectedly into the gathering of bewildered and fearful disciples, regathering them by the Spirit's power (Jn. 20:19-31). This community of amazed and grateful believers soon comes to be filled with joy, power, well-being, divine gifts, and generosity (Acts 4:32-35[11]). For the body of believers, in the train of Jesus' resurrection comes communion with God

---

[10] C. Norman Kraus rightly cautions that biblical language about the Spirit is "experiential and functional rather than philosophical and analytical. The Spirit is identified with God and Christ's presence and activity. He is God (or Christ) at work in and through the new messianic community and the world at large, furthering the mission of Christ.... What we want to affirm is the full divinity of the Spirit's presence and work among us (Phil. 2:13; Rom. 8:9-11; 1 Cor. 6:19) without adopting all the philosophical shibboleths of the Greek tradition [three 'persons,' e. g.]" (*God Our Savior*, Herald Press, 1991, 133, 136).

[11] This text underscores that the ideal of the faith community is not rooted in guilt, as though a "communistic" style of economic life and a set of behavioral legalisms are

and with each other. The church is the company of the committed.[12]
The teaching of 1 John 1:1-2:2 is that the gathering of resurrection
people is a remarkable community characterized by light, truth, righteousness, and a burden for the need of the world. All is by the loving
grace of the God who remains present as the enabling Spirit of Christ.

Between Easter and Eschaton

Eschatology, the study of "end things," should not be relegated
to the last pages of Christian theology. Eschatology, biblically understood, is more theologically pervasive and profound than merely
laying out the nature and even chronology of the events that finally
will bring to a climax the whole divine program for the history of
humanity and all creation. Yes, there will be a consummation to the
biblical story of salvation history. The primary biblical concern, however, is hardly to satisfy human curiosity about the future. It is to highlight that God's reign and future intent already have broken into our
history in Jesus Christ and should make a difference *now*, as it certainly will *then*.

In the Gospel of John the phrase "eternal life" means much more
than unending existence. "Eternal" in the New Testament means
"pertaining to an age," or life with the quality that reflects God's age
to come in its fullness. In part this future of God is available for experiencing now by Spirit-enlivened believers. John's great thought is
that eternal life already is the possession of those who come to Christ
and find new birth by the Spirit. Jesus came that abundant life might
be available in the present (10:10). God gave the Son, a Self-giving
out of profound love so that everyone who believes might have this
life eternal (3:16). The good news of Easter is that in Christ we too
may be raised to newness of life, now, in accord with and in the service of that age yet to come.

---

commanded as law. It is rooted rather in resurrection power and grace, making the church
an eschatological community living with standards and potentials in contrast with the surrounding culture. Sharing is not to appease guilt, but to affirm and live the resurrection
life by the power of the Spirit.

[12] See Elton Trueblood, *The Company of the Committed* (N.Y.: Harper, 1961).

The story of Christian believers today is to be an unfolding drama of the fallen creation on its way, by God's grace, to regaining the true holiness of God's intention. The church is to embody the reality seen in and inaugurated by the first coming of Christ. Says Paul, God in Christ "has made known to us the mystery of his will" (Eph. 1:9). This mystery now is an assured vision of the Christ-shaped future rooted in the gospel of the Jesus already come among us. It brings to believers the needed direction and inspiration for their journey through history. Sinners become new creatures and divine agents only as personal stories are caught up in and reshaped by the truth of the biblical story of God in Christ.

Eschatology is a central concern of biblical writers and so should be an essential perspective that permeates Christian truth as a whole. Rather than being "the tail end of a doctrinal system,"[13] it is of the essence of the life of faith. Leading representatives of the theology of hope (J. Moltmann, W. Pannenberg, etc.) stress both the reality of the full consummation yet ahead and the present implications of such a hope. This interactive emphasis helps to overcome the false dichotomy often seen between this-worldly and other-worldly orientations of Christian vision and life.

That which yet will be opens the door of hope and power in relation to what might come to be even now in our troubled times. Paul makes clear that such sanctification of the present is the work of the Spirit. The divine goal is the enablement of ethical character and action patterned after the likeness of Christ (1 Thess. 2:13; 4:3ff). Paul is elaborating the full implications of life in the new age, the age that already is inaugurated by Christ and now is being activated by the Spirit in the lives of the believing church.

Delwin Brown says it well: "If we are to be faithful to our confidence in a God who through us is able to do more than we ask, more even than we can imagine, then we must emphatically reject any effort to put a limit on the kind of personal and social transformation that might be accomplished in history, even in our own time."[14]

---

[13] Clark Pinnock, in Pinnock and Delwin Brown, *Theological Crossfire* (Grand Rapids: Zondervan, 1990), 221.

[14] Ibid., 236.

Stanley Grenz elaborates further on such Christian optimism: "Because of their awareness of the significance of the present in the light of the future, those who acknowledge the lordship of Christ seek throughout this epoch (time between the *already* of Christ's first coming and the *not yet* of the full realization of God's future) to proclaim in word and action by the power of the Holy Spirit the good news about the reign of God."[15]

The biblical revelation leads from the vision of the resurrected Christ to an enduring hope that inspires and enables *present mission*. At the heart of this vision, hope, mission, inspiration, and enablement is the Spirit of God, the Sustainer, the One who stays with us in the interim time. This crucial interim, now, the era of the church, lies between the comings of Christ and is the time of living out the mission of Christ. Now is the Age of the Spirit.

As seen in the early chapters of Acts, the function of the Spirit is to make it possible for the believing community to live already, at least in part, in the not yet of the full reign of God. That reign, already inaugurated in our midst, calls for self-less loving and giving, which is why it is so difficult for the rich to enter the kingdom (Matt. 19:24). When one's investments are in the present order, usually there is little commitment to being a pilgrim journeying eagerly toward full realization of a new order of things. When investments are in the age to come, there is freedom to impact the present by a pilgrim existence that contrasts with and speaks prophetically to the world. The church is to be a journeying band of "resident aliens."[16]

The events of that first Christian Pentecost are a central part of the drama of the incarnation. In fact, the whole story of Jesus is the historic baseline, the "and it came to pass" of God's promises through the prophets (Heb. 1:1-2). But the fullness of the good news about the coming of the Christ is that the incarnational work of God extends from Jesus to this very moment. The announcement that now brings great joy is about a continuing narrative of what God did and *is doing*. The full gospel is the news that in Christ the "power of God for

---

[15] Stanley Grenz, *The Millennial Maze* (InterVarsity Press, 1992), 200.

[16] See Stanley Hauerwas and William Willimon, *Resident Aliens* (Nashville: Abingdon Press, 1989).

salvation" (Rom. 1:16) can become present reality for all who will receive. The relevance of the historic gospel is that it can and should be received and represented *now*.[17]

What happened at Pentecost provided "the connecting link between past and present. The continuity between the historical presence of Jesus and our present salvation was disclosed in the living presence of the Spirit of Christ."[18] The kingdom of God announced and embodied by Jesus is not forced to await some future millennium. There is the potential of meaningful kingdom fulfillment in the present, made possible by the outpouring of the Spirit on waiting disciples. We who choose to wait on the coming God have the promise that we *will receive* (Acts 1:8). Being filled with power from on high is a significant part of the Christian good news! God came in Christ–and still comes in the Spirit!

Christians can wait in hope and live distinctive lives of sacrificial service because they have God's promise and the Spirit, the downpayment on that promise's final fulfillment. In Romans 8:22 Paul says that believers groan in travail with the whole creation, waiting for the day when the creation will be freed from its bondage. Meanwhile, we have the first fruits of the Spirit. We dare to hope because the triumph of goodness, grace, love, and justice does not depend ultimately on us, but on the power and work of the Spirit.

Having made the harsh but justified judgment that much of what passes for traditional Christian theology "is in reality the result

---

[17] The Anabaptist or Believers' Church tradition judges that true reformation of the church must include holiness. Christian faith is not merely what church members believe. It is who they now are and how they now live, especially as a faith community in contrast to the world. See Alan Kreider, *Journey Towards Holiness* (Scottdale, Pa.: Herald Press, 1987). John Wesley showed an increasingly close affinity with this tradition later in his life (see Howard Snyder, *The Radical Wesley*, Inter-Varsity, 1980). Howard Snyder identifies four broad correlations between Wesley's understanding of the Christian life and what is characteristic of "charismatic" movements: (1) the stress on God's grace in the life of the church; (2) the significant role of the Holy Spirit in theology; (3) the emphasis on the church as community; and (4) the tension between the vision of the church and its institutional expressions (see Snyder, with Daniel Runyon, *The Divided Flame: Wesleyans and the Charismatic Renewal*, Grand Rapids: Zondervan, 1986, 54-64).

[18] C. Norman Kraus, *The Community of the Spirit* (Scottdale, Pa.: Herald Press, 1993), 13.

of the alliance between the church and the power structures of society," Justo González went on to speak for an ethnic roundtable of Christians representing the world's oppressed. They believe in the church because they believe in God's future. They hope, "not because we trust our own programs of reformation, and even less because we trust its structures and committees, but because we trust in the Holy Spirit."[19]

Neglect and distrust of the work of the Holy Spirit, however, have been far too common in Christian church history. In many cases the church has opposed movements that have stressed the presence and power of the Spirit, movements like the Montanists of the second century, the Waldensians of the twelfth century, the radical reformers of the sixteenth century, and the Charismatic and Christian base communities of our own time. In the case of Montanus (ca. 180), who claimed to be the Comforter Jesus had promised, official church response went far beyond dealing with this obvious extreme. Particularly in the Latin church, spiritual gifts now were to be restricted to the control of properly credentialed clergy–a dramatic institutionalization of simple New Testament teaching. Such overreaction and artificial restriction of spiritual gifts, often understandably prompted by genuine abuses,[20] usually has had damaging effects on both Christian life and theology. Despite the lingering problems of human sin, even within the "visible" church, the Spirit (not creed or clergy) is to be Lord of the church!

---

[19] Justo González, *Out of Every Tribe & Nation* (Nashville: Abingdon Press, 1992), 115.

[20] Two unacceptable extremes often have emerged. One is disconnecting the Spirit from the teachings and work of the historical Jesus, allowing an unchecked mysticism, a "spiritual" religion like at Corinth where the rootage in Christ was getting buried in unchecked emotional experiences. The other is identifying the Spirit with universal reason, human enlightenment and aspiration, an attribute of the creation apart from the transcendent being of God (or identified as God reduced to immanence only). Creation and the Spirit are to be identified closely, but never are they identical. Through the Spirit the gift of life was and is granted (Ps. 104:29-30). All forms of life are to be treated with respect. Creation is to be preserved in dignity without a sacralization of nature. The Holy Spirit gives life, but is not to be identified with and limited to biological life, human consciousness, or a creative impulse inherent in the creation itself.

Experiencing the Spirit

Christian theology always seems to seek equilibrium. Particular thinkers, schools of thinkers, or even whole periods in church history have tended to emphasize one thing in order to balance a perceived overemphasis on the opposite in the recent past. For instance, Protestant "orthodoxy" in the generations following the great Protestant reformers of the sixteenth century came to place emphasis on highly creedalized doctrinal thinking and church life. Soon that brought the reaction of Pietism with its stress on the subjective, individualistic dimension of truth and life. The sanctification of the inner life through the Holy Spirit thus gained the spotlight, down playing the importance of objective, intellectual, and organizational precision at the doctrinal and institutional levels.

In turn, as time passed the pendulum continued to swing. The subjective tendency of Christian Pietism evolved into the liberalism of the nineteenth century. The result so weakened orthodoxy's hold on the German universities that soon "Enlightenment" thinkers came to prevail. Immanuel Kant (1724-1804), reared in a Pietist home, saw his critical philosophy as an enlightened form of Pietism. Modern secularism began to champion in its own way the realm of the subjective. The emergence of such "modernism" can be seen as an implicit translation of the doctrine of the Spirit into secular terms.[21] Spiritual "experience," without firm roots in the biblical revelation, holds much negative potential.

By the twentieth century it was time for another reversal, one that would counter the severe swing of this subjectivistic stream. Karl Barth (1886-1968) came to view human consciousness methodology as a threat to the Christian faith because it subordinates the historic biblical witness to the immediacies of Christian experience. Barth taught that "God alone is the absolute Subject of his own revelation to humanity. Jesus Christ is the absolute focal point of the self-revealing God."[22] With the focus now falling on the historic Christ,

---

[21] Georg Hegel, *Reason In History*, trans. by Robert Hartman (N. Y.: The Bobbs-Merrill Co., 1953), 25.

[22] Laurence Wood, "From Barth's Trinitarian Christology To Moltmann's Trinitarian Pneumatology," *The Asbury Theological Journal* (Spring 1993), 50.

Barth's massive *Church Dogmatics* was designed largely to counter Schleiermacher's liberalism. Barth feared subjectivism and above all wanted to avoid the trap of equating pneumatology (study of the Holy Spirit) with anthropology (study of humanity). This corrective of Barth, so influential on Christian theology through the middle of the twentieth century, also got out of balance, as Barth himself admitted late in his life. He realized that, in countering the excess of spiritualized religion, he himself had failed to develop a significant theology of the Spirit.[23]

Barth called for someone to balance his own lack of teaching at this crucial point. Who would step forward? Jürgen Moltmann, a student of Barth, answered the call and now has managed a doctrine of the Holy Spirit that largely is free of the kind of subjectivism rightly refuted by his teacher.[24] The freeing factor is that with Moltmann "the revelation of God is not a private affair, subjectively imagined to happen in a non-historical moment of self-disclosure [Barth]. Rather, the revelation of God is a real historical happening in the concrete world and can be affirmed with rational integrity."[25]

Given the biblical narrative with its historically objective foundations, Christian theology again appears ready to be rebalanced. One can reintroduce confidently the role of spiritual experience and a theology of the Holy Spirit without yielding to the extremes sometimes characteristic of Pietism, the liberalisms emerging from Schleiermacher, or an existentialistic modernism.[26] The twentieth

---

[23] Karl Barth, *The Theology of Schleiermacher*, trans. Geoffrey Bromiley (Grand Rapids: Eerdmans, 1982), 279.

[24] Jürgen Moltmann's *Theology of Hope* (1964), praised widely as theologically groundbreaking, suffered from absence of attention to the Holy Spirit. In 1992, however, he released *The Spirit of Life* (Minneapolis: Fortress Press), rectifying the earlier omission. He now has come into serious conversation with the Spirit-oriented work of John Wesley.

[25] Wood, op. cit., 52.

[26] In the eighteenth century John Wesley balanced well the objective and subjective in Christian faith. He had been influenced early by Pietism, but two hundred years before Barth he also had come to distrust "mysticism" for reasons similar to Barth's. Even so, the importance of "assurance" and inward cleansing by the work of the Spirit was taught by Wesley as essential for Christians. See Robert G. Tuttle, Jr., *Mysticism in the Wesleyan Tradition* (Grand Rapids: Francis Asbury Press, 1989).

century has seen an unprecedented "charismatic" renewal. Obviously the search is on to rediscover the living reality of authentic Christian faith with its Spirit-centered power. A part of this contemporary search are movements like the Church of God (Anderson) and the Brethren in Christ.[27] These Christians, while affirming objective revelation in history as mediated by the biblical witness, nonetheless have been in the vanguard of a "radical" renewal based on the biblical witness and life in the Spirit.[28]

Life in the Spirit, authentic Christian spirituality, has come to be viewed widely by Christians as important.[29] It has to do with internalizing and implementing the gospel. It calls for human stories to be transformed by exposure to the biblical story. Not some vague mysticism, Christian spirituality centers in the historic Jesus, mediated to current believers by the Spirit of God. Believers are to affirm Jesus as truth's norm and life's guide, finding their lives in the Spirit of Jesus. This focus has specific foundation and clear intent. The focus is the biblical revelation; the intent is present fulfillment of Christ's mission in the world by life in the Spirit.

The general malaise of mainline Protestantism in the final years of the twentieth century will not be addressed successfully by mere revisions of church structures and programs. The vitality of Christian

---

[27] The narrative histories of these two movements emphasize in their very titles the necessary journeying with the Spirit that should lead to new life in the Spirit and discipleship obedience enabled by the Spirit (*Quest for Holiness and Unity* by John Smith, Warner Press, 1980, and *Quest for Piety and Obedience* by Carlton Wittlinger, Evangel Press, 1978).

[28] For the historical roots of the "pentecostal" movement emerging in the nineteenth century, see Donald Dayton, *Theological Roots of Pentecostalism* (Hendrickson Publishers, 1987). For discussion of how the Church of God movement relates to this emergence, see Barry Callen, *Contours of a Cause* (Anderson University School of Theology, 1995). This "radical" renewal is likewise needed today in the United Methodist Church, one major carrier of the Wesleyan tradition (see Stephen Seamands, *Holiness of Heart and Life*, Abingdon Press, 1990).

[29] The many reasons for renewed interest today in the Holy Spirit include: (1) reaction to the depersonalization of modern society; (2) hunger for a personally meaningful relationship to God, one adequate to face the crises of our times; (3) realization that activism on behalf of ecumenism and social justice finally collapses if its foundations are only structural and programmatic; (4) the fact of the dramatic rise of various forms of pentecostalism and Christian base communities, especially in the third world; and (5) new appreciation for the central role of the Holy Spirit throughout the biblical narrative.

life is absent without the Spirit. To be spiritual is not merely to med-
itate, retreat, and pray frequently and in prescribed manners. Christian life in the Spirit is "seeking to live out of the future that the Spirit makes present.... The question is...whether we are willing to live
out of that spirituality which, by the presence of the Holy Spirit,
makes us the people of the Reign of God." Shall we indeed be a Pentecost people? Who is a spiritual person in a truly Christian sense?
The spiritual person is the one "in whom the Spirit of the Lord
dwells."[30]

The Spirit As God Present

A crucial transition occurs in the Apostles' Creed when historic
memory moves to contemporary meaning. Having affirmed as sacred
memory that Jesus was conceived, born, suffered, crucified, dead,
buried, descended, risen, and ascended, the creed dramatically shifts
to meaning in the present tense. This same Jesus now is "seated at the
right hand of the Father" (1 Pet. 3:22). This being "seated" is the time
of the church's life, bracketed by the past events of the Christ on earth
and the anticipation of Christ's coming again "to judge the living and
the dead." Between formative past and culminating future is the *present of the Spirit*, the reigning and ruling, enlivening and gifting of the
Spirit of Christ. In the gift of the Holy Spirit, explains Jürgen Moltmann, word and sacrament, ministries and divine gifts "become comprehensible as the revelations and powers of Christ and his future. As
the emblematic revelations of Christ they are the messianic media-
tions of salvation. As glorifications of Christ they are actions of hope
pointing towards the kingdom."[31]

Paul raised the pivotal questions in Romans 8:33-35, concluding that no one and nothing can separate believers from the powerful
love of Christ, the One who now sits at the right hand of God and
ministers through the Spirit. Ephesians 1:20-21 likewise affirms that
Christ currently has complete authority. First Peter 3:22, noting that

---

[30] Justo González, *Mañana: Christian Theology from a Hispanic Perspective*
(Nashville: Abingdon Press, 1990), 158, 163, 167.

[31] Jürgen Moltmann, *The Church in the Power of the Spirit* (N.Y.: Harper & Row,
1977), 205-206.

Christ now is at the right hand of God, gives assurance that any persecution can be endured if one is steadfast in faith.

It was common in the biblical world for sitting to be the body language of authority.[32] For Jesus to be "sitting" suggests not his relaxation, but his aggressive activity in exercising authority by the very power of God. Here is belief that sustains the faithful between the resurrection and final return of Jesus. This Jesus is the Lord of the between time. Indeed, "it is by fixing our attention on the one who is the true authority for life and history that we learn to turn away from a life of compulsion (Col. 3:5) and division (3:8) and deceit (3:9), and turn instead to a life formed by forgiveness, peace, and gratitude (3:12-17)."[33] Life formed in this new way, on the pattern of Christ, is the work of Christ's Spirit. The Spirit is God present lovingly and powerfully in our nows.

Genuine Christian living comes from knowing that, in the time of our own existence, the biblical story of God-with-us moves steadily forward, featuring Christ sitting at the Father's right hand on our behalf. The Christ of the New Testament church is not the absent Christ, once here in Jesus and now gone with Jesus. He "has never resigned his position as head of the church and vested the governmental authority in a self-perpetuating clerical caste.... He administers it himself through his Holy Spirit.... The basis of every man's authority and responsibility is, therefore, not human appointment or official position, but the divine call, gifts, and qualifications that he possesses."[34] Life with Christ and for Christ's mission is enabled by life in Christ's Spirit.[35]

---

[32] Note: Ex. 18:13; 2 Kings 25:28; Da. 7:9; Matt. 5:1; 13:1-2; 20:21; 23:2. A current example with similar meaning is referring to the one in charge of a group as the "chair" of the committee.

[33] Theodore Jennings, Jr., *Loyalty to God* (Nashville: Abingdon Press, 1992), 155.

[34] F. G. Smith, *The Last Reformation* (Anderson, Ind.: Gospel Trumpet Co., 1919), 135.

[35] The Spirit of Christ is the Spirit of *life*, a new order of creation in Christ (2 Cor. 5:17), the Spirit of *wisdom* which is the mind of Christ (1 Cor. 2:10-16), the Spirit of *power* with the death-overcoming resurrection potency of Christ (Eph. 1:19-20), and the Spirit of *love* and *peace*. See development of these in C. Norman Kraus, *God Our Savior*, 1991, 154-157.

Much theological confusion is avoided when the Spirit of God is understood in a trinitarian relation to God the Creator and God the Redeemer. To speak of the Holy Spirit in Christian theology is to speak of the Spirit of the triune God, not just of any spirit. The Apostles' Creed is stated in three articles, God the Father, Jesus the Son, and the Holy Spirit, with the third defined by and identified intimately with the first two. The creed speaks of the "Holy" Spirit, the One associated with the eternal One, God Almighty. The Spirit is the *ruach* of God, the *pneuma* of God, the divine breath, wind, living power that (who) creates, liberates, and enables those of faith to anticipate and represent the present reign of God on earth.[36]

The Spirit of God is none other than the Spirit of Jesus. Jesus spoke of "the Spirit of truth" (Jn. 14:17; 15:26), the One who brings home to willing believers the truth of the gospel, the same truth that is in Jesus. The Spirit of truth leads disciples into all the truth (Jn. 16:13), the fullness of truth as taught by and embodied in Jesus. Jesus said he would teach the disciples "all things" (Jn. 14:26). The Spirit continues the fulfillment of this promise, unfolding but not superceding the revelation in Christ. The story that the Spirit narrates in our time is none other than the biblical story that centers in Jesus.

We are not called to idealize some heavenly power thought of so ambiguously that it can be shaped easily by our own emotions, desires, even illusions. The Holy Spirit is God, "God in so far as God is near to human beings and the world, indeed becomes an inner force as the power which grasps but cannot be grasped, the force which creates life but also brings judgment, the grace which gives, but is under

---

[36] The metaphor "wind," when used biblically for the Spirit of God, was not intended to reduce God to a natural force. To speak of God as wind reminded Israel of the power that blew over the chaos and brought ordered creation and the dynamism of God, the wind that divided the sea as God called a people out of Egyptian slavery (Ex. 14:21). Recall that Israel was framed geographically by the Mediterranean Sea on the west and great deserts on the east. Wind from the east scorched and parched the land, highlighting in biblical thought the transitoriness of life (Isa. 40:7) and the action of God in destroying human pride (Ps. 103:15-18; Jer. 4:11). Wind from the west brought coolness and life-giving rain, a picture of the refreshing and nourishing ministry of God's Spirit (Hos. 6:3).

no one's control."[37] This Spirit is that of Jesus, meaning that any spirit that leads people to forgetfulness of the neighbor, that encourages escape from the world into the heavens of contemplation cannot be the Spirit of Jesus who "suffered under Pontius Pilate." The gift of the Spirit is for the enablement of true Christian identity and effective Christian mission in the practicalities of this world. The presence of God's Spirit is not a private possession for personal enjoyment, but a means of empowering the church in its mission so that together God's people can witness about Christ, work for Christ, and be in the world Christ's way.

Jesus Christ, crucified and resurrected, is the center of the biblical revelation, the substance of the Christian good news. This glorious center, however, is not a static point on the long storyline of God's choice to be with us. Jesus is both historically definitive and dynamic. Jesus *was* and *is*. The gospel announces a present reality. The New Testament highlights Pentecost as the pivot between past and present. There is continuity between the Jesus who once was in the flesh and our salvation now disclosed and made possible by the living presence of the Spirit of Christ.

It would appear that Luke intentionally uses parallel language in describing the Spirit's work in first preparing the human body of the Messiah, Jesus, and later Christ's new body, the church, to carry on the life of Christ. An angel told Mary: "The Holy Spirit will come upon you, and the power of the Most High will overshadow you" (Lk. 1:35). In Acts 1:8 Jesus is reported to have informed his disciples: "You will receive power when the Holy Spirit has come upon you." Obviously there is close association between the ministry of Jesus, which is the work of the Spirit (Lk. 3:22; 5:1, 18), and the ministry of the church in the life of the Spirit.

Jesus and the Spirit are interdependent. On one hand, Jesus is the gift of the Spirit. He was conceived by the Spirit (Matt. 1:20; Lk. 1:35), anointed for ministry by the Spirit (Lk. 4:18ff), and raised from the dead by the Spirit (Rom. 1:4). On the other hand, the Spirit is identified as the gift of the risen Christ. The Spirit is the One who

---

[37] Hans Küng, *Credo: The Apostles' Creed Explained for Today* (Doubleday, 1993), 125.

teaches us what is the mind of Christ (1 Cor. 2:16), pours the love of God into our hearts (Rom. 5:5), empowers our new life in Christ (Rom. 8:11), and motivates and equips us for discipleship and service (Rom. 8:14). The Spirit makes Christ known, present, and effectual by re-presenting him to believers and, through believers, to the world.

Biblical imagery for the Spirit's work is rich and varied. As there are several metaphors that seek to express the meaning of the work of Christ (see chapter five), various metaphors seek to express dimensions of the human experience of the work of the Spirit. These metaphors have been grouped into the personal (Lord, Mother, Judge), the formative (energy, space, gestalt), movement (tempest, fire, love), and mystical (light, water, fertility).[38] All of these describe vital functions of the Spirit, beginning with "the Lord, the giver of life" as stated in the Nicene Creed.

What really happened at Pentecost (Acts 2)? There appeared the Spirit as wind and fire. Being formed by this energy was the new covenant community of the Spirit. At Pentecost persons who were "born under law" (Gal. 4:1-4) became part of a new community of the Spirit. A fundamental difference between the old and new covenants is "the shift from Torah (law) to Spirit as the formative basis of community."[39]

The ongoing story of the Christ is the evolving narrative of the Spirit. The Spirit creates a new community, a Jesus community. Individuals are privileged to receive the Spirit and thereby are gifted to participate in the biblical story as they join in the *koinonia* (fellowship) of the Spirit through repentance and baptism (Acts 2:38).[40] Despite the pervasive individualism of our time, the Bible insists on individual-in-community. The continuation of the ministry of Christ has been given to a Spirit-filled new community, Christ's body, the church, and not simply to individual members of it (Matt. 16:18-19; 28:19-20).

---

[38] Jürgen Moltmann, *The Spirit of Life* (Fortress Press, 1992), 270ff.

[39] C. Norman Kraus, *The Community of the Spirit*, rev. ed. (Scottdale, Pa.: Herald Press, 1993), 25-26.

[40] Note that, despite common perception to the contrary, the fellowship of the church is not fundamentally a network of familiar, fulfilling, and fun relationships among church members. It first is to be relationship with the Spirit of God, a relationship that enables all good things within the body of believers.

Words from two hymns reflect this commitment to the continuing sovereignty and ongoing inspiration of the God who has chosen to come preciously near. Prays the first: "Fill me with Thy presence now, Lord, Thyself in me reveal; At Thy feet I humbly bow, To receive the holy seal."[41] The other whispers this prayer: "In me now reveal Thy glory, Let Thy might be ever shown; Keep me from the world's defilement, Sacred for Thyself alone." Repeats the chorus: "Spirit holy, Spirit holy, All my being now possess; Lead me, rule me, work within me, Through my life Thy will express."[42] Here are authentic and distinctly Christian prayers for Spirit inspiration in the presentness of human life[43] and church mission.

Before time itself ever was, there was God. God chose to create and to interact with that which was created. Demonstrated in Israel and most clearly in Jesus Christ is the persistent intent of God to be Self-revealing and creation-redeeming. The Spirit of God is the divine agency of interaction with creation. This Spirit is God with us, instructing, inspiring, directing, re-creating, and sustaining, carrying forward the story of Jesus in ways that can revolutionize our troubled human stories. The Spirit is the sovereign God active even now on behalf of all God's beloved children. The only appropriate human response is worship—and a yielding of full control to the Spirit of Christ who is Lord of all!

This divine Spirit, the very One now present to extend Christ's victory by delivering from the destructive forces in the world, is the same One who first created the world. The creation passages of Genesis 1-2:4 likely developed during Judah's Babylonian captivity and functioned first as a faith witness to the creator God who had not abandoned the creation. Did God still have the capacity and the will to restore Israel in such dire circumstances? The Genesis answer is

---

[41] Daniel Warner and Andrew Byers, "Fill Me with Thy Spirit, Lord," verse 5, in *Worship the Lord: Hymnal of the Church of God* (Anderson, Ind.: Warner Press, 1989), 269.

[42] Charles Naylor and Andrew Byers, "Spirit Holy," verse 4 and chorus, in *Worship the Lord*, 267.

[43] The personal pronouns in these two hymns reflect the individualized focus of American revivalism. The corporate dimension of the Spirit-community should not be lost in any isolated series of private spiritual experiences.

"yes!" The God who originally created stood then and stands now ready to recreate in response to human faith and faithfulness. The God who was Creator of heaven and earth and who was present in Jesus Christ is still the One with us as the Holy Spirit. As always, the Spirit is the presence of divine loving grace.

We who believe must not resign ourselves to the perverted way things now are. Christians are called instead to become living signs in the world of the present activity of God in overcoming evil in all its forms. The biblical theme of God's creation is eschatological in character and soteriological in focus–the not-yet already is, all for the purpose of our salvation. The principal object of our faith is not God's formation of the world out of the originally formless chaos. Rather, it is the new creation (Gal. 6:15), the call to be faithful to what God now intends to become reality in the believer (2 Cor. 5:17) and among the believers as the church on mission. This life of faith, in its anticipation of the new heaven and earth (Isa. 65:17, 66:22; 2 Pet. 3:13), is itself to become a present agent of that which is yet to come. The phrase "creator of heaven and earth" in the classic creeds sends us "not toward a primordial past, but toward the ultimate future which has already been inaugurated in the life and death and destiny of Jesus."[44]

As the ancient Apostles' Creed begins, "I believe in God, the Father Almighty." The precise meaning of the identity of God as "Father" and as "Almighty" comes to be known only by awareness of the life and work of God's Son, Jesus Christ. In turn, the meaning of that life and the fruits of that work are mediated to and brought alive in believers only through the Spirit of God. By God staying with us and providing for all our needs, we can launch out on divine mission. We can serve in liberating faith because "the Spirit takes the benefit of Christ's reconciling work and brings pardon *for* the believer and then power *in* the believer."[45] This pardon and power are the foundations of the Christian life.

---

[44] Theodore Jennings, Jr., *Loyalty To God*, 1992, 54.

[45] Gabriel Fackre, *Ecumenical Faith in Evangelical Perspective* (Eerdmans, 1993), 113. In the tradition of the American "holiness" movement in general, "justification" and "sanctification" have been conceived somewhat separately. This highlights

Foundations of the Christian Life

For Paul (1 Cor. 14) a congregation of Christians is the place where the Spirit of God is manifest in a wealth of spiritual powers (*charismata*), the energies of new life in Christ (1 Cor. 12:6, 11). The whole people of God is to be filled with the living force of God's enabling presence. God is present as the Spirit, giving gifts of ministering grace. The Spirit of God is the power of the resurrection, the divine power of creation and re-creation (Rom. 8:11; 4:17). As the power of the resurrection, "the Spirit is the reviving presence of the future of eternal life in the midst of the history of death; he is the presence of the future of the new creation in the midst of the dying life of this world and its evil state."[46]

The work of the Spirit is the creation of new life. The Gospel of John identifies the Spirit as the agent of the second birth of all believers in Christ (Jn. 3:3-8).[47] The Spirit also liberates (2 Cor. 3:17), a continuation of the freeing work of Christ (Gal. 5:1). This liberation is a grace-granted freedom from guilt, legalism, and eventually even death. It also is a freedom to act, to risk as a servant, to live in gratitude, hope, and joy rather than in self-seeking and self-justification. Such liberation is intended to lead not to erratic individualism, but to new and Spirit-disciplined community. The Spirit unites believers to Christ and to each other, launching a new communal existence, the church of Christ.

Salvation understood broadly includes the three-part deliverance "immediately from the *penalty* of sin, progressively from the *plague* of sin, and eschatologically from the very *presence* of sin and its

---

the differing and often not simultaneous human experiences of "pardon for" and "power in" the believer. This more comprehensive view of the work of the Spirit is based on the work of Christ and is necessary for effective Christian living and mission. See below under "Sanctification."

[46] Jürgen Moltmann, *The Church in the Power of the Spirit* (N.Y.: Harper and Row, 1977), 295.

[47] Jesus told Nicodemus that one sees the kingdom of God only by being born of "water and the spirit" (Jn. 3:5). He was emphasizing that "the way into life is not by human striving...but by a work of the Spirit of God.... Jesus did not come simply to tell people to try harder but to bring them new life by the Spirit" (Leon Morris, *New Testament Theology*, Academie Books, Zondervan, 1986, 258).

effects."[48] In relation to individual believers, then, the work of the Spirit involves justification (removal of penalty), sanctification (removal of plague), and vocation (sending on mission).[49] Being delivered from sin's very presence (glorification) waits the time beyond this life.

We will review briefly these foundations of the Christian life, with justification, sanctification, and vocation all enabled and authenticated by the fruit and gifts of the Spirit of God.

1. Justification. Christian life is grounded in the loving grace of God. It is based on the completed work of Christ made effective by the continuing work of the Spirit. With the assumption of the open door of prevenient grace and the goal of transformation into the likeness of Christ, justification begins with God's forgiveness that releases the contrite heart from the guilt of committed sin. Regeneration or rebirth is then received through faith alone (Rom. 3:23-28). Believers are justified, restored to right relationship with God by God's initiative of sheer, unmerited grace (*sola gratia*), and by the response of faith and trust (*sola fide*).

For Christians, justification is the declaration of God that a believer who trusts in Christ's atoning work on the cross is now accounted righteous before God. This is because one now is in Christ and thus has entered into a restored relation with God. By an act of God's free grace the sinner becomes absolved from guilt and is accepted as righteous in light of Jesus Christ. Justification before God does not result "from higher commitment to greater ideals or more advanced actualization of good character or better performance of the demands of the law. It is solely due to a verdict rendered that reveals God's attitude toward the sinner whose life is hid in Christ."[50]

---

[48] Randy Maddox, *Responsible Grace: John Wesley's Practical Theology* (Nashville: Kingswood Books, Abingdon Press, 1994), 143. See John Wesley's 1765 sermon "The Scripture Way of Salvation."

[49] This three-part approach to viewing the Christian life follows in general the outline of Karl Barth's description (*Church Dogmatics*, IV/1-3).

[50] Thomas Oden, *Life in the Spirit*, systematic theology, vol. 3 (San Francisco: Harper, 1992), 109. The Augsburg Confession (1530) defined justification normative-

Salvation is righted relationship. It is being "saved" by true friendship with Jesus. In the Gospel of John a friend is pictured as more than a mere acquaintance. Friendship is full of the deep relatedness of empathy that expresses itself in mutual struggle and support. Jesus refers to his disciples as friends (Jn. 15:15). Friends of Jesus are those who know that they are loved and chosen by their Lord, the One who laid down his life for them (Jn. 15:13). Friends of Jesus are those who, in the fullness of right relationship, love as they are loved and find their own pathway brightened by the divine presence (Jn. 14:26). Friends of Jesus are those whose lives have been renewed because they have been captured by the transforming power of the God known through the biblical revelation. They have followed the plot of the biblical story from Abraham to the cross and empty tomb of Jesus, and now, in the Spirit's coming, they are finding the light of Friend Jesus, ever present as the Spirit, to guide their way in this world and beyond. It is all by divine grace, made effective by the human response of faith and faithfulness.

It is important that the church not misread Scripture and itself assume the place of the initiative of God in forgiving sins. Jesus called for his disciples to receive the Holy Spirit and then announced that "if you forgive the sins of any, they are forgiven them; if you retain the sins of any, they are retained" (Jn. 20:23). The observation of Leon Morris about this verse is crucial: "The verbs...are both in the perfect tense. Jesus is saying that when the Spirit-filled church pronounces that such and such sins are forgiven, it will be found that forgiveness has already taken place. He [Jesus] is not giving the church the power to do it then and there. The Spirit enables the church to declare authoritatively what God has done in the matter of forgiving or withholding forgiveness."[51]

---

ly for Protestant theology: "...we cannot obtain forgiveness of sin and righteousness before God by our own merits, works, or satisfactions, but that we receive forgiveness of sin and become righteous before God by grace, for Christ's sake, through faith, when we believe that Christ suffered for us and that for his sake our sin is forgiven, and righteousness and eternal life are given to us. For God will regard and reckon this faith as righteousness, as Paul says in Romans 3:21-26 and 4:5."

[51] Leon Morris, *New Testament Theology*, 265. Boyce Blackwelder agrees with Morris. Fearing "sacerdotalism," the placing in the hands of establishment Christianity the apparent power to forgive sins, Blackwelder also turns to Greek grammar. The "if you

We humans continue to pursue many futile attempts at self-justification. How desperately we need and want lives that are meaningful and acceptable. We think and work in ways we hope will win the approval of others. The drive to belong and succeed is strong in our competitive Western societies. We strive to "make it," to acquire or accomplish in order to feel understood, valued, and loved. Paul Tillich addresses this with his fresh statement of the Christian doctrine of justification as taught earlier and so vigorously by Martin Luther and John Calvin. "Just accept the fact that you are accepted," Tillich says, "accepted by a power that is greater than you."[52] We sinners are made right with God only by the loving grace of God.

2. Sanctification. John and Charles Wesley certainly were committed to the central concern of the Western church for human justification before God. They also argue that people cannot be delivered from the *power* of sin (its plague) until first they are delivered from the *guilt* of sin (its penalty). Even so, the burden of the Methodist revival was "Christian perfection." This attempt to unite "pardon" and "participation" may be John Wesley's greatest contribution to the ecumenical dialogue.[53] He bridged the Western and Eastern churches, especially by acceptance of the Greek Orthodox stress on "deification," a human participation in the divine life that increasingly transfigures the believer into the image of Christ.[54] Saving grace is both grace as *justifying pardon* and grace as *sanctifying power*. Wayward humans are to be put right with God and made like God.

---

retain" then the sins "are retained," he argues, are not simple future tenses. They are "future perfect passive participles" to be translated "whatever you may bind on earth shall have been bound in heaven." See his *Light from the Greek New Testament* (Warner Press, 1958, 75; reprint Baker Book House, 1976). Whether or not the significance of the grammar used is overdrawn, the central point is significant. No earthly institution or its representative can make pronouncements which heaven is bound to ratify.

[52] Paul Tillich, *The Shaking of the Foundations* (N.Y.: Scribner's, 1948), 162.

[53] See Albert Outler, "The Place of Wesley in the Christian Tradition," in K. A. Rowe, ed., *The Place of Wesley in the Christian Tradition* (Metuchen, N.J.: Scarecrow, 1976), 30.

[54] See Randy Maddox, "John Wesley and Eastern Orthodoxy" in *The Asbury Theological Journal* 45:2 (Fall 1990), 39-40.

Sanctifying grace is the culminating phase of the Christian teaching of present salvation. Jesus prayed that those justified persons who already were his disciples might also be sanctified by God's presence and truth (Jn. 17:17). The church's task is to teach and live "so that we may present everyone mature [*teleion*] in Christ" (Col. 1:28).[55] The purpose of the work of the Holy Spirit is to enable believers to become "holy" by their loving and serving God as originally intended.

Some historical perspective is helpful. The Brethren in Christ and Church of God (Anderson) movements, for instance, have sought to be "sects" in the sense defined by Ernst Troeltsch. He defined a sect sociologically as a voluntary society composed of Christians who have been born anew and are committed to living a distinctive life separate from the sordidness of this world.[56] In this sense the Free (Anabaptist) or Believers' Church tradition has been sectarian, stressing the central place of holiness. Through spiritual rebirth and discipline within their ranks, such Christians have sought to keep the church pure and unblemished from the world. This is the way and work of the Spirit.

In America, the Baptists, Methodists, and "Christians" (Stone-Campbell movement) often led the way. The age-old paradox prevailed. How can the church be *in* but not *of* the world, serving the world without sharing its perverted values? How can holiness be a practical reality, a real separation from the world, without leading to social irrelevance? The New Testament, especially the parts written by Paul, argue that the answer lies with the church living in the power of the Spirit, the present power of the messianic age now dawned in Jesus Christ. To be "holy" is to be truly "in Christ" through the Spirit.

The work of Christ on the cross addresses more than humanity's juridical (legal) status before God, justifying past sin by divine grace. It also intends a re-creation of fallen and now forgiven humanity. The

---

[55] The concept of "perfect" is misleading today since it often is taken to mean flawless being and performance. John Wesley spoke often of "perfect love" (see Mildred Wynkoop, *A Theology of Love: The Dynamic of Wesleyanism*, Kansas City: Beacon Hill Press, 1972, 294-301).

[56] Ernst Troeltsch, *The Social Teachings of the Christian Churches and Groups* (London: Allen and Unwin, 1931), 2:993.

already justified are to be filled with the Spirit of love (Rom. 5:5) so that they can give thanks always (Eph. 5:18-21) and grow up into the likeness of Christ (Eph. 4:15). Justifying grace "works *for* the sinner; sanctifying grace works *in* the penitent faithful.... Justifying grace is juridically a *finished* work of the Son on the cross, while sanctifying grace is actively a *continuing* and current work of the Spirit in our hearts and social processes."[57] The former brings change in a person's relative position before God; the latter effects a real change in the believer's actual being in relation to God.[58]

To be holy is costly to self-centered egos and middle-class lifestyles in prosperous societies. To walk the path of holiness is necessarily to break with the habits of comfortable religion. It is to "renounce the 'cheap grace' that only gives a religious sugar-coating to our worldliness and instead embrace the grace that will cost us our life and give us deliverance not only from the guilt but also from the *power* of sin." It entails "a turn toward the despised, the forsaken, the marginalized, the poor, the least of these."[59] It is to follow humbly the God of the cross into the sordidness of a lost world as new creations in the Christ of the cross.

To be holy is to move beyond the prior question "what must I do to be saved?" to the equally crucial "what must I be and do now that I am saved?" To avoid the demands of the second question surely is to reflect negatively on any accomplishment of the first. In the ministry of John the Baptist people were challenged to turn *from* past sins and receive forgiveness. With the announcement that God's kingdom had come near in the person of Jesus the Christ (Mk. 1:14-20), Jesus called people to also turn *toward* the new reality of the pre-

---

[57] Thomas Oden, *Life in the Spirit* (Harper, 1992), 218.

[58] Real change is regeneration, actual new life. Justification, the forgiveness of sin, is the necessary preface to or first stage of actual rebirth. Regeneration involves reorganization of a believer's motive life by the work of the Spirit so that the prevailing motive becomes love for God and loyalty to Jesus Christ. Such reorganization is sanctification, the larger outworking of justification. John Wesley insisted that God graciously has provided both pardon for sin and an empowering, "perfecting" Presence, the Holy Spirit in the lives of believers and in the church.

[59] Theodore W. Jennings, Jr., "The Meaning of Discipleship in Wesley and the New Testament," *Quarterly Review: A Journal of Theological Resources for Ministry* (Spring 1993), 18.

sent reign of God. Beyond forgiveness, faith enables access to the power of the kingdom of God for inner healing and active service. After forgiveness is to come "the quest for piety and obedience."[60]

One's understanding of the nature of sin controls the understanding of holiness. Thinking of sin primarily as violation of a set of behavioral expectations is to risk a seeking of righteousness by human works and to limit holiness to those few (if any!) people who somehow function at a flawless level in relation to these expectations. Thinking of sin only as a pattern of sinful acts committed is to tempt a limiting of the view of salvation to only the forgiveness of these acts, a commercial transaction whereby human wrong is redeemed by the grace of God's love. Thinking biblically, however, sin is seen more in personal and relational terms. Rather than being a negative "thing" within the person, a heavenly score sheet registered against an absolute standard, sin is the deliberate turning away from God, defective or perverted love, violation of the covenant relationship. Thus, "if sin is the orientation of the whole person away from God, then holiness is the whole person turned in love to God. It is not merely the absence of sin, but the presence of the God-given love for God."[61] It is genuinely restored relationship.

The proper approach to conceiving Christian holiness is focusing on restored relationship. In this view, believers are free from the dilemmas of perfectionism that have plagued many holiness seekers. The sanctifying goal is a perfect love characteristic of restored relationship, not perfect performance in spite of human frailty, ignorance, and immaturity. The issue is the set of the will, the focus of one's true affection. John Wesley's phrase "perfect love" should be thought of as mature, life-restoring relationship to God. In this light, Mildred Bangs Wynkoop correctly defines sin as "love locked into a false center, the self," and holiness as "love locked into the True Center, Jesus Christ our Lord."[62]

---

[60] See the story of the Brethren in Christ by Carlton Wittlinger titled *Quest for Piety and Obedience* (Nappanee, Ind.: Evangel Press, 1978).

[61] Kenneth Jones, *Commitment to Holiness* (Anderson, Ind.: Warner Press, 1985), 73.

[62] Mildred Bangs Wynkoop, *A Theology of Love* (Kansas City: Beacon Hill Press, 1972), 158.

Justification is the foundation of Christian life; sanctification continues the reclaiming of the once fallen by the process of set-apartness unto God, the reestablishment of right relationship, perfecting love. This process of becoming holy should not be thought of as moral flawlessness or isolated otherworldliness, but as a pattern of maturing into Christ-likeness, a releasing from the compulsive power of self-centeredness so that the believer may genuinely love God and neighbor. Such is the goal, possible only by the sanctifying grace ministered by God's Spirit. The goal is not achieved easily or instantly. Wisdom warns that "if we respect the freedom of God's grace and the limitless disguises that sin assumes, we will avoid oversimplification in our portrayals of the process of growth in Christian life."[63]

There is growth when faith and obedience are exercised. As justification is a gift of God's grace, a gift effective only when matched by the human response of accepting faith, so sanctification is a divine gift effective only when enriched by the believer's faithful use of the available means by which grace is made operational (see chapter seven). Sanctification, a divine gift of the Spirit, is nonetheless a human task. When responding to grace, the believer becomes responsible to the purposes of that grace.

One unfortunate aspect of much preaching on sanctification in many American camp meetings has been the stress on emotionalism and immediacy of expected result. While there certainly is a point of human decision and commitment, there also is a process of discipline and development. In much of American revivalism, holiness teaching has focused on a very individual experience, often disconnected from the disciplining and nurturing church context. Becoming "holy" also was thought to be realized in one crisis experience, sometimes to the near exclusion of its progressive dimension. This altered the better balance held by John Wesley generations earlier. Wesley's long life appears to have experienced stages of developing thought here, but

---

[63] Daniel Migliore, *Faith Seeking Understanding* (Grand Rapids: Eerdmans, 1991), 178. Migliore lists marks that characterize real growth in sanctifying grace. They are maturing (1) as hearers of the Word of God, (2) in prayer, (3) in freedom, (4) in solidarity, and (5) in thankfulness and joy (178-182).

"his later descriptions...lay much more emphasis on the gradual nature of salvation and the interrelationship of its different facets.... [These facets], not an ordered series of discrete states, ...are intertwined facets of an overarching purpose–our gradual recovery of the holiness that God has always intended for us."[64]

Teaching about holiness, when solidified in a given cultural setting, easily becomes more reflective of the time and place than of the work of God's Spirit. The Church of God movement (Anderson), for instance, emerged from the nineteenth-century holiness movement and focused heavily on a quest for both the holiness and unity of all Christians by the power of the Spirit. But legalisms of several kinds soon evolved, encouraging in more recent generations a near silencing of this doctrinal emphasis once so central in the movement. Very recently, especially in the movement's international dialogues on doctrine, the urgent need for holiness emphasis has resurfaced, now with greater recognition of the care needed to avoid earlier distortions.[65] The goal is to be captured by God, not by culture! While never easy, this goal of God for human restoration is hardly optional. It is a central work of the Spirit and basic to the full meaning of being "saved."

Modernity has secularized the concept of sanctification, reducing it to moral improvement or the political gains of upward social mobility. This has resulted in biblical emphases being "cut and squeezed into pop metaphors of psychological growth or stress reduction or creative management."[66] But to sanctify, in biblical understanding, is to set apart for holy use. Today Christians must learn again to resist being shaped by the pervasive and powerful secular culture. Instead, by faith in the Spirit's work, believers are called to become

---

[64] Randy Maddox, *Responsible Grace: John Wesley's Practical Theology* (Nashville: Kingswood Books, Abingdon Press, 1994), 158.

[65] Recent International Dialogues on Doctrine of the Church of God movement (Anderson) have focused on "Pentecost and the Church" (Nairobi, Kenya, 1983), "Gifts of the Spirit" (Seoul, South Korea, 1987), "Sanctification" (Wiesbaden, Germany, 1991), and "Christian Unity: God's Will and Our Role" (Sydney, Australia, 1995). These dialogues are sponsored and convened by the School of Theology of Anderson University.

[66] Thomas Oden, *Life in the Spirit*, 1992, 212.

set apart *by* God and *for* God, to be resident aliens in this world,[67] to be shaped by the distinctive reading of reality that is Jesus Christ, to be pilgrims through this life, formed by the biblical view of life's fallenness and the potential newness in Jesus Christ.

Isaiah 6:1-8 serves as a window through which the church today can gain again a vision of the biblical understanding of holiness. This understanding avoids any insistence on experiential formulas like "a second work of grace" that often force the work of the Spirit into overly rigid categories and time frames. This prophetic vision centers rather in the dynamics of an unholy person (people) encountering a holy God. The emphasis is on the life impact of opening oneself humbly to the God who is high, glorious, powerful, pure, and Self-giving love.[68]

To be holy is to allow one's life to be focused by transforming grace around an Isaiah-like vision of a holy God and of one's sinful self that becomes painfully revealed by shocking comparison. It is a grace-granted renewal in the image of God, prompted by a transforming vision of God. Personal and church renewal come when unholy people are touched by the divine fire so that they become a holy people (humble, righteous, sent, serving). When asked the meaning of Christian perfection or entire sanctification, John Wesley typically responded with "loving God with the whole heart, soul, mind, and strength and our neighbor as ourselves." Holiness is "that dynamic level of maturing within the process of sanctification characteristic of 'adult' Christian life."[69] With love assumed as the essence of Christian life, the intended Christian "perfection" is the love of God ruling the attitudes, words, and actions of a committed believer. Salvation is to be seen eschatologically, that is, within the context of the

---

[67] See Stanley Hauerwas and William Willimon, *Resident Aliens* (Nashville: Abingdon Press, 1989), for a prophetic statement of the call to holiness in the setting of the competitive capitalistic cultures of today.

[68] For an exposition of these divine characteristics and their relevance for the renewal of contemporary Christian believers, see Stephen Seamands, *Holiness of Heart and Life* (Nashville: Abingdon Press, 1990). Alan Kreider expands this with three provocative "snapshots" of holiness based on the narratives of Exodus 15, Isaiah 6-7, and Acts 4 (*Journey Towards Holiness*, Scottdale, Pa.: Herald Press, 19-26).

[69] Randy Maddox, *Responsible Grace* (Abingdon Press, 1994), 187.

coming to human history in Christ of the reign of God, resulting in the potential of a new order of human existence.

Holiness is not a static adoration of the holy (distant) God or a perfect performance in relation to some catalog of right and wrong actions. It is renewed life on the move, transforming and being transformed into the image of the Holy One who is active in the midst of our world. It is a believer whose personal life story has merged with the biblical story of the God who yet journeys among us. As Isaiah learned, experiencing holiness soon sends on mission ("here am I, send me!"). The God who is "majestic in holiness" (Ex. 15:11) invites people both to enter the divine character (sanctification) and to take part in God's holy actions (mission). Holiness erodes resistance to God's sovereignty and liberates women and men from all forms of bondage. It is restored relationship, the victory of grace over the power of evil.

3. Vocation. God justifies and sanctifies human life by the power of the Spirit for the immediate purpose of Christian discipleship. To neglect mission and focus only on experiences of the Spirit is to pervert the life of grace by yielding to spiritual narcissism. Election by God is a calling to service, not an invitation to privilege or self-serving spiritual "experiences." The justifying and sanctifying Spirit is the Spirit of the crucified Christ. The assurance of the Spirit "does not lead to a dream of worlds beyond this world; it leads ever more deeply into Christ's sufferings and into earthly discipleship."[70] Grace received is responsibility assumed. Service is costly; grace is loving and free, but never cheap and without resulting responsibility.[71]

John Wesley's concern clearly was centered more on the *fruit* of the Spirit (see below) and less on the *gifts* of the Spirit, especially a gift like "tongues" that easily becomes self-serving and not beneficial to the church's mission. Fruit is inevitable if faith is authentic. In fact,

---

[70] Jürgen Moltmann, *The Church in the Power of the Spirit* (N.Y.: Harper, 1977), 299.

[71] See Dietrich Bonhoeffer, *The Cost of Discipleship* (London: SCM Press, 1959). The dramatic life of Bonhoeffer, including his martyrdom at Nazi hands, is a story of grace received and lived out in a costly discipleship.

the fruit that flows from faith is an essential part of what "salvation" means. Claiming to be "saved" without exhibiting the Christ-life is to profess a lie (1 Jn. 2:9-11). From the "Radical" (Anabaptist) Christian tradition comes the view that salvation is "to walk in the resurrection" (Schleitheim, 1527). Christian conduct, rather than merely a consequence of salvation, is itself basic to the very meaning of salvation. The "salvific gift of God and its human answer in following Jesus were [are] two sides of one reality."[72]

What God has accomplished in the past, especially in the work of Christ, is intended to send believers on a journey outward to others and forward to the completion of God's redemptive work in the world. Christian life is "more than acceptance of the forgiveness of sins and personal transformation. It also is the vocation to participate in the preparation of all creation for the coming of a new community of justice, freedom, and peace in partnership with the Triune God."[73] To be walking by Christ's Spirit is to have enhanced the capacity for truly loving others in the full range of their lives. We become a reflection of the God of loving grace.[74]

Precedent for such "worldly" vocation is found in the faith tradition which Jesus shared. The ancient Hebrews have been described as an "energetic, robust, and, at times, even turbulent people." For them, "truth was not so much an idea to be contemplated as an experience to be lived, a deed to be done."[75] Israel's religion was a "puptent" faith that followed a God on the move, with the followers being God's "movable treasure" (cf. Ex. 19:5).

While it is clear that Christian disciples are to be liberated agents of Christ on mission in this world, it sometimes is less clear how best to express such sacrificial discipleship. Basic at least are having (1) the mind of Christ as pattern and (2) the enabling Spirit of Christ as power.

---

[72] James McClendon, *Systematic Theology: Doctrine* (Nashville: Abingdon Press, 1994), 118.

[73] Daniel Migliore, op. cit., 184.

[74] Laurence Wood defines love as "our capacity to reach beyond ourselves to penetrate the lives of others and embrace them as part of our own reality" (*Truly Ourselves: Truly the Spirit's*, Grand Rapids: Francis Asbury Press, 1989, 75).

[75] Marvin Wilson, *Our Father Abraham* (Grand Rapids: Eerdmans, 1989), 136.

John Wesley's teaching of "Christian perfection" links doctrine and life closely together, thus closing the inappropriate gap between thought and act, creedal commitment and compassionate application. Having a "heart strangely warmed" by the Spirit is seen as a social-ethical call to warm a chilled world by the embodied love of God. The manner of love's expression is to be controlled by the way of Jesus Christ in the world. Jesus is the norm of the Christian's life—and his way is radically different from the standard messianic expectations of his time or the typical way the world and even the church functions in our time.

The first Christian disciples had to reorient their understanding of the way God expresses power in the midst of human history so that they could have the mind of Christ in their own living. "If they had been endowed with the gift of the Spirit before that gift had manifested its full range of meaning in Jesus," warns Ray Dunning, "they would have doubtless become raging nationalists, swinging weapons like Samson of old."[76] While life in the Spirit is essential, so is its being understood as one with the historical story of Jesus.

The Spirit of God sends the believing community on mission in the Spirit's way. The community goes in the Spirit, that is, in the present power of the messianic age already dawned in Jesus Christ. The Spirit "moves us through enemy territory toward God's final victory, along the way offering us a quickening foretaste of the glory to come." But the Spirit's leading is into, not out of this present world. The Spirit "always directs us to the Crucified One and thus into the way of the cross." So we are put on mission *for* Christ, *by* the Spirit of Christ, and *like* Christ. Like Christ? Yes, "the Spirit implants in our hearts the strength to follow the way of weakness, the power to receive and care for the powerless, the peace to endure and absorb hostility."[77] Such is the vocation of those who follow the way of the cross, the way of Jesus.

---

[76] H. Ray Dunning, *Grace, Faith and Holiness* (Kansas City: Beacon Hill Press, 1988), 415.

[77] C. Leonard Allen, *The Cruciform Church* (Abilene Christian University Press, 1990), 163.

4. Fruit and Gifts. God loves the community of Christ and intends to equip this church to fulfill its divinely assigned tasks. A key dimension of this equipping is the giving of divine gifts to enable divine service, thus building up the church for its service in the world. This too is the work of the Spirit. So, "do not be foolish, but understand what the will of the Lord is. Do not get drunk with wine, for that is debauchery; but be filled with the Spirit..." (Eph. 5:17-18).

The relationship between Jesus and the Spirit is theologically crucial. This relationship provides the test by which the "spirits" of teachers can be discerned (1 Jn. 4:2). The test for "prophets" who claim to speak by the Spirit is whether they recognize and affirm the significance of Jesus' humanity. The test for the authenticity of spiritual gifts is their value in the service of the continuing mission of Jesus (1 Cor. 12). Above all, "the test is whether faith produces in us the love of Christ."[78]

In 1985 widely reported abuses of presumed divine gifts led the General Assembly of the Church of God movement (Anderson) to establish a national study committee on this subject. The resulting 1986 committee report reads in part:

> Which gift or how many gifts a person is given is not a factor in that person's salvation or sanctification. What is a factor is the reception of the Gift, that of the Holy Spirit (Acts 1:8 and Romans 8:9).... Congregations are urged to teach the central importance of the work of the Holy Spirit in the lives of believers and in the process of genuine Christian worship.[79]

To be holy and in Christ's service is first to receive the greatest gift from God. This gift is the indwelling presence of the Holy Spirit, God actually with us. Believers are judged holy only because of God's presence, and because of the privilege of belonging to God. Sin

---

[78] C. Norman Kraus, *God Our Savior* (Scottdale, Pa.: Herald Press, 1991), 147-148.

[79] As in Barry Callen, ed., *Thinking and Acting Together* (Anderson, Ind.: Leadership Council of the Church of God and Warner Press, 1992), 108-109.

can be avoided only because believers are being sanctified by divine presence and help. We can find our way through dark, difficult places because of divine guidance. We can do whatever God desires because the Holy Spirit is with us to strengthen and give us the abilities we cannot have in our own strength. The presence of the Holy Spirit and our active life in the Spirit are crucial to the maturing of individual Christians and to the accomplishment of the mission of the church in every age. A lack of the power of Pentecost explains much of the emptiness which the current church renewal and charismatic movements are seeking to fill.

The emergence of the *fruit* of the Spirit (Gal. 5:22-23) should be a goal and is the privilege of all Christian believers, precisely because the fruit are the expected expressions or reflections of the presence of the Spirit. The *gifts* of the Spirit, however, are given only as the Spirit chooses (1 Cor. 12:11), not as any person desires or has a right to expect. These gifts are intended primarily for service so that the church may be strengthened and made more effective in its mission.

Self-gratification by use of a divine gift or public exhibition of such a gift for its own sake are inappropriate in church life (1 Cor. 14).[80] Unfortunately, the abuse of gifts has been all too common in church history. The two dangers that seem to persist are either "claiming that every Christian must have one of these gifts, especially speaking in tongues, or that any who do have them must be either demon-possessed or insane."[81]

A range of divine gifts appears in the New Testament.[82] Those named apparently are representative only, since the Holy Spirit qualifies each believer and congregation to accomplish whatever kingdom task is at hand. Love is said to be supreme, superceding all forms of spiritual individualism. Gifts are given to the church for the building

---

[80] This paragraph is adapted from the report of the Study Committee on Glossolalia made to and accepted by the General Assembly of the Church of God movement, June, 1986. It represents the traditional viewpoint of this movement that sees spiritual gifts as essential to church life, although great caution is expressed, like in the New Testament, about an often abused gift like "speaking in tongues."

[81] Frederick Norris, *The Apostolic Faith: Protestants and Roman Catholics* (Collegeville, Minn.: The Liturgical Press, 1992), 99.

[82] See Rom. 12:4-6; 1 Cor. 12:8-10; 12:28-30; Eph. 4:11.

up of the body of Christ (Eph. 4:11-12). They are present as God sees need and provides the capacity to meet it. The fruit of the Spirit (Gal. 5:19-23), however, are characteristics of the Spirit and thus are inherent in the Christian life and always should be present.[83] Where the Spirit truly is, in that place or person there should be authentic reflections that are Spirit-like.

To summarize, by God's grace and through God's Spirit sinful men and women are enabled to experience restored relationship with God. The restoration involves the forgiveness of sin's guilt (justification), the renewal of existence in the image of Christ (sanctification), and engagement in Christ's service (vocation). All of these are supported by the fruit of the Spirit's presence and the gifts of the Spirit's strengthening and equipping for the challenges at hand.

Renewed stress on the role of the Spirit in Christian life is absolutely essential for today's church. The need and possibility are stated well:

> Without the Holy Spirit, God is far away,
> Christ stays in the past,
> the Gospel is a dead letter,
> the Church is simply an organization,
> authority is a matter of domination,
> mission a matter of propaganda,
> the liturgy is no more than an evocation,
> Christian living a slave morality.
>
> But in the Holy Spirit:
> the cosmos is resurrected and groans
> with the birth pangs of the Kingdom,
> the risen Christ is there,
> the Gospel is the power of life,
> the Church shows forth the life of the Trinity,
> authority is a liberating service,
> mission is a Pentecost,

---

[83] See an excellent commentary on the Galatians 5 passage by William Barclay, *Flesh and Spirit* (Nashville: Abingdon Press, 1962).

the liturgy is both memorial and anticipation, and human action is deified.[84]

May it be so in the church of our time!

Contexts for the Spirit's Work

The loving grace of God is the forgiving source of justification and the empowering source of sanctification and service. Therefore, there should be optimism about the possibility of human and social transformation, even in our world.[85] But this transforming grace of God involves human responsibility, introducing a necessary realism about the degree to which it really will occur in particular lives. God's grace requires reception, participation, and embodiment. John Wesley's understanding of the relation of divine grace and human responsibility is instructive:

> ...our very capacity for growth in Christ-likeness (new birth) is contingent upon God's gracious pardoning prevenience (initial justification), while the continuance of God's acceptance (final justification) becomes contingent upon our responsive growth in Christ-likeness (sanctification).[86]

There are contexts in which the saving and sustaining grace of God are especially available and most effectively operational. Considerable caution is appropriate when offices, rituals, and structures

---

[84] Metropolitan Ignatios of Latakia, address to the World Council of Churches' Assembly in Uppsala in 1968, as quoted in *Ecumenism and Charismatic Renewal* (Ann Arbor: Servant Books, 1978), 34.

[85] Social reform or social action is too seldom seen by some conservative Christians as a work of the Spirit. Yet, interestingly, it is precisely the Pentecostal and Holiness groups within conservative Protestantism [in fact, the whole Anabaptist tradition] who have often been at the forefront of crusty issues like slavery and women's liberation.... Indeed, among both Protestants and Roman Catholics it is not only exhilarating experiences of the Spirit and a wealth of virtues, but also a life of active wall-busting which is one mark of the Spirit" (Frederick Norris, op. cit., 107).

[86] As in Randy Maddox, *Responsible Grace*, 1994, 172.

307

arise in the church's life to claim control of the dispensing of God's grace. Even so, God's nurturing and guiding of believers often occurs best through particular "means" that have been made available.

These means or appointed contexts for responsive growth in Christ-likeness are available for the purpose of Christians fulfilling their responsibility to the divine goals of available grace. These means or contexts include regular attention to the Bible (the reliable record of the story of divine grace active in human history), the church (the primary context for Christian growth and service), and the "sacraments" or ordinances (dramatic re-enactments of the memories, meanings, and implications of the grace of God in Christ).

Through intentional immersion in this record, this believing community, and this celebration of God's grace recognized and received, Christian believers become established in the faith. The Spirit's work of sanctifying proceeds. We who take regular advantage of the opportunities of God's sustaining and sending grace are enabled increasingly to be Spirit infilled, Spirit shaped, Spirit inspired and equipped for life and service in God's kingdom.

We now turn to consideration of these special settings in which the Spirit of God chooses especially to work.

CHAPTER SEVEN

SPIRIT:
TELLER OF THE STORY

—

"We believe in one holy catholic and apostolic church. We
confess one baptism for the forgiveness of sins. We look
for the resurrection of the dead, and the life of the
age to come. Amen."

—

The church is the community of Christ, the body that realizes its own nature and fulfills its own purpose only as it remembers Christ, is formed by Christ's Spirit, and faithfully serves Christ in the world. The church is brought into being by the saving power of God that always should be recalled through the biblical story and newly known through direct experience with the current work of the Spirit. The church exists to be a servant of the divine presence and power that now are at work in human hearts and history.

God's church is "one holy, catholic, and apostolic" body of believers. It is to be unified, distinct from the world, a church of people from all nations that is rooted in the original witness of Christ's apostles. This church is to be formed in memory and motivated by hope. It remembers Jesus Christ and looks for the age to come. In the meantime, it confesses belief, e.g., in baptism, a pivotal practice related to the forgiveness of sins. To understand the nature of this relationship, one needs to understand the manner in which the Spirit works.

The biblical revelation is to be remembered and joined, heard and retold, visualized and re-enacted, celebrated and embodied. The good news in Jesus Christ is a narrative that was oral and communal before it became a written and fixed text. People, however, are more than rememberers and thinkers, more than readers and doers. We humans live by symbols and rituals that portray formative memory and help draw the whole person into present commitment, intentional growth, and inspired mission. The church's "remembrance, exploration, and struggle are in celebration as well as assessment, sacrament as well as sermon."[1]

All Christian celebration, when biblically-informed and enlivened by God's Spirit, can become an avenue for the working of God's sanctifying and sustaining grace. There is no adequate understanding of the Spirit's work apart from consideration of the primary means through which that work typically is done. These means feature the church as context, the Bible as source of guidance, and certain practices as vivid portrayals of what God the Spirit has done, is doing, and yet will do.

A Story-Formed Community

Speaking sociologically, any community, including the church, needs to choose leaders, order its life, and maintain regular practices that keep its identity visible and support its mission. Speaking theologically, such ordering and practicing in the church need to relate closely to the gospel message that creates and sends this Christ community. The church's roots, fruits, and symbols should interrelate so that each supports and reflects the others. If authentic, they all are gracious actions of the Spirit and essential disciplines of the people of God.

---

[1] Delwin Brown, in Clark Pinnock and Brown, *Theological Crossfire* (Grand Rapids: Zondervan, 1990), 186. Thomas Oden notes that the church's acts of mercy often relate to providing the basics of clean bodies and full stomachs to the alienated and poor. In introducing his discussion of Christian baptism and the Lord's supper, Oden says: "Nothing is more prized to the hungry and homeless than a bath and a meal. Nothing is more characteristic of the church's essential identity and self-ordering than bathing and feeding" (*Life in the Spirit*, Harper, 1992, 274).

For the Pentecost people of Christ, the Spirit-formed community of believers, the religious practices of baptism, the Lord's supper, and foot washing have biblical origins and are associated directly with the ministry of Jesus. Especially the first two of these have been central to the life of most Christian church bodies over the centuries, although they have been understood to be related to the life of believers in significantly different ways. The ordinances or sacraments[2] of the church are vital means by which most Christians affirm that "God not only creates the physical realm, but also operates in and through it, blessing it with His own holy presence."[3]

It has been common in Protestant circles to say that the true church exists wherever the sacraments are celebrated and the word of good news in Jesus Christ is preached faithfully. Since the church is sustained from generation to generation by telling, hearing, receiving, and living out the biblical story of God in Christ, the church could not exist without the story. Certain practices keep presenting the story in a way that has the grace-filled potential of constantly forming the church into the image of Christ. They are sacred, not in themselves, but only as the Spirit works through them to form, strengthen, and send the church on Christ's mission.

Through baptism, for example, new believers acknowledge gratefully having heard the saving story of Jesus and submit themselves to becoming part of this story through personal participation in Jesus' death, resurrection, and ongoing mission. In baptism, believers declare that "Jesus' story now constitutes our own identity and life."[4] Persons made new in Christ declare unity with Christ, a per-

---

[2] See below for discussion of an often perceived theological problem with use of the word "sacrament." The word is from the Latin *sacramentum,* meaning "a consecrating." The idea of a sacrament is that certain ceremonies are said to mediate the divine into human experience. Particular rites become consecrated, officially recognized as regular means whereby God's grace reaches the participant. Churches that stress individual religious experience often downgrade the significance of such rites. This is partly a reaction to sacramentarianism, the view that sacraments automatically impart divine grace if one merely participates in them.

[3] Michael Lodahl, *The Story of God: Wesleyan Theology and Biblical Narrative* (Kansas City: Beacon Hill Press, 1994), 177.

[4] Stanley Grenz, *Theology for the Community of God* (Nashville: Broadman & Holman, 1994), 679.

sonal participation in Good Friday and Resurrection Sunday, immersion into a death to the sinful life and a launching into new life by God's grace (Rom. 6:3-8).

The very act of baptism tells again the Jesus story, rooted in the past and now renewed in the present. The act, in part, is testimony from the individual and strength for the church. The baptismal process of immersion is a dramatic picture showing the Jesus story again to the church and affirming the Spirit's present work in applying the story. For this reason, immersion as a method of baptism is preferred since it so clearly re-enacts the story (Rom. 6:4).

The Lord's supper also dramatizes for our memory what the Lord Jesus has done and at the same time, by the Spirit's ministry, draws believers into the present benefits of his sacrifice and resurrection. Through Christ's continuing presence in the remembering and participating church, thanks (*eucharist*) is given to God by those now representing God in this world. The eucharist, or grateful celebration of the Lord's supper, provides

> a lens through which the scriptural narrative of the death of Jesus may be read. It provides a focus of identity for the Christian community. It affirms that this is *our* story. It declares that we *belong* to this story. It asserts that the community of faith and its individual members possess deep and stable roots, firmly grounded in the history of the world.[5]

Such focus and grounding rest on earlier chapters of the biblical story as told in the Hebrew Scriptures ("Old Testament"). Annually the Hebrews celebrated the Passover, a highly symbolic meal that retold the formative story of escape from the Egyptian Pharaoh, and thus encouraged fresh experiencing of God's gracious deliverance. This ritualistic recalling of dramatic past events supplied to Israel a vision for new life in the present. Repeatedly in the Law are appeals

---

[5] Alister McGrath, *Spirituality in an Age of Change* (Grand Rapids: Zondervan, 1994), 72.

for Jews of later generations to remember the Exodus: "Take heed to yourselves, lest you forget..." (Deut. 4:20, 23). Remembering would be a reminder of God's faithfulness and a fresh motive for present action as God's liberated and liberating people (Ex. 22:21-23; 23:9).

Similarly, such recalling in the Lord's supper of the liberating work of Christ draws into the present the power of the age to come. The power of symbols recaptures and in a sense repeats the past, bringing transformation of participants. While symbols can become idols, they also can be media that portray and convey the message. The ancient tradition of the Jewish meal, commemorating the exodus from Egypt and the covenant at Sinai, "ended by celebrating a new exodus from the Egypt of sin and the establishment of a new testament in the blood of God himself soon to be shed."[6] The Lord's supper is the Christian celebration of the present reality of this new testament.

Believers who recall and celebrate the biblical story of liberation through participation in baptism and the Lord's supper often also submit humbly in an action like communal foot washing. This act remembers Jesus (Jn. 13:3-9), symbolizes his distinctive way in the world (Phil. 2:7-8), and calls all disciples to the same path of lowly service that led Jesus willingly to a cross. More than mere words, here is a tactile testimony, a visual lesson, a grace-laden door of faithfulness and dedicated discipleship.

These traditional church practices, baptism, the Lord's supper, and foot washing, are not magical moments guaranteed to bestow divine grace. But they are celebrations and enacted memories characteristic of faithful Christian people. Through them Christians have special opportunity to hear, feel,[7] taste, act out, and thereby are nur-

---

[6] Thomas Oden, *Life in the Spirit* (Harper, 1992), 275.

[7] In earlier decades of the history of the Church of God movement (Anderson), Enoch Byrum was known widely for having the gift of healing. Sometimes he mailed a handkerchief anointed with oil to a distant sick saint as a visible symbol of prayer support and hope. Historian Merle Strege admits that "something must be said for the kind of presence we know only through touching.... Far from magical charms, they [anointed articles] offered the touch of 'presence' for which souls thirst" (in *Vital Christianity*, April, 1989, 29).

tured by the biblical story of God in Christ.[8] These practices are a dramatic joining of history and nature, of the Christian revelation and everyday life. Through thoughtful participation, the Spirit helps believers better learn who they are and gain inspiration to pursue what they yet should be. Such practices underline further the principle of incarnational integrity so vital for Christian theology. Since in Jesus the "Word became flesh" (Jn. 1:14),[9] it is clear that the material reality of this world is capable of functioning as a vehicle of the Holy Spirit's continuing presence and work. The church is to be an embodiment of God's active presence in the world.

The church is a story-formed community, a people on a pilgrimage through time, directed by the shaping force and motivating goal of the biblical story of God in Jesus Christ. A basic problem in recent centuries is that Western culture has been excessively book oriented. People have been convinced that they are to read and write the truth. Christian worship, especially in conservative Protestant circles, too often has been reduced to a flurry of words. Sacred story is turned into extended doctrinal statements and long preaching sessions, sometimes even producing people "who use the biblical story as pornography (a subject turned into an object) or as idolatry (a means turned into an end)."[10]

Now Western culture is slowly recovering sight and sound as basic means of communication and learning.[11] It is time in the church

---

[8] In John 6:32-40 we learn that the heart of Christian faith is the "flesh" of Jesus sacrificed for the world. So, symbolically, we are instructed to "eat" and "drink" of Jesus' flesh and blood, drawing on the very life of Jesus to gain our own "eternal life." To ingest the elements of the Lord's supper has potential to bind one in a unique way to the Christ of God.

[9] Jesus has been called the "primordial sacrament" (Edward Schillebeeckx, *Christ the Sacrament of Encounter with God,* N.Y.: Sheed & Ward, 1963, 13-39). In Christ is the primary sacrament, the decisive meeting of a redeeming God and a fallen creation. Though now changing, in recent generations the Christian sacraments have been undercut by a rationalistic concept of the Word of God that reduces divine presence and revelation to inspired information about divine things. If the core categories of Christian theology are relational in nature, then sacraments should play a key role in Christian life.

[10] John Westerhoff, *A Pilgrim People* (The Seabury Press, 1984), 8.

[11] Recently music has been presented as one effective medium through which to explore the whole communication task of the Christian preacher in our "post-modern" time. See Barry Callen, ed., *Sharing Heaven's Music: The Heart of Christian Preaching* (Nashville: Abingdon Press, 1995).

to resurrect the rituals that come from the hands of Jesus, that touch all our senses, visualizing the heart of the biblical story, helping to form and send God's people.

Salvation is made possible only by the grace of God. Even so, one or more formalized worship practices of the church often have been seen as helpful, possibly even essential mediators, channels, nurturers, symbols, and signs of salvation. Such revered rituals as baptism, the Lord's supper, and foot washing are full of Christian meaning, tradition, symbolism, and New Testament rootage. Since they often are contexts in which the Spirit chooses to work, they deserve careful consideration. A crucial part of this consideration is determining how they are to be understood in relation to the ongoing work of the God of loving grace. Are they (1) graphic *responses* to divine grace, (2) symbolic *reflections* of this grace, and/or (3) available and even required *channels* and *means* of receiving this grace? Further, is the reference to *saving* grace and/or to *sanctifying* and *sustaining* grace?

Responses to these questions vary and pose a major obstacle to Christian unity in modern times. How central are these practices supposed to be in the church's life and what role(s) should they play in an individual's conversion to Christ and subsequent spiritual growth and discipleship? We will seek to answer these questions below; but first, since Christian wisdom is to be biblically directed, we give attention the Bible-Spirit relationship. What is the Spirit's work in helping believers benefit from the teaching of Scripture on traditional church practices or any other subject?

A Spirit Reading of Scripture

The Holy Spirit is key to the illumination needed for discovering the current significance of Scripture for the Christian life. The original Inspirer of the biblical story surely is in the best position to assist with its contemporary understanding and application. We hear Christ say, "Let anyone who has an ear listen to what the Spirit is saying to the churches" (Rev. 3:22).

The Bible is authoritative for Christians, but wherein does this authority lie? Approaching the answer requires a recognition that many "evangelicals" of recent generations have not evidenced. This recognition sees a close link between the reader of a biblical text and that reader's perception of the meaning and authority of that text.[12] Who and where we are as we read, in fact our whole cultural setting, is very influential on what we understand by our reading. Capitalizing on this link without capitulating to its distorting tendencies is a central work of the Holy Spirit.

Christians, especially "evangelicals" in their reaction to classic liberalism, have tended to be more interested in the *inspiration* than the *illumination* of the biblical text (authority vested in the text as received as opposed to awareness of the text's special significance for life now). Fearing what easily can be the unbridled subjectivism of a reader-driven interpretation, evangelicals tend to focus on historical exegesis, seeking to affirm and protect the authority of the biblical text as originally inspired. They often "ignore the fact that readers bring interests and presuppositions to the text and settle comfortably into a positivist framework of interpretation, viewing the text as stationary object and the reader as detached examiner."[13]

By contrast, many leaders of European Pietism in the seventeenth and eighteenth centuries taught that only the spiritually prepared biblical reader will understand the text properly. In other words, there is an intimate connection between holiness of text, holiness of interpreter, and quality and significance of interpretation. More recently, with good reason Mary Ford has rejected the characteristic Enlight-

---

[12] Note: "A Wesleyan hermeneutic, though it gives priority to the Scriptures as the basis of all beliefs, assumes that all truth is existentially perceived and appropriated. One does not simply come to the Scriptures with a blank mind and then rationalistically interpret the Bible. The Bible is always interpreted through experience, tradition and reason. This is not a subjectivizing of the biblical revelation, but a frank acknowledgment that all truth is mediated in a larger context, rather than merely through a logical and rationalistic framework. This personal-relational dimension is a decisive exegetical and theological presupposition for a Wesleyan hermeneutic. Hence the crucible of life is the laboratory for testing our interpretation of Scripture" (Laurence Wood, "The Wesleyan View" in Donald Alexander, ed., *Christian Spirituality: Five Views of Sanctification,* InterVarsity Press, 1988, 95-96).

[13] Clark Pinnock, "The Role of the Spirit in Interpretation," *Journal of the Evangelical Theological Society* 36:4 (December 1993), 492.

enment ideal of reading Scripture in an "objective" way. Rather, the knowledge that is intended for conveyance by the Bible, spiritual knowledge of God and of the path to restored relationship with God and God's work, comes only through a faith-full reading that is inspired by the Spirit and conducted in the context of the believing community.[14] Therefore, Stanley Grenz rightly calls for "the reorientation of the doctrine of Scripture under the doctrine of the Holy Spirit."[15]

The model of the ancient Apostles' Creed is wise, making the triune God the organizing principle for systematic theology and addressing the content and interpretation of revelation within and not prior to consideration of the being and work of God. In this way the Bible comes to be seen as a dynamic instrument of the Spirit's work, not a static deposit of propositional truths to be considered in advance of and even separate from a focus on the past and present work of the Spirit. Instead of exclusive attention being given to the past action of the Spirit in inspiring the biblical authors (insuring the adequacy of their writing in relation to divine intent), there also is need to recognize the Spirit's present work in speaking through the Scriptures to illumine appropriate interpretation and fresh application.

The canon of biblical materials is itself the result of the Spirit's inspiration of original composition and illumination of Israel and the church as they sought ongoing meaning in changing circumstances. Church perception of relevant meaning today rests both on initial divine inspiration, a tradition of divine illumination in the church, and the ongoing illumination work of the Spirit. There is a close relation between Scripture and the believing community, to the extent of saying that, energized at all stages by the Spirit, the Bible is both a product of the community of faith and a constant resource for that community's fresh belief and application. Consequently, "a closer connection between inspiration and illumination would lead

---

[14] Mary Ford, "Seeing, But Not Perceiving: Crisis and Context in Biblical Studies," *St. Vladimir's Theological Quarterly* 35:2-3 (1991), 122.

[15] Stanley Grenz, *Revisioning Evangelical Theology* (InterVarsity Press, 1993), 114. These paragraphs are indebted in part to this work of Grenz, especially his chapter 5.

evangelicals to a more profound, Spirit-focused rather than text-focused understanding of the nature of biblical trustworthiness."[16]

A central truth taught in the Book of Acts is that the Spirit of God creates a new social reality, the church, the body of believers brought into being by the Spirit's renewing and infilling. The gift of the Spirit, then, is not to be seen merely as an individualistic privilege. It is not best received, understood, and employed in isolation from the community of believers. Rather, it is a personal gift that creates "an organic connection with other Spirit-filled persons."[17] It is the living, growing, serving body of Christ. Within this body, the Spirit works to open the Bible anew. Believers need the book of God, the Spirit of God, and the church of God in which the Spirit still speaks.

The divine dimension of the biblical materials is bound closely to the present illumination provided by the Spirit of God. This was the case when these materials were first written, when later they were edited and then compiled and canonized within the church's life, and when still later they were freshly understood and newly applied. Rather than the truth of God in Scripture being restricted narrowly to fixed concepts and their exact way of statement and precise point of application, there is a more Spirit-oriented dynamism inherent in the process of interpretation. According to 2 Timothy 3:16-17, God "inspires," breathes into the Scripture, thereby keeping it alive, faith producing, and church directing as times and cultures change.[18]

This ongoing illumination of the Spirit of God need not be an open door to unchecked subjectivism among Christians. Brevard Childs provides one helpful way of avoiding this persistent danger. He approaches biblical understanding by examining the process of the

---

[16] Grenz, *Revisioning Evagelical Theology*, 124. Also see F. F. Bruce, *The Canon of Scripture* (InterVarsity, 1988), 281-282,

[17] H. Ray Dunning, *Grace, Faith and Holiness* (Kansas City: Beacon Hill Press, 1988, 492.

[18] The simple and rigid logic of the verbal inspiration (inerrancy) theory of the Bible is inadequate to convey the mutually interactive relationship between Bible and Spirit. If the Spirit only inspired and then fixed forever the very words of Scripture, the exact "facts" of revelation, then we are taken "back to the Jewish scribal position, which assumed that the prophetic Spirit had been withdrawn from Israel" (C. Norman Kraus, *God Our Savior,* 158). Such is not the case with the Pentecost people, the church of Christ's Spirit.

original formation of Scripture as we now have it, particularly the patterns of interpretation and reinterpretation evident over the generations within that very process. Scripture displays examples of its own reinterpretation in ways judged by the faithful community of the past as appropriate to the ongoing and authoritative work of the original inspiring and then later illuminating Spirit. The Spirit enables the interpretation of the Bible as authoritative Scripture through "the canonical context of the church."[19]

The Scriptures play the foundational role of being the "constitution of an ongoing community"[20] because they are the product of the faith's formative stage and because they provide the narrative that presents properly the pivotal events and foundational realities that make the church God's church. The *significance* of a biblical text sometimes changes, but not its *meaning*. In the Bible is the revelation of God's work in the world, the very revelation that the Spirit is prepared to use to bring new life and to form true Christian community in every time and setting. Through the retelling of this biblical revelation of primal events,[21] "the Spirit re-creates the past within the present life of the community. And the texts thus provide paradigms and categories by means of which the community under the direction of the Spirit can come to understand and respond to the challenges of life in the present."[22]

---

[19] Brevard Childs, *Biblical Theology in Crisis* (Philadelphia: Westminster Press, 1970), 104. Drawing on Edmund Clowney, *Preaching and Biblical Theology* (1961), and assuming the Protestant principle that the Bible is its own best interpreter, Richard Lints expands helpfully on three "horizons of interpretation," the textual, ephocal, and canonical (*The Fabric of Theology*, Eerdmans, 1993, 293-310). These horizons are (1) the immediate context of a biblical passage, (2) the context of the period of revelation in which it falls, and (3) the context of the entirety of biblical revelation. Under the guidance of the Spirit, these horizons help an interpreter discipline the questions asked of a text and determine the current relevance of the points made in a text. Regarding any passage, one asks: Is it in the flow of the biblical story of salvation? What does it add to the story? How is it illumined by looking at it in light of the whole of the story, especially Jesus Christ? The Spirit's role is crucial in answering such central questions.

[20] Francis Schussler Fiorenza, "The Crisis of Scriptural Authority," *Interpretation* 44 (October, 1990), 363.

[21] Of central significance are the exodus, exile, and messianic expectation of the Hebrews, and the life, teachings, death, and resurrection of Jesus.

[22] Stanley Grenz, *Revisioning Evangelical Theology* (InterVarsity, 1993), 127.

While the biblical text is indispensable, at all points it is the work of the Spirit that is primary, breathing authority into the text and illuminating its relevance for the community of its contemporary readers. The biblical canon is closed, the historic narrative being complete and adequate. Yet, in a sense, it is very much open. The openness rests on the sure base that the canon and the challenge of its present significance in the church are both controlled by the power of the Spirit. The Bible is servant to the work of the Spirit. The Spirit's goal is to illumine the Word for the church so that it sheds needed light on her life and mission. Good theology is biblical and pilgrim theology. We should care both about what the Bible says and where it points for life and mission now. Theology that takes the path of discovery requires both the Spirit's historic inspiration and present illumination of the biblical text. According to Jürgen Moltmann:

> Scripture points beyond itself to the history of the coming kingdom of God. This history is the history of the Spirit, which brings together God's people for the coming kingdom, communicates the powers of healing, and preserves and establishes creation for the day of glory. Holy scripture is no self-contained system of a heavenly doctrine, but promise open to its own fulfillment.[23]

The formative events of Christian faith happened in a very different place and a long time ago. How can they be made understandable now? How can they function relevantly in a technology-driven, post-Christian, secularized world? Paul Tillich, representative of a common kind Christian theology in recent decades, concentrated his theological work on deciding how the traditional message of the faith can be refocused best for the people of our time. He saw the twentieth century as a time when the world was disintegrating and people were being victimized by the existential anxieties of guilt, meaninglessness, and death. Faith is essential, but, judged Tillich, an adequate faith has to be reconceptualized and culturally conditioned to the times (newly illuminated).

---

[23] Jürgen Moltmann, *History and the Triune God,* 67.

John Wesley lived in an earlier century when the challenge to "make relevant" the ancient gospel was different only in details. Wesley's way of going about the task differs somewhat from Tillich's. Wesley also faced culture, credibility, and communication gaps. In addition, he recognized the need of facing a *spiritual gap*. Men and women of any age are "dead in trespasses and sins." The only hope of their responding to God's reality and redeeming presence is the gracious work of the Holy Spirit. This is made possible by "prevenient grace," insisted Wesley, divine grace given when we sinners are yet "dead," unworthy, unable to recognize and respond to God's love apart from divine grace. Such gracious enablement provides a way that the gulf of sin, time, and culture can be bridged.

God speaks through the divine Word, Jesus, as narrated biblically and brought to life for us by the Spirit. Granted, theological vocabulary must fit the times. Wesley sought to speak plain truth to plain people in plain language.[24] He relied on the ministry of the Spirit to "quicken" the Word and bring "assurance" to the soul. Wesley's chosen option was not to adopt a new God-concept, discarding all those being judged by many others as not compatible with the spirit of the age. He relied on the Holy Spirit, the presentness of the God of all times, to contemporize without distorting the message. In the person of the Spirit, the God who always was still is! God can be known only as God assists with the knowing. Such assistance comes when believers are prepared to allow God to be God.

So far as the theological task is concerned, the Spirit functions in two interrelated ways. One is to preserve the purity of the gospel as witnessed to dependably by the Bible. The other is to make current that gospel in thought, language, and life application appropriate in each new time and place. The church in changing times is tempted either to compromise the gospel to "fit" the times (heavy on context) or to retreat with the gospel in isolation from the times (heavy on text). The Spirit works in either case, making available the promise of illumination that always involves a move toward the right relationship

---

[24] Edward Sugden, *Wesley's Standard Sermons* (London: The Epworth Press, 1968), 30.

between text and context, the Word then (Jesus) and the same Word alive and communicating now (Spirit of Jesus).

The integrity of this crucial balance is easily compromised. The rightful authority of inspired Scripture sometimes is narrowed to focus only on the words of the biblical text. John Calvin taught that the Word is the *object* and the *instrument* of the Spirit's witness. This opens the way for "Protestant Orthodoxy to place most of the weight on the former, so that the authority and power of the written Word lay in the inspiration of its writers rather than in that of its hearers."[25] John Wesley rightly saw the inner testimony of the Holy Spirit as "the primary basis for the authority of Scripture and the authenticating factor of its inspiredness."[26] In other words, before Scripture can play its revealing role, the same Spirit who originally inspired its writers must now inspire its readers. The Word and Spirit fulfill coordinate and interdependent tasks. The written Word cannot work automatically without the Spirit, and seldom does the Spirit work autonomously apart from the written Word.

Here is a radical addition to what often passes as adequate Christian orthodoxy. Just as we fallen humans are "dead" in our sins until enabled by God's prevenient grace to respond to the offer of forgiveness, the written Word also lies dormant until enlivened by the Spirit for present readers. In the words on the Bible's sacred pages lie the essential records, the crucial salvation story, and normative interpretations of the meaning of God's pivotal acts in human history. But proper perception, existential power, and contemporary cultural relevance rely on the present work of the Spirit. God's Spirit, who first inspired the Word, now chooses to dwell within the searching heart to inspire again, witnessing afresh to the truth and current significance of Scripture. Always, it is the Spirit of God and not the book who is God. The book, clearly essential as an instrument of revelation, does not supplant the Spirit who remains the inspirer, the One revealed and the One revealing.

---

[25] Rob Staples, "Wesleyan Perspectives on the Doctrine of the Holy Spirit," in A. Deasley and R. Shelton, eds., *The Spirit and the New Age,* vol. 5 of the *Wesleyan Theological Perspectives* series (Anderson, Ind.: Warner Press, 1986), 211.

[26] R. Larry Shelton, "John Wesley's Approach to Scripture in Historical Perspective," *Wesleyan Theological Journal* (Spring 1981), 36.

The integrity of God's ongoing activity in the interpretative process should never be compromised. Since the written Word is divinely inspired and normative, the revealing of the Spirit never is contrary to it. Even so, the foundation is theism, not biblicism. The letter of the Word is dead apart from the dynamic of the divine, the Spirit. The Christian tradition, paradoxically, is both a fixed and yet an unfinished journey guided surely by the Spirit. All along the way, Christian doctrine is "revisable but not reversible; it develops along the line of the trajectory that comes from its origins.... Underneath this conviction is the trust that the Holy Spirit is present in the church in the ministerial work of the tradition, in the sense of rightness of direction."[27]

Charles Wesley put it well in his hymns that were intended to be sung or prayed before the reading of Scripture. For instance:

> Come, Holy Ghost, for moved by Thee
> The prophets wrote and spoke;
> Unlock the truth, Thyself the key,
> Unseal the sacred book.

Or again, reflecting the work of the Spirit in bringing light to that first primeval darkness (Gen. 1:3), Charles prays in inspired verse:

> Expand Thy wings, celestial Dove,
> Brood o'er our nature's night;
> On our disordered spirits move,
> And let there now be light![28]

Instruments of the Spirit

Already we have spoken of the Bible and the church as special instruments of the Spirit's current work of conveying and embodying the good news of God in Jesus Christ. We now return to the question

---

[27] Gabriel Fackre, *Ecumenical Faith in Evangelical Perspective* (Eerdmans, 1993), 67-68.

[28] As quoted by T. Crichton Mitchell, *Charles Wesley: Man with the Dancing Heart* (Kansas City: Beacon Hill Press, 1994), 137-138.

of the place of baptism, the Lord's supper, and foot washing in the grace-giving ministry of the Spirit of God. With the Bible assumed as foundational, the Spirit's ongoing illumination of the Bible's present significance as essential, and the context of the church as vital, how are such practices to be understood within church life? Recognizing that interpretation of biblical teaching is influenced strongly by church and cultural contexts, a brief review of such contexts is helpful.

The Believers' Church approach to "sacramental" issues is seen clearly in its historic witness to Christian baptism. This witness can be traced back at least to the sixteenth century. The Schleitheim Articles (1527) is a theological declaration that played a significant role in consolidating the Swiss and South German streams of the early Anabaptist movement. The first article of this statement of faith freshly addressed baptism at a time when witness was needed to counter an institutionally entrenched and clergy controlled view of baptism as a "means of grace."[29]

Soon Menno Simons (1496-1561)[30] spoke about baptism in a way similar to the Articles, with a confessional form of his view appearing in the 1632 Dordrecht Articles. In the 1539 essay "Christian Baptism," Menno said that baptism is a sign of obedience that proceeds from faith. Regeneration (new birth in Christ) comes by faith in God's Word rather than by receiving the sacrament at the hands of established clergy. Baptism follows regeneration instead of effecting it. Similarly, when Russell Byrum (1889-1980) identified the church as "the aggregate of those who have been regenerated,"[31] regeneration and not sacraments as such were said to be God's criterion for placing members in the church through the work of saving grace.

---

[29] The Schleitheim Articles stress that baptism is for those who understand the gospel's demands (thus no infants), witness to sins forgiven through Christ, and express desire to follow Christ in a life of dedicated discipleship (see Marlin Miller, "The Mennonites" in Merle Strege, ed., *Baptism and Church,* Grand Rapids: Sagamore Books, 1986, 16-17).

[30] "Mennonite" derives from his name.

[31] Russell Byrum, *Christian Theology,* rev. ed. (Anderson, Ind.: Warner Press, 1925, 1982), 424.

The church is "where Christian experience makes you a member."[32] The central question is not whether baptism makes one a Christian instead of repentance and actual regeneration, but whether nonetheless there is a crucial link between baptism and church membership. Responding affirmatively, the Believers' Church tradition sees a corporate dimension of baptism.[33] Beyond confession of personal faith and a promise to answer the call to discipleship, in some settings the candidate for baptism is asked: "Will you be loyal to the church, upholding her by your prayers and your presence, your substance and your service?" Insisting that "the covenant with God through Christ cannot be separated from the covenant with brothers and sisters," there is the Brethren practice of laying on of hands immediately following baptism, symbolizing the truth that "the Spirit comes to us through the lives of others in the body of Christ."[34] Baptism, among other things, is the believer's ordination to ministry, a

---

[32] The intent of this slogan, commonly used in the Church of God movement (Anderson), is to oppose a view like Walter Scott's "five finger exercise" made famous during his evangelistic preaching on the Western Reserve (northeast Ohio, 1827-1830). With the sequence significant, Scott taught faith, repentance, baptism, remission of sins, and the gift of the Holy Spirit (counted on five fingers). The Church of God movement and many other Wesleyan and Anabaptist bodies have understood, to the contrary, that the remission of sins necessarily precedes baptism. Alexander Campbell, famous associate of Scott, held a complex and often misunderstood view of this subject. He complained that "some of my brethren...have given to baptism an undue eminence–a sort of pardon-procuring, rather than pardon-certifying and enjoying efficacy" (*Millennial Harbinger*, 1840, 544-45). But he also wrote that, as long as previous faith and repentance are present so that salvation is by faith and not by any merit-producing work, baptism "is the means of receiving a formal, distinct, and specific absolution, or release from guilt" (*The Christian System*, 1839, 61-62). Rather than merely a sign, baptism was seen by Campbell as a step in the saving process, the time when sins are remitted and the gift of the Spirit given (see: *Christian Baptist*, April 7, 1828, 82). Baptism was said to complete one's adoption into the family of God. It is "a sign of God's grace toward us and a way of our saying 'yes!' to that grace" (Clark Williamson, *Baptism: Embodiment of the Gospel*, St. Louis: Christian Board of Education, 1987, 37).

[33] Note: "The influences of pietist, revivalist and charismatic renewal movements...have frequently contributed to what sometimes amounts to an overemphasis on the subjective and individual dimensions of Christian baptism in Mennonite teaching and practice" (Marlin Miller, "Baptism in the Mennonite Tradition," *Mennonite Quarterly Review*, July, 1990, 236). The same could be said about many similar bodies. While personal experience with the Spirit is essential, it does not replace the need for the communal context, discipline, and practices through which the Spirit works.

[34] Dale Brown, "The Brethren," in Merle Strege, ed., *Baptism and Church* (Grand Rapids: Sagamore Books, 1986), 33.

highlighting of the priesthood of all believers, a commitment to belonging to Christ's body, the church.

An overarching perspective is needed to assist in sorting out the many issues that arise about the sacramental practices of the church. Here is one perspective of particular value:

> There are some symbolic acts of obedience and experience with Christ that are [should be] commonly practiced.... When one becomes a Christian one makes a public testimony to this new relationship with Christ through baptism. This is the baptism of believers by immersion in water after they have reached an age of accountability. A high experience of worship for the Christian is the Lord's supper, where the bread symbolizes Christ's body broken for us and the wine...symbolizes his blood shed for us.... A third commonly practiced custom of this sort, symbolizing obedience and practical, humble service to one's brother and sister and the servant role of the church, is foot washing.[35]

Here one sees the broad perspective generally held by Believers' Church movements. Baptism, the Lord's supper, and foot washing are understood as: (1) symbolic acts of obedience reflective both of what God has done in individual lives and how these lives then are to be lived in the community of God's new covenant; (2) experience-engendered acts growing out of one's prior saving experience with Christ; and (3) acts expected of believers because they are commanded by Christ and normally should occur in the context of the church's worship. Such understandings necessarily have vital relation to Christian discipleship. These ritual acts dramatize to the world the nature of the spiritual conversion (immersion into Christ), the basis of that conversion (the work of Christ), and the result of that conversion (a life of humble service in the manner of Christ).

---

[35] Titled *So This Is the Church of God,* booklet of the Leadership Council of the Church of God (Anderson), as found in Barry Callen, *The First Century* (Anderson, Ind.: Warner Press, 1979), I:303-304.

This broad perspective is to be viewed in light of the two tendencies that have been apparent from the earliest times in the church's interpretation of the ordinances or sacraments. One tendency emphasizes the *objective reality* of God's grace received in and through the ritual acts themselves. Particular rites are believed to be divinely appointed. When administered properly, they convey divine grace and even salvation by their very operation (*ex opere operato*). This objectifying tendency is seen in Ignatius, Augustine, and clearly in the traditional Roman Catholic doctrine of transubstantiation (the loaf and cup of the Lord's supper are said to become the actual body and blood of Christ). The word "sacrament" often is associated with this objectifying tendency. Focus is on the effectiveness of the act itself at the hands of official church leaders.

The other tendency emphasizes the *subjective reality*, the priority of the believer's faith response to the grace of God. These sacred practices are said to be less the means of something being done to or for the believer and more the means by which believers express gratitude and witness to grace already received by faith. Baptism and the Lord's supper are basically human rather than divine acts.[36] Thus, the word "ordinance" has gained wide use. The intent is to focus on human response to and celebration of divine grace, not on any claimed grace-conveying ability of the rites themselves, especially when the rites are controlled by a church establishment and linked to citizenship in a country.

Viewing baptism and the Lord's supper as *merely* ordinances, however, can lead to as much loss to the church as the almost magical view of sacraments as automatic grace conveyors. Some perspective from the history of Christian theology can be helpful.

The theology of the Lord's supper has tended to focus on two questions ever since the Middle Ages. First, what is the nature and

---

[36] Whether the focus is on divine or human action has been crucial in deciding the issue of baptizing infants. There have been two streams of interpretation, both claiming biblical support. The Free Methodist Church, e.g., affirms both streams, seeing them as complementary and needed for theological completeness. The tradition that practices infant baptism points to the priority of grace over faith and stresses God's initiative in humans coming to Christ. The tradition espousing believers' baptism only (infants are "dedicated") emphasizes the believer's response to God's grace. The first highlights the corporate dimension of life in Christ, the second the individual.

degree of the real divine presence in the elements (bread and wine)? Second, in what way is the ceremony itself a sacrifice? Within Roman Catholicism stress came to be placed on the objective presence of Jesus and the immediate effectiveness of his sacrifice freshly made in the rite itself, known in this setting as the "Mass." Thomas Aquinas, e.g., taught that remission of sin could be obtained thereby. The Protestant Reformers of the sixteenth century complained that such developments undercut the role of faith and placed God-like power in the hands of the priestly hierarchy. Zwingli, the Swiss reformer (1484-1531), argued that communion is only a memorial of Jesus' death. The focus should not be on "this is my body," but on "do this in remembrance of me." John Calvin (1509 1564) joined Martin Luther (1483-1546) in teaching the real presence of Christ in the holy meal, but separated from him by insisting that the presence was through the energy of the Spirit.

Since the historic Vatican Council II of the Roman Catholic Church (1962-1965), there has been a considerable ecumenical convergence of these objective and subjective views. The main features of this convergence are: (1) emphasis on the inseparability of Word and sacraments; (2) trinitarian and christocentric interpretation of both the proclamation of the Word and the celebration of the sacraments; (3) effort to interpret the sacraments by understanding the whole creation as a sacramental universe;[37] and (4) concern to make explicit the connection between the sacraments, Christian life, and Christian ethics.[38]

Obviously an adequate view requires taking seriously all that Jesus said and did, not building doctrine in reaction to someone else's overemphasis. In biblical thought a symbol and name actually participate in the reality each signifies. The biblical authors assumed

---

[37] See William Temple, "The Sacramental Universe," chap. 19 of *Nature, Man and God*, Gifford Lectures, University of Glasgow, 1932-1934 (London: Macmillan & Co., 1964).

[38] Daniel Migliore, *Faith Seeking Understanding*, 1991, 214. This latter point of convergence, linking faith to life, is especially characteristic of the Believers' Church tradition. One thinker representing this tradition is attempting to develop an alternative both to medieval sacramentalism and a modern rejection of any sacramental understanding (George Beasley-Murray, *Baptism in the New Testament*, Eerdmans, 1962).

that the symbolic acts they practiced in some sense facilitated participation in the reality signified by the rites. Thus the current convergence of objective and subjective emphases suggests a fresh and hopeful balance in forming an overall perspective that is biblically based and seasoned by the wisdom of the whole tradition of God's people.

The Believers' Church tradition has tended toward the approach of subjective reality and remains cautious about any convergence of views.[39] It has emphasized a volunteeristic view of faith, the church, and sacramental church practices. Its traditional emphasis, conditioned in part by the historical context of its origin, has been away from all humanly conditioned church establishments (including clerically dominated religious rites) and toward the freely chosen gathering of Christian believers who, as a direct consequence of their individual salvation experiences, have come to comprise the true church.

An essential biblical paradox is captured in John Wesley's view that a Christian sacrament, to be fully authentic, must include both *inward work* and *outward sign*. To be baptized without the inner experience of true repentance and the acceptance by faith of God's regenerating grace in Christ certainly fails to be adequate. To be truly repentant and renewed, on the other hand, and not be baptized fails to complete the cycle of memory, symbolism, witness, and the full blessing of a God-intended ordinance. There is, then, a sense of sacramental necessity in order for the wholeness of grace to be realized in the lives of believers. For Wesley, "baptism was far more than a human testimony to one's faith, and the Eucharist [Lord's supper] was far more than a memorial of Christ's death. A sacrament was *a means whereby we receive* inward grace."[40] It was an instrument of the Spirit's ongoing work of loving grace.

---

[39] Especially in its early Anabaptist expression, the central issue was the choice between choosing the faith or being born into it without personal choice because of state-church alliances. Often the choice for personal faith led to death at the hands of the state. As seen in ancient and modern times, the combining of church and state can lead to dramatic loss of personal freedom and widespread violence sanctioned by both church and state.

[40] Rob Staples, *Outward Sign and Inward Grace* (Kansas City: Beacon Hill Press, 1991), 58. To be clear, the grace so received is sanctifying and sustaining, not saving grace.

Wesley's understanding of growth in the Christian life involves what he referred to as the "means of grace." These means are appointed spiritual disciplines that can facilitate God's grace as it continues its sanctifying (healing) work in the believer's life. Wesley's pastoral theology centered in his encouraging believers to discipline their lives methodically ("methodists") by practicing habits designed to enable spiritual growth. A believer moves forward in the life of faith by appropriating the means instituted by God for the Spirit's work of renewing believers in the image of Christ and sending them on the mission of Christ.

The general view of John Wesley, strongly influenced by his Anglican association, brings a corrective to the occasional overreactions of radical reformationism. These overreactions to "liturgical" religion sometimes dispense entirely with established forms. They fear that the very mechanics of these forms can distract believers from focusing on the real presence of Christ and encourage them to get caught up in the sterility of church authoritarianism.[41] Wesley's more balanced view is that baptism and the Lord's supper are central means of grace and are necessary, "if not to the *being,* at least to the *well-being* of a Church."[42] Note this about Wesley's own experience:

> After Aldersgate the ordinances of the church glowed with the living power of the Spirit for Wesley. The interesting thing is that the Lord's supper took on deeper meaning for Wesley, not less, after his heart-warming experience. Rather than trading off the sacramental means of grace for the direct intimacy of his newfound experience of God, he thrived on them as nourishment for the new life of God in his soul. Here is yet another instance of Wesley's joining the old and new, the institutional and charismatic.[43]

[41] See Wilmer Cooper, *A Living Faith: An Historical Study of Quaker Beliefs* (Richmond, Ind.: Friends United Press, 1990), especially chap. 7, "Quakers and the Sacraments."

[42] John Wesley, "An Earnest Appeal to Men of Reason and Religion," *Works* (Oxford ed.) XI, 78. Says Randy Maddox: "...while God's grace offered in the sacraments must be responsively received, Wesley was equally convinced that our response-ability is progressively nurtured by this very grace" (*Responsible Grace*, 1994, 196).

[43] Howard Snyder, *The Radical Wesley* (InterVarsity, 1980), 102-103.

The outward practice is never the bringer of salvation, but it does signify and is able to nourish that salvation. Therefore, outward practices such as baptism and the Lord's supper should be kept in their place–but they do have an important place, one not necessarily limited to symbolism and memory alone. They are to be instruments of the Spirit.

Table, Towel, and Eschaton

Biblical teaching appears to call for a believer, having repented and been justified before God, to take full advantage of the continuing ordinances (sacraments) of the Christian faith (adopting a general Wesleyan view, but under the cautious eye of Believers' Church concerns). One should appreciate Wesley's emphasis on "means of grace" for spiritual growth, even in the midst of the effort to avoid their common institutional distortions. The purposes of baptism, the Lord's supper, and foot washing, while not the means for accomplishing initial or final salvation, nonetheless are significant to the health and fruitfulness of that salvation. They are means of graphic remembrance, public witness, corporate identity building, and ongoing personal sanctification. In short,

> ...participation in the ordinances facilitates the symbolic retelling of the old, old story of God's action in Jesus and the declaration of his glorious future. As we tell the story, we are transported into the past, and we anticipate the future. We symbolically experience Christ's death and resurrection, which constitutes the foundation for our own future triumph over sin and death. As we are reminded of the past and are caught up in the vision of God's future, we gain a sense of the connectedness of all history. Through this, the Spirit confirms in us that we are moving ever onward toward full participation in God's intention for us. This reminder provides a transcendent vantage point and a sense of our ultimate identity through which the Spirit empowers us for living in the here and now.[44]

[44] Stanley Grenz, *Theology for the Community of God* (Nashville: Broadman &

One ecumenical convergence in recent decades has been substantial agreement on the close relationship between Christian eschatology, the symbolic and celebrative life of the church, and the church's calling in the world. Baptism, the Lord's supper, and foot washing are not to be practiced merely out of reverence for tradition or because they have aesthetic value. In these observances the biblical story is retold, visualized, brought to life again, and acted out, affirming Christians in their identity and vocation. Baptism shows the new life in Christ; the Lord's supper recalls the basis for that life; foot washing[45] acts out the purpose and distinctive servant style of that life.

God's acts of revelation and grace in the past (e.g., Israel's exodus and Jesus' death and resurrection) constitute the wonderful biblical story of salvation. That is good news. More good news is that this story *goes on.* Such revelation and grace are renewed regularly in the sacramental life of God's people. This life is to be a visible sign of the people of God as it rehearses and rejoices in its grace-granted identity and is nurtured for its present mission as redemptive representatives of God's kingdom come and coming.

As God's people in the world, the church is to be a sign of the divine kingdom already present. In spite of its imperfections, the church is to point beyond itself to the vision which it seeks to embody. This pointing is dramatized in the remembering, celebrating, witnessing, and serving inherent in baptism, the Lord's supper, and foot washing.

1. Baptism. Baptism gives vivid expression to a new believer's having been convicted of sin, turned in penitence from sin to new life in Christ, and thus become a member of God's people on mission. Through baptism the individual witnesses to personal renewal by the Spirit in the presence of the believing community, and thereby brings new strength and encouragement to the body of believers. Baptism "involves our immersion into the critical moments of Jesus' own story, and making that story our own through symbolic action–an

---

Holman, 1994), 674-675.

[45] The ecumenical consensus, while affirming the centrality of Christian servanthood, does not usually include the practice of foot washing as such. It is affirmed more commonly in segments of the Believers' Church tradition.

action that itself is baptized in the Holy Spirit of God."[46] In this way baptism is a witness of renewal and a means of continuing renewal.

Baptism into Christ also is to choose solidarity with Christ in his redemptive reach to a lost world.[47] It signifies membership in the one church that is committed to defying the destructive barriers that sin has erected between human beings. It is public initiation into God's people and into a life of radical discipleship that is defined by the story of Christ's life, death, and resurrection.

Christian baptism is properly reserved for those who consciously have exercised faith in the saving work of Christ. When practical, it ought to be administered by immersion in water since, according to New Testament language, precedent, and expressed symbolism, such a process is most appropriate. It retells graphically the story of salvation in Christ and appears expressly intended.[48] Baptism is a ceremonial representation of the burial and resurrection of our Lord, dramatizing the believer's having followed Christ in such death and resurrection (Gal. 2:20; Col. 2:12; Rom. 6:2-4). Submitting to baptism does not insure some automatic transfer of saving grace apart from repentance and faith. In the presence of repentance, faith, and saving grace, however, baptism can be a means of growth in the grace that builds and sustains new life in Christ. In the New Testament, baptism is associated closely with receiving the Spirit of God and launching into new life in the Spirit.

---

[46] Michael Lodahl, *The Story of God: Wesleyan Theology and Biblical Narrative* (Kansas City: Beacon Hill Press, 1994), 180.

[47] Theodore Jennings interprets the phrase "the communion of saints" in the Apostles' Creed to mean "an intimate relation between persons whether within or without the Church, a solidarity based on their commitment to the justice of God.... The test of this justice is not religious or doctrinal, but a commitment to the neighbor, especially the poor, the oppressed, the afflicted.... The discernment and celebration of this solidarity is one of the most critical tasks facing us in our pluralistic world" (*Loyalty to God*, Abingdon Press, 1992, 195-199). See Matthew 7:21 and 25:31-46.

[48] Such a conclusion is only one reading of New Testament teaching. Not all Christians share this reading, of course. Here is a clear example of the tension evident in the traditional idealism of movement's like the Church of God (Anderson). On the one hand, this movement's stance is "no creed but the Bible." On the other hand, movement leaders have been clear that the "immersion" reading of the Bible is the correct reading (almost a creedal stance since viable alternatives of biblical interpretation, while existing, have been frowned upon if espoused by movement leaders).

The ethical implications of salvation are clear. The Christian who emerges from the waters of baptism should demonstrate a changed character. Once set apart for God and enrolled in the family of God, the baptized Christian is "empowered by the Holy Spirit to turn full attention to the service of God in all areas of personal and social life."[49] Not merely a "birth ceremony," and surely not a "safe-conduct badge for the dying," Christian baptism is "the commissioning of disciples setting out on their faith journey."[50]

The eschatological significance of Christian baptism is crucial. The practice appears suddenly and dramatically in the New Testament, signifying identification with the coming kingdom of God and abandonment of all reliance on traditional religious identity for salvation (Matt. 3:9; Lk. 3:8). It demonstrates that believers are heirs of the kingdom by divine grace (1 Cor. 6:9-11; Jn. 3:3-5). Baptismal candidates do more than witness to an inner spiritual experience. They commit to life in the body of Christ, kingdom life possible only through the power of the Spirit.

In the account of life in the early church found in the Book of Acts, one sees the close association of baptism and the gift of the Spirit. This closeness indicates the ready availability of the Spirit to the believer who witnesses and commits in the present to faithful service as a representative of the kingdom that is yet to come in its fullness. In baptism, Christians receive the Spirit as the "first fruits" (Rom. 8:23) of the harvest still ahead.[51]

2. Lord's Supper. The Lord's supper is full of significance for ongoing Christian renewal. The biblical story, the full narrative of God's plan for the redemption of creation, is here portrayed dramatically. The central elements of any story are setting, theme, plot, and resolution. We see these in this celebration as human history (setting), rescue of humankind from self-destruction (theme), God's redemp-

---

[49] Mark Toulouse, *Joined in Discipleship* (St. Louis: Chalice Press, 1992), 115.

[50] James McClendon, *Systematic Theology: Doctrine* (Nashville: Abingdon Press, 1994), 391.

[51] This is not to imply that the Spirit is absent from a person prior to baptism (at conversion, for instance). It is to say that baptism is that symbolic moment when the Spirit's presence is especially acknowledged, celebrated, and confirmed.

tive entry into human history, especially in the costly work of Jesus Christ (plot), and the final judgment and consummation of the king-dom of God (resolution). Stated otherwise:

Setting ....Thanksgiving to the Father (creation)
              Give thanks to God for bread (1 Cor. 11:24)
Theme ....Memorial of the Son (redemption)
              This is Jesus' body given for us (1 Cor. 11:24)
Plot ....Communion of the Faithful (church)
              We are one body as we partake together
              (1 Cor. 10:16-17)
Resolution....Meal of the kingdom (eschatology)
              Do this until he comes again (1 Cor. 11:26)

This common meal has become sacred for Christians. Christ is unusually present with the church as in this way it recalls his work and anticipates the heavenly banquet that symbolizes the eventual com-pletion of God's purposes for creation.[52] The way of the cross is understood to be the way that the church also is to be in and to serve this world.[53] Sharing life with others, even at great cost to oneself, is God's way of working, and should be the way for God's people.

First Corinthians 11:20-34 highlights three dimensions of the Lord's supper that transform and redirect past reality into present mis-sion. The meal of Christ is at once a sanctifying, a social, and a sedi-tious sacrament. This spiritual celebration necessarily makes per-sonal, community, and political statements. By the power of the age to come, faithful participation remembers (re-members), alters destructive relationships by "discerning the body of Christ," and rejects the prevailing values of the world in favor of those of the com-

---

[52] Christ's death and resurrection are not only first-century events. In part through the Lord's supper, they also are to become a present happening. James Evans notes that this radical presentness is the meaning of the African-American spiritual "Were You There When They Crucified My Lord?" (*We Have Been Believers*, Fortress Press, 1992, 140).

[53] See C. Leonard Allen, *The Cruciform Church* (Abilene Christian University Press, 1990).

ing kingdom.[54] A contemporary prayer associated with the Lord's supper properly states the intended focus on mission:

> Deliver us from the presumption of coming to this table for solace only, and not for strength; for pardon only, and not for renewal. Let the grace of this Holy Communion make us one body, one spirit in Christ, that we may worthily serve the world in his name.[55]

From the beginning of the church's existence the Lord's supper has had social and mission significance. It is a visible expression of the kingdom of God, a sharing of the life that flows from the self-giving of Jesus. Jesus' own continuing presence in the Spirit is the basis of this sharing, this acting out of a righted relationship. We who believe participate by remembering, receiving, responding, and rejoicing. For the presence of Jesus in the meal to be meaningful in the present, out faith must be active since "he cannot be anywhere in this sacramental way unless he is being willingly received."[56] Jesus is present in the faithful community since the supper of the Lord is a banquet of those who are both rejoicing in the kingdom's presence and practicing kingdom life on the way to the final consummation.

The supper is a love-feast of community celebration (Acts 2:42, 46) staged in light of the eschatological banquet prophesied by Isaiah (25:6-8) and already begun in Jesus (Acts 10:40-41; Lk. 24:30-31; Jn. 21:9-14). The sacrificial Christ who is made known to us in the breaking of the bread and sharing of the cup is the very One who will be the host at the great feast of the Lamb! The Lamb now on the altar is alone worthy "to receive power and wealth and wisdom and might and honor and glory and blessing!" (Rev. 5:12). This very Lamb, one day to be recognized by all, is now the church's Lord. Such present lordship enables the church to "symbolize the future of the divine

---

[54] Robert Mulholland, Jr., "Discerning the Body," in *Weavings: A Journal of the Christian Spiritual Life* (May/June, 1993), 20-26.

[55] *The Book of Common Prayer*, the Episcopal Church (N. Y.: Church Hymnal Corporation, 1977, 372, Rite II, Prayer C).

[56] Thomas Finger, *Christian Theology* (Scottdale, Pa.: Herald Press, 1989), II:339, 341.

kingdom that Jesus came to proclaim."[57] It all is the work of the Spirit, the God of loving grace who is sanctifying and sustaining those who believe.

3. Foot washing. There is a third rite of faith visualization that has powerful mission imagery for the church. It is intensely relational, graphic, humbling, an acted story of how restored relationships now are to be among believers and how the church now should be in the world. Jesus washed the feet of his disciples and directed that they do the same (Jn. 13:14-15).[58] Even if this command is understood as an aspect of the Lord's supper and not necessarily a specific and separate sacrament for the church,[59] the symbolism of sacrificial sharing and serving should not be lost. Washing of feet is a truly sacramental scene, an occasion for enacting liturgically the humility called forth by the meal of the Lord. Kingdom life is servant life.[60] Acceptance in theory of the Lord's sacrificial provision for sinful humankind is not enough. What also is required is bodily action at the most mundane levels of life (feet, food, housing, employment, human dignity).

[57] Wolfhart Pannenberg, *Christian Spirituality* (Westminster Press, 1983), 36. Pannenberg says worship is at the center of the church's life. In worship, especially in the Lord's supper, "the Christian community anticipates and symbolically celebrates the praise of God's glory that will be consummated in the eschatological renewal of all creation in the new Jerusalem.... The mere existence of the church delimits the claims of any present political organization on the life of its members" (36).

[58] See John Winebrenner, *The Ordinances: Baptism, Feet Washing, and the Lord's Supper* (written 1860, available from Churches of God Publications, Findlay, Ohio, 3rd printing, 1982). Russell Byrum insists that "in comparison, neither baptism nor the Lord's supper has surer marks of being an ordinance than does foot washing" (*Christian Theology*, Warner Press, 1925, 1982, 500). He says this practice teaches a spiritual truth by means of an "object lesson." It is a "visible word" about humility and service (504).

[59] Stanley Grenz echoes the judgment common in the Christian community. While noting the explicit command of Jesus (Jn. 13: 14-15), he nonetheless says that "the early church did not understand this statement as enjoining on the community the physical act of foot washing" (*Theology for the Community of God*, 676). He quickly adds, however, that "it represents the kind of humility that we should emulate" (676).

[60] The *We Believe* doctrinal statement of the Churches of God: General Conference [Winebrennarian], Findlay, Ohio, 1986, affirms foot washing as (1) a celebration of the incarnation, (2) a reminder of the Christian calling to be servants, (3) an expression of the love Christians have for one another, (4) a reminder of the need for Christians to minister and be ministered to, and (5) a help in preparation for the Lord's supper (35-37).

Christians are to be in the world in Christ's way and by the Spirit's power (service through weakness and self-giving). The age to come, already having been inaugurated in Christ, is to make the Christian community a sacramental sign to the world. As the church remembers, re-enacts, rejoices, and lives out the life of God's kingdom, it becomes a divine agent that knows and participates in "breaking the power of cancelled sin."[61]

4. Sacredness of Daily Living. Christians finally are called from the water, table, and towel to the streets and workplaces of the world. The biblical story celebrated in worship requires translation into "social holiness" (Wesley), worldly good news. It provides orthodox roots that are to flower into radical discipleship. One element of the "Chicago Call" to the church today captures a "radical" concern of truly "orthodox" Christians:

> We decry the poverty of sacramental understanding among evangelicals. This is largely due to the loss of our continuity with the teaching of many of the Fathers and Reformers and results in the deterioration of sacramental life in our churches. Also, the failure to appreciate the sacramental nature of God's activity in the world often leads us to disregard the sacredness of daily living.[62]

The adequacy of the symbol-only view of the Lord's supper has been questioned often. The "anamnesis" or "remembrance" of "do this in remembrance of me" (1 Cor. 11:24) is not merely a mental recollection of what Christ once did on our behalf. It is rather a re-calling and re-presenting of a key redemptive event in the past "so that it becomes living, powerful and operative."[63] This word points to "an

---

[61] This phrase, familiar in the Wesleyan tradition, comes from the hymn "O for a Thousand Tongues to Sing" by Charles Wesley.

[62] "The Chicago Call: An Appeal to Evangelicals," as in *Christianity Today* (June 17, 1977), 29. For expansion of the theological themes of this Call, see Robert Webber and Donald Bloesch, *The Orthodox Evangelicals* (Nashville: Thomas Nelson, 1978).

[63] Neville Clark, *An Approach to the Theology of the Sacraments* (London: SCM Press, 1956), 62.

active recalling to mind and heart, a bringing back to the present moment."[64] Believers who traditionally have highlighted the memorial interpretation of this meal should appreciate also the present realism imbedded in the rich biblical motif of remembrance.[65]

The worship of the first Christians was modeled after a Jewish pattern which included praising, thanking, glorifying, and acknowledging God for God's saving deeds. These deeds were remembered, not simply as events having taken place in the past, but also as the efficacious representing of this sacred past as God's present redemptive reality. From such God-centered worship, practiced in the midst of real and often troubled life, Israel was and today's church should be confirmed in its identity. It church is to be God's people, people assured that the Spirit of God is yet present and yet works as the God of loving grace powerfully among us. The sacred practices of the church objectify God's presence and God's aim. Their intent is to invite response, not to cause salvation. The grace extended in baptism and the Lord's supper is an invitation that emerges from God's real presence. It is a gracious lure by which we can begin to make sense of the past, especially the cross of Jesus, and begin responding to God's future.

Baptism, the Lord's supper and, for some Christians, foot washing play the dual roles of (1) recalling vividly pivotal past events in salvation history and (2) bringing these events forward into the church's believing, living present. A visual retelling of the biblical story assists in the reliving of the story. The events are remembered and rehearsed in such a reverent and participatory way that God's presence is just as near in the current moment as it was in the initial event recorded in Scripture. While the past is foundational, the pre-

---

[64] Richard Harrison, Jr., "Early Disciples Sacramental Theology: Catholic, Reformed, and Free," in Kenneth Lawrence, ed., *Classic Themes of Disciples Theology* (Fort Worth: Texas Christian University Press, 1986), 77-78. Says Laurence Stookey, "for ancient Jews and early Christians (the first of whom were all Jews), remembrance was a corporate act in which the event remembered was experienced anew through ritual repetition. To remember was to do something, not to think about something" (*Eucharist: Christ's Feast With the Church,* Abingdon Press, 1993, 28).

[65] Paul Mickey, "Process Theology and Wesleyan Thought: An Evangelical Perspective," in Theodore Runyon, ed., *Wesleyan Theology Today: A Bicentennial Theological Consultation,* Nashville, United Methodist Publishing House, 1985, 78).

sent is the focus of God's ongoing will and work, empowered by the sure hope of the yet coming kingdom of God.

God of Grace, God of Glory

True Christian worship covers the full range of the being of God as known in the biblical story–the sovereign God, revealed in Christ, now in the world by the Spirit. In true worship, the past of this story is recalled, the present of this story is acknowledged, and its future implications are engaged. Jesus really was present with the early church (Acts 1:1-5), empowering for witness and service in all the world. As the pages of the Bible are engaged with dedicated mind, cleansed heart, and yielded will, the Spirit of God graciously reveals their current significance. In the waters of baptism, the elements of the Lord's supper, and the humility of the washing of feet, the God of creation, crucifixion, resurrection, and final triumph is present still!

Such divine presence is God the Spirit. We are privileged as believers to pray in the Spirit (Eph. 5:18; 6:18), the Spirit through whom we are inspired to cry "Abba! Father!" (Rom. 8:15), as did Jesus the Son. Filled with the Spirit, we are to give thanks to God in the name of Christ (Eph. 5:18-20). We can approach God with confidence, knowing that, through Christ in the Spirit, we have first been loved (1 Jn. 4:10) and sought (Matt. 18:10-14) by this most gracious God. It is the Spirit who leads us in giving glory and worship to God.

Both the Apostles' and Nicene Creeds end with a simple "Amen." In gratitude and hope, the whole assembly of believers is to express a "YES!", a "SO BE IT!" to the God revealed to us as Father, Son, and Holy Spirit. Believers are sinners who have heard and now become part of the biblical story of the sovereign God who stands and creates, the sacrificing God who stoops in Jesus and saves, the ever-present God the Spirit who stays and sustains.

Now we who believe have been changed by this God who is the source of loving grace, who in Jesus is the initiative of loving grace, and who in the Spirit is the presence of loving grace. Thus, we who are in Christ wait for that time when we shall join the heavenly chorus that cries out: "Hallelujah! For the Lord our God the Almighty reigns. Let us rejoice and exult and give him the glory, for the marriage of the Lamb has come..." (Rev. 19:6b-7a).

In the beginning, reports Genesis 1:1, there was God in the sovereign act of creating. At the end, Revelation 22 pictures the Alpha-and-Omega God in the act of inviting all who wish to take the water of life as a gift (22:20). In the meantime, through the sanctifying and sustaining ministry of the Spirit, now graciously active among us all, we have this promise: "the grace of the Lord Jesus [will] be with all the saints" (22:21).

Therefore, with the New Testament writer, "I commend you to God and to the message that is able to build you up and to give you the inheritance among all who are sanctified" (Acts 20:32).

Index of Persons

Index of Biblical References